The Anthropology of Christianity

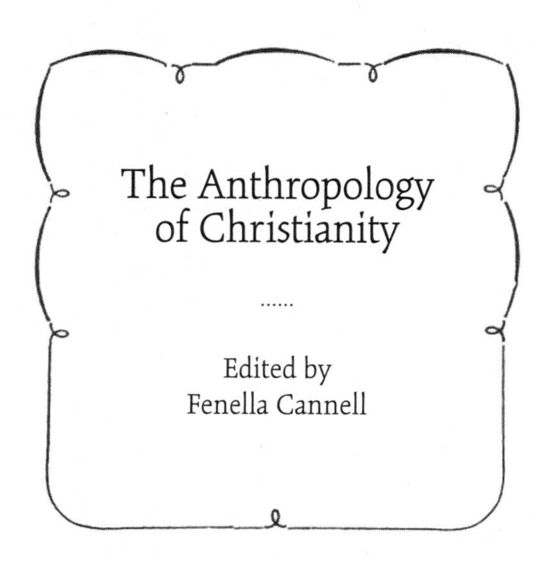

The Anthropology of Christianity

......

Edited by
Fenella Cannell

Duke University Press
DURHAM & LONDON 2006

2nd printing, 2007

Printed in the United States of America on acid-free paper ∞
Designed by Jennifer Hill
Typeset in Fournier by Keystone Typesetting, Inc.
Library of Congress Cataloging-in-Publication Data
appear on the last printed page of this book.

For S. P. J., with love and thanks

Contents

Acknowledgments

This volume originated with two workshops, held at Manchester University and the London School of Economics, and thanks go first to all the participants, including Maia Green and our two LSE discussants, William A. Christian Jr. and Patricia Spyer. The ideas presented in the introduction have been through a long process of evolution that has included courses I have taught in the anthropology of Christianity, and I would like to thank all my students at LSE who have helped me to think further about the issues involved. I would also like to thank Maurice Bloch for originally encouraging me to teach on this subject. Parts of the introduction and chapter 4 are based on research conducted with the assistance of grants from the British Academy and the Economic and Social Research Council (grant no. R000239016), whose support is gratefully acknowledged. I would also like to thank colleagues at Cornell University for providing, on three occasions, an ideal academic base and for their warm hospitality. Among the many individuals to whom thanks are due, I would like to mention in particular Danilyn Rutherford and Simon Jarvis, who patiently read and helpfully commented on the introduction in several drafts, and the two anonymous readers for Duke University Press.

···Introduction···

The Anthropology of Christianity

Fenella Cannell

Just because something is "well-known," it does not always follow that it is known.—G. W. F. Hegel

What difference does Christianity make? What difference does it make to how people at different times and in different places understand themselves and the world? And what difference does it make to the kinds of questions we are able to ask about social process?

Anthropology and Christianity

Propositions about the difference made by Christianity played a critical role in the fashioning of the broad comparativist theories of society that founded sociology and anthropology. For Émile Durkheim, Marcel Mauss, and Max Weber, each in their different ways, the characterization of the new social sciences as distinctively secular never precluded a clear recognition of the importance of Christianity. Mauss ([1938] 1985) considered Christianity decisive in the formation of modern Western understandings of the self. For Durkheim, Judeo-Christian religions constituted one important stage in the development and progressive abstraction of the "conscience collective," before the humanist values he predicted would emerge in later modernity. For Weber ([1930] 1992), while all world religions involved features of systematization and innovative thinking that might promote social change, the "elective affinity" between capitalism and Calvinist Christianity in Europe had produced Western modernity's distinctive forms.

Durkheim and his nephew Mauss were, of course, both nonpracticing and agnostic members of originally Jewish families, within a French culture divided between Catholicism and secularist republicanism that still contained powerful anti-Semitic tendencies.[1] Weber was an agnostic of Christian background, teaching and writing in Weimar Germany. For all three of them, it seems, the world in which they lived appeared to be becoming less religiously observant, and yet religious practice as the norm also seemed a recent, almost tangible memory. This modernist sense of being just "after" religion marks the tone of all three in some way, while Durkheim and Mauss were obviously doubly outside conventional Christianity.[2]

It is now commonplace to observe that each of these writers was a social evolutionist, at least in the loose sense of speaking of one form of society giving rise to another, more complex and less "primitive" form, over time.[3] Criticism of the evaluative aspect of social evolutionism, which ranks one person or community as more "advanced" than another, has been a constant feature of anthropological writing for many years. It is also widely understood that such models are teleological, in that they assume that societies are all tending toward the goal of some singular civilization.

It is certainly true that each of these writers invoked a sense of the development of history through successive stages; indeed, each one proposed that Christianity played a key role in the creation of a series of complex but definite one-way changes in social process. It is also well recognized, however, that all three of these writers were skeptical about the advantages of modernity; Mauss's most famous work, *The Gift* ([1924] 1990), in particular is best read as a critique of capitalist ideology (see Parry 1986), while Weber's prose is darkly evocative of the "iron cage" of contemporary work practices and bureaucratic systems that have lost sight of the values they were intended to serve. They were not, therefore, teleologists in the sense of assuming that society was tending toward some straightforwardly "higher" goal. Moreover Weber was explicit in insisting that the patterns of historical development followed by European modernization would not necessarily be replicated in other parts of the world.

This makes it somewhat ironic, therefore, that anthropological and sociological approaches to Christianity have long tended to become mired in a highly teleological reading of the foundational anthropologists, and in particular certain kinds of readings of Weber. The prevailing orthodoxy for several decades has been a focus on the seeming inevitability of secularization and of the advance of global modernity, while Christianity has been identified as, above all, a kind of secondary or contributory aspect of such changes. In the process, there has often been a tendency to assume that Christianity is an "obvious" or "known" phenomenon that does not require fresh and constantly renewed examination.

Alongside the general preoccupation with charting processes of modernization, there has been a widespread although not total disciplinary bias within anthropology in favor of the claim to be exercising a completely secular analytical approach. As the theologian John Milbank has succinctly noted, this claim is a fiction: "Once there was no 'secular' . . . The secular as a domain had to be instituted or *imagined*" (1990: 9). This invention was given a distinctive form in the modern social sciences. While this idea of a secular anthropology and sociology certainly does derive from Durkheim, again it is ironic that the treatment of religious topics in foundational anthropology was on the whole much less hostile than has been the case in some later writing.[4] As a significant minority of commentators have noted (Bowie 2002; E. Turner 1992; Engelke 2002), anthropology sometimes seems exaggeratedly resistant to the possibility of taking seriously the religious experiences of others. Religious phenomena in anthropology may be described in detail, but must be explained on the basis that they have no foundation in reality, but are epiphenomena of "real" underlying sociological, political, economic, or other material causes. It is not necessary to be a believer in any faith, or to abandon an interest in sociological enquiry, to wonder why the discipline has needed to protest quite so much about such widely distributed aspects of human experience.

In the context of this disciplinary nervousness about religious experience in general, the topic of Christianity has provoked more anxiety than most other religious topics. It has seemed at once the most tediously familiar and the most threatening of the religious traditions for a social science that has developed within contexts in which the heritage of European philosophy, and therefore of Christianity, tends to predominate. Unease about the political affiliations of some types of Christian practice, especially in the United States in the period after the rise of the Moral Majority, has produced the kind of situation described by Susan Harding (1991) in her accounts of Jerry Falwell's church, as the problem of studying liberal anthropology's "repugnant social other." In addition, the understandable desire to acknowledge the complex part played in European and American history by Jewish, Islamic, and other religious traditions has sometimes resulted in blanket suspicion of all intellectual interest in Christianity and the variety of Christian practice around the world. As I found when I embarked on some recent research on Mormonism in the United States, it is surprising how many colleagues assume that a research interest in a topic in Christianity implies that one must be a closet evangelist, or at least "in danger" of being converted—an assumption that would not be made about anthropologists working with most groups of people around the world.[5]

For these and other reasons, I would suggest that Christianity has functioned in some ways as "the repressed" of anthropology over the period of the formation of the discipline. And, as the repressed always does, it keeps on staging returns. The complexity of the relationship between Christianity and anthropology has in fact been pointed out early, well and repeatedly, if only by a few. It is noted, for example, by E. E. Evans-Pritchard (1960), in a typically acute essay delivered to a religious audience after his conversion to Catholicism. Both Malcolm Ruel (1982) and Jean Pouillon (1982) analyzed the difficulties of employing the word *belief* in anthropology, given the specifically Christian theological freight of that term, which tends to distort many other kinds of religious reality. More recently, and again from the acknowledged perspective of a Catholic convert, Edith Turner (1992) has sought to develop an anthropological method which allows the possibility that religious phenomena might be real, while at the same time maintaining high standards of ethnographic accuracy. There have also, from the earliest period of anthropology, been some ethnographers who became fascinated by the "syncretic" and missionary Christianities they observed, and who analyzed these in important accounts.

The curious fact is, however, that these insights remained marginal to mainstream anthropology and sociology for a long period and indeed have come to be more widely read again only relatively recently. With a more recent wave of prestigious commentators, including most famously two brilliant contributions by Talal Asad (1993) and Marshall Sahlins (1996), the topic of Christianity has started to move to a more central place again on the disciplinary agenda. Asad, drawing on Foucault, has written of the genealogy of the idea of religion in anthropology, analyzing elements taken from the history of both Christianity and Islam. In an important article on the native anthropology of Western cosmology, Sahlins has observed the extent to which assumptions about the world that inform the intellectual frameworks in which we operate are drawn from the Christian theology of human "fallenness" and its consequences, including a world that exists in a state of lack.

This book had its inception in teaching and collegiate workshops that took place at about the time that this new wave of writing on Christianity was beginning. The ideas presented here are not based directly on either Asad or Sahlins, although they share more common ground with the latter.

The book contains eleven original essays on localities in different parts of the world where people consider themselves to be Christians. It makes no claims to ethnographic completeness. We have, for example, no contribution solely devoted to continental Africa.[6] It does, however, offer a significant contribution to the range of comparative material available explicitly addressing what it means for people to be Christian. The authors included here argue from diverse and sometimes opposed theoretical positions. They are united in taking the Christianity of their informants seriously as a cultural fact and in refusing to marginalize it in their accounts of the areas in which they work. This means setting aside the assumption that we know in advance what Christian experience, practice, or belief might be. We offer eleven fresh accounts of particular, local[7] Christianities as they are lived, in all their imaginative force: a bodybuilding Jesus, a nonimmortal God, a fetishized Bible, Scripture study as "normal science." Together they begin to suggest ways anthropology might begin to renew its thinking about a religion whose very proximity has hitherto rendered it only imperfectly perceptible.

At the same time, this book makes a contribution to the questions asked by Milbank, Evans-Pritchard, and Sahlins, among others. How has anthropology's attitude to Christianity—which we understand as both an attempt to separate from Christian metaphysics and a simultaneous assimilation of key ideas derived from those metaphysics—limited the development of the discipline? What in fact is the relationship between anthropology and Christianity?

In considering this question, it is necessary to reach some provisional working definition of the term *Christianity* itself. This is more difficult than it might first appear. Some theoretical discussion in the social sciences rests on the supposition that Christianity has clear, inherent properties leading to repeatable effects when it is introduced into other societies around the world. On the other hand, some anthropologists have reacted against strong predictive theories of the effects of the introduction of Christianity, and might argue that most of the supposedly defining features of Christianity are chimerical, and can as well apply to many other sorts of religious practice, whether within the so-called world religions or not.

One among many possible examples of this kind of tension would be the diverse views taken on the effects of Christianization on attitudes to the dead. Meyer Fortes (1970, 1979), following an earlier article by Max Gluckman (1937), had placed much stress on the idea that ancestral religion stood in contrast to later world religions. In particular, ancestral religions should not be confused with cults of the dead. Ancestral religions were supposed to be distinguished by the focus of the ancestors on participation in the lives of their living descendants. There was little or no elaboration of ideas about where or how the ancestors went after death (in a way, they were still among the living).

This was contrasted with the situation in salvationist religions, where the fate of the dead person and their arrival in the afterlife was of key importance. In such situations, as in Catholic Europe, the living might pay attention to the dead, but with the main aim of changing the situation of the dead souls (e.g., getting them out of Purgatory by saying Mass) rather than changing the situation of the living.

It is not in doubt that the Christian church as it evolved introduced deliberate policies and practices designed to manage believers' attitudes to their dead, and these teachings changed over time, perhaps most famously with the elaboration of the Catholic doctrine of Purgatory, and with the challenge to that doctrine at the time of the Protestant Reformation (see Le Goff 1986; Schmitt 2000). Some writers questioned the basis of the Fortesian comparison, by pointing out that the terminology of "belief" ill described what was central to African ancestor worship in particular (Kopitoff 1968). More recent writing in a cognitivist tradition has challenged the paradigm in a different way, suggesting that such differences may be less significant than underlying cognitive similarities. This work proposes that all humans consider the dead as gone or as having some kind of continued existence, depending on the eliciting context (see Bloch 2002). While in this example the two kinds of approach are not necessarily incompatible, it is clear that the cognitivist analysis allows for a much greater degree of skepticism about any homogeneous or automatic effects following from Christianization.

Many of the contributions to this volume balance these models of what Christianity does against the specificities of local interpretations, and they do so in diverse ways. My own approach in this introduction, as well as of related work elsewhere (Cannell 2005b), is that Christianity is not an arbitrary construct, but that it is a historically complex one. It is *not* impossible to speak meaningfully about Christianity, but it *is* important to be as specific as possible about what kind of Christianity one means. Christianity—more perhaps even than other salvationist religions—is also a complex object in a different sense. This is because, as historians of the early church such as Peter Brown (1988), Caroline Walker-Bynum (1996), and Averil Cameron (1991) have clearly shown, part of its distinctive character is that it is essentially built on a paradox. The central doctrines of the Christian faith are the Incarnation (by which God became human flesh in Christ) and the Resurrection (by which, following Christ's redemptive death on the Cross, all Christians are promised physical resurrection at the Last Judgment). Although most writing on Christianity in the social sciences has focused on its ascetic aspects, on the ways in which Christian teaching tends to elevate the spirit above the flesh, Christian doctrine in fact always also has this other aspect, in which the flesh is an essential part of redemption. As Brown in particular shows, this ambivalence exists not just in theory, but as part of the lived practice and experience of Christians.

We will not be specifically concerned in this volume with institutional church history, since so much has already been written on this topic by those better qualified to do so. We will be concerned, however, to take up the insight of Brown and others, and to use it to question the ascetic stereotype of Christianity as it has become embedded in anthropology. I would moreover suggest that a recognition of the centrally paradoxical nature of Christian teaching allows us to move some way further in conceptualizing its historical development and, of special concern to anthropologists, local encounters with missionary Christianities.

The nature of this contradiction is such that even where particular Christian churches have, at given times and places, adopted certain theological positions as orthodox and policed them as such, the unorthodox position remains hanging in the air, readable between the lines in Scripture, and implied as the logical opposite of what is most insisted upon by the authorities. Hence the heretical is constantly reoccurring and being reinvented in new forms. Such recurring inventions may take place in the heartlands of Europe or America, or they may develop in fascinating and variable ways in quite different cultural contexts.

This introduction explores the range of issues briefly anticipated here, under several headings. First, I review in more detail some of the contexts in which Christianity was for many years marginalized in the ethnographic account. Second, we contribute to the debate on the relationship between anthropology and Christianity when we consider carefully the proposition, central to all dominant anthropological views of Christianity, that transcendence is at the center of the religion, and suggest a link between this idea of transcendence, and the idea of Christianity as a religion of radical discontinuity. Third, we review the diversity of Christian practice described in the contributions to this book, which challenge both the notion that Christianity is a merely arbitrary category, and the notion that it is a completely homogeneous phenomenon. Fourth, we consider and reevaluate the defining place that ideas about orthodoxy and conversion hold in the ethnography of Christianity. Fifth, we consider the problems inherent in defining Christianity through theories that prioritize narratives of modernity. Finally, we ask whether it is possible to draw on anthropology's origins to formulate a revived understanding of the relation between the discipline and Christianity and also ask whether we should move beyond the paradigm of Christianity as the "impossible religion."

Ethnography without Christianity

Perhaps surprisingly, Christianity was the last major area of religious activity to be explored in ethnographic writing. Since Durkheim, if not before, the attention of anthropologists has been directed as much to the supposed elementary forms of the religious life as to the supposed underlying structures of kinship, and with a similar assumption: that by examining what was prior to and other than our own society, we would uncover simultaneously what was universal in the composition of human interaction and what was distinctive about both the worlds of both the examined and the examiners. So much is familiar. Less often remarked, however, is the way in which the investigation of Christianity was pushed to the margins of this inquiry. While anthropology proceeded from the examination of "primitive" religions to the analysis of world religions such as Hinduism, Buddhism, and Islam, the study of Christian areas of the world was, generally, considered the least urgent object of study.

Two kinds of enquiry were theoretically open to anthropologists of religion. They might have examined Christian practice at home, especially in various European or American contexts. Or they could have worked on the Christianization of colonial populations in other continents. Different limiting factors seem to have been at work in each case. An instructive instance of the disincentives to focusing on Christianity at home is offered by the beginnings of interest in Mediterranean ethnography in the late 1950s and early 1960s (e.g., Campbell 1964). When young ethnographers began to imagine that interesting fieldwork sites could lie closer to home than the Trobriand Islands, they felt obliged to justify their choice by emphasizing the difference and distinctiveness of the apparently more familiar cultures they were studying—an imperative that probably also influenced the choice of a relatively remote pastoral culture for Campbell's groundbreaking study. In the resulting paradigm of the Mediterranean, this cultural distinctiveness came to be guaranteed by reference to so-called shame and honor behaviors, and to the rigid gender divisions through which these were supposed to operate. Perhaps in part because men were seen as the active enforcers of this culture, women were at first thought of as having less to say. When Ernestine Friedl first went to the field (Friedl 1962), she was assured by her supervisors that Greek women would have nothing "cultural" to tell her.[8] These culturally unmarked women were usually associated with specifically Christian activities. In Julian Pitt-Rivers's innovative *People of the Sierra*, which in 1954 dealt seriously for almost the first time with Spanish small town ethnography, cultural activities are strongly gendered as male, while women are regarded as those to whom society has assigned the role of appeasing the church by a demonstration of orthodox religious observance. A kind of functional division is assumed between the sexes. The black-clad, rosary-telling women of these Mediterranean ethnographies are figures of conformity rather than of local "cultural" autonomy and resistance. Of course such ethnographies reflected in part a real gendering of roles within some Catholic communities in Europe, in which women may often have adopted a role of greater observance and piety, while men (especially in peasant communities) indulged in a flamboyant anticlericalism in which the priest was set up as the butt of jokes from "real males" (Pina-Cabral 1986: 117). But it is also clearly true that this is not always a predictable or sufficient account of Catholic practice in such communities; compare the accounts of male religious enthusiasm in Christian 1972, for example. In advancing the well-known division between male culture and female domesticity, some of these early ethnographers also made a less widely noticed assignment of Christian practice to the female and therefore implicitly noncultural sphere.

A complementary deficit in the consideration of Christian experience can be found even in that feminist scholarship which helped to correct the assumption that women had nothing to say. Marina Warner (1976) argued that women in Catholic countries through different historical periods were oppressed through the church's romance with the figure of Mary. Because Mary was unique in being both virgin and mother, she necessarily made women aware of their own failure to emulate her. Catholic women were thus said to understand themselves, at the instruction of the church, as being centrally and inevitably failures. Certainly, Christian theologians have reproduced over long historical periods both an emphasis on the value of female virginity, which can easily produce a somewhat punitive form of asceticism (Brown 1988), and an attitude to the superior spiritual authority of men that, while not without space for alternative interpretations, might reasonably be called patriarchal. However, it is now clear that women's experience of Mary and Christ is historically and regionally variable (Walker-Bynum 1987); that the appeal of Mary for some Catholics may lie instead in a differently constructed notion of her mediatory, almost mediumlike powers (Bloch 1994); and that Catholic women may invert the notion of Mary as model, choosing instead to understand Mary as a woman whose experiences are modeled on their own, most human, experiences of maternal love and grief (Cannell 1991, 1999). Warner tends to identify the whole of Catholic religious experience (women's or men's) with the policies of the church, as though the pronouncements of the Vatican could perfectly determine the experience of Catholics. This has a curious result. The view that women are entirely subject to formation by the church ends by replicating a view of female Catholic experience worthy of the most austere of the Desert Fathers.

Some exceptional anthropologists gradually began to give illuminating accounts of European Catholicism (e.g., Christian 1972; Catedra 1992). These, though, have been mainly focused on rural and peasant communities in the south that could be seen as sufficiently distant from the industrial northwest to allow for an analytic distance from the academy. Protestant Europe and the United States have proved even more difficult for anthropologists to tackle. Both Weber's legacy and modern folk theory tend to lead to the assumption that late market capitalism is formed by Protestantism at the most profound, if secularized, level. But with the return of Protestant groups to the center of the political stage in the American New Right of the 1980s, some anthropologists began seriously to address these issues (Ginsburg 1989; Harding 1981, 1984). This kind of work is now beginning to be published at length (Harding 2000; Coleman 2000; McDannell 1995) and represents a crucial development, but such writers are still few in number. For many anthropologists, it seems that, unless special circumstances bring it into view, Christianity is still an occluded object.

The treatment of Christianity away from home developed slightly differently. For the British Africanists of the mid-twentieth century, for instance, the dominant models of lineage, tribe, and ancestor worship tended to focus attention away from the issues of Christian missionization, as the notion of honor cultures had eclipsed interest in Mediterranean Christianity. Nevertheless, there were astute and distinguished ethnographers of that period, such as Monica Wilson, whose interest in Christian conversion and social change led to an important early publication (M. Wilson 1971). Wilson tended to view Christianity in terms of its role in social transformation, but James Fernandez (1982) provided an example of the exploration of a distinctive African Christian imaginary in his richly detailed study of Fang syncretic Pentecostalism.

However, in mainstream anthropological circles the most influential view of African Christianity has probably been that provided by Jean and John Comaroff. And it is arguable that this major body of work, despite its valuable accounts of the reception of missionization in South Africa, ultimately subordinates the exploration of Christianity to the narrative of modernization.

Anthropological interest in colonialisms and postcolonialisms has of course both stimulated and required a nuanced view of local Christianities. Yet Christianity often took on a curious relation to that catchword of Marxist-influenced anthropology in the 1980s, "resistance." Jean Comaroff's earlier work (Comaroff 1985), for instance, explores some of the resonances of Tshidi Pentecostalist practice. She offers an illuminating discussion of the combination of Tshidi and U.S. Pentecostalist spatial symbolisms. Yet it is clear that what mainly interests her is the way in which (by, for example, recapitulating the color symbolism of precolonial Tshidi initiation rites) Tshidi Pentecostalist ritual resists incorporation into an "orthodox" Christian practice. Pentecostalism's role in resistance from the margin to the processes of nineteenth-century U.S. industrialization makes it an appropriate signifier for black experience in South Africa. As other Christian experience in Tshidi regions is not easily construed as a vehicle for "resistance," it remains unexplored. The religion of Tshidi Wesleyans is associated with a direct capitulation to the values of the white, colonialist, and industrializing state under apartheid. The Comaroffs' more recent historical works on South African Christianity draw attention to the particularity of Christian agents as they meet forms of local understanding (Comaroff and Comaroff 1991). But despite the value of this work and its wealth of illuminating historical detail, Christianity is nevertheless primarily identified with colonial agency and the compulsory imposition of modernity. A number of other questions, including the question of whether there are intrinsic dynamics of change and transformation within Christian theology itself, are thereby somewhat sidelined, and the association between Christian experience and subjugated orthodoxies—in this case the orthodoxies of modernity—is maintained. Many anthropologists who become interested in Christianity, then, do so almost against their will, initially seeing it as a kind of secondary phenomenon or top coat that has been applied by external forces to the cultures they are studying. This is particularly and understandably true when Christianity has been forced upon people by the actions of the state or of colonial missionaries. With honorable exceptions, anthropology has tended to come at the problem of the significance of Christianity rather simplistically, and has even tended to view it as a homogeneous thing, often covered by the label "the church," whose main distinguishing feature is taken to be its hostility to local patterns of understanding and behavior.

One key body of work for a different kind of anthropology of Christianity, then, may be work by historians on the early church, as it defined itself first as a quasi-millenarian sect within the Roman Empire, and then became at much-debated times and by a series of strange, uneven transformations the official religion of the empire itself. Peter Brown's work on Romano-Christian burials (1981), to take only one of the most famous examples, has subtly and convincingly demonstrated how the relationship of Roman citizens to their ancestors was transformed into the origins of the first Christian saint cults. Both Brown and Averil Cameron are among those historians who have begun to build up a concrete picture of how such shifts in social imagination actually came about (Brown 1988; Cameron 1991). Historians have focused on some of the central dilemmas of Christianity as it created itself as a changing social force—what for instance, could replace the cult of the first Christian martyrs as Christians ceased to be persecuted; how would those strands of Christianity whose millenarian, otherworldly tone most stressed the repudiation of existing kinship ties be reconciled with the continuity of Christian communities that actually emerged? How could it be that Christianity was inevitably thought through the concepts and intellectual methods of late Classical education, and by those who had been educated in it, but yet developed something new to say? How did the essential paradox of Christianity—its elevation of death to triumph—work to prevent the total assimilation of an evolving Christian theology to secular Roman modes of thinking after Constantine?

Such work forces us to acknowledge the extreme complexity of the questions being asked. The notion of transcendence usually taken to be characteristic of Christianity, for instance, can certainly be traced not only to Christianity but also to the Platonic philosophies of the Greeks and Romans, and perhaps also the Stoic philosophies of Rome, each of which in different ways argued for the existence of a set of abstract moral principles (Justice, etc.) that stood above social obligations, might come into conflict with them, and might require a man to choose them above such social obligations. The demand that a human being cultivate an internal barometer of such matters—that he create his own view of himself in terms of his relation to a form of conscience separable from social rules and obligations—certainly foreshadowed the development of the subjectivity that has usually been presented as distinctively Christian. Insofar as influential early Christian converts of the Roman Empire were themselves steeped in such teachings, they can also be said to have made Christianity in crucial ways. Similarly, the influence of the contemporary Judaism out of which early Christianity grew, and the relationship between Jewish, Latin, and Hellenistic strands in the early church, is itself a complex and intensely debated field in theological and historical scholarship (Ehrman 2000, 613–16).

As Cameron (1991) has pointed out, therefore, the questions which anthropologists, if they are at all alert, ought to be asking themselves—what, in any situation is Christianity, and how can one possibly discern its lineaments from that of the social context in which it lives—are not only the questions of historical colleagues, they are also the questions of Christian thinkers, teachers and officials at all periods in the history of the church. Therefore, the writings of the early fathers on heresy, and of the officials of the Inquisition not only in its later flamboyant stages but also in the centuries of gradual development in the Middle Ages, can all be read as the pursuit of an answer to this question from different points of view. Moreover, as Averil Cameron has noted (albeit with reference to a Kuhnian notion of paradigm shift, rather than an anthropological notion of social transformation), the evolution of the early church is one of the most important potential areas on which historians, like many anthropologists, are working on the dynamics of what used to be called "culture contact" (Cameron 1991).

The difficulties facing such a renewal of attention, however, are serious indeed. Christianity's comparative invisibility as an interpretative problem for contemporary ethnography, a problem with its own contours, not identical with those of modernity, is by no means a problem of recent origin. It has tangled and still strong roots in the long emergence of social science and social theory themselves out of deist, and then Enlightenment, critique of religion. Social science takes some of its earliest and most important steps toward a separate disciplinary identity by means of a unilateral declaration of independence from metaphysics, including Christian theology[9]—a declaration which, however, it has proved easier to make than to fulfill. I now turn briefly to consider some aspects of that prehistory which had particular consequences for current anthropological thinking about Christianity.

Christianity as Radical Discontinuity

The idea that Christianity constructs, through the Incarnation, an absolutely new relation between man and the world might be said to be the central proposition of the religion. This proposition has itself had a fateful influence upon critical conceptions of Christianity. One of the most powerful—as well as influential, albeit diffusely—formulations of the thesis of Christianity's qualitative distinctiveness is found in the work of the German philosopher G. W. F. Hegel. Hegel's interest in the history of religion developed out of a structural contrast between classical, especially Greek, religion[10] and the Judeo-Christian tradition. The many aspects of this contrast turned on the difference between a form of religion in which the divine was present in the world and one in which the divine was essentially thought of as belonging to a world transcending, superior to, and radically incommensurable with the world of time and space. Thus while in Greek religion as Hegel imagined it there could be no statue of (say) Pallas Athena, in which Athena was not in some way actually present, in Christianity a statue of the Virgin Mary is intended in essence as a representation of what is not there—an evocation of the divine beyond this world, and a means to approach it that is necessary precisely because of the distance separating mortals from an ineffable God:

> "The divine" in Christianity is supposed to be present in consciousness only, never in life. This is true of the ecstatic unifications of the dreamer who renounces all multiplicity of life . . . and who is conscious of God alone and so could shake off the opposition between his own personality [and God] only in death. It is equally true later. . . . This is either the felt opposition in all actions and expressions of life which purchase their righteousness with the sense of the servitude and the nullity of their opposition, as happened in the Catholic church, or the opposition of God [to the fate of the world] in mere more or less pious thoughts, as happens in the Protestant church; either the opposition between a hating God and life, which is thus taken as either a disgrace or a crime, as in some Protestant sects, or the opposition between a benevolent God and life, with its joys, which are thus merely something received. (Hegel [1807] 1975: 301)

Leaving aside the details of Hegel's chronology and typology of various Christian formations for the moment, we can see here the kernel of much later thinking about the difference Christianity makes. The separation of man from the divine—the origin of the "unhappy consciousness" that recognizes this loss—sets up problems to which anthropologists and historians have recurred again and again in accounts of Christian thinking, including the need for mediation with this distant God, the centrality of a salvationist emphasis in which death (the only place in which man and God can be reunited) becomes the crucial defining moment of life, the setting up of a hierarchy between life and afterlife, with crucial implications for ideas about economy and exchange, and the creation of a new notion of interiority that has its origins in the need of the Christian to consider the fate of his or her own soul.[11]

Hegel's influence spread in many diffuse ways in nineteenth-century thought, and it is often powerfully evident even in the work of those who had read little or nothing of his writing, or who are not known as Hegelian thinkers. We could observe, for instance, how closely Durkheim's account of Christianity, within his own argument about the development from mechanical to organic social solidarity, appears to follow the logic elaborated by Hegel.

Like Hegel, Durkheim in *The Division of Labour in Society* ([1893] 1997) makes a strong contrast between Christianity and Greek and Roman religions, which, again in an explicitly developmental framework that we will find in all these models, he thought of as intermediate between animism and Christianity. "Gradually," according to Durkheim, "the religious forces became detached from the things of which they were at first only the attributes." Over history, he thinks, people stopped worshipping the divine element in rocks and other features of the natural world and started worshipping spirits on their own "but still present in space and near to us." For the Greeks, the gods had moved further away to Olympus and only rarely intervened in human life, but were still present and accessible in their temples and statues. "But," he writes, "it is only with Christianity that God finally goes beyond space; his kingdom is no longer of this world. The dissociation of nature and the divine becomes so complete that it even degenerates into hostility. At the same time, the nature of divinity becomes more general and abstract, for it is formed not from sensation as it was in the beginning, but from ideas. The God of humanity is necessarily not so comprehensible as those of a city or clan" (230–31).

Although it refers explicitly neither to Hegel nor to Durkheim, the continuity of this line of thought can be seen, for instance, in the important 1972 essay by Edmund Leach on the dynamics of Christianity in social process, "Melchisedech and the Emperor: Icons of Subversion and Orthodoxy." Leach begins this essay[12] by claiming that "the origin of Christianity lay in a wide-ranging cultural situation rather than in any single event" (Leach [1972] 1983: 68). The "wide-ranging cultural situation" is that of a continuous "oscillation" in Christian practice between the cropping up of small, democratic and radical cults (some of which we might call millennial), which challenge the authority of the church, and which he claims share certain structural features with the original Christian community in its earliest form, and the establishment out of and against these cults, of a more hierarchical and institutional church structure, which can be closely linked with rather authoritarian state forms beginning with the Roman Empire, to which it may lend legitimation. Leach links this political "oscillation" to an essential ambiguity in the structure of Christian thought. Like Hegel and Durkheim, Leach argues that Christianity's radical separation between man and God lies behind this oscillation. Two extreme, opposed positions were logically possible within the doctrine of the Incarnation:

> At one extreme, it was held that Christ was always God and his human form only an appearance; at the other, the human Christ and the divine Logos, though housed in one fleshly body, were separate rather than fused. . . . doctrines of the latter kind . . . imply that any inspired human prophet who

> feels himself to be possessed by the Holy Spirit is really no different, in kind, from Christ himself. Hence the Incarnation ceases to be a unique historical event in the past; it becomes a perpetually repeatable event belonging to the present. (Leach [1972] 1983: 75)

Such dilemmas were, thinks Leach, central to many of the arguments about the Arian "doctrine" (later heresy), which the Council of Nicaea firmly established as what one recent historian has called Christianity's "archetypal heresy" (R. Williams 1987).[13] For Leach, the argument that each person of the Trinity was eternally and equally God reinforced the nonrepeatability of the Incarnation. Since no man could rival Christ's union with the divine, God's power was to be channeled through established intermediaries, especially through the priesthood and the emperors who could be consecrated only by them. Yet the possibility of direct union with the divine could be repressed only partially and is continually liable to revive in, for example, inspirational Protestantism (Leach [1972] 1983: 88).

Whatever the accuracy of Leach's account of historical Arianism, we may for now simply note the influence of his general line of thinking, traceable back to Hegel; the struggle over the mediation of divine power is one of the aspects of local Christianities that has been best documented in ethnographic writing. The pioneering work of William Christian on Spanish Catholicism and other writing on saints' cults in Catholicism, on alternative forms of priests, and on struggles to achieve church endorsement for locally chosen mediators has highlighted the extent to which struggles for control of mediation may be taking place not episodically, but continuously (Pina-Cabral 1986; Catedra 1992; Christian 1972, 1992; Ladurie 1981; P. Brown 1988; Cannell 1999). The work of Pina-Cabral, in particular, lucidly formulates a particular kind of insight into European popular Christianity. Pina-Cabral describes for the Portuguese Alto Minho region the characteristic cults of the "incorrupt bodies" (local people popularly declared saints because their bodies are found not to have decayed after burial), the "noneaters" (local people said to subsist on the Communion wafer alone), and other connected practices. He declares, "The Portuguese peasant, like all Christians, lives in a fallen world, one of hardship and despair, permanently threatened by impending death. Yet he believes that there is a state of perennial life which can already be achieved in this world. To overcome this contradiction, he has recourse to entities which, because they are not clearly classifiable as dead or alive, can be used as mediators" (Pina-Cabral 1986: 235).[14]

The mediation of the power of a God withdrawn from the world of mortal men thus becomes a key trope in the anthropology of Christianity. The same perception also drives most anthropological treatments of ascetic practices in Christianity; because God has withdrawn from the world, spirit and matter have become opposites that can never again be fully reconciled. Moreover, spirit may be perceived as "beyond" and "better than" flesh, since spirit is that of which God is made.[15] This becomes the reason for fasting and other forms of self-mortification, in which the person limits the claims of the flesh in order to increase the space in himself that is given to the spirit, and thus come a little closer to the divine ideal. And the irreconcilable divergence between spirit and flesh, or spirit and matter, becomes in turn, it is argued, the basis for many other kinds of dualistic opposition in which one element is thought of as "beyond" the other, including symbolic oppositions between the genders.

However important this focus on mediation and asceticism has become, however, the definition of Christianity as determined by transcendence in Hegel's sense was also taken up in a range of connected propositions about changes in human understanding of the universe and of the self. At this point we need to remind ourselves of one such aspect, which is perhaps best known to anthropologists through the work of Mauss on the concept of the person (1938), but more recently discussed in the important volume edited by Carrithers, Collins, and Lukes (1985), *The Category of the Person*. Mauss was particularly interested in the effects of Christianity in creating a new concept of the socially defined self or, in Mauss's terms, "person." Here, as in *The Gift*, Mauss relied (like the early kinship theorists) on material drawn from comparative law and contracts. Working from the evidence of the "rules" of a society, he claimed, it would be possible to extrapolate its values, and to trace the development of the definition of what constituted the person, legally and ethically understood. His essay is therefore concerned with the movement from the *personnage* of tribal society, who is no less a self, but simply a different kind of self, to the birth of conscience as a sense of interiority connected with morality. While, like a number of other commentators both ancient and modern, Mauss saw this shift as being in several ways foreshadowed in Greek Platonic and Roman philosophy, he was also like them in attributing the most important change to the influence to Christianity: "It is Christians who have made a metaphysical entity of the 'moral person' (*personne morale*) after they become aware of its religious power. Our own notion of the human person is still basically the Christian one" (358).

So obvious was the truth of this argument to Mauss that he dealt with the Christian person in a page and a half, remarking that he could here do no better than to rely on long labors already undertaken by the theologians (Mauss [1938] 1985: 358). He notes, however, the importance of the Trinitarian controversy. In it the concept of the person passed through a crucial stage: "Unity of the three persons—of the Trinity—unity of the two natures of Christ. It is from the notion of the 'one' that the notion of the 'person' (*personne*) was created—I believe that it will long remain so—for the divine person, but at the same time for the human person, substance and mode, body and soul, consciousness and act" (20). From this, all later Western philosophy on the development of the person as "psychological being" has taken its starting point (361).

As N. J. Allen (1985: 41) points out, Mauss's much-criticized (and easily criticized) evolutionist framework for the comparison of societies is not a reason to discard all the observations of his essay. Much of what he suggests about the West is translatable into the terms of historical investigation, rather than a priori assertion. It is worth comparing the thesis with Foucault's account of the growth of the "scientia sexualis" in *The History of Sexuality* (1976). While Mauss proposes a developmental paradigm of societies, which perhaps still implicitly retains some notion of the progressive movement of history, for Foucault the history of the self can be excavated only archaeologically, by means of the examination of the discontinuously successive forms of knowledge-power that have produced it. Nevertheless, Foucault's excavations still place Christianity in a crucial position in the creation of the modern self, a position that it occupies for him in part because he sees it as producing a form of interiority that foreshadows and enables the growth of modern psychological and psychoanalytic regimes. "The confession," says Foucault, "became one of the West's most highly valued techniques for producing truth . . . Western man has become a confessing animal" (60). The contemporary belief in sexuality as the key and hidden foundational truth about identity grows for Foucault out of the Christian sacrament of confession, which teaches people to believe in the reality of something hidden, inaccessible at first not only to their interrogator, but also to themselves, which must be brought slowly into the light of day as a form of offering (61–79).[16]

Like the philosophers who preceded him (but of course unlike Mauss and Durkheim), Foucault is in fact discussing the history of Western "power/knowledge," and not undertaking a comparative exercise across cultures.[17] Here we should note that we have moved from the original notion of transcendence as the "unhappy consciousness" to theories (both before and after Foucault) in which what unfolds from that is the notion of personal interiority.

Whether considered as a fact or as an illusion, this notion of interiority has been applied especially to the analysis of Protestant, and particularly Calvinist, thought and cultures. And these, in turn, have been widely considered at least since Weber ([1930] 1992) to have been formative in the creation of the modern Western person under capitalism. Weber's thesis is, of course, that it was the ironic fate of seventeenth-century European Puritanism finally to run its course as a religion and become absorbed in the development of capitalist process. Once-religious concepts, such as the "calling," are uncannily transformed in secular capitalism, he argues, so that they retain much of their power as tools of self-fashioning, while being emptied of the otherworldly impulse which previously gave them real meaning.

This famous text is often remembered in the social sciences as a *locus classicus* for Weber as a prophet of universal secular modernity. This view traduces both Weber's careful historicism and his genuine interest in religious experience. We should also remember, however, another aspect of Weber's argument, which is that it, too, assumes the logic of asceticism in Christianity. That is, in Weber a Protestant variant of Catholic ascetic practice becomes the work ethic, and a Protestant transformation of the Catholic ascetic religious vocation becomes the calling in Protestant, and later secular, daily professional life.

An interesting inversion of Weber's secularization argument has been offered by Louis Dumont (1985: 93–122) in an essay inspired by Mauss's essay on the person. Some elements of Dumont's argument are familiar. He again traces the notion of the person as an interior, reflexive self back to Platonism and Stoicism, via Christian conceptions of the soul under the early church controversies. The Calvinist reading of God as Will, most clearly shown in the doctrine of predestination, completes the creation of the capitalist individual. The Calvinist person has internalized the duty to imitate God thus conceived of as Divine Will and must therefore act on himself in continual self-fashioning, in order to show forth a reflection of the Almighty.

If Weber's is a secularization theory of modernity, Dumont's can thus be said to be in a sense a Christianization theory. Certainly, both point to the internalization of asceticism and its accommodation with the world:

Weber's worldly ascetic and Dumont's *homo economicus* share much of their genealogy. Yet there is also a key difference of emphasis. For Dumont, the modern state is "a transformed church." With Calvinist theology, a model of the individual that was originally developed in the context of asceticism and orientation to the life beyond becomes the central type of the modern person. The Calvinist vision of God as above all Will produces the notion of the Christian as necessarily imitating God through a process of the constant exercise of the will in the processes of self-fashioning. These theoretically equal individuals, the *homo aequalis* to a South Asian *homo hierarchicus*, are increasingly imagined as the basis of the state. For Dumont, the foundation of the modern state in individualism is precisely what most deeply attests to its fundamentally ecclesial character.

One of the most important explicit attempts to define the question of the relationship between the ideology of capitalism and the ideology of Christianity (although here subsumed within the general category of "salvationist religions") is offered in Parry 1986. In this article, Jonathan Parry offers a rereading of Mauss that draws attention to Mauss's insistence on the notion of gift versus commodity as an artifact of contemporary Western ideology. In Parry's reading, Mauss's work on the Maori and other famous examples is really intended to demonstrate not that gift societies preceded commodity societies, but rather that an absolute gift-commodity opposition had little purchase in precapitalist societies and is an artifact of capitalism.

Parry proposes that there is a link between the contrast between altruism and business and the introduction of an economy of salvation. (His 1994 work on Hinduism makes it clear that this is not confined to Christianity, but also readable in other "world religions.") The idea of salvation is correlated with a realm of exchange that is superior to (and transcendent of) ordinary, earthly exchange, and whose distinguishing feature is that it is premised on unidirectional transactions, in which gifts pass out of the worldly frame and into the beyond. Such gifts are therefore not in any ordinary sense reciprocated, although the believer may hope that the reward for altruism will be salvation in the next life; that his gift will, as it were, be converted from one economy to the other on the condition that he acts in the spirit of the heavenly economy while still on earth. But Parry (1986) suggests that, like the mutually dependent gift and commodity identified by Mauss, such an unearthly economy can exist only in opposition to a still-acknowledged worldly economy in which ordinary reciprocation and sociality play a much greater part. Parry's punctilious style of argument enables us to isolate what in many other works is somewhat blurred over—that is, the complexity of the suggested connections between Christianity and the late capitalism of which this bifurcated ideology is typical.

This suggestion is of course in some ways consonant with the Weberian story of capitalism and the rise of Protestantism. But while Weber's is essentially a trajectory of modernization, in which Christianity plays an ironic if intimate part that ultimately leads toward the disenchantment of the world, theses like Parry's and Dumont's suggest a more complex and active role for Christian thought and Christian institutions.

Diverse Christianities

Fundamental to any understanding of Christianity's diversity today is the opposition between broadly Protestant and Catholic Christianities. Four of the essays included here concern parts of the world that are predominantly Roman Catholic, and seven concern areas that are predominantly Protestant. All are committed to a historically particular understanding of Christianity. Anthropologists writing on Catholicisms have long had available the example of William Christian's work, which has shown that popular Catholicism cannot be described without an integrated account not only of the impact of changes in Vatican policy and teaching at the local level, but also of the distinct histories of the different religious orders and their varied relationships to forms of religious practice.

Among these, the nineteenth-century Jesuits were central actors in the construction of local practice in Tamil South India, as described by David Mosse in this volume. Mosse argues that South Indian Catholic personhood had been and still is widely enacted in dramatic rituals of possession and exorcism, in which Hindu demons are expelled by Catholic saints. These saints are themselves governed by a nonviolent Christ within a hierarchical model of Christian divinity reminiscent of caste, and Mosse associates this pattern with the accommodationist policies of the Jesuits who converted this area in the seventeenth and eighteenth centuries, but who were eventually disgraced and expelled. When reformed French Jesuits returned to Tamil South India in the nineteenth century, it was as the agents of the new orthodoxy of personal agency and personal responsibility, which took an austere attitude to both saints and spirits. These priests demanded that local Catholics replace explanations of personal suffering centered on demonic possession, with those in which the sin or folly of the individual was the cause, and confession was central to the cure. Exorcism remained an area of tension within this form of Catholicism, as while resisting local demand as largely frivolous, the Jesuits were never able to divorce themselves entirely from the possibility of a "legitimate" need for exorcism, since this of course continues to be acknowledged in contemporary Catholic doctrine.

The devotion to the Sacred Heart found ubiquitously in Catholic fishing households in Kerala, as described by Cecilia Busby, apparently carried with it few such orthodoxies of an interiorized Catholic practice. The area seems to have retained the relatively relaxed attitude to religious accommodation that characterized its first Portuguese Jesuit priests in the sixteenth century. Indeed, Busby describes the logic of the Keralan Sacred Heart as being driven by an idea of renewable, material power. She further argues that the Sacred Heart is not construed just in terms of local Hindu ideas of religious power (*shakti*), but also in terms of local (Dravidian) kinship, best understood as a processual flow of gendered substance.

By contrast with these essays from South Asia, Olivia Harris and I both write on areas originally converted and predominantly organized by Franciscans as part of the late-sixteenth-century expansion of the Spanish Empire. The particular interest of the Reformation and Counter-Reformation Franciscans in a structuring of time into the ages of the Father, Son, and (in millennial time) Holy Ghost has been studied by historians including Phelan (1959, 1970). What has most often been said of the Catholic practice both of the Laymi area and of historic Bicol is that given the relative shortage of priests, native or syncretic concepts have survived in the absence of complete institutional control. However, this kind of statement reveals very little of the logic of such interactions or of the ways in which local peoples were responding to specifically Franciscan ideas. Both the Laymi preoccupation with successive epochs and the Bicolano reference to ages of the Father, Son, and Holy Ghost clearly demonstrate this interaction, but time has been construed differently in each area. For the Laymi, epochal time is central to their understanding of their own Christianity; in Bicol, it is a more marginal concept, evoked most often in discussions of the decline of virilocal marriage and associated kinship forms, not of religious conduct (Cannell 1999: 52–54). Franciscan doctrine features in the Bicol ethnography primarily as a message evaded; while eighteenth-century Franciscan sermons stressed the risen Christ (as

Danilo Gerona explained to me) and the nineteenth-century reformers stressed the transcendent God, I argue here and elsewhere (Cannell 1999: 133–200) that Bicol Catholics are deeply devoted to a "dead Christ" and are little concerned with the economy of salvation.

If Catholicism is diverse despite the central control of the Vatican, the multiplicity of Protestant churches is even more so. Most of the mainstream Protestantisms that figure in this volume are either Lutheran or Calvinist (rather than Anglican or Episcopalian). Two of them are directly historically linked: both Danilyn Rutherford and Webb Keane discuss areas of the former New Order Indonesia, which were colonized by the Dutch and converted by Dutch and German missionaries. Harvey Whitehouse's discussion of Papua New Guinea is also mainly centered on mainstream Protestant practice. The Fijians discussed by Christina Toren are strong Methodists, the Malagasy described by Eva Keller are Seventh-Day Adventists, the Piro of Peter Gow's essay were converted by the secretive Summer Institute of Linguistics (SIL), whose public and non-missionary arm is the Wycliffe Society, which works on the translation of Bibles into native languages, and the Swedish arm of the Word of Life group (described by Simon Coleman) is one of a proliferating number of charismatic Faith churches, based in the United States.

All these churches define themselves against Catholicism, and they share a good deal of theological common ground. But they have also diverged widely from each other. Methodists follow the emphases of the English brothers John and Charles Wesley, whose eighteenth-century movement stressed the need for revival of both spiritual experience and social conscience in Christian practice, and whose view of the need for Christians to work all their lives at "perfecting" themselves in Christlike conduct softened the teaching on salvation through grace alone. Seventh-Day Adventism, often regarded by other Protestant churches as a cult, is one of a group of churches that emerged around modern-day prophets in the religious revivals of East Coast mid-nineteenth-century America. The SIL, although in many ways sui generis, especially in how little is known of its teachings, belongs to the aggressive American Protestant missionization of third world countries. It is clearly linked to a nineteenth- and twentieth-century politics in the United States both ambitious of global influence and deeply suspicious of and competitive with Roman Catholicism, especially when the latter is apparently connected with socialist or Communist regimes. The Faith movement of which the Word of Life Church forms a part, on the other hand, is a form of religious revivalism that is part of America's religious discourse with itself as much as with outsiders. As Coleman points out, it aims to address the dissatisfactions many people have with religious experience within the mainstream churches and deliberately proposes a different view of the relationship of faith and the physical world.

It is also important to bear in mind that Roman Catholicism and Protestantism did not cease to oppose and mutually define each other at the time of the Reformation. Indeed, much that is central about the tone of religious teachings in any given period is a product of the relationship between the two, especially because the Catholic Church has at times sought to disarm its Protestant critics by selective imitation. The asceticism and (relative) rationalism of the nineteenth-century French Jesuits described by Mosse in this volume, for example, in many ways evoke stereotypical mainstream Protestantism of the period. One could also look at instances of innovation in church policy. The Catholic Church of the twentieth century became increasingly concerned that it was losing ground to Protestant missionaries in Latin America and other traditional Catholic strongholds. This perception influenced moves around the period of Vatican II away from hierarchical and conservative styles of pastoral authority at local level and the replacement of the Latin Mass with services in local languages. All the Christians in this volume are indirectly linked together through the complex shared histories of the churches to which they belong.

Orthodoxy and Conversion

Anthropologists and sociologists looking at Christianity have often expressed the inherent difficulty of deciding whether nonstandard Christian practice is or isn't really Christian. On the one hand, they are aware that Christianity is a changeable phenomenon; on the other, it seems somehow unsatisfactory to class together all sorts of practices and beliefs that have little resemblance to each other, or to metropolitan or theological Christianity. This problem has been particularly acute in the study of convert populations, a domain of special interest to anthropology. Robert Hefner concludes that conversion is best defined as "not a deeply systematic reorganization of personal meanings" but a "new locus of self-identification" (1993: 17), while Charles Stewart and Rosalind Shaw (1994: 2) tackle the issue by proposing a reclamation of the term *syncretism* from its pejorative connotations to describe religious synthesis and urging alertness to the ways in which political capital can be claimed through the construction of either mixed or pure identities.

This amended, nonpejorative language of syncretism points in useful directions, for example by reminding us that the Catholic Church has always had its own theory of syncretism and its acceptable limits, currently known as inculturation theory. Inculturation theory presents quite a sophisticated attitude to local culture, claiming that local forms of approaching God may all be acceptable, and even necessary, as long as the presence of a transcendent deity presiding over all is acknowledged.[18] This definition would cover many of the cases presented in this volume, but it would not cover all of them. As I show in my essay on the Philippines, Bicolano Catholics have only a very muted and ambiguous interest in the economy of salvation, and in most contexts they do not focus on the transcendent idea of God.[19] Yet given their profound devotional engagement with Christ and the Catholic saints, it would make no sense to say that they are not Christians. I shall argue that while the idea of transcendence usually defines the limits of Christianity's own self-definition, not all local Christianities are Christian in this way (nor do they all put together all the elements that have been identified as belonging to transcendence). Indeed, while most of the exported Christianities have historically been transcendent Christianities, Christian thinking has always carried other selves within it.

The question of how far one can go without ceasing to become a Christian has always been the subject of active and explicit debate in missionizing churches. The original function of the medieval Catholic Inquisition was to distinguish what was mere superstition in European folk practice from what was pernicious error, idolatry, or heresy. The Catholic Church has taken a relatively tolerant approach since Vatican II. Protestant churches have sometimes been less permissive about continuities in existing social customs. Much has depended in each case on what the church defines as religion and what it allows as culture in a particular locale. Yet this distinction, as a number of anthropologists have recognized, is problematic because it is in itself a characteristic of Christian thinking and tends to be meaningless in many other systems. Missionary decisions as to what custom could harmlessly remain and what must be abandoned have therefore tended to seem arbitrary from the point of view of the people they are serving, and have often, as in the case of the *korwar* described by Rutherford, or the Fijian funerals of Toren's chapter, provided the opportunity for much greater continuities of thought than the missionaries had ever intended.

This volume joins this debate by supplying a comparative ethnography of orthodoxy itself. The contributors do not ask simply whether the people they describe are "orthodox" by mainstream Western standards; they also ask to what extent, if at all, different groups share the mainstream Christian interest in "orthodoxy" and boundary maintenance. For the Bicolano Catholics about whom I write, four centuries of Roman Catholicism have rendered familiar the idea of "religion" as a separate sphere of life. It is also well known that several commonly held ideas are not popular with the clergy, and this is a cause of some anxiety. Thus far, one could say that Bicolanos are interested in the orthodox.

On the other hand, these anxieties come into play only because people engage daily in activities on which the Catholic Church frowns—most notably, spirit mediumship and healing. For most people, dealing with the spirits is not undertaken in a mood of countercultural defiance toward the church and the priest; rather, there is constant discussion of how the two can actually be reconciled. Thus, while acknowledging that priests say that spirits are "demons," ordinary Catholic Bicolanos give a wide variety of reasons for continuing to treat with them. They will say, for instance, that while other spirit mediums may deal with evil spirits, they themselves deal only with good, Catholic ones. Or they may explain that although spirits are of a lower order of powers than Christ and the saints, they are "all under God" and that the efficacy they have in healing is in fact given to them by God himself (Cannell 1999: 134). Spirit mediums are in fact among the most regular devotees at saints' shrines and pilgrimage sites, although they, like most Bicolanos, may not flock so eagerly to confession and other activities directed by the priest, usually placing more importance on religious devotions carried out at home. Somewhat comparable situations seem to exist in both Kerala, as described by Busby, and Tamil South India, as described by Mosse, for in each of these places local Catholics are much less concerned than their priests to separate Catholic worship from local Hindu traditions and are in fact resistant to pressures toward increased exclusivity of worship.

On the closely associated point of whether or not local Christians are interested in the idea of conversion, we have two strongly contrasting examples in this volume. The Piro of Amazonian Peru demonstrate an impressive indifference to it, closely analyzed by Gow. From the point of view of Christian missionaries, the Piro are a kind of ultimate challenge; they resisted several prolonged attempts to convert them, made by both Catholics and Protestants, before being suddenly and dramatically won over by the SIL. Gow explains that for the Piro, the idea of conversion had so little relevance that they immediately forgot it, claiming that they "have always been" Christians. The Piro do recall the advent of the SIL but describe it primarily as a reorganization of social relations—or rather, seen through a shamanic lens, a restoration of proper social and trade relations—with whites through which the Piro have gained access to goods and education earlier withheld from them by rubber plantation owners.

For the Bolivian Laymi, at the other extreme, the idea of conversion to Christianity is so compelling that they constantly dwell upon it, and particularly on the idea of its incompleteness. According to Harris, not only do Andean saints' shrines have to be periodically "charged" with the power of the Mass to prevent them turning against the community, but the Laymi doubt that they themselves can ever be absolutely proper Christians, a self-perception that seems to fill them with melancholia rather than with defiance. Laymi rituals play out again and again the problematic and unresolved relationship between a Christianity clearly understood as dominant and ancestral powers that nonetheless cannot be entirely abandoned. Christianity, then, does not always and equally convert people to the idea of conversion.

The difficulty of understanding the force of conversion and orthodoxy in particular ethnographic contexts is finely illustrated in Christina Toren's piece on Fijian Methodism. Toren's piece is important because the people with whom she worked are, by the standards of mainstream Methodism, highly observant and correct Methodists. Unlike many of the other groups of people discussed here, Fijian Methodists do not express understandings of Christian teaching that are in obvious tension with those of their church authorities, nor do they avoid church services or deliberately relocate religious activity away from those areas where ministers have close control. On the contrary, as Toren shows, they are regular churchgoers and encourage their children to attend Sunday school. Indeed, Fijian adults say that there is no contradiction between "the way according to the church" and "the way of the land," and they argue that their children are learning the two together. This is a case, then, not only of orthodoxy but also of orthopraxy. Yet Toren argues convincingly that Fijian Methodists' conception of God is ultimately shaped after the pattern of Fijian chiefs, whose power is not otherworldly in origin but is dependent on the support, attendance, and compassion of their followers. For Toren, this equivalence is maintained through the attitude to kin learned in daily interaction, and in rituals such as funerals for dead relatives. These rituals are most emphatically not anti-Christian; they follow the Methodist liturgy and are directed toward the Christian God. However, Toren shows that a child gradually learns, as he or she grows up, a set of procedures for dealing with the immediate bereavement, the treatment of the body, the gathering of the mourners, and the conduct of the funeral. Through following these procedures, children learn the emotion of social compassion and share in the experience of attendance on God that is at the center of Fijian worship.

Toren's example illustrates possible shortcomings in some accounts of colonial Christian conversion as the "discipline of the body." The tendency of these (usually Foucauldian-leaning) accounts is to suggest that while Christian doctrine may fall on uncomprehending ears in non-Western milieus, profound changes in subjectivity can be and are wrought mainly through the drilling of convert bodies in Christian practices. Neither of these propositions seems to hold true in Fiji. First, here as in many Christian locales, doctrinal content is in fact of considerable interest to convert populations. Yet, second, neither the embracing of this doctrine nor the following of Christian bodily observances of all kinds has resulted in the Fijians having the same idea of divine power as Charles Wesley did. It might be objected, of course, that if disciplinary regimes were extended to Fijian kinship practices, we would see a more thoroughgoing change in outlook. The historical fact is, however, that this has not happened,[20] and that it seems that neither orthodoxy nor orthopraxy automatically produces such changes.

If Toren's piece directs us to consider that the meaning of orthodoxy is not self-evident, so too with perhaps even more force does Keller's account of pious and observant Seventh-Day Adventists in Madagascar. Keller's essay resonates with two of the central arguments of this book: first, that it is not sufficient to assume that we know in advance what Christian experience is—even when popular practice appears to be most highly conformist to the standards of the church concerned; second, that it is unhelpful to treat Christianity as simply a secondary phenomenon of underlying political or economic change. Keller argues against explanations of conversion to Adventism which claim that it is a reaction to slave status, an attempt to reestablish dislocated communities in conditions of urban migration, or has some other clear socioeconomic cause. Indeed, her informants gain no particular advantage from conversion, and she argues that their continued adherence to their religion must therefore be explained in terms of the religious experience itself. Keller's ethnography of Adventist Scriptural study provides an illuminating sense of the intellectual excitement and satisfaction of Adventists engaged on the pursuit of truth.

Adventist worship emerges in this account as surprisingly cerebral; indeed, Keller notes that Adventists look down on what they view as the extreme emotionalism and drama of neighboring Malagasy Pentecostalists. This draws our attention to a final connected point: religious engagement in Christianity can come in a wide variety of forms. The intense expressiveness that the analytical Adventists shun is precisely what attracts the members of the Word of Life Church, for whom the ideal worship form is speaking in tongues, which frees spiritual and ecstatic communication from the shackles of any single language or specific semantic content. The devotional intensity of Bicolano Catholics' relationship with the dead Christ is expressed in dreams, visions, stories, and the singing of the *Pasion*; the commitment of Mosse's South Indian Catholics is expressed through exorcism; Biak Protestants compose hymns on the model of traditional *wor*. Anthropology needs to develop further a comparative ethnography of devotional practice, without privileging some forms over others. In the existing literature, accounts of mainstream Protestant worship tend to be particularly flat. It may sometimes be true, as both Whitehouse and Keane argue here of Protestant services they describe, and as has also been claimed of mainstream Catholic liturgy, that public worship can at times be mechanical, drained of affect, and can become boring even to its participants. Such routinization may even be a deliberate policy on the part of church leaders, in the interests of member control. But we have also seen that these conformist appearances can be deceptive and that (as Keane has also shown) even where they are true, they do not necessarily exclude a deep engagement with questions of Christian faith; this is expressed in other contexts, including debate with missionaries and church leaders.

The Problem of Modernity

Like some other recent work, this is skeptical of the proposition that the modern world will see religions declining and religious faith ceding to secularism. This dissenting opinion is not confined to students of fundamentalisms but has certainly been given support by the recent interest in Christian, Islamic, and Hindu movements thus classed together.

Susan Harding's important book on Jerry Falwell's Southern Baptists explores some of the ways in which these movements have been tied to explicit and politicized discourses on modernity. Agreeing with other authors that American Biblical Fundamentalists had been placed through most of the twentieth century in the symbolic position of the other of modern secularism, she explores in detail the attempt made by Falwell to break out of that position and occupy the widest possible terrain in American cultural and economic life, without making any change of doctrinal direction toward liberal secularism. For Harding, this attempt was made through a characteristic deployment of rhetorical language that functions through preaching and conversion, through moral campaigns, and through mass marketing and the creation of a "sacrificial economy": "*God does miracles because people give sacrificially*; because they obey God and act on faith" (Harding 2000: 124). Even the occasional doubts of Falwell's own congregation as to his financial probity worked to his advantage. They challenged believers to assert the faith, which would bring them blessings in return.

This area of literature, then, is concerned with what one might call the further adventures of the Protestant-capitalist nexus originally identified by Weber. Here we must be careful in our attributions. Weber himself certainly described "elective affinities" between Puritanism and its apparent converse, capitalism, and certainly also argued that the alliance between the two had led, strangely, toward secular modernity in the West. But Weber did not thereby commit himself to the view that modernity could take only this one possible form; nor did Weber regard the study of religion as of little interest except insofar as it contributed toward the study of secularization. Still less did Weber take a triumphalist view of the process of secularization; witness his melancholic account of the modern capitalist caught in the "iron cage" of asceticism without religion, a meaningless drive toward wealth-creation (Weber [1930] 1992: 182).

While some neo-Weberian commentators have retained the nuance and complexity of Weber's own attitude to social change, it is ironic that other forms of neo-Weberian analysis have appeared to lend weight to accounts of the inevitable spread of modernity and globalization, in which religion is treated as a topic clearly subsidiary to the processes of secularization, and where the claims of modernity as an ideology in itself are never properly analyzed. Even for balanced and clear-minded commentators such as the sociologist Steve Bruce, the idea that secularism succeeds a religious outlook is understood as factually established beyond serious question, while attempts to qualify that idea are for Bruce simply revisionist tinkering (Bruce 1996: 6–7).[21] Such tendencies appear even in work of considerable historical and ethnographic sophistication, such is the power of the notion that the key "meaning" of Christianity is that, like John the Baptist, it ushers in a mightier reality that will succeed it.[22]

But a lesson we can derive from Harding's material is that Weber's ideas have themselves fed into a widely held folk theory in Europe and America. Harding's ethnography is based on the fact that for many ordinary Americans, whether they practiced a faith or not, the idea that the world was becoming less religious as it became more modern was accepted as fact. So too, perhaps less explicitly, was the idea that mainstream religions were weakening in the contemporary world, and that Protestant churches were perhaps more liable to such draining of vigor than Catholic ones.[23] Thus, Falwell's fundamentalism is pitted not only against a truly secular modernity, but also against more liberal and culturally mainstream Protestant churches—churches regularly described as progressive. The practice of one's religion is always conceived of in contemporary America as in some way a defensive (if not offensive) reaction to the threatened erosions of the modern world. The ethnography Harding gives us therefore makes an important point for our purposes: all those concerned are acting as though some crude version of Weber's theory of secularization were an absolute truth. They are enacting one particular myth about modernity; they all believe in the essential opposition of modernity to Christianity, or at least fear it might be true. So in considering the relation between the two, we have to reckon up not only how far it may be true that institutions and ideas have changed in the ways Weber predicted, in any given locality, but also how far it might be true that the people in these localities believed that this would be so and therefore to some extent enacted that belief as history. In that sense, ironically, Weber himself has been treated as a prophet.

This returns us to a point close to that made by Mauss on capitalism and brilliantly explicated by Parry (1986): the most tightly tied bond between Christianity and modernity is at the level of the ideology of modernity. Thus, neo-Weberian arguments that proceed from the actual links between modernity and Christianity in the West to propose that the same developments will proceed everywhere are flawed. This proposition is in fact part of the ideology of modernity itself.[24]

Coleman's contribution to this volume considers a further development of this complex of ideas about Protestantism and modernity. The Faith Christians with whom he works constitute a church of more recent origin than the Southern Baptists, and they define some of their central understandings of divine power differently. While the separation of language from materiality is crucial to Harding's account of Falwell's church, Coleman argues that Word of Life Church members precisely elide the distinction between language and spirit and the body. Placing an emphasis on the spoken word, rather than the Bible text, Faith Christians conceive of language as objectified and corporeal; that is, language is not opposed to the physical world (cf. Cannell, Rutherford, Keller, and Keane in this volume). "To read and listen to inspired language is to fill the self with such language, even in a physical sense," Coleman writes. "To 'speak out' is to give an aspect of the stored self." Faith Christians conceive of both the media and the world of monetary exchange as arenas that can be dealienated by the extension into them of the self thus understood. Faith Christians regularly make gifts of alms, but these are ideally made to strangers and not to members of the church community who might be expected to return them. The gift instead stands as a token of one's spiritual growth, and its giving away is part of a contract with God. By this act of faith, the giver is insured that God will bless him with further accumulation, and that his self will therefore not be lost in the anonymous world of capital. Word of Life members are therefore refusing the central ideological opposition between gift and commodity that capitalism proposes. Significantly, they are doing so simply with the resources of capitalist Protestantism itself, and not (as in Pina-Cabral's argument) by engaging an alternative folk tradition that will supply the deficiencies of a transcendent Christianity's discourse on the body. Coleman's account shows how such Christians accept the economic structure of capitalism as inevitable, yet refuse to allow it to be an "impersonal" power, reconstruing it as ruled by a higher contract between God and Christians inserted within it. While conservative Protestants achieve similar outcomes without contesting the separation of spirit and matter, however, Faith Christians take a different route, asserting that money must in the end partake of the same nature as prayer, and thus cannot act independently of it.

The single issue over which the contributors in this volume most diverge is that of the relationship between Christianity and modernity. These differences are, perhaps, partly accounted for by the areas in which they are working. Those who work in regions dominated by mainstream Protestantism—especially where it collaborated with a colonial regime like that of the Dutch in Indonesia—are probably especially inclined to focus on these questions. In doing so, they are responding both to the strong Weberian tradition of analysis, which of course traced the connection between Calvinism and the rise of the capitalist work ethic back to the seventeenth-century Netherlands, and to the stated intentions of the Dutch government and missionaries themselves. Moreover, many local informants will themselves discuss their Christianity in terms of "being modern," especially when, as was the case in New Order Indonesia, the postcolonial government explicitly demanded that all its citizens should modernize themselves by acquiring a world religion. The link between Protestantism and discourses of modernity is, therefore, in some parts of the world a demonstrable historical fact.

I suggest that to say this is not, however, the same as claiming that disenchantment and modernization are proceeding everywhere and in similar ways where conversion takes place. Harvey Whitehouse takes up a position at one extreme on this question, arguing in relation to his Melanesian evidence that there is such a thing as a universal transformative effect of the introduction of Christianity, and that the introduction of Protestantism in Papua New Guinea supplies the paradigm. For Whitehouse, conversion to Protestantism introduced a new and distinct form of cognitive experience for Melanesians, centered around the learning and reproduction of text-based religious liturgies. Standardization and replicability enabled the rapid spread of these new forms, in an account highly reminiscent of Weberian rationalization. However, there are key differences in Whitehouse's argument. For him, these new religious forms are defined primarily by their cognitive features. This is not simply a matter of institutional transformation, nor changes in the group identification of individual converts, but a literal acquisition of a new way of thinking by a population. However, this radical new form of religion or thought does not simply displace and replace preexistent forms. Older forms of Melanesian religion, exercised in rituals that evoke a different, more bodily and sensory based and less abstract kind of cognition, continue to exist alongside the new forms. Indeed, Whitehouse argues elsewhere (1995) that the new rationalized religion is itself inherently limited in its appeal because it cannot tap into these sensory and emotional forms of cognition.

Webb Keane also sees evidence in Sumba of the gradual intrusion of specifically Protestant formulations of interiority and agency, here supported by the demands of the Indonesian state. For Keane the transformation is by no means as sudden or wholesale as Whitehouse suggests it has been in Melanesia but is conducted through a complex series of renegotiations of meaning that, for both missionaries and Sumbanese Protestants, center on differing understandings of the power of words and other symbolic communication. Here and elsewhere (e.g., Keane 1998), Keane shows that Protestant anxieties focused on what they saw as native idolatry, which implied a confusion between God and images of gods, between spirit and matter. The Sumbanese, on the other hand, objected to the Protestant notion that God always hears our prayers; for them, this seemed to be placing an almost idolatrous reliance on words themselves rather than recognizing the uncertain nature of all communication with the divine. Keane further develops in this volume the insight that although distinctive Sumbanese understandings of the relationship of words, things, and agency still continue, many local people are being increasingly called on to enact attitudes, such as sincerity of speech and intention, that rely on Protestant notions of authenticity and moralized interiority. For Keane, this is occurring even though the absolute body/spirit distinction toward which the missionaries are striving is less realistic than the categories through which his Sumbanese informants view the world, and even though he thinks that modernity is a destination at which no one ever fully arrives.

It is perhaps Danilyn Rutherford's ethnography of Biak—poised between Indonesia and Melanesia—that offers some of the most serious obstacles to the narrative of Christianity as inevitably promoting modernity. Paying careful attention to the ways in which missionaries were addressing the Dutch faith revival back home as well as their immediate Biak audience, Rutherford outlines an evangelizing movement based equally on a belief in the working of the Word of God on the inner person and on the example of self-disciplined labor set by the missionaries in building houses and other appurtenances of civilization. While mass conversions in Biak apparently confirmed the success of this campaign, and while Biaks certainly entered with some willingness, even enthusiasm, into the disciplinary regimes of modernity—in some cases competing to send brothers to Jakarta to become government officials—the effects were not what the missionaries had anticipated. Rather than the Word of God doing its work as "a vehicle of meaning that would sink into the souls of men everywhere," the Bible in Biak came to be treated as booty. The authority behind the Bible was understood by Biaks not as a single, omnipotent voice of God, but as a mysterious absence, an untranslatable potential. Power continued to be understood by Biaks, Rutherford writes, as "the lure of the ancestral . . . of kinship . . . and of the foreign"—something that had left Biak and gone missing, but which constantly promised to return in surprising forms, available for appropriation.

Here in fact is the crux of the matter for Rutherford. For the missionaries, conversion to Christianity was envisaged as a single, blazing revelation of a universal Truth. This Truth is expected to have a permanently transformative effect on men's minds, but "the surprise that leads to conversion should be the heathens' last," since once the Truth is known, nothing can surpass or supersede it. Biaks, however, refused to be surprised by surprise; given their understanding of how power works, that arrival of the new was exactly what they had learned to expect. Rather than disrupting the categories through which they understood the world, rather than appearing as something beyond local truth, the advent of Christianity suggested to the Biaks that they had been right all along.

This example is suggestive in a number of ways. One might briefly reflect on the nature of the Christian missionary encounter in general, from the point of view of the missionaries. Most Christian missionaries take with them as explicit theology the idea that they are the bearers of a unique Truth, knowledge about God, which is different in kind and potential to any other knowledge. Whatever their level of tolerance of local practices, most of them also believe that this Truth is communicable to all God's creatures, so that all of them may have access to the promise of Salvation. They also believe themselves in the power of conversion, perhaps on the Pauline model. Light enters the soul and nothing is ever the same again.

Missionaries often experienced discomfort and dislocation in areas where conversion was persistently declined, or where they feared it had been accepted for the wrong reasons. In discouragement, missionaries have generally taken refuge in two alternative conclusions. Either God is testing his servants, spiritually refining them by withholding success, or there are powerful forces working against them: the devil is struggling to keep souls out of heaven, perhaps. Sometimes, however, the confusion felt by missionaries is extreme. They may even abandon the perception (which, as Nicholas Thomas [1994] has pointed out, has often been an advantage of Christianity over secular colonialism) that people of all races are equally human under God and wrestle with the temptation to view their potential converts themselves as devils, or alternatively, as less than human, sullen, deanimated.

Encounters with cultures whose ontologies fit poorly with Christianity's most basic and unrecognized assumptions tend to trigger such destabilizing effects. We have already noted the attention anthropologists have paid to missionary misunderstandings. Missionaries in Madagascar rejoiced when the Merina abandoned their "idols" (*sampy*) without realizing that sampy are always disposable and renewable in Merina culture (Bloch 1986: 21). The narrow definition of religion that most Christian missionaries shared led them to disregard kinship practices in many parts of the world, although in fact these were integral aspects of local ideas of power, fertility and renewal, and so on. But in addition to these misunderstandings, one can see in some cases a process of more radical lack of fit between the unspoken ontology of Christianity and that of local systems of thought with which it comes into contact.

Christian missionaries have been relatively comfortable with systems that do not place value on the idea of a single, exclusive Truth; competition with other divinities has been a familiar problem for Christianity since its inception. But systems of thought that place no emphasis on moral interiority of the particular kind that Christians call the soul have been more confusing. Early Philippine missionaries rejoiced over the readiness of their Tagalog, Bikol, and Visayan converts to enter into the rituals and gestures of repentance, yet Vicente Rafael (1988: 100) has convincingly shown that they were soon bewildered and frustrated by their parishioners' refusal to understand the point of the sacrament of confession. Rafael has argued that a different set of understandings of the "inside" of a person and the ways in which someone entered into relations of exchange with others were persistently at work in the postconversion Christian Philippines, and I have argued in this volume that Rafael may even have understated his case in some respects. Against Keane's interesting account of how Protestant missionaries are working to encourage behaviors in their Sumbanese converts that produce in them the notion of "sincere" interiority, we can therefore place the example of the Philippines where the chain of connections soul-guilt-repentance-salvation / damnation does not appear to have been completed even in the course of more than four hundred years.

Most unsettling of all, perhaps, are those groups of people who, like the Piro and Biak discussed in this volume, accept Christianity but reject that idea that in becoming Christian something both unprecedented and unrepeatable has occurred. Societies that recount conversion as part of a narrative of traumatic change—as is the case in many parts of the Andes—are much more readily comprehensible from a Christian perspective than those that "forget" it has happened, or which construe it as just one in a series of similar foreign arrivals in the past and the future.

At work here, I would suggest, is an underrecognized link between Christian ideas of time and event and Christian ideas of transcendence. It is clear that the idea of the unique and irreversible event in many ways has to underlie the idea of transcendence. The dominant Christian ideas of personal conversion depend on a break in time. Conversion changes the individual, and however much he might backslide, the event itself cannot be undone.[25] We might say that the hierarchical relation of the "world beyond" and the "world of the here and now" established in a salvationist Christianity has a temporal dimension. Time following conversion is not just time after but time beyond. Even though he has not yet entered eternal time, the convert is thought to be touched by the transcendent and enter into its economy. But because it is less explicit in Christian doctrine than other ideas about time, such as the various eschatologies and end-time scenarios or the regeneration of the world at the crucifixion (Bloch and Parry 1982: 14) or other ideas about the implications of transcendence, such as the need not to mistake matter for spirit, this assumption of nonreversible event may be the most disturbing when it is contradicted. In Rutherford's language, the "shock" of Christian revelation was intended for the Biak converts but rebounded instead on the missionaries.

Universal theories suffer from the difficulty that they need to be applicable in all cases. It should be clear from this section that I would not claim with Whitehouse (and the neo-Weberians) that Christianity is rightly seen as inevitably a modernizing force, even if in some parts of the Protestant world processes akin to what Weber described as "rationalization" are in progress. It seems to me in fact that the proposition is placed the wrong way around. It may be that the history of modernity is inextricably bound up with the history of Christianity, but this does not mean that the meaning of Christianity is sufficiently explained by the history of modernity. The potential for meaning contained in Christian doctrine is in fact demonstrably always in excess of any particular social situation to which it might be considered functional.

In the hunt for "a view of our origins"—that is, a glimpse of the origins of capitalist thought—we may first ignore every other aspect of our own Christian history and then think of Christianities of conversion only in terms of the teleologies of modernity or global capitalism. Christian experience cannot be seen properly if it is tied exclusively to a supposedly destined trajectory of modernity, nor indeed to a postmodernity that so often tacitly repeats the logic of modernity (Osborne 1995: 3–4). Talal Asad's important 1993 study persuasively understands the category of religion as a product of Christian thinking that has entered anthropological theory. Yet might it not also be the case that the use of the term *modernity* itself has become superstitious in the social sciences?[26] Insofar as it implies an irreversible break with the past, after which the world is utterly transformed in mysterious ways, it is itself modeled on the Christian idea of conversion. Is it possible that anthropologists, as well as missionaries, find difficult the idea that one might encounter a transcendental Truth without becoming part of its logic?

Beyond the Impossible Religion

Most theories of Christianity and its effects consider it as a religion of transcendence, and for the greater part of this introduction this is what we have also been doing. God withdraws from man, and as a consequence man is left in a state of incompleteness that can be resolved only at death, when he will pass into the other world. From this view are derived those minority of arguments in recent anthropology that have asked about the character of Christian thinking as such, rather than its connection to modernity. Many of these arguments, such as those by Pina-Cabral, emphasize the inevitably dualistic character of Christianity (particularly its mind/body split) and propose that ascetic Christianity deals badly with issues related to bodily life: folk beliefs and figures of local power drawn from outside the Christian repertoire, such as ancestors, are then said to be called into service to supply the deficiency. Similar arguments have also been applied to situations in which Christianity is present together with another complex religious tradition (see, e.g., Stewart 1997: 204–31; Ileto 1979; and Rafael 1988).

Many of these arguments draw on Bloch and Parry's influential formulation of the significance of mortuary ritual (1982). In that collection, the editors propose that funerals are ritual mechanisms through which, symbolically and ideologically speaking, the continuity of the community is asserted over the disruption caused by the death of an individual member of that community. Mortuary ritual enfolds a range of symbolic assertions that death is not incomprehensible and arbitrary, but is ordered, anticipated, or even chosen, and forms part of a wider whole of renewal. In the process, the authority structure of a society is legitimated, and the collection makes a very strong connection between the supernatural powers that a society venerates, and the sources of political power and—still more—political legitimacy.

The primary objective of the Bloch and Parry volume is to look not at Christianity, but at universals in religious processes, which for the purposes of their argument are there defined almost entirely as ritual processes.[27] Nevertheless, a consideration of the approach taken in that work to Christianity is relevant here, not only because the book has been widely influential, but because it prompts a direct confrontation with some of the most difficult issues we have been attempting to raise in this introduction.

The central example given in the Bloch and Parry volume of a Christian context is Olivia Harris's rich essay on the Catholic Laymi (1982). Harris states that the Laymi maintain an "uneasy truce" between Laymi ancestors, who remain charged with important aspects of the reproduction of fertility, and the Catholic saints and deity (73). Thus far, the book seems to conform to the "impossible religion" model of Christianity we have already discussed. Elsewhere in Bloch's own work, Christianity features as a religion inimical to natural kinship and superimposes on it a logic of superior, church-authorized artificial kinship terms (Bloch and Guggenheim 1981). However, for Bloch this tendency in Christianity is only an instance of a tendency in almost all religious ritual; for him, almost all religion[28] is in this sense seen as impossible, since all ritual applies a transcendental logic whereby the value of a real life beyond this world is asserted at the expense of the immediate and mortal world.

Bloch's first two books, on the ethnography of the Merina of Madagascar (Bloch 1971, 1986) are in fact concerned with Christian populations, since the Merina have long been Protestant converts, while their former slaves mostly became Catholics. However, in some ways Bloch's account of the Merina suffers from the same indifference to the properties and significance of this Christian experience, as many of the other Marxist-influenced works cited in the early part of this introduction; indeed, for the most part, Malagasy Christianity is of interest to Bloch only insofar as it seems to him to have been entirely absorbed into the preexisting forms of Merina social organization and ancestral religion, whose ideological resilience is one of his central topics.[29]

Because of this characteristic lack of interest in local Christianity per se, it is in some ways difficult to assess Bloch's claims. Certainly, Bloch demonstrates a powerful transcendental logic in Merina religion, which repeatedly stresses that the ancestors are the only source of moral good and of the "real life"; however, he never explicitly discusses whether any of this transcendentalism is due to the influence of Christianity on Merina social logic, rather than vice versa. We might also ask whether he has fully recognized that the model of the transcendent which defines this analysis of ritual is itself a profoundly Christian model; in one sense, indeed, the work belongs to that long tradition of antireligious social science that incorporates Christian models by its refusal of them.[30]

At the same time, the Bloch and Parry thesis that (in effect) transcendent logic is a property of ritual in general, rather than Christianity or "world religions" in particular (however much these might have their own forms of the transcendental), serves as an important counterbalance to the assumed contrast between "world religions" and "local religions" that follows from the kind of Christian exceptionalism we have traced back to the diffuse originary influence of Hegel.[31] It may be that we need to reassess the notion that Christianity is so easily distinguished from other religions by its celebration of the impossible world beyond, and to think of the attitude that religions take to transcendence understood in this way as much more of a continuum.

If transcendence is not necessarily exclusively Christian, then it is even more clearly true to say that Christianity is not exclusively a religion of transcendence.

Once again, we may take our cue from historians of the early church, including Brown (1988), Cameron (1991) and others. For scholars of this period, while the Christian church was becoming established in the Roman Empire and in post-Rome Europe, there are of course intense debates about continuity of thought and tradition. But these debates tend to be less heavily burdened with the teleologies of modernity, and somewhat less inclined to blur the "Christian" and the "Western." Historians of this period see with clarity that Christian doctrine is not a monolith but a constantly evolving object, in which what is orthodox for one generation may come to be defined as heretical in the next, depending not only on the development of theological controversy but also on the history of the struggle for authority within the emergent central authorities of the church.

The central dilemmas of Christian theology are clearly visible in the period in which the division between heresy and orthodoxy was first defined. The Trinitarian controversy; the problems over the nature and limitations of reason in Christian discourse; the sense of unspeakable mystery, with the consequent relativization of the role of verbal debate and the rise in the role of visual imagery and imagistic speech but its counterpart in the mystical notion of the Word—these sources of tension are already present in the late classical world Cameron describes. From these debates emerged the dominant paradigm of Christianity as the religion of transcendence, but this paradigm always carried with it, even if only as negation, the other possible visions of Christianity that existed in relationship to it. Some later heretical movements, like the Pyrrennean Catharism described by Ladurie (1981), are said to have a direct historical connection with earlier heretical thinking (in this case, Manicheanism). But such genealogical connectedness was not necessary for the reemergence of similar problems. One might see the endless return of the problem of idolatry, from the iconoclastic controversies of Byzantium to the perplexities of Sumbanese Calvinists, as just one instance of Christian doctrine being haunted by its own expurgated other self.

Heresy—a term only ever applied as abuse—thus has a much more complex history than orthodox narratives would sometimes have us believe (Williams 1987; Wiles 1996). As Peter Brown has shown, the ambiguity of the Christian message could never be entirely eliminated. Even ascetic Christianity was never entirely hostile to the body; indeed, asceticism's intense focus on the body could convert it into a privileged site of spiritual struggle as well as of spiritual peril. Contemporary Christian movements, such as the Seventh-Day Adventism discussed in this volume by Keller, or American Mormonism (the Church of Jesus Christ of Latter-Day Saints), on which I am currently conducting research, also propose, in different ways, a vision of the afterlife far less distant than that of mainstream Christianities. The Mormon Celestial Kingdom is unhesitatingly described by most ordinary Mormons as "very much like this world," only perfected, and Mormon doctrine states that it will literally be this world, renewed and transfigured at the final Resurrection. Moreover it is a unique and central teaching of Mormonism that kinship will be not abandoned but completed in the next world.

One response to such examples is to dismiss the Adventists and the

Latter-Day Saints as cults: their teachings can have no bearing on the essential nature of Christianity. Yet this assessment has little more analytical weight than does the label *heresy*. Although there are elements of innovation in both churches (based on the teachings of their respective prophets), however, there are also overwhelming elements of continuity with earlier Christian teaching. Indeed, all of Mormon teaching and prophecy is cast as a further revelation of the meaning of the Old and New Testaments and a restoration of parts of that meaning which have been lost. Mormonism therefore draws both on earlier forms of orthodox Christianity and, as John Brooke has argued (1996),[32] also on those Christian traditions that were themselves marginalized and considered heretical in English and American Puritanism.

Even transcendent Christianity, therefore, was never unambiguously otherworldly, and even orthodox Christianity contained within it the shadows of its own alternative ways of thinking. Christianity is a complex historical object whose parameters are by no means arbitrary but which also cannot plausibly be described except as being in tension with itself. Thus, as Reynaldo Ileto (1979), for example, has elegantly demonstrated, Christianity's meaning is always underdetermined by any single historical, social, or ideological context in which it is deployed; its meaning inevitably exceeds such contexts, even if, as in the case Ileto gives us, it is deployed by power holders for the purposes of domination, and even if most of the potential interpretations of Christian doctrine inevitably remain unrealized in social action at any one time. Thus we must be cautious of anthropological paradigms of Christianity that present it as solely an ascetic tradition, rather than as a fundamentally paradoxical tradition, a fault of which even Sahlin's magnificent article "The Sadness of Sweetness" (1996) is partly guilty.[33]

The implications for anthropological studies of non-Western Christianities are twofold. First, when a locality encounters Christianity, it is never obvious in advance what that "Christianity" is; it can be defined only in reference to its own historical development. Second, however unyieldingly orthodox the form of Christianity that may be visited on another culture, it can never contain only a single message with single possibilities of interpretation, because Christian doctrine is in itself paradoxical. Although anthropologists may recognize in theory that Christianity has this complex character, in practice, as we have seen, most anthropological writing tends to revert to a rather simplistic modeling. The concept of a distinctive formulation of the transcendent is powerful in Christianity, and is a predominant, although always historically developing, idea in most forms of orthodox Christian thinking, including most colonial Christianities. It is therefore appropriately a central focus of anthropological discussion. However, encounters between Christianity and local cultures cannot in fact be adequately typified as encounters between transcendent and nontranscendent religious conceptions, both because the transcendent may not be the sole preserve of Christianity and other world religions, and because Christian thinking itself is never solely or unequivocally otherworldly.

One belief which all orthodox Christians, together with those they dismissed as heretics, held in common was a belief in Christian exceptionalism. Christianity, like Judaism, has taught that it is an unprecedented and a singular revelation of the truth, a "new song" sung to the Lord. It is when this vision of itself is met with indifference by another culture that Christian thinking seems to fall into most confusion. As anthropologists, we may in part have this expectation about Christianity embedded into our own theoretical expectations. Christianity always makes a difference, but that difference may not be as one-dimensional as we have supposed.

A central aspect of the tradition of Christian exceptionalism that we have been considering here is the transferal of that exceptionalism onto the trope of modernity. We saw that the model of the unrepeatable event in Christianity, after which the world is irreversibly changed, is key to the understanding of conversion as well as to Christian cosmology and eschatology.[34] I have argued that this notion of the event after which nothing is ever the same again has become annexed by the ideology of modernity. In anthropology, this has happened perhaps above all through the medium of neo-Weberian interpretations. Yet Weber himself was profoundly interested in religious experience and saw the ebbing away of religion in contemporary capitalism as by no means a cause for celebration. I have argued that what began as a critical hypothesis offered by Weber (that secularization paradoxically proceeds through Protestant ethics and institutions)—a hypothesis that certainly illuminates historical change in some places and times—has become confused with a widespread popular conviction that religion is inevitably inimical to modernity, and that for better or worse modernity is winning. This conviction, which ought to be regarded as an ethnographic datum about the ideology of the West, has instead become lodged in much sociological and anthropological writing as though it were established fact. That only a minority of writers have been skeptical of these arguments must certainly be due to the peculiar relationship between anthropology and theology noted at the beginning of this introduction. Anthropology, as part of social science, defined itself in its origins as what theology was not; since the theology it was repudiating was specifically Christian theology, anthropological theory has always carried within it ideas profoundly shaped by that act of rejection, from which there can therefore never be a complete separation. Moreover, because of this uneasy relationship, anthropology has on the whole been less successful at considering Christianity as an ethnographic object than at considering any other religion in this way.

What answer, then, could we make to the question posed at the beginning of this introduction: What may we take from the legacy of the founders of the discipline? Durkheim, Mauss, and Weber all regarded the arrival of a transcendent Christianity as an irreversible moment of transformation, and each built this perspective in different ways into sociology: because this seemed to them to be well known and well established, because debates over the nature of Christianity were still politically sensitive ground, and because the thrust of their inquiring energies lay elsewhere. Yet they also shared a deep sense of the importance of understanding the history and theology of Christianity. Mauss read widely on the history of the Christian church; Durkheim debated issues in religion with Catholic friends such as Charles Péguy; Weber's immersion in nineteenth-century debates about the nature and history of Christian revelation is obvious. This sense of engagement has to an important extent been lost in recent anthropological writing. Anthropologists have in certain ways remembered the letter and forgotten this spirit of their mentors. This has tended to promote the inflexible attachment of the study of Christianity to a theory of modernity, and a downgrading of any serious engagement with what Christianity, in all its historical particularity, might mean. We might do well to recover some of the serious comedy of Marx's *German Ideology* (Marx and Engels 1970). That text is not only a critique of religion but also a critique of the critique of religion. Marx, who lacked a paid position as an explainer of society, understood better than perhaps anyone else before or since the depth of the subterranean connections between Christianity and its ideological and sociological critics and investigators. If we can stop presupposing that Christianity changes everything forever, we may be able to begin to see the experiences of Christianity, in all their diversity, complexity, and singularity, for what they are.

Notes

1 As demonstrated by the Dreyfus affair, on which Durkheim wrote (1969).

2 This serves as a powerful reminder of the many ways in which Christianity is absolutely rooted in Judaism, both historically and theologically. For Mauss and Durkheim, interestingly, it sometimes seems as though the extensive analysis of such similarities is being lightly stepped around, in favor of an emphasis on the distinctive features of Christianity as such.

3 The dominant intellectual evolutionist model is Lamarkian and not strictly Darwinian.

4 One thinks here, for instance, of Weber's almost wistful remark that he had "no ear" for religion (Weber [1919] 1946), or of Mauss's doctoral thesis (published as Mauss 2004) on types of prayer.

5 Whenever I teach a course on the anthropology of Christianity, my students without fail are curious to know what my own religious position is; in the interests of transparency, it may be useful to the reader to know that I am not a member of, or a regular attender at, any church (although I have a Methodist family background), and that I would describe myself as a sympathetic agnostic who takes seriously the religious experiences of others and is open to the possibility that these might at some point occur even in my own life.

6 This particular omission is purely a matter of the contingent history of this volume. Our original contributors included the Africanist Maia Green, who has done fine work on Pogoro Catholic Christianity in Tanzania (e.g., Green 2003), but who was later unfortunately prevented from pursuing her contribution because of work commitments abroad. I will take this opportunity to acknowledge, in the absence of this essay, some of the other recent work written on Christian groups, particularly Pentecostals, in Africa, including Peel 2000, Meyer 1998, and Englund 2002.

7 That is, contributors are attentive both to local cultural practice and to the particular type of Christianity prevailing in the area they study. Clearly, one needs to know not only which church or religious order is involved, but also at what period and with what specific doctrinal and social emphases it arrived in a locality, as well as how these have evolved. For a concise and useful review of the long-standing general debates in the anthropology of world religions about the relationship between the global and the local, see Stewart and Shaw 1994: 13–17.

8 This tendency was of course part of the wider (and well-known) debate in the anthropology of the period about the theorization of gender and the independence or otherwise of women's perspectives in different cultures, which it is not the intention of this introduction to reproduce here.

9 Among other key references on this complex area, see Milbank 1990, which critically discusses the claims of social science to have freed itself from

religious thought. Some of the analysis offered here, although arising from a different impetus, coincides closely with some of Milbank's arguments, especially his reading of the influence of Weberian sociology. However, I would not wish to go as far as Milbank in a despairing dismissal of the social sciences tout court, or to share Milbank's conclusion that, because it is incompletely self-recognizing, all social science thinking is vacuous insofar as it differs from historical thinking. One element in Milbank's impatience with social science, it seems to me, is a lack of familiarity with those elements that are concerned with ethnographic empirical work, and their ability to generate relevant theoretical questions.

10 Hegel, like other authors since, proposed that Christian developments were partly anticipated by elements of later classical philosophy, especially Platonism (in relation to the idea of the soul) and Stoicism. However, the central point for our discussion is that Christianity is always perceived in these theories as a paradigm shift; it is not necessary to argue that none of its elements had existed in any previous system.

11 Of course, the whole notion of transcendence arguably applies to the wider Judeo-Christian tradition, and not just to Christianity. Interestingly enough, Judaism (and related topics, including anti-Semitism within the history of the discipline) have also been understudied within anthropology.

12 The essay appears to me to have provided continuing theoretical impetus behind much more recent collections, such as the important volume *Shamanism, History and the State* (Humphrey and Thomas 1994).

13 Rowan Williams (1987: 14) points out that Leach may himself have misrecognized Arianism, and that Arius's own doctrine was different, and more conservative, than the Arian heresy, which was an artifact constructed post hoc by Arius's enemies. While historically important, this observation does not affect our argument here.

14 Like most other anthropologists writing in this area, Pina-Cabral does not explicitly refer to his debt to Hegel or, indeed, Leach, and he may not be aware of it; his immediate reference here is to the work of Maurice Bloch on death, funerals, and fertility (Pina-Cabral 1986: 224). The way in which Bloch's work of this period itself incorporates certain assumptions about transcendence is discussed below. Bloch's work in itself, however, in some ways demonstrates the influence of Leach's teaching on this point.

15 I say "may be" because it has long been clear from the scholarship that such extreme positions are taken only at certain times within Christianity, and that even in apparently dramatic ascetic practices there may be a significant symbolic space that is given to the flesh, and which revalidates it at least in some degree (Walker-Bynum 1987). See later in this chapter. The point is that after the inception of the unhappy consciousness there can supposedly never be a perfect reconciliation between flesh and spirit, and indeed, that the contrast between those two categories can never again be unthought.

16 For an outstanding account of the use of, and reaction to, the confessional as

a colonial instrument intended to create a new, Christian interiority, see Rafael 1988, chapter 3. Rafael's argument is discussed in more detail in my essay in this volume.

17 Foucault does make occasional contrastive references to ancient Hindu traditions of attitudes to the body.

18 Some Protestant churches have been less tolerant, although this is also highly variable.

19 This argument takes off from Rafael's (1988) important account of the contracting of Catholic hierarchies of power in the Tagalog areas of conversion. See my essay in this volume for an account of Rafael's argument and the similarities and differences of my own interpretation of the Bicol region.

20 It often appears to be the case that nineteenth- and twentieth-century missionary colonialism misrecognized the significance of local kinship rituals and underestimated the degree to which religious meaning was embedded in family practices, therefore placing people under less pressure to alter or abandon this kind of activity. However, in other instances, kinship ritual *has* become intensely targeted—for example, when it is linked to missionary concerns with sexual respectability, or to population control, and / or when it is identified as being linked to the rituals of the local state (see, e.g., Kendall 1996 and Pemberton 1994).

21 Bruce (1996: 6) cites himself as a robust defender of the secularization theories of Talcott-Parsons, Peter Berger, and others, as well as of Weber—that is to say, of a particular reading of Weber. Much of his argument depends on developing a contrast between a historically earlier world of greater church participation and a modern world of increasingly individualistic beliefs. The argument thus bypasses the kind of examination being made in this volume. Bruce concedes that in some parts of the world, including America, religious participation remains high, but he argues that in fact American religion is increasingly concerned with the "mundane" (147). The idea that it is a simple matter to identify the mundane is one I and others would contest (see McDannell 1995).

22 One recent example might be Albert Schrauwers's accomplished and scholarly account of To Pamona Protestants, *Colonial "Reformation" in the Highlands of Central Sulawesi, Indonesia* (2000). The argument is driven by the notion of "the rationalization of a world religion in the periphery" (16), derived from Weber refracted through Foucault and others. The focus is on Christianity effectively understood as the Calvinist Church, its relationship to "pillarized" Dutch society, and its disciplinary and discourse-creating effects, all of which are understood as tending toward rationalized modernity. While Schrauwers is right to argue that new, often coercive, definitions of religion are generated in colonialism, this volume would want to make more analytic space for the potentially unexpected and underdetermined nature of such encounters, and for the importance of local interpretations of Christian teachings. Lorraine Aragon's *Fields of the Lord*, also on highland Sulawesi Protestants (Aragon 2000), provides an interesting comparison.

23 This kind of assessment could be viewed as the corollary of the Protestant (and Protestant-secular) perspective on Catholicism as superstition. It is as though the Protestant world fears that Catholicism might retain more power against modernity by dint of those very practices that Protestants have for centuries condemned as magical or idolatrous. Thus many Protestants appear at some level to have internalized Weber's theory that Protestantism leads to secularism. This move anticipates in some ways the secular world's classification of fundamentalisms and contemporary cults as irrational fanaticism.

24 In pursuit of a new perspective on Christianity in anthropology, we are again treading here in the difficult terrain of the actual historical relationship between Christianity, capitalism, and modernity. We might note that one answer to the question implied in Parry's brilliant 1986 rereading of Mauss discussed above—whether it is world religions or capitalism that introduces the dualistic split between the idea of the free gift and the idea of interested exchange—is that, at least in the West, it is both, simply because capitalism is never free of the language of Christianity, however far back in time you push capitalism. This is presumably one part of what Milbank (1990) means by calling capitalism a heretical deviation from what he defines as real (i.e., Augustinian) Christianity. (See also Jarvis 2000.) As I argue here, however, it does not follow that the whole history of Christianity can be adequately conveyed by the history of capitalism (or of modernity).

25 Of course, this is to some extent a simplification: most Christians recognize that the enlightenment produced by conversion needs to be cared for and can be lost sight of. Mormons, and perhaps other Christians, sometimes talk as though conversion were at least in theory a continuous process rather than a one-off event. Yet, these ruminations are mainly sidelights on the central Christian perception that conversion itself (like the Incarnation) is an irreversible event; nothing can undo the fact that it has happened.

26 Talal Asad (1993: 54) also concentrates his discussion on the transcendental and ascetic forms of Catholic Christianity. For Asad, to make this comment is precisely to miss the point of his argument, because he is attempting to establish that the category of religion itself (and Christianity as a generative example of it) is misconceived, in that religions are inserted in such different ways in relations of power, economics, and personhood in different places and periods as to have no meaningful connection with each other. I cannot ultimately see how the Foucauldian category of knowledge-power, which replaces other explanatory categories, itself escapes these objections. To this extent, I think, Asad's analysis ultimately shares some of the problems of the less subtle ways of reducing religion to power that we have already discussed. Nonetheless, Asad provides an attentive, highly original, and illuminating reading of various Christian formations and communities. For another interesting set of comments on the relationship between anthropology and Christianity that share some ground with the current discussion, see Robbins 2003.

27 Both these authors are of course perfectly well aware of fields of religious activity that do not fall within the usual definition of ritual. Yet for their arguments, especially as defined at the period of the 1982 volume here discussed, as well as in Bloch 1986 and elsewhere, ritual is really the most important problem in the analysis of religion, because it defines the intersection between religion and power.

28 An exception would be some religious practices in unusually egalitarian societies.

29 That is, topics of Merina kinship and state formation; Merina Protestant churches turn out to be structured by Merina kinship (endogamous demes). (Bloch 1971).

30 This is a particularly well-established tradition in France. Much of Pascal Boyer's 2001 work on religion as a dysfunctional by-product of forms of cognition certainly has this ancestry.

31 The tension between the idea that the transcendent is in some important sense brought into being with world religions, and the idea that it belongs to all ritual insofar as it describes the mystifying power of ritual, does not appear to have been much remarked upon by those who have used Bloch and Parry's work in ethnographies of Christian locales.

32 This book is very highly regarded academically but is considered by some devout members of the Latter-Day Saints Church to be anti-Mormon in tone. Critics point out, with some justification perhaps, that many of the elements Brooke points to as having their origins in hermeticism are in fact scripturally derived; to me, these two possibilities do not seem mutually exclusive.

33 Sahlins's arguments are often compatible with the line taken here. However, while the interdependent relationship between postlapsarian Augustinianism and unorthodox Christian theology is set aside in Sahlins's article, it is essential to the argument offered here. I also feel, as Sahlins seemingly does not, that it is impossible for anthropology to step outside its theological inheritance entirely, even in the process of critiquing it. See also Cannell 2005b.

34 Bloch and Parry in the same volume (1982) offer some interesting remarks comparing Christian symbols of death and regeneration (the crucifixion and resurrection) with Hindu cyclical cosmologies. These remarks bear the hallmarks of Parry's attentive work on Hindu asceticism. Although it is true that Christianity has its own symbolism of eternal cycles, to my mind this comparison omits a consideration of the equal importance in Christianity of the idea of the unalterable transformation in time (that is, with the advent of the Messiah).

···One···

The Eternal Return of Conversion

Christianity as Contested Domain in Highland Bolivia

Olivia Harris

There is a recurrent moment in the ritual offerings of the peasants of Northern Potosí that expresses an ambiguity in their identity as Christians.[1] It occurs during sacrifices to the spirits of the landscape who ensure fertility—the mountains, the earth, powerful places such as waterfalls, springs, or spots where lightning has killed a living creature. The offerings are prepared at night. All the ingredients are raw and no salt is used. After the night of ritual libations of rum and chewing coca leaf, the officiants sacrifice one or more animals from their flocks, then, at the first light of dawn, they hasten up the mountainside carrying the blood and other offerings to a designated spot and spread them out on the ground with more libations. Before the first rays of the sun appear above the horizon everybody runs away, leaving the powers of the landscape to come and enjoy their food. Nobody must look back. As the sun rises the celebrants offer each other a formal greeting, and then return to the village.

In an obvious sense, made familiar by Van Gennep's and Leach's analysis of the time of ritual, the end of all ritual performances is marked by such a break, signaling a return to everyday life. But for indigenous peasants in Northern Potosí, the time of ritual is the time when humans enter into intense communication with spirits often known as "devils" (*yawlu*), in an Aymara version of the Spanish term *diablo*. The dilemma is, to what extent is this "devil worship" part of their Christianity, and to what extent is it antithetical, or at least incompatible? In fact, to write about practical Christianity is always to face a conundrum. What to include and what to exclude? This conundrum is of course nothing new. It lies, for example, at the heart of sixteenth-century debates about which aspects of native practice in the New World were harmless superstitions and which were idolatry, inspired by Satan himself (Cervantes 1994: 25–33, 57–62). In fact it is an inevitable consequence of a religious system that wishes to maintain clear boundaries between what is acceptable and what is not. My uncertainty about what aspects of ritual practice in Northern Potosí should count as Christian therefore seems to me diagnostic of something important about Christianity in general, whatever the denomination, rather than the stumbling block it initially appeared to be.

The Scope of Christianity

Perhaps the least ambiguous place to begin a discussion of popular Christianity is with God himself, where the catechism and the creed begin. As all commentators on Andean religion have noted, God is the sun (father sun, *tata inti*), an identification that draws both on the solar imagery of Christian iconography, and on the sun deity at the heart of Inca statecraft and the imperial religion (Platt 1987). For the peasants of Northern Potosí, the sun has given humans everything that makes life possible, in particular the crops and livestock on which the peasant economy depends, and the minerals in the earth that are brought forth by the work of miners. He is "our father" (*awksa*), "little father" (*tatituy*), "our Lord father" (*tata mustramu*) or "the sovereign father" (*tata suwirana*), who protects people when they go on a journey, or when they fall ill, and he is normally the first to be honored whenever they make ritual offerings to the sources of power. Without him, I was told, we would have nothing. The dawn ritual of feeding the "devils," then, which ends with formal greetings as the sun's rays rise above the horizon, represents also a turning toward God.

But God is not eternal. He has not been there since the beginning of time. The present age is the time of the Christians (*Kristiyanu timpu*), but before the dawning of the Christian sun there was a previous, weaker sun that survives as the moon. That was the time of the *chullpas*, the remote ancestors whose monumental tombs mark today's landscapes, and whose remains are unearthed from time to time, reminding the living of their existence and their extraordinary powers. Known in other Andean regions literally as "gentiles" (*gentiles*), these ancestors from a previous age were destroyed by the rising of the Christian sun, which burned them dry.[2] In some accounts from this region, the rising of the sun / God is recounted explicitly as a battle with the Devil (the term used is *supay*; see G. Taylor 1980; Dillon and Abercrombie 1988; Stobart 1995: 33–34). The moon today is part of God, a manifestation of his female aspect, his "wife."

This temporal scheme will frame my discussion of popular Christianity in Northern Potosí. As a conversion religion, Christianity creates an absolute break between a pre-Christian past and the present, with its hope of salvation. In the Andes, as in other American civilizations, the idea that time could be divided into distinct epochs separated by moments of violence or destruction was already well established before the coming of the Christians (Brotherston 1992). But the sixteenth-century missionaries demanded a denial of the past, and the pre-Christian ancestors, in more absolute terms than those that underwrote indigenous temporal schemes. Moreover, worship of the dead was central to pre-Columbian religious practice. Bodies were preserved by various techniques of mummification and dehydration and were located at all the nodes of power and significance, such as mountaintops, crossroads, and fields (Arriaga [1621] 1920; MacCormack 1991). Therefore, the relegation of the dead to purgatory, and the requirement that the newly baptized Christians reject their gentile ancestors, posed theological problems for which many of today's practices can be seen as an ongoing attempt at resolution.

One of the recurring themes in accounts of popular Christianity in the Andean region, from the sixteenth century to the present day, is whether the indigenous peasants can be called Christians at all (Mills 1997). The very phrase "popular Christianity" is oxymoronic, since it suggests deviation from a supposed orthodoxy, a contested domain. This is inevitable in so literate a religion, and one in which many denominations still require an exceptional level of education for the priesthood. But I suspect there is more at stake. Surely the very exalted conditions laid down for what constitutes a good Christian, or even a good enough Christian, mean that this state is almost unattainable. This may well be part of the reason for the schismatic and competitive tendencies within Christianity as a whole (Herrin 1987). In a situation of constitutive ambiguity, how better to confirm your own faith than by contrasting it with the lesser or misguided faith of others?

One of the best and earliest accounts of popular Christianity in the

Bolivian Highlands, written by a Canadian Oblate missionary priest in the 1960s, is wryly titled *On les croyait chrétiens* (*We Thought They Were Christians*) (Monast 1969). Researchers, including myself, have often showed more interest in those aspects of Andean popular religion that seem like relics of paganism (from the perspective of the church), or continuities of pre-Colombian religious forms (from the perspective of historians and anthropologists). One of my aims here is therefore to explore what the indigenous peasants mean when they identify themselves as Christians, especially since there are many points of ambivalence where a unified religious system is hard to sustain and the objects of worship, the sources of power, and ritual practices seem to be duplicated to produce something approaching two parallel religious domains. I shall discuss this particularly in relation to ideas and practices concerning the dead, in order to bring out what seems to me to be a central dilemma in Christian conversion, whether Catholic or Protestant.

Communicating with God

HEARING MASS

God, the source of justice, of order, and of morality, oversees the world and the present Christian epoch. The peasants of Northern Potosí consider themselves to be good Christians, although they are aware that this view is rarely shared by outsiders. One of the main ways in which they celebrate their Christian devotion is by hearing Mass (*mis isapaña*) in one of the colonial pueblos with their vast churches and extensive ritual calendars, or alternatively in one of the newer churches in the mining regions. God's power is concentrated in churches that can be a distance from the rural communities, so in order to receive God's blessing people must travel, usually on foot, to the nearest church attended by a priest. But while Sunday is usually kept as a day of rest (*warta*), the peasants do not attend Mass every week. Especially for those who live a long way from the nearest priest, as is the case for all the communities in which I have lived, people go to hear Mass for particular reasons, articulating time both as a personal passage through the stages of life and death, and as the communal passage from one season to the next in the cycle of patronal feasts and saints' days. So both the time of the individual and the time of the community are structured by hearing the Mass and receiving blessing.

In the personal life cycle, a baby's entry into the community is confirmed when it is baptized in church with its "naming godparents" (*sutiyir parinu/marina*) standing by.[3] Later in their lives, children acquire more godparents, both when their parents pay for a Mass for the child's health (*misa de salud*) in order to transfer some of the godparent's vitality to the child, and when they marry. After death the close kin offer a Mass for the dead person (the *misa de nueve dias*, supposedly celebrated nine days after the death, but often many months later). And at two successive feasts of the dead at All Saints in early November, the kin offer a Mass for the dead soul in order to settle it into its new afterlife. The second of these masses, the "Mass of the rug" (*misa jant'aku*),[4] lays the Christian soul to rest.

In these sacraments that succor people through their life, God's blessing is received through hearing Mass. The performativity of the Mass is probably clearest in baptism. Even though the brief ritual of naming the child with salt and the sign of the cross is valid, it is essential that it be confirmed later by a full baptism in church, in order to incorporate the baby as part of God's order, part of human society. Before this it belongs to the domain of the wild and fertile mountain deities, associated with the pre-Christian ancestors (*chullpas*) who eat without salt. The term used to refer to babies who die before they are baptized—"little moor" (*muru wawa*)—is a clear indication that they do not belong to the Christian community.[5] But in the other life-cycle rituals hearing Mass is also an essential element for the proper performance of passage from one state to another. In cases where people fail to do it, problems may arise, and on occasion the diviner may diagnose the cause of a problem (e.g., illness, loss) as the failure to hear Mass.

Since the peasants never take communion, hearing the words spoken by the priest is central to the significance of Mass. However, although the Aymara word used to express attendance at Mass is "to listen" (*isapaña*), I have not heard peasants emphasize the words of the Mass as such. According to Monast, for the Aymara of Carangas the Mass is a special form of long prayer (1969: 178–79). If this is correct, it is a communication to, rather than from God, and the blessing received in return is not materialized through sound. At the same time, people consider that through the Mass, God and the saints are "fed" with the bread and wine, just as the mountain and earth spirits are "fed" with blood sacrifice. From this perspective, the efficacious part of the Mass is the food that is offered, which satisfies God's hunger.[6]

Moreover, paying for a mass is crucial for its efficacy. In giving money or gifts in kind, people make a reciprocal offering to God that ensures the success of their participation, and they require a receipt from the priest as material evidence that the proper transaction has taken place. During the patronal feast of Muruq'umarka, one of the Laymi hamlets in which I lived, I watched the Jesuit priest who had arrived from the mining town of Uncia spend several hours receiving requests for Mass. The payments were mainly in produce, since it was the height of the harvest season. By the time he left, his jeep was loaded high with sacks of potatoes, beans, and chickens. On this occasion Padre Jaime accepted to play the role the peasants required of him. However there were ongoing tensions. As a Spanish member of a missionary order, and moreover as an individual passionately committed to the service of the poor, he often refused to accept payment for masses and chose to finance his ministry by donations from Europe. The peasants resented this bitterly, and when they went to town to hear Mass, those from the Muruq'umarka region often made the much longer and less convenient journey to the colonial pueblo of Chayanta, where the priest was Bolivian, not from a religious order, and charged high rates for saying Mass since this was his main source of income.[7] It is in paying for the Mass, then, that peasants participate in the feeding of God and the saints and are able to receive their blessing through hearing the holy words.

Padre Jaime exemplified other tensions, too. As a member of a sophisticated European order, he saw the Mass as an intensely personal and spiritual encounter with the deity. In his view, the peasants did not and could not understand the meaning of the Mass and used it as a magical instrument for gaining specific ends. As such he considered it a waste of time, if not downright superstitious, to say Mass in the Indian communities, and he avoided doing so whenever he could, preferring to preach about practical issues such as the need to build a medical post and send children to school, as well as basic Christian virtues. His reluctance to say Mass, let alone to receive money for doing so, was an ongoing source of friction which the peasants saw as a refusal to enter into normal reciprocal relationships, that was endangering their livelihood and well-being. So even attendance at Mass is a contested domain in which the authenticity of the peasants' faith may be called into question.

It is not just human beings themselves who depend on the blessing of their Sovereign Father through the Mass for their passage through life. It is equally important for the multiple sources of power associated with God (*tyusa parti*—God's sphere) in the Andean cosmos to hear Mass and be replenished by it. The household shrines (small domestic altarpieces—*retablos*—locally known as *tiwishuna*, from the Spanish *devoción*)[8] lose their power to bless unless they are periodically regenerated through hearing Mass. The staff of office (*vara*, known locally as *tata santo roma*, holy father Rome) must also be taken to Mass each year by the community officer who holds it, in order to replenish its authority. Likewise the images of the saints, the banners (*istantarti*, standards) representing avocations of the virgin, and the shawls and other clothing of the miraculous saints from larger shrines that are kept in each community as a way of distributing the powers of the miracles. All these dwell in village churches and calvary chapels and must hear Mass regularly (usually once a year), or else they become angry and turn their powers against the community.[9]

PILGRIMAGE AND PENANCE

While ordinary Sunday masses are sufficient to celebrate and confirm aspects of the life cycle, those for replenishing collective sources of well-being are associated with the concentrated power of "miracles." A miracle (*milawru*) is a local shrine of a particular saint. Even very small local shrines can have the quality of miracle, but the "great miracles" (*jach'a milawru*) are centers of annual pilgrimage whose power and blessing are widely recognized in the region, and in some cases beyond it. These great miracles have exceptional powers and are also credited with specialized skills, and they are usually referred to by the place itself, with the name of the saint taken for granted.[10] Saints as miracles are intensely localized, identified not just with the place, but with the very soil and landscape. In many pilgrimages, part of the efficacy of the miracle derives from stuff picked up off the ground—earth, stones, sheep droppings—which are talismans of whatever it is people desire. They take these objects home with them and make offerings to them, often during a three-year cycle.[11] For example, Tata Phanakhachis brings children to the infertile; Mamita Pitunisa confers special skills on the women weavers who worship her; Mamita Urqupiña brings wealth; and Tata Killakasa is a great doctor who heals the sick. Each saint has a particular function, for which people make offerings. Thus Mamita Candelaria in Chayanta is the miracle of the fertile potatoes; Tata san Antonio in Qalaqala protects llamas; Tata San Juan in Carasi is the patron of sheep.[12] At the same time, saints are intercessors with God. I have often heard it said that people worship a particular saint or virgin because he or she is "good at beseeching God on our behalf" (*sum mayt'asi Tyusat jiwasataki*).

Saints, whether great miracles or small ones, are God's children and called "little father" (*tatituy*) or "little mother" (*mamita*). Most "little mothers," such as Mamita Rosario, Mamita Asunta (Assumption), or Mamita Waralupi (Guadaloupe), are advocations of the Virgin.[13] As many commentators have pointed out, the evangelization of the Andean region focused especially on the cult of the saints. The Protestant denial of the efficacy of the saints had led to its reaffirmation by Rome, and it was also deeply embedded in the popular religion in which most of the priests had been raised in Spain. Moreover, the moments of the liturgy centered on the life of Christ were fixed dates, and therefore celebrated only in the main parish church, whereas the saints' days allowed for more flexibility and were the occasion when priests could visit and attend to their flock living far from the main parish church (Marzal 1983: 262, 275). For these reasons Jesus Christ himself is not a significant figure in local forms of Christianity. Some people barely recognize the name, although the suffering Christ on the cross is a saint of great importance known as Tata San Exaltashuna (Holy Father Exaltation).

People make invocations to the "miracles" throughout the year. However, their powers are most efficacious at the time of their annual feast day. It is the moment when peasant communities journey together to renew the powers of their "devotions" and protectors, and their contact with God. Within each community, households rotate the responsibility for sponsoring a feast, with all the expenses associated with journeying to the shrine and providing the entire community with food and enough drink to ensure the required state of intoxication for all who participate.

At the feast of Saint James in the valley town of Torotoro, in 1973, the musicians of each community marched around the main square, in and out of beer shops, and at the entrance to the church itself, competing to outplay each other. Inside the church people were burning incense and candles, chewing wads of coca leaf that they then spat onto the mud floor, and pouring libations and drinks from jugs of chicha and bottles of cheap rum. In the midst of the deafening noise, with drunken men sobbing and occasionally falling on the floor, people milling about, and self-righteous townspeople telling everyone to be quiet and show some respect, the priest said Mass at the high altar. A huge queue pushed to the front to be splashed with holy water. The priest in question was an idealistic young Spaniard who had been in the area only four months and was shocked to the core by the clash between his way and theirs.

The most intensely ritualized occasions on which the peasants go to Mass are the patronal feasts when ritual battles (*tinkus*) are celebrated. Tinkus have traditionally been the centerpiece of many fiestas at miraculous shrines, but not at all. For example, at the shrine of the Virgin of Guadaloupe at Pitunisa, near San Pedro de Buena Vista, people said that *mamita* would be angry if they fought. While the uneven incidence of tinkus may be merely the result of sporadic attempts to ban them as brutal and unworthy of a civilized country,[14] it may also be that they are held during feasts to promote the fertility of the crops and livestock. They are often interpreted as a blood sacrifice for the earth deity (*pachamama*) and the mountains, who are responsible for the fertility of land and livestock; by contrast, the virgin of Pitunisa's miraculous powers are particularly associated with weaving skills.

When there is a tinku, the married couple who sponsor the feast and provide days of banquets and liquor for the whole community go in solemn procession to the church bearing the hamlet's crosses to hear Mass. Much of the community accompanies them. The men of fighting age form a military band playing long bamboo panpipes (*suqusu* or *jula-jula*) commanded by the "major" (*mayura*), and a couple of unmarried girls (*mit'ani*) march at the front waving white banners. When they pass hamlets on their way, people bring out their sacred images to be blessed by the sound of the pipes. The music is based on old Gregorian chants, and at designated points along their route (*ch'isiraya*) the band stops to perform spiral and circular dances and then kneel, doffing their caps and facing east to ask pardon (*pirun mayt'asiña*) from our father the sun, and make the sign of the cross.

Several things are striking about this act of penance. The bamboo pipes communicate directly with God, playing a genre of tunes known as *nuwina*,[15] and the very name of the group that goes to the tinku—*wayli*, from the Spanish *baile*, meaning a dance—indicates that communication with God takes place not only through words but also through musical sound and movement. Moreover, this act of penance is a collective one involving—symbolically if not arithmetically—the whole community, and contrary to Catholic orthodoxy it is performed without the mediation of a priest.[16]

It seems that on most occasions people ask pardon from God for their sinful state, rather than for particular shortcomings. On the one hand, human beings are generically sinful; on the other, one of the major attributes of God is to punish (van den Berg 1990: 239), and disasters that afflict a whole community (such as drought, epidemic, or mudslide) are usually said to be punishment from God (*kastiku*). But people do not use the Mass as a means of seeking pardon for sins.[17]

Another important element of the *wayli* that marches to do battle at the saints' feast days is the crosses that are carried in this military procession to hear Mass. In each of the two communities I know best, two large crucifixes are kept in the calvary chapel. They are painted with a series of motifs relating to the Passion, for example a ladder, nails, a cock, the sun, but not the image of the dying Christ, which, as I have already indicated, is a separate saint. Crosses were powerful symbols in the Andean region long before the coming of the Christians, invoking notions of order and balance and therefore serving as guardians, for example of the community, or of the food crops (Urton 1981: 129–50). Those that are taken to hear Mass during the tinku are dressed as warriors. For example, in the highland village of Muruq'umarka, the bigger cross, known as Tata San Ijsimu (the Spanish *eximio* means distinguished, eminent, and is an epithet of the Host), was taken to the tinku during the potato sowing season in October,[18] dressed in a red poncho, a woolen sash, and a helmet (*muntira*). When we stopped on the journey, the bottom of the cross rested on a garment provided by the feast sponsor, since it must never touch the ground. Tata San Ijsimu was also important in another feast to bring rain to the planted potato fields at the end of November (*rama phista*).

This cross was a physical, local manifestation of God himself, manifested in the Host. Similarly, in the valley community of Saychani where I also lived, one of the crosses was a manifestation of God, but in this case in his capacity as healer—Santiago or Saint James—known in Saychani as Tata Kimsa Mujuna (Father Three Boundary Markers).[19] In both cases the God/cross was partnered with a second, lesser cross, though the details differed. In Muruq'umarka the second, smaller cross was called Tata San Phulurisa (Holy Father Flowers), and he was said to be the wife (*warmi*) of Tata San Ijsimu. He played an important role in the feast of Carnival, which is also the celebration of the first fruits of the harvest. In Saychani the paired cross was called Tata San Sebastián (Holy Father Sebastian) and was said to be the older brother of—and less powerful than—Tata Kimsa Mujuna.[20]

In these examples we find the typical Andean dualisms. Everything is doubled, usually as male/female or older/younger division (and, as often occurs, the female partner is not exclusively gendered as female). Even God is doubled, as male/female (the sun and the moon, Tata San Ijsimu in Muruq'umarka and his "wife" Holy Father Flowers) or as older/younger brother. In some senses God takes the form of the universal parents, father and mother to everything in this world, who themselves have no parents. At the same time some conceptual effort is made to align with a monotheistic principle, in the idea of God as superior and different. For example, in the chullpa myth the moon (today the sun/God's female counterpart) is represented as less powerful, the deity of a previous age. Again, in the case of the paired crosses just mentioned, only the husband or younger brother is thought to be God, while the wife or elder brother is not.

At the same time, these examples indicate that in some manifestations, God is present in material form, and moreover that in certain rituals such as the penance, the peasants communicate directly with him, and not through the mediation of the priests. At the same time it is the priests, especially the foreign, modernizing priests, who repeatedly denounce the superstitious practices of the peasants whom they serve.

Colonial Christianity and Devil Worship

While the very figure of God is in some senses multiple or paired, there are also forms of doubling and duplication that take us right outside the realm of things pertaining to God, and it is here that accusations of continued paganism carry most weight. There are many powers in the cosmos that must not go to Mass—in fact, in order to function properly, they must be kept apart from it and not participate in the circulation of blessing that derives from paying for and hearing the Mass. These include representations of the mountain gods and the earth (at least in some manifestations), the powerful stones that serve as guardians of the community and the household flocks, and the shrines where a living being has been struck dead by lightning.

These powers are often referred to generically as *saxras*. Their domain is one of chaos, fertility, danger, the possibility of great wealth, but also of destruction. It is associated with the inner, hidden world (*manqha pacha*) in contrast to the upper world (*alax pacha*) of God and the saints. These beings, like those of the upper world, get hungry and must be fed, but while the upper sphere of God (*tyusa parti*) is nourished with the bread and wine of the Mass (and the payments of those who attend), the *saxras* consume the blood of sacrificial animals, a drink made with the flour of white maize kernels, and llama fat. If they do not receive these raw offerings, made at dawn before the sun rises, they may eat their human devotees instead, causing illness and death.

Given that these powers of the inner world are also known as devils (Harris 1982, 1989, 2000), it is not surprising that visually they are sometimes depicted through the European iconography of the devil. For example, the devils who live deep inside the mines of the Potosí region take the form of horned men with bulbous eyes and erect penis, to whom the miners must make constant offerings to avoid their anger and court their favor. And in rural communities, too, people cover themselves with black goatskins to dance as the devils of Carnival (goats are traditionally associated with the devil in European folklore). Moreover, the antipathy of the Catholic devil to salt is echoed in the way that Andean devils eat sacrificial food without salt. However, it is not easy to define who and what these devils are.

Indeed, within Christian theology as a whole, there is no unitary understanding of the devil, whether historically or today (Forsyth 1987; D. Taylor 1985). Fernando Cervantes has argued persuasively that in sixteenth-century Mexico the inquisitors and theologians had little success in instilling their own notions of the devil as the cosmic antagonist of God. Sacrifices to pre-Christian deities were idolatrous, since they violated the First Commandment, and therefore could only be described as devil worship. But ironically it was this very identification of sacrifice with devil worship that led indigenous people to embrace the devil as part of their pantheon, since they could not renounce the practice of sacrifice, and were anyhow predisposed to understand deities as a combination of positive and negative characteristics. The notion of the devil that took root, then, was more medieval than post-Tridentine, subservient to God and even susceptible to manipulation through natural means (Cervantes 1994; MacCormack 1991: 40). It is likely that a similar process took place in Andean Christianity, since it is especially through sacrifice and offerings that people communicate with those powers they call generically devils today. Devils in Northern Potosí are the sources of fertility, chaos, danger, and luck.

It is tempting to interpret this inner domain of the devils as what remains of pre-Christian religious forms, driven into clandestinity and demonized from the sixteenth century onward by the absolutist demands of the new religion. And there are indeed some elements of the devils' sphere today that resonate strongly with sixteenth-century Spanish accounts of pagan Andean practice. However, at the same time, a contrast between the sky and earth cults already existed, and so did the contrast between light and dark, order and disorder, so that affinities between a pre-Christian religiosity and present practice can also be detected in what peasants today call "God's sphere," such as the close identification between the Christian god and the Inca sun/lightning god (Bouysse-Cassagne and Harris 1988). On the other hand, the inner world of the devils is also deeply infused with Christian imagery and associations, so that a stratigraphical approach to the historical depth of different aspects of worship cannot be applied (Abercrombie 1998: 110–16; Bouysse-Cassagne 1997). There is no unambiguous mapping of Christian practices with God's sphere and of pre-Christian practices with the devils' sphere.[21]

Nonetheless, the early colonial history of evangelization in the Andes is generally recounted as one of poignant contrast. One of the emblematic stories recounts how the priest Valverde, who accompanied Pizarro to Peru, offered the Inca king Atahuallpa a Bible to indicate the source of the true religion. Atahuallpa held it to his ears, and when the Bible failed to speak he threw it to the ground in disgust. This moment of mutual incomprehension when the Spanish and Incas first met resulted in the imposition of Christianity by force. Crucial to this version of history is the evidence of the "extirpations of idolatry": the violent rooting out of pagan practices by priests drawing on the techniques of the Inquisition (Duviols 1971). However, it seems that the experience of extirpation was limited to certain areas of Peru, and evangelization occurred in a far more accepting and less dramatic form in many parts of the Andean region (Mills 1997). It seems likely in the case of highland Bolivia that evangelization was initially a matter of *Realpolitik*, and then conducted in close cooperation with the native ruling classes. For example, in a document relating to the 1570s, Don Fernando Ayavire, the ruler of the northernmost part of what is today Northern Potosí, boasted that he used his authority to persuade his people to abandon their "dancing and drunkenness"—in other words their pagan rites—and that he accompanied the Jesuit priests on Sunday mornings in the mining city of Potosí, rounding up the Indians to go and hear Mass (Platt, Bouysse-Cassagne, and Harris 2006).[22] Although many scholars have written of the "resistance" of Andean peoples to Christian evangelization, examples such as this evoke a far less polarized situation: not either/or so much as both/and.

The configuration of the religious domain today is still affected by a number of colonial policies. For example, a key decision taken by the Crown in the late sixteenth century was to bar Indians and mestizos from the priesthood, ironically on the grounds that their commitment to the vow of chastity and celibacy was questionable. This ruling was only partially relaxed in the eighteenth century (Meiklejohn 1988: 133). As a result, priests were always outsiders, of Spanish descent even if born in the Americas. This policy may well have encouraged the development—or continuation—of two distinct religious domains, one related to the outer and upper world of the celestial deity, serviced by foreigners, the other related to an inner clandestine world serviced by Indian priests, spirit mediums, or diviners, and focused on the unpredictable powers that renew the fertility of the earth and the well-being of the flocks. Moreover, there was always a shortage of priests to serve the rural areas, and those that there were had to travel long distances to say Mass in the different chapels within their parish. There are many myths told in which a priest arrives late for Mass and is confronted by the wrath of the local Indian lord.[23] But it would be wrong to conclude from this that priests and the Church they represented were simply identified with the colonial administration and its abuses. Szeminski, for one, has convincingly argued that even at the height of anti-Spanish feeling during the Great Insurrection of 1780, priests were largely exempt from attack (Szeminski 1988).

Many other distinguishing features of popular Andean Catholicism that today's reformist priesthood finds problematic also derive from the strategies of the colonial evangelizers. The fiestas of patronal and miraculous saints are an obvious example, promoted by a combination of different interests in the sixteenth and seventeenth centuries. Priests found them an effective vehicle for evangelization, colonial functionaries saw them as a means to regroup the dispersed population in concentrated settlements, and indigenous groups themselves were thereby able to reinvent their world through the new organizational forms that accompanied the cult of the saints, such as religious confraternities (*cofradías*) (Saignes 1995; Marzal 1991: 240).[24]

The attitude of peasants today with regard to the Mass is another example, in the sense that their presence at the Mass is as listeners, and to be blessed with holy water. The colonial grounding of this is clear. In the first centuries of evangelization, hearing Mass and the catechism were probably the central means of participation in Christian worship.[25] Some priests even refused to allow Indians to take communion and neglected to teach them the meaning of the gospel and the new faith, although many kept a strict check on which of their flock had confessed and taken communion at Easter and which had not, a practice that apparently died out only at the beginning of the nineteenth century (Meiklejohn 1988: 258; Marzal 1983: 288, 301–2).

On the other hand, today most Catholic priests who serve the Bolivian countryside reinforce the sense that some aspects of indigenous worship are not only backward and superstitious but unacceptable in a more absolute sense, although some of them merely turn a blind eye. The peasants also perceive the incompatibility between attendance at Mass and some of the rites they practice to ensure fertility and the prosperity of their communities. Many stories are told of rituals hurriedly broken off and concealed when the priest arrives (e.g., Abercrombie 1998: 103–7).[26] In some contexts there must be no mention of saints' names, or the use of the cross, for fear of offending the devils (as, for example, Nash records [1979: 7] for the mining communities of Oruro). But while in some respects they are viewed as incompatible, in others the domain of God (*tyusa parti*) and that of the devils (*saxra parti*) mirror and duplicate each other. The very term used in Aymara for the ceremony of feeding the *saxra*—*misa*—is the same as the Mass,[27] and the spirit medium who presides over the Mass for the devils is often referred to during the ceremony as "father priest" (*tata cura*).

Pilgrimage shrines often reflect this doubling process. Near the colonial city of Potosí, for example, there is a chapel dedicated to Saint Bartolomew on a rocky promontory, and thousands journey there for his feast day on August 24. Right below the chapel in the rock there is a huge "cave of the devil." After hearing Mass in the chapel, the devotees climb the mountainside above both chapel and cave to collect stones that represent the wealth that they desire in the coming years, pouring libations simultaneously for both saint and devil.

What we can detect in this complex field is a general distinction between two spiritual spheres or worlds, which operates differentially according to context. Sometimes the two worlds are so close as to be virtually identified; at other times a sharp contrast is enacted. Sometimes parallelism is emphasized, at other times radical alterity. Moreover, while the relationship between the two has generally been seen in terms of opposition and alternation, there are also senses in which the complementarity between them can be expressed in terms of a transformatory dynamic. This is the argument of Henry Stobart (1995: 116), for example, who in analyzing the mythical and ritual associations of music through the course of the annual cycle in Northern Potosí notes how the different powers of saints and devils are uppermost at different moments of the agricultural calendar, and are embodied by people at different stages of the life cycle; from this perspective, the ritual cycle involves a process of transformation from one to the other.

Increasingly, however, external religious functionaries do not turn a blind eye. Since the beginning of the twentieth century, the colonial model of Christian practice has been under attack in the Andean region. The first Protestant missionaries arrived in Bolivia at the very end of the nineteenth and beginning of the twentieth centuries (Ströbele-Gregor 1989: 120; Gill 1993: 184), and Baptists were active in Northern Potosí by the 1920s from their base in Torotoro. There have not at the time of writing been large-scale conversions to the different Protestant churches in the region, but everywhere there are a few who refuse to join in the fiestas, refuse to drink, who go out to work in their fields on saints' days but never on a Sunday, and who get together to read the Bible, pray, and sing hymns each week. Often those who convert have worked as migrants in the towns, and above all they wish to avoid the periodic bouts of drunkenness and the accompanying violence associated with fiestas. One of the things that unites Protestants—or *evangélicos* as they are normally called—is their repudiation of their previous religious practices as devil worship.[28]

In Latin America as a whole, the postwar period saw the recruitment of foreign Catholic priests in large numbers, especially from the religious orders, both in response to the challenge from different Protestant churches and as a solution to the long-term decline in local recruitment to the priesthood. They brought with them a conception of the religious life, the person, and the sacraments that was radically different from the colonial Christianity that had become institutionalized over the centuries. In some countries this Reform Catholicism had a profound impact on rural Christianity, training local men as catechists to promulgate the new ideas, notably Guatemala, where the Catholic Action movement became a major player in the civil war (R. Wilson 1995). In Bolivia the more radical wing of the Catholic Church has been more influential from the 1970s onward, involved as much in the organizing of peasant unions, development work, the funding of NGOs, the building of latrines and hospitals, and the promotion of chemical fertilizers as with spiritual transformation. Since the late 1980s this was partly superseded by an interest in local forms of popular Christianity and the forms of spirituality embodied in apparently pagan practices. At the same time, the strength of the indigenous movement in Bolivia has led to a revalorization of "Andean religion" with which some—but only some—missionary priests are sympathetic (Albo 1991; Marzal 1991; van den Berg 1990). In any event, the new wave of reform has reignited the debate on whether the indigenous rural peasants of the Andes can be called proper Christians, or whether a new conversion is required.

The Ambiguities of the Dead

The peasants of Northern Potosí consider themselves to be proper Christians. And yet at the same time many have lingering doubts, and in some ways they have internalized the view that outsiders have of them. I discussed the Protestants with Pedro Mamani as we returned from dispatching the soul of one of his kinswomen at the end of the feast of the dead. He put it bluntly: "We drink beer, we fight, we talk with the devil, so we don't go to heaven. The Protestants do none of these things, so they do go to heaven."

In many contexts, the souls of the dead can be identified directly with the devils' domain and are implicitly integrated with the pre-Christian ancestors, the chullpas who were destroyed by the rising of the Christian sun. They are a major force for the growing crops, since it is they who bring the rains at the beginning of November when they are collectively welcomed back into the community of the living. At the end of the rainy season, they take on the guise of devils in the feast of Carnival, embodying the vegetation and the new crops that are about to be harvested. Carnival is known as the feast of the devils, and at the end of a week of intense celebration, accompanied by the *pinkillu* flutes that sing mournful songs to the dead, the souls of the dead are dispatched to return to Tacna Marka, the place of the dead (Harris 1982). In Tacna Marka they cultivate chili peppers for the living.[29] By contrast, the souls of those who die as children are called "little angels" and fly straight to heaven because they have not sinned—that is, they are not old enough to drink beer, fight, talk with the devil, and commit other sinful acts of adults.

Yet at the same time, the souls of the dead are also part of the Christian world. As I have already indicated, masses are offered for them in order to make sure that they reach their final destination, even though this is not the Christian heaven. One of the most striking moments of the ritual calendar when the domains of God and the devils seem temporarily to fuse is the feast of the dead at All Saints (November 1), when everybody assembles in the graveyard. The air is heavy with the sound of the pinkillu flutes that are played throughout the rainy season from November to February. High stepped altars, covered with foodstuffs, have been erected to the memory of those who have died within the previous two years. Their living kinsfolk beg the people thronging the graveyard to pray, and they reciprocate with coca leaf, food, beer, and rum. When I asked why the altars were stepped and what we were praying for, people usually replied that this was to help the soul reach heaven.

On many occasions when people pray to God or the saints, or indeed to the devils, they use Aymara. They may ask for protection on a journey, help in starting something such as building a house or weaving a cloth, or health for themselves, their kin, and their livestock. But at the feast of the dead they pray in Latin, or at least in Spanish, not in their language but in God's, spoken also by the priests as God's intermediaries. They rarely know the literal meaning of these prayers, but every adult should know how to pray.[30] To my knowledge, in addition to the feast of the dead, the occasions when it is important to pray in Latin or Spanish are to perform the initial rites of baptism a few days after a baby's birth, and for some curing rituals. People were mystified that I could pray neither in Spanish nor in Latin, and they found my English recitations a poor substitute. Being able to pray extensively in Spanish or Latin is a skill that can bring rewards. In urban graveyards there are people—sometimes young children—who work for money reciting prayers in Latin for the souls of the dead.[31]

Praying in Latin or Spanish is, I conclude, a means of appropriating the intermediary function of the priest.[32] It is not clear to me whether the prayers are directed to God or to the dead themselves. The fact that flute players pray with music and are paid in kind suggests that the prayers may communicate with the dead, since pinkillu flutes are the means for communicating with the dead.[33] On the other hand, on the occasions when I have witnessed the spirit medium speak to the soul of a recently deceased person, Aymara was the language of communication. Indeed, there may not be a simple answer as to who is the recipient of these prayers in Latin and Spanish during the feast of the dead. It may be yet more evidence of the ambiguous position of the dead souls, alternating between the Christian identity they maintained while alive and their gradual incorporation into the world of the devils who play such an important role in the promotion of the fertility of the crops.[34] At All Saints people pray for the souls of the departed; but by Carnival these same souls have been transformed into devils who are dangerous, chaotic, and at the same time figures of play and of fertility.

The Eternal Return of Conversion

This doubling and duplication across the two domains of God and the devils in traditional Andean Christianity might be interpreted as a classic instance of syncretism, in which two distinct religious traditions are joined in a new and creative synthesis.[35] The developing anthropology and historiography of popular Christianity takes as a major theme the issue of how the globalizing, universalizing force of Christian missionary activity becomes embedded in new localisms, how new meanings are forged through the mutual incorporation of non-Christian and Christian cultural practices (e.g., James and Johnson 1988; Mosse 1994a). However, in the Andean context, the debate is still conducted often in terms of whether or not the peasants can be said to be proper Christians at all, and it is a debate of intense concern to many different parties.

The shock experienced by many dedicated missionary priests coming from Europe has already been mentioned. With their modernizing ethos, they see it as their duty to save the peasants from their ignorance. By contrast, those whose position derives from the critique of colonialism are eager to demonstrate that the retention of pre-Christian elements in popular Andean Christianity is a form of resistance, and that many aspects of contemporary practice are the continuation of pre-Christian religion with a superficial change of nomenclature. For townspeople and the educated elite, the religious practices of the indigenous peasants of Northern Potosí—their fights, their sacrifices, their drunkenness—are a continuing source of embarrassment and outrage, leading to denunciation and occasional attempts at prohibition. These concerns reproduce directly the attempts of earlier generations to civilize and control the Indians. The Bourbon reforms of the mid-eighteenth century, for example, led to repeated attempts to abolish religious fiestas (Sala i Vila 1994). Similarly, the liberal governments of the late nineteenth century were preoccupied with the squandering of resources and loss of working days caused by the drunken fiestas (Irurozqui Victoriano 1994). Anthropologists and historians are not immune from the intensity of this debate. They may respect the evident fact that the peasants think of themselves as Christians, but at the same time it is hard for us not to see the continual parallels between present-day practices and elements of pre-Christian practice as revealed in sixteenth- and seventeenth-century writings by Spanish chroniclers and other missionary priests.

Historians have begun to flesh out the term *conversion* and show what a lengthy and complex process the Christianization of the Andes was. It is clear that policies differed markedly from one period to another, as did the criteria for what constituted adequate Christian practice, and the different approaches of the various religious orders and the secular priesthood also played an important part. Today the debate has been recast between traditionalists, reformers, and populists within the Catholic Church, the far more stringent demands of most Protestant churches, the strong indigenous movement in Bolivia, and local elites concerned to promote a more modern culture. Christianity, in short, has been and still is a contested domain, for all its claims to absolute truth and absolute rules.

And yet the terms set by the different contestations as to what is and is not real Christianity rarely allow for mutual recognition and respect. A concern with defining orthodoxy has always been a constitutive part of Christianity and certainly was at the forefront in the evangelization of the Andean region. Church leaders remained preoccupied with the continuation of idolatry even in the many areas where virulent campaigns were not carried out (Mills 1994: 114). And although the terminology and the precise doctrinal concerns have changed, the preoccupations remain. Tristan Platt (1987: 144) notes the concern at continuing "superstition" in eighteenth-century Bolivia. Today the fundamentalist Protestants identify the practices of Andean Christianity as devil worship, while reformist Catholics see it as paganism, resulting more from ignorance and the failings of previous generations of priests than from the seductions of the devil.

A constitutive element of Christianity is the uncertainty whether members of the faith have fully cast off the "old Adam," the sins of previous existence, and the worship of pagan gods. In the sixteenth-century Andes, even the most passionate adherents to the new faith might be visited by nightmare visions calling them back to the old ways, as Frank Salomon has so vividly described (1990). Even in the Christian heartlands of Europe, there is an ambivalent recognition that practitioners of popular Christianity continue to worship pagan elements to this day (Stewart 1991; Pina-Cabral 1992).

Given the radical demands of Christian epistemology, with its exclusivity, its policing of the boundaries of truth, and its constant search for unity and orthodoxy, I would argue that a preoccupation with who is and who is not a true Christian is a typical attribute of the religion across denominational boundaries. The peasants of Northern Potosí are themselves not entirely immune from this concern, exploring through their myths the ambiguities of whether they, or their frequent adversaries, the mestizo townspeople, are the true Christians.

In other respects, the paradoxes of their own commitment to the Christian faith and its irresolvability are lived out in repeated ritual performances. In many ways the religious practice of the peasants constitutes a "single total field," as Tambiah (1970) argues for the heterodox practices of Buddhist peasants in northeast Thailand. But they know that aspects of their religious practice must be hidden from the priests and are guarded in what they will reveal to outsiders. Undoubtedly many things are not only hidden from outsiders but also protected in metaphor from the dangers of verbal exegesis as such. The clandestinity of much of their religious practice has a number of sources. In part it takes the form of gradual revelation for the committed typical of mystery religions. In part it derives from the domestic nature of many rituals, whose efficacy would be undermined if anyone from outside the immediate kin and residence group participated or even saw from a distance. But in part it is also secret because people know that outsiders consider it to be transgressive.

Perhaps the clearest way in which the tension between the two domains is reenacted is when there is a clear break from the time of ritual and a return to everyday life. I described one such moment at the beginning of this essay. Another even more dramatic experience of rupture comes at the end of Carnival. After more than a week of festivities, the devils are dispatched outside inhabited space. The flutes that sing to the dead are thrown on one side. Those that have impersonated the ancestors and devils (*kiramayku* and *kirat'alya*) throw off their disguise, and everybody returns to their homes singing the joyful songs of the dry season, accompanied by men playing *charangos* (small mandolins).

These moments of ritual severance, where people break off communication with the devils, can perhaps be seen as an eternal return to the point of conversion. The process of abandoning the pre-Christian ancestors and other deities, which I have suggested remains incomplete, is reduced to a moment. A similar sense of rupture can be found in the chullpa myth, when the dawning of the Christian sun immediately kills all the previous inhabitants of the earth. This myth, told widely throughout the central Andes, constitutes in many senses a myth of origin, explaining how the time of the Christians started and contrasting the people of today with the pre-Christian population. In ritual and in myth there is an eternal return to the experience of conversion. My echoing of Mircea Eliade's famous essay ([1954] 1989) is deliberate but ironic, for in Eliade the "eternal return" of ritual is a return to the cosmogony itself, while the experience of conversion to Christianity would constitute precisely the kind of historical event he saw as antithetical to the integrative and therapeutic qualities of archaic ritual.

We can see in the complexities of Andean Christianity a profound meditation on the implications of conversion and its ambiguities. There are many reasons the return to the moment of conversion may be particularly pronounced in the Andean region. In particular, pre-Christian religious practice was centrally focused on the worship of ancestors, mummified or otherwise preserved, and the ritual calendar was intricately imbricated with the agricultural cycle, so that the continuation of agricultural production involved the continuation of rituals to ensure its success, albeit in a modified form.

However, I suggest that a concern with the incompleteness of conversion is a leitmotif of Christianity in a much more general sense. Much has been written about the forms of temporality peculiar to Christian doctrines, in particular the pronounced emphasis on linearity both as a narrative of salvation and as an eschatology (e.g., Eliade [1954] 1989; S. Brandon 1964). But the way in which Christian time is derived from a complete rupture with the past has not received the attention it deserves.[36] This radical break requires converts to renounce whatever they previously held sacred, including close kin ties. For most human populations, respect for their ancestors operates as a powerful metaphor of continuity between past and present. Therefore, conversion to Christianity produces discontinuity. For the recently converted, this discontinuity constitutes an existential dilemma that is hard to resolve. The rejected pagan ancestors may come back to haunt the living. But this tension in different professions of Christianity is not restricted to the recently converted. Even where loyalty to the pre-Christian ancestors as such has disintegrated, the permanent threat of sin, of backsliding, means that the drama of conversion is constantly reenacted, whether through baptism, the confession of sins, or reconversion. For some, the ambiguities of conversion may be displaced onto the pagan other through missionary endeavors. For others, particularly in charismatic sects, conversion is a permanent process, constantly renewed in ecstatic confession and renunciation of the Devil (Lehmann 1996: 139). It is this poignant but dynamic tension at the heart of Christian faith that is illustrated so clearly by the attempt to knit past and present, mountain ancestors and solar deity, and communion with saints and with devils in popular Andean Christianity.

......

Notes

I thank the participants in the Christianity workshops organized by Fenella Cannell and Maia Green in 1996 and 1998, and also the Social Anthropology Research Seminar at the University of Oxford, for their comments on earlier drafts of this essay.

1 The western part of the region where my research has been based—in particular the Laymi *ayllu*—was until recently Aymara-speaking but is experiencing language shift to Quechua. It is notable that ritual language remains largely Aymara. The main fieldwork on which this chapter is based was carried out during extended stays in 1972–74 and 1986–87, as well as on a number of shorter visits. While obviously there have been enormous changes in indigenous communities, I am confident that at the time of writing (2000) the practices and beliefs that I describe were still current. For this reason I use the ethnographic present.

2 This belief is grounded in the material reality of chullpa remains, since before the Christian evangelization of the Andean region the dead were regularly mummified by desiccation and worshipped by the living.

3 Babies are "baptized" within a few days of birth by a high-status layperson in the local community (e.g., the anthropologist). In this ceremony the baby is defined as a Christian by the salt placed on its lips, the sign of the cross in water on its forehead, and by the recitation of prayers from the breviary.

4 *Jant'aku* is any cloth or skin used to ensure that people do not sit or lie directly on the ground.

5 In fact, as we have seen, parents ensure that an initial rite of baptism is performed within the rural community a few days after the baby's birth, if priests are far away. Otherwise, if the baby dies, it must be buried in the wild for the mountain deities to consume, and its spirit may cause trouble to the living in the future. This initial rite is confirmed later by a full baptism in church.

6 This idea perhaps accords with some theological conceptualizations of the Mass as a "living sacrifice" on the part of the congregation, although belief that God is fed with the bread and wine of the Mass is remote from orthodox understanding of the Mass as a reenactment of the sacrifice of Christ by which the congregation is spiritually nourished.

7 There may be other reasons that the peasants did not make explicit, for example that they have a special historical relationship with Chayanta and its patronal saints (Platt, Bouysse-Cassagne, and Harris 2006).

8 The term *devotion*, which properly refers to the attitude of the worshipper, has in this instance been transferred wholesale to the holy image (see Christian 1972: 47).

9 Conversely, the Mass can also be used as a way of warding off evil and harm. A Canadian Oblate priest working in the mining district of Northern Potosí told me that he had been approached by a peasant asking him to say Mass "for a head" (*cabezapaj*). Mystified, he asked what was meant by this. In reply the man opened his bundle and produced a severed human head, which was causing him and his family a lot of trouble. The priest refused to offer Mass on this occasion. Monast also reports (1969: 211) that he was asked sometimes to say a "cursing mass" (*misa de maldición*), and he too refused. The implication is that some Bolivian priests would accede to such requests.

10 Many myths recount how a particular image came to live in a particular spot. Often this involves wandering from one place to another, or being stolen by jealous neighbors, until the saint decides for itself where it will live (Morote Best 1988; Sallnow 1987).

11 In the late 1980s, when enthusiasm for Mamita Urqupiña (August 15) near the city of Cochabamba was at its height, the Bolivian national airline issued advertisements in the papers, warning that passengers trying to board a plane with large rocks from the shrine in their hand luggage would be prevented from doing so.

12 In Sallnow's account (1987: 54–55), the role of miracles in popular Catholicism in the Cusco region is rather different, more in line with the theological notion of thaumaturgy.

13 One female saint who is regularly invoked—Santa Barbara, the patron of artillery, identified as one of the triple aspects of the lightning deity—is in fact treated as male.

14 The modernizing campaigns both of the reformist priesthood and of secular officials such as teachers and subprefects have led by the beginning of the twenty-first century to the suppression of most tinkus in Northern Potosí.

15 From the Spanish *novena*, a supplicatory act of worship, originally a pilgrimage of nine days (Christian 1972: 60).

16 Penance in Catholic Christianity is a sacrament mediated by the priest, and so it was in colonial practice (Marzal 1983: 285–86). In the standard Confessional of 1585, the question "Have you confessed with any native sorcerer?" was the third question pertaining to the First Commandment, signaling its importance (Barnes 1992: 75). The collective nature of the act of penance described here is in marked contrast to individual confession, which is very uncommon for the peasants, unless they have been trained as catechists by the Reform clergy.

17 At the feast of the virgin of Pitunisa, after performing the ritual of penance on the journey, people tied knots in the *ichu* grass above the shrine to "tie up their sins" (*juch ch'inuña*) and leave them behind there. In addition to the calendrical feasts, the ritual of "asking pardon" of God may be performed with the bamboo pipes at other moments of crisis.

18 The tinku this cross was taken to was that of Mamita Rosario in the colonial village of Aymaya, patron of the potato crops, the staple food of the highland populations.

19 The nails painted on these large crucifixes are interpreted by the peasants as *anti*, the rattles made of a composite of metal objects used by spirit mediums to call up the spirits. Hence the particular association of the cross—and its painted images of objects associated with the Passion—with curing. Saint James was identified from the earliest arrival of the Spanish with the lightning god Illapa, closely identified with the sun, whose powers are especially used in healing (Silverblatt 1988; Platt 1997). The round stones used by the spirit mediums are said to be the "bullets" or slingshot of the lightning god, and they must also hear Mass in order to retain their efficacy (Platt 1987).

20 While Tata Kimsa Mujuna is a miracle, Tata San Sebastián is only a devotion.

21 In this respect Andean Catholicism is quite different from the pattern found in more fundamentalist branches of Christian practice. Birgit Meyer's analysis of Ewe Pentecostalism in Ghana is a particularly clear example of the unambiguous association of the Devil with the past and with pre-Christian practices (1999).

22 There is evidence in the historical sources for the presence of a number of different orders in the region in the mid-sixteenth century—Franciscans, Jesuits, and Mercedarians, as well as secular priests (Platt, Bouysse-Cassagne, and Harris 2006).

23 Stories of this kind are analyzed in Howard-Malverde 1990 and Molina Rivero 1986.

24 As William Christian (1972) has noted for Spain, aspects of religious cults that are today seen as deriving from the "little" tradition of a local peasantry in fact correspond to what was official church policy in previous periods.

25 Sixteenth-century documents are full of references to the need to ensure that the Indians "hear Mass."

26 Such stories usually refer to moments when an animal is being sacrificed in the community; the rejection of blood sacrifice is of course a leitmotif of both the Old and the New Testaments.

27 The ritual feeding of the *saxras* is usually written as *mesa*, the Spanish word for table, in order to avoid identifying it with the Mass. However, in Aymara there is no phonetic distinction between *i* and *e*.

28 See Kamsteeg 1993. In practice there is often backsliding among protestant converts, especially in rural communities, where access to community land and cooperative labor is closely linked to the periodic sacrificial offerings to the landscape deities (Spier 1993).

29 Tacna Marka exists in geographical reality as a town on the southern Peruvian coast to the west of the Andean chain. It is a matter for speculation why the Laymis identify this place as the place of the dead, a view that does not seem to be widely shared by other groups in northern Potosí.

30 Monast reports the belief in Carangas that people should not get married

until they know how to pray in Spanish or Latin (1969: 227–28; see also Irurozqui 1994: 392).

31 In La Paz I have participated in curing sessions with a famous healer who recited Padre Nuestro and Ave Maria some thirty times each. He had been a sacristan in his earlier life, so he knew much of the prayer book by heart, and this was one of the sources of his powers as a healer.

32 This interpretation is reinforced by the observation of Paula Sainz during his visit to Chayanta (the colonial name of Northern Potosí) in 1795, that at the feast of All Saints the priest and his assistants would go among the drunken peasants praying for the souls of the dead and receiving a *real* coin for each prayer (quoted in Sala i Vila 1994: 347).

33 Monast reports (1969: 45) that in Carangas masses for the souls are offered to the dead themselves, rather than to God in the name of the soul. Similarly, Christian notes (1972: 94) that until the twentieth century it was accepted practice in parts of Spain to pray directly to, as opposed to for, the souls in Purgatory.

34 Saignes has argued (1989) that in sixteenth-century Bolivia the use of the Spanish language by indigenous people in drunken rituals was a means of communicating with their native gods. Similarly, Penny Harvey (1991) suggests that the common use of Spanish in drunken speech in the Peruvian Andes is both a means of reflecting on the ambiguities of power and a means of expressing the potency of the "animate landscape"—what I refer to as the devils.

35 But I have argued elsewhere (Harris 1995) that the concept of syncretism is inherently contradictory, since it evokes the incompatible points of origin of the two blended traditions in a way that destabilizes the status of the new mix.

36 Nock's 1933 theological study of the significance of conversion is an excellent early text. Recently the studies of anthropologists such as Meyer 1998, van Dijk 2000, and Engelke 2004 concerning fundamentalist and evangelical groups in different parts of Africa have highlighted the temporal schemes involved in conversion, or in van Dijk's case, reconversion. However, the case I am considering is very different, since it concerns not new converts but people whose Christianity goes back four centuries or more.

···Two···

Renewable Icons

Concepts of Religious Power in a Fishing Village in South India

Cecilia Busby

The coastal road in south Kerala runs through an almost unbroken line of fishing villages, each consisting in the main of hundreds of small thatched huts, nestling under the ubiquitous palm trees. Small lanes run between them, down to the beach, and along the road women with fish baskets on their head or men with an outboard motor or a block of ice are common sights. What catches the eye, though, and takes the villages out of the ordinary, are the huge and impressive churches that emerge from the trees at regular intervals—one to each village, and often the only sign that one has passed from one village to the next. These are large, and often vividly painted bright white or red, sometimes like gothic cathedrals, but always towering above the small houses, with a prominent cross outside or a saint's shrine. They are unmistakably Catholic, and there are other signs, too, of the dominant religion in this area: the names of the paths that crisscross the village—St. Mary's Lane, All Saints Lane; the wayside shrine to St. Peter ("The Fisher King"); the shrine to the Holy Family next to the bus stop. In fact, three-quarters of the fishing community in this region of Kerala are Latin Catholic Mukkuvars, and the area has been dominated by Catholicism since the sixteenth-century mass conversions by St. Francis Xavier, a Portuguese Jesuit.

In this chapter, I want to look at the ways in which Christianity among the Mukkuvar, while still recognizably Christianity, is fundamentally connected to very local understandings of the nature of people and power. One of the most potent symbols for the ways in which these understandings interact is the image or icon of the Sacred Heart of Jesus that can be found in every home, the efficacy of which is regularly "renewed" by the local priest in a ceremony that reinvests religious power in the family shrine.

In a country where an overwhelming majority of the population is Hindu, it is difficult to understand Christianity without reference to parallel Hindu practices and beliefs. Thus much of the anthropology of Christianity in India has centered around the issue of to what extent Christians show evidence of caste practices, or accommodate their forms of worship to Hindu cultural idioms.[1] Here I want to try to understand Christianity in the fishing community in relation to implicit notions of the person, substance, and power, notions that are in some ways recognizably Indian but which must also be accepted as fully a part of local understandings of Christianity. These notions particularly center on the perception and manipulation of religious power, and while parallels can be clearly drawn with Hinduism, there are also strong parallels, at another level, with European Catholicism.

Catholicism in the Fishing Community of Kerala

Although one of the smallest states in India, Kerala is in fact one of the most cosmopolitan, with a large non-Hindu population. As well as a Christian and Muslim community, there are the remnants of a Jewish community, all of which have a long history in the state. The ports of the Malabar coast have served as centers for commercial exchange between China and Arabia and the West since well before the first century AD, with the state itself also exporting pepper, spices, ivory, and hardwoods.

There are a number of separate Christian groups in Kerala, associated with different caste groups and periods of conversion and for the most part maintaining separate church organizations (Fuller 1976). The state claims a Christian presence from the very earliest days, with the St. Thomas or Syrian Christians reputedly converted by the apostle before his martyrdom in Tamil Nadu in AD 72. This group for the most part follows the Syrian rites, suggesting a strong connection with West Asia through trading links, and was certainly well established around the coastal ports by the sixth century. Although subdivided among themselves into various sects—Protestant, Catholic, Marthomite, Syrian Orthodox, and so on—they form in general an elite among the Christians, claiming the status of upper-caste Hindu Nairs, from whom they were supposedly converted. Apart from the Syrian Christians, the other two large groups of Christians in Kerala are the Latin Catholics and the New Christians. This latter is the group of mostly low-caste or untouchable Hindus converted by English missionaries in the nineteenth and twentieth centuries; they are mostly to be found in the inland agricultural villages, particularly in the south and central regions. Conversion to Christianity has not altered their caste status, and they remain very low in local hierarchies, with separate churches from the Syrian Christians even where they share the same village.

Separate from these groups both ecclesiastically and geographically, the Latin Catholics of Kerala are found almost exclusively among the fishing villages in the coastal regions of the state, particularly in the southernmost district of Trivandrum. They were converted to Catholicism during the period of Portuguese colonialism in the area, which reached its height in the sixteenth century when St. Francis Xavier, one of the first Jesuits, came over to Kerala, and had outstanding success in converting the Mukkuvar and Arayan fishing castes. By the end of the sixteenth century the coastal regions of Kerala and Tamil Nadu contained some 45,000 baptized Roman Catholics.

Conversion to Christianity in Hindu caste society has often been part of a strategy of denial of or escape from low caste status, though it has rarely been successful in these terms. While the fishing community is undoubtedly considered low caste by the rest of Kerala society, conversion here may have been so phenomenally successful because it was a way of articulating a pervasive sense of difference between the fishing community and the majority agricultural community. Geographically on the margins, the periphery of the agricultural community, and outside the dense web of social and economic exchange, debt, obligation, and power relations that bind the castes together in agricultural villages, the fishing community maintains a sense of separation, of identity outside the hierarchy of caste and as far as possible independent from it. This sense of separation, based both on spatial separation and on the independence made possible by their occupation, has been further expressed by the fishing community through an identity as Catholic, and thus non-Hindu.[2]

Catholicism in the villages is immensely strong, and there is little doubt of most people's unquestioning faith. The huge, elaborate churches that dominate the villages are paid for almost entirely out of village funds. The church takes a tithe from every family, with 3 percent of the daily catch handed over to the church treasury and ideally used for the good of the community. The money is used for running church schools, village festivals, the church administration, decoration and upkeep, and so on. Although there may be questions asked if the priest is seen to use this money exclusively to his own ends, very few people would question the ultimate right of the church to demand this money, and most claim to give it with pride. On Sundays, there is no fishing and no selling, and virtually the entire village will attend the morning mass. On other days, it is mostly a smaller number of women who go, but there are numerous prayer groups who meet at other times. Every house in the village also has an image of the Sacred Heart of Jesus, before which they will often gather to say family prayers.

Women are the most prominent churchgoers, but they also play an important part in the economy in this region as fish sellers, and as a result are often more familiar with the world beyond the village than are their men. Women, even where they are not vendors, still control family finances. Men hand over their earnings to their wives, who give them money for their needs and make most of the day-to-day decisions of household economy. Women are also prominent in dealing with credit, which is extremely important in a fishing economy, and they are central also in kin networks. The community is predominantly matrilocal, with a great deal of marriages between people from different villages, so that while men may be settled relatively far from their natal kin, women tend to stay within close proximity to their mother and their sisters.[3]

It is in fact in the matter of marriage, and more particularly kinship, that we begin to see the importance of local understandings of person and substance. Marriage here is frequently between close relatives, in many cases first cousins, and the tracing of relatedness here indicates very particular notions of substance and gender, notions with certain implications for local conceptions of Christianity.

The Church and the Flesh

Although the tracing of links of kinship may at first seem rather far removed from the concerns of religion, it is significant partly because it is bound up with ideas about personhood, procreation, marriage, and sexual relationships—areas into which the Catholic Church particularly has never feared to tread. The kinship terminology among the Mukkuvar is

Dravidian, as it is across much of south India, and there is a marriage preference for the first cross cousin, that is, the mother's brother's child or the father's sister's child. In fact, a significant proportion of marriages in each generation are with this relative, although most will be with a classificatory cross cousin more distantly related.

Underlying these marriage preferences and the terminology that gives rise to them is an understanding of relatedness that is rather far from European Catholic ideas about consanguinity. There is an emphasis here on gendered substance, and particularly on the different ways in which mothers and fathers are substantially connected to their children, the one through female blood and milk, the other through male blood or semen. These distinctions, as I have argued elsewhere (Busby 1997, 2000), are responsible for the distinctions between parallel cousins, who are like siblings, and cross cousins, who are hardly related and hence are ideal marriage partners. There is in general here a concern with links of substance and with transfers of substance between people, not only through birth but through eating, exchange, and the transfer of sexual fluids through intercourse. The underlying matrix is south Indian, and the concerns echo those which E. V. Daniel (1984), M. Trawick (1990) and Caroline Osella (1993), among others, have described for south Indian Hindus.

Thus in Marianad there is a common conception that husband and wife become one body, one flesh. Though this accords with the church's teachings, we should see it rather as arising out of a specifically south Indian understanding of the nature of exchange and substance. Rather than a spiritual identity created by the act of marriage in the sight of God, it is a specifically substantial identity brought about by the sharing of food and the exchange of sexual fluids. In absorbing parts of each other's substance, husband and wife become part of each other.[4] This is demonstrated and reinforced in the fishing community by the fact that husband and wife eat together from the same plate, and each can in different contexts be represented as responsible for feeding the other and providing for them.[5]

The effects of these ideas of kinship and person in religious belief in the fishing community can be seen particularly in formulations of the relative importance of Mary, God, and Jesus, while in ideas about Mary and her relationship with Kadalamma, the sea goddess, we also see strong underlying notions about femininity and power. I want to explore these two issues before going on to look at notions about substance and transfer of power that again reveal assumptions about people, things, and divinity which are often held in common with local Hindus.

The Holy Family and the Holy Trinity

There is a strong emphasis in European Christianity on the patrilineal principle. As Carol Delaney has argued in her 1991 study of procreation beliefs and religion in Turkey, both Islam and Christianity emphasize the importance of the male seed in initiating the "divine spark" of life and relegate women to the position of vessels, or, in a common metaphor, the field or soil in which the seed grows. Delaney relates this to the emphasis in both religions on a single male God. Although Catholicism finds a more significant place for the worship of a female divine in the person of the Virgin, nevertheless she is not herself God, nor is she equal in the parenting of Christ, being rather just a worthy vessel.

In the Dravidian system, however, maternity is equal with paternity, and women are related to their children substantially, through the blood and milk they pass on to them, just as men are related through semen. In talking of the relative importance of mothers, one man drew on the metaphor of seed but compared the woman not to the passive field, but to the farmer: "If you sow some seeds on the field, is that enough for the plants to grow? Anybody can do that, but it takes the hands of an expert farmer to water it, to give it the right space, look after it, and make it grow. The mother is like the farmer."

This strong position of women in notions of procreation and relatedness is reflected in the importance given in the community to Mary. In general, for the Mukkuvar, the deity whom they worship, whom they see as *their* God, is Jesus Christ, and they will more often refer to Jesus (*Yesu*) or to Christ (*Kartava*) than to God (*Devum*). Mary is likewise extremely important as the mother of Christ, and her role as mother is seen as central. She is understood to have the kind of strong and loving relationship with her son that mothers do, so that what she asks of him he cannot refuse. However, she is not simply an adjunct to either Jesus or God but is also worshipped and prayed to by the Mukkuvar in her own right, as their Mother, Mariamma.[6]

Women in particular call on Mary and feel that, as a mother, she best understands them. It can seem a very personal relationship; as one woman told me, "When I first wake in the morning I think of her, I ask her how she is, how is her Son, to be remembered to him. . . . I depend entirely on them, the Mother and the Son." Rather than seeing Mary as an impossible ideal (see Warner 1976) to which they must somehow live up, women in Marianad seem to depend on her to understand them and their troubles, to identify with *them*, rather than the other way around. She is the one who comforts and understands them, through her own knowledge of what it is to be a mother (see Fenella Cannell's introduction to this volume).

Men, too, recognize Mary as an important figure. For Simon, a fisherman, "When you go to sea, you pray on the beach. You make the sign of the cross on the water and on your forehead and then say Our Father and Hail Mary. The Mother looks after you at sea also. You remember the Father, the Son, and the Mother. You rely on the Mother's power [*ammayude shakti*]." Men, however, also identify with Joseph. As one woman explained, "You pray above all to Jesus, but then to other saints: women will most often pray to Mary, and men to Joseph." Joseph, like Mary, will often be called upon at sea. One man told the story of his uncle, who was lost at sea in a storm and called out for St. Joseph to save him. He was guided back to shore by an old man, who then disappeared, "so he knew that it was Joseph himself who had saved him."

The importance of Joseph is interesting, for it points to another way in which the relationship between God and Mary is altered in the fishing community. The emphasis in Dravidian kinship on bilaterality accords not only with a greater respect for Mary in her own right, but also with a tendency to emphasize Christ's two parents. Where European Christianity commonly focuses either on the Mother and the Son, or on the Father and the Son, in Marianad there is more often talk of the three: Mary, Joseph, and Jesus, or else the Mother, Father, and Son. In fact there is often a slight elision here, so that when talking of the Mother, Father, and Son it is not quite clear whether it is God or Joseph who is intended, and at some level the two become identified as one. Thus in the course of a more general theological discussion one older man explained: "Although with different names, there is only one supreme being. I believe in that one God. The power is one; we understand it in different forms. Joseph, Mary, and Christ, you have them as three but they are all one and the same." The elevation of both Mary and Joseph, and their identification with forms of God, is startling.[7]

The figure of Mary is an interesting one in other ways, however, for as we saw above she is considered to possess shakti, divine power, in her own right, and in many ways can be considered a deity comparable to Hindu goddesses; in ideas of Mary and in her relation to another female deity worshipped by the Mukkuvar, Kadalamma, we see the close interrelationship of Christianity here with more widespread local religious concepts and ideas of gender.

Mary and Kadalamma

When men set out to sea, they pray to Christ and may call on Mary to protect them. But many will also dip their hands in the sea and raise them up in homage to Kadalamma, the Sea Mother / Goddess, calling on her to save them from danger or trouble at sea. Kadalamma is a deity worshipped also by the Hindu fishermen along this coast; she is clearly not seen as a Christian deity or saint, yet her worship is understood by the majority in the Latin fishing community as compatible with their faith.[8] As one fisherman expressed it, "Kadalamma is a form of God. We pray to God and we call on her, the Sea, as a kind of witness to the prayer." For others, Kadalamma was something separate and apart from the Christian deities, but, as their Mother, she also approved of their worship of Christ and ultimately was herself seen as subject to the greater power of God, who created everything.

Like Mary, Kadalamma is a female goddess and thus possesses divine power, shakti. *Shakti* is the Hindu term most commonly used to refer to the power of any deity, but it is particularly the "immanent, manifest and acknowledged energy or power of the divine" (Pocock 1973: 88)—the power to act in the world. As such, shakti is seen as a preeminently feminine power, incarnated in goddesses, in contrast to the transcendent power of male gods; indeed, male gods require their female consorts or counterparts in order to act in the world (Fuller 1992: 44). Goddesses, because they themselves embody shakti, can stand alone, but the consequences of such female power being untamed or uncontrolled by a male consort are often dangerous.

Kadalamma is typical of south Indian village goddesses worshipped as Mother who are nevertheless clearly single and childless. Like such goddesses, she is not cooled and tamed by a spouse; she is both more powerful and more easily angered because the heat of her female sexual energy remains undissipated through marriage. Her power is therefore dangerous, capricious, and ambivalent, containing both life and death. Like the sea, she can both give and withhold; she is both a protective and a nurturing force, and also one swift to anger and with vast destructive potential.

By contrast, Mary, Mariamma, is never seen as a destructive or revengeful force, but rather as always benevolent. Her power is exerted only to the good, and she is seen as a loving and protective mother to her children. Crucial here is the representation of Mary not only as mother but also as wife, and her wifeliness is emphasized, as we have seen, in the unusually strong emphasis on the Holy Family and the figure of St. Joseph. As a wife, she is comparable to the Hindu spouse goddesses, who have been calmed by marriage and whose power is channeled into benevolent fertility and blessing.

The two deities, then, Mary and Kadalamma, represent two alternative visions of feminine power, both commonly found across the region: the one the auspicious, controlled power of married women, the other the potentially dangerous but also creative power of untamed female sexuality. Mary is unquestionably the more important of the two among the Mukkuvar, worshipped by men and women alike, and with jurisdiction over all areas of life, while Kadalamma has a more restricted power, associated with the sea and of particular importance to men. Nevertheless, we see in the juxtaposition of these two figures of worship important themes that underlie local Hindu concepts of femininity and the divine.[9]

Shakti, while associated here with female power, is also commonly used as a term for divine power more generally. Looking more closely at people's understandings of the nature of religious power, and the transfer and manipulation of that power, can give us further insight into the effects in Mukkuvar Catholicism of local ideas about people, substance, and divinity.

Substances and Power

In India, ethnosociological studies have highlighted a tendency toward what could be called substantialism (Vasavi 1994: 287)—that is, the tendency to imbue qualities that Western ethnoscience would consider abstract or nonmaterial with a certain material essence and a concern with the effects of flow or exchange of such qualities between people and things (e.g., Marriott 1976; Marriott and Inden 1977). People in South Asia, in this view, continually engage in transfers of coded substance through marriage, kinship, services, and food transactions. These become part of their person and thus their nature. There are two main implications of this view of the person: first that the person is a relatively fluid and permeable entity, "channeling and transforming heterogeneous, ever-flowing, changing substances" (Marriott and Inden 1977: 233), and, related to this, that the person is substantially connected to others and is not therefore a stable, bounded individual but rather a "dividual," constantly giving out and receiving parts of the self from others.

The idea of the fluid person has been explored in south India by Daniel (1984), who argues that this understanding of the person as open to diverse substantial influences underlies Tamil preoccupation with the maintenance of equilibrium through the search for compatibility. For his Tamil informants, the compatibility of person and place, person and house, and husband and wife are all crucial to well-being because of the strong substantial influences that each can have on the other. Ultimately all are connected, all are one, so that, as with Marriott's understanding, there are no individuals here.

Notions of people as dividual clearly exist alongside other clear notions of individuality and boundedness (McHugh 1989; Mines 1994), and the contrast with the West can be overdrawn. If the Indian person is not an entirely fluid and malleable entity, neither is the Western person always understood as the hard-edged autonomous individual of Western philosophy.[10] Talk of the transfer of substances or of fluidity hovers uneasily on the borderlines between the literal and the metaphoric. Yet there remains a clear sense that the materiality of essences and natures is more emphasized here, that the idiom of material transfer of qualities is widely available. Thus qualities such as love, or sin, are commonly understood in substantial terms, as capable of being passed on in transactions between people.[11] The character of a man who works in the steel mills is seen as likely to be strong and unbending, taking its qualities from the material he works with (Osella 1993: 283). Husbands and wives, who eat food from the same plate, are commonly understood to feel the same emotions (Busby 2000: 171).

Cannell, talking of Christianity in Bicol, notes that the phenomenon of imitation and the use of imitation to reduce or negate hierarchy have a long history in the region. In seeking to understand the nature of Bicolano Catholicism, Cannell argues that it is such "*processes*, rather than a fixed cultural *content*," which are of most relevance (Cannell 1995: 379). The point is important. For the Mukkuvar Catholics of Kerala, historical continuity as well as connections with their Hindu neighbors are indeed to be found most strongly in processes rather than content[12]—in this case, processes that privilege a substantialism or materialization of religious power and a concern with incorporation and transfer of that power.

Religious power in this community is very commonly metaphorized through an idiom of substance, which is seen as capable of being exchanged and passed on, and which is paradigmatically materialized in objects. The term for religious power, as I have noted, is *shakti*, the word also used in Hinduism, and this form of power, as we have seen, is paradigmatically understood as immanent: an active capacity operating in this world to material effect.

This representation or understanding of divine power as shakti, and thus as material, immanent, and at the same time importantly transferable, is at the heart of many religious practices in Marianad. Thus the Catholic Mass has an immediate resonance for the fishing community: the transfer of power or divinity through the exchange with God, the ingestion of his substance. People in Marianad consume the Host as the body of Christ and thus share something of substance with the divine. They have little difficulty with the idea that this wafer is both food and body, that it is both a sign and a reality, because these are concepts that can be found at the heart of their understanding of relations between ordinary people. As one woman told me, "To take the Host [*appam*, bread] is to take part in something divine. It *is* the body of Christ, we believe that."

Baptism also is exceptionally important in Marianad, for it is the point at which the child becomes "the child of God." "Only after this," one woman told me, "are they accepted as Christian. . . . After this they become God's child, then God loves them." The sprinkling of holy water over the baby, and the words said by the priest, remove sin not only from the child but also, by association, from the parents and replace the sin with the substance of God.

Perhaps one of the most striking examples of the understanding of religious power in Marianad is, however, the practice associated with family shrines, particularly the pictures or icons of the Sacred Heart of Jesus—practices also found in substance transfers at more famous pilgrimage shrines.

Renewable Icons and Dripping Crucifixes

The presence of a number of printed, colored images of Mary or the Holy Family or the saints is a ubiquitous feature of the houses in Marianad, even the poorest, and such images are displayed prominently, closely grouped together with the few family photographs. In addition, each house in the village has an image of the Sacred Heart of Jesus, a framed picture that is fixed to the wall. There is usually a small shelf beneath it on which are kept small statues bought from pilgrimage sites, and on which at some point in the day a candle or a lamp will be lit for the image; some people keep a small electric light permanently on above the picture. Often the image will be decorated with flowers or incense will be burned, and the family will pray in front of it or say the rosary. The other pictures in the house will vary from family to family, depending on their preferences, their favorite saints. The Sacred Heart, however, is a must; as one person put it, "It's almost like a rule."

This is the one image in the house that is consecrated by the priest, and though other pictures are seen to have some power, this is the one that is most powerful, has the most shakti. As one woman told me, "The Sacred Heart has power [*shakti*]. It has the most power. It's there because God should dwell in your house." The presence of the image brings the presence of God into the house, it blesses and looks after the inhabitants, and praying before the picture is almost as good as praying in the church.

What makes the materialization of divine power within the image particularly interesting in this case is the perception that after a certain time this power begins to run out, that it needs to be regularly renewed. Ideally every year, but mostly every two or three years, the priest will be called in to perform a renewal ceremony, to reconsecrate the image, and this ceremony is specifically seen as increasing the shakti of the image, which will have begun to diminish. He will lead the family in prayers before the image, calling on God to bless the house with his presence, to be there so that He may hear when they call on Him, and he will sprinkle the image and the people in the house with holy water.

The belief that the power of the Sacred Heart begins to wear out after a certain length of time implies an extraordinarily materialistic understanding of the manifestation of power within the object. It is as though the ceremony fills the image with a certain, finite amount of power, and this is gradually used up by the demands and prayers of the family before it, in the tricky business of warding off evil and danger from the household. In renewing the shakti of the image, there is a transfer of divine power from the central source of the church, in the person of the priest, through his presence in the house, and importantly through the medium of the holy water sprinkled on the picture and absorbed by it, another substantial transfer.

While the image is not itself the object of worship, it is a "repository of divine power" through which the deity can be accessed. One man explained to me the power of the pictures in his home:

> You see, if you meditate on this image, and pray in front of it, then you can see God. If I concentrate on this picture on the wall [of Our Lady of Health] then in my mind I can easily evoke the real form of the Mother. You have the image to see something through it, and the image is not the end; you are not actually worshipping the image, you are worshipping God. God is seen in many forms, but it is all just one supreme being; the power is one, we understand it in different forms.

We have here practices that are strikingly parallel to those of Hindus, particularly in the idea of consecration and installation of shakti in images but also in the concern with sight, with seeing God through the image, which is also central to Hindu worship of deities. The sight of images, *darsan*, is considered to be one very powerful way of receiving power or blessing from a deity, and such sight is considered a material, substantial transfer. For Diane Eck (1980: 9), seeing, in the Hindu tradition, is a kind of touch, "a going forth of the sight towards the object. Sight touches it and acquires its form. Touch is the ultimate connection by which the visible yields to being grasped. While the eye touches the object, the vitality that pulsates in it is communicated."

While the visual sense is certainly important in Marianad, there is also a distinct emphasis here on the transfer of power through touch, through direct or mediated physical contact with an image. On the evening of Good Friday during my fieldwork in Marianad, as part of the Easter festivities, a bier with an image of Christ's body on it was carried around the perimeter of the village and along the beach, where lights and decorations had been erected. The entire village (apart from those in the procession) lined up in single file, kneeling, along the route, so that the bier was carried over their heads. As it passed, each of them reached up to touch the underside, and then touch their hands to their head and face. After the bier had passed, they stood up, and some even hurried to the head of the line to kneel once again and obtain a double blessing.

I witnessed another striking example of the power of such touch at the church in Manapad, a fishing village on the coast of Tamil Nadu, which is a popular pilgrimage site. The church here is dedicated to Christ, and particularly to the image of Christ's sufferings on the cross. The shrine to the left of the altar depicts Christ with the crown of thorns, hanging on the cross. His wooden body is covered with realistically painted wounds and trickles of blood. The large wooden cross that dominates the altar is said to drip permanently with oil, and there is a small passageway behind the altar that runs under the cross, allowing people to witness this for themselves.

What struck me when I went with a group of villagers on a pilgrimage was the importance here of touch and physical contact. Seeing and being present were not, it seemed, enough. As people approached the shrine of Christ, they reached up toward the statue and touched its feet, with great reverence, before touching their hands to their face. The motion was almost one of wiping, as though they were drawing the power out of the image and transferring it to themselves, rubbing it onto themselves. Similarly, as the long queues passed along the passage behind the altar, they reached up to touch both sides of the cross suspended above them and rubbed the oil that had been transferred onto their faces and into their hair. This, I was told, had great shakti, and would protect against illness.

In addition to the shrine at the church, Manapad has fourteen crosses scattered around the village, forming a set of stations of the cross surrounding the church. People told me that if you rub a little oil onto each of these crosses and then scrape it back off into the bottle, the power of the crosses goes into the oil, and it can then be used for healing. Several of my companions did indeed visit each cross to collect a bottle of the sacred oil. Again, not only is power itself made manifest within objects, but the transfer of power also takes a material form.

Strikingly similar ideas about divine power, and the presence of such power in objects, are found in Hinduism. Susan Wadley (1975), discussing the importance of the concept of shakti in a north Indian village, emphasizes the ways in which this notion of power is understood as substantial, present in objects and people. All living things contain some of this divine energy; thus, as we have noted, women particularly are said to embody shakti, one reason they must be carefully controlled through marriage. In this sense, there is less an absolute disjunction between humanity and the gods than a difference of degree, of scale. At the same time, the substantial nature of shakti leads to a concern with its transfer, with interactions between worshipper and deity in which some part of the deity's power is obtained. Deities in India, Wadley argues, are mainly embodied in images or objects because "interaction with deities requires the exchange of substance, and substance cannot be exchanged with unembodied powerful beings" (146).

Ambiguities surround the matter of whether such an image or object embodies or merely represents the deity. At one level, the image is there merely as a "channel through which the deity can communicate with the worshipper and through which the worshipper can visualize the deity" (Brockington 1992: 29), but at the same time, most Hindus would perceive the image as "an actual embodiment of the sacred" (29), and thus as a "repository of divine power" (Fuller 1992: 60). For Fuller:

> The relationship between a deity and its image is commonly explained in terms of the power, *shakti*, possessed by all deities. . . . According to this explanation, the image actually contains some or all of the deity's power, so that the purpose of the consecration is to install that power in a particular location, the image. There is no limit to the number of separate images within which the deity's power can be installed and the deity is never shackled by locating its power in images. Hence an image itself cannot be equated with the corresponding deity; the object of worship is not the image, but the deity whose power is inside it. Devotees who gaze upon an image . . . are touched by the power flowing out of the image.

According to Fuller, the images within a temple, which are normally sculptures, "are not normally considered to be sacred objects until they have been consecrated by installing divine power within them" (58). In the home, a picture of a deity may often substitute for a sculpture, and Fuller notes that "in millions of poorer homes, the household shrine contains only pictures of the family's favorite deities, which are consecrated and worshipped just like [sculpted] images" (59).

The exchange of substance or power with such embodied deities takes place in a number of ways, but one of the most common is through the distribution of *prasad*, and a clear parallel may be made here with the Catholic communion. In the Hindu ritual, water or ash may be given to worshippers to put on their body, or food that has been offered to the god may be given to be eaten; in either case the prasad, which is imbued with the divinity and power of the god, with shakti, is transferred to and absorbed by the worshipper. This process helps to effect "identity between deity and worshipper" for at least a short time (Fuller 1992: 75).

While I have concentrated here on the manifestation of power in objects, there are contexts where it is not objects that are powerful but words; yet here, too, the substantialization of that power seems inescapable.

Confessions of a *Mantravadi*

An older man in Marianad, one who had a particularly theological bent and with whom I often discussed religion, was also a healer, a *mantravadi* (often translated by locals as a "magician," but meaning only one who uses mantras, ritual chants). He gave me some examples of mantras that he knew, for healing or for warding off ghosts and evil spirits. The Christian symbolism is strong, but so also are more classically Hindu references,[13] while the form itself is identical to Hindu mantras. Yet for Paulos the use of these mantras, and their efficacy, is bound up with his faith as a Christian. He saved his daughter from dying of a hemorrhage during her first labor, "chanting over her and holding her ankle" until the nurse came. If not for this, he believes, she would not have been saved—"and this was confirmed when a fortune teller came to the house later and said that if it were not for my great belief in Christ my daughter would have died."

For all that these are words of power, rather than objects, however, they make themselves manifest in the world in the materiality of the body and its flow or otherwise of blood. For some mantras, the efficacy is in fact bound up with the transfer of words to substance. Thus in the case of one mantra to promote a healthy birth, the mantra is written on a piece of paper. "Then you hold the paper over your mouth, close to your mouth, cupped in your hands, and chant into it alternately the mantra and the Hail Mary—seven times, like the seven arrows in Mary's heart." The paper is then rolled up very tight and tied with three threads, once in the middle and once at the two ends. It is worn by the pregnant woman on a chain around her neck until the delivery is over, and Paulos assured me of its efficacy to prevent a cesarean: "It is a mighty one, I used it once and it worked."[14]

The notion that words have a power to transform material reality, and thus the implicit materiality of the words themselves, is found to some extent also in understandings of confession and the baptism ceremony. In the latter, although the holy water sprinkled on the child is one medium through which God's power is incorporated into the child, the words said by the priest are also important, especially for the parents. They make the responses to the priest, they agree to bring the child to God, and, as Paulos told me, "When you say those words, it removes your sin, it removes the sin of the parents as well as the child." Similarly, in confession, which is communal and takes place during the course of the Mass, before communion, the release of sin and the release of the words of confession are one and the same. As Paulos explained: "If you can feel the remorse, if you can really cry it out, then the sin goes out of you and you are cleansed."[15] The breath that contains the words, of mantra or of confession, contains also the essence of power or the essence of sin and carries it away from the person that speaks it.

People and Powers: Christianity in South India

There are significant ways, then, in which many of the meanings and practices of Catholicism in Marianad take their force from implicit understandings of the nature of people, substance, and divine power, and these are clearly understandings that are held in common with south Indian Hindus. David Mosse (1994a, 1994b) has characterized a similar situation among Christians in rural Tamil Nadu as one in which Christianity is a matter of content rather than form.

In his analysis of Christianity as it developed in the district of Ramnad, where the Jesuits of the Madurai mission were active in the seventeenth and eighteenth centuries, Mosse shows how a deliberate accommodation with Hindu cultural practices was seen as the surest way to ensure conversion from Hindu religion. Thus the priests tolerated caste divisions, and practices such as the giving of honors at festivals, because the more important issue to them was to whom worship was offered—that it was to God rather than to a Hindu deity. As Mosse puts it, "What mattered was not the *form* but the *object* of worship" (1994b: 91, emphasis added). However, ironically, as Mosse notes, "what the Jesuit missionaries failed to appreciate was the extent to which for actors themselves meaning lay not in the religio-cultural content (saint rather than deity, church rather than temple) but in the ritual form." This is not only a matter of caste practices and the marking of hierarchy through ritual. Underlying this system was "a conception of divine power (of saints and deities) as localized, material, and not clearly distinguished from the secular power of the king" (90). Not only can Hindu and Christian be seen to share notions of divine power, but there are also shared conceptions of the dead and ways in which the cults of saints in the region are "conceived and ordered by principles held in common with village Hinduism" (91).

One distinct difference between Mukkuvar Christians and those in rural Ramnad studied by Mosse is the absence among the Mukkuvar of any substantial caste hierarchy: they are a single-caste community, and one that moreover is not tied into the web of intercaste exchange and dependency relations that characterize agricultural villages. Thus the clearest arena in which Catholicism in Ramnad draws on Hindu ritual forms and beliefs, caste-related practices, is absent. Absent too in Marianad is any significant concern with purity or pollution: thus menstruating women are not barred from cooking, for example. However, there are many ways in which Catholicism in Marianad fits Mosse's model of content rather than form. The absence of caste-related pollution practices reveals, as we have seen, a number of underlying notions about people, substances, and power that are clearly part of a local south Indian cultural matrix.

It is particularly striking that people's own descriptions of their religion seem to imply that they see it as just one among a number of possible variants, rather than as the one true faith. For most people, they are Christians because Christ is *their* God. Rather than seeing Christianity as a religion that negates all others, that makes other beliefs simply wrong, paganism or worse, Mukkuvar Catholics present it more as a question of a choice, that they have chosen to worship Christ and the Christian saints out of all the possibilities and that this distinguishes them from people who have, rather, chosen to worship the Hindu deities. Their attitude to Hindu deities for the most part resembles that of the upper-caste man to a low-caste village goddess, described by Pocock: "I said, 'Don't you believe in the *mata*?' He looked at me as though I were mad and said, 'Of course I do, I just don't worship her, that's all' " (1973, 65).

Christianity here, then, is not "right," where other religions or gods are "wrong" or misguided. Rather it is one choice of deity among many; it is localized, bound tightly to a notion of identity. Christianity is the religion exclusively of the fishing community, and the Christian God is *their* God.[16] This view of Christianity and Christ allows space in the fishing community's cosmology for other, non-Christian deities, and particularly, as we have seen, for the worship of the sea goddess Kadalamma.

Catholicism in Marianad is not only essentially polytheistic but also pluralist. It clearly shares a number of important themes, understandings, and practices with local Hinduism. In this sense, it is a specific, localized form of Christianity that could be considered, as Susan Bayly (1989) has argued for both Christianity and Islam in south India, an Indian religious system. However, it would be a mistake to draw the contrast too strongly between Christianity in India and in Europe. In Europe, too, Christianity is in many respects a localized religion, drawing on specific sets of ideas about the nature of people and powers, on particular histories and articulations of identity (see Christian 1981). Moreover, Catholicism in Marianad and Catholicism in rural Spain (see Christian 1989), for example, are recognizably engaging with essentially the same set of religious concerns, ideologies, and structures, and there are of course as a result strong resonances and similarities in people's beliefs and practices. Thus, for example, the Sacred Heart, which takes so central a place in Marianad, is a specific devotion of the Catholic Church that was widely promulgated and disseminated in the early part of the twentieth century. The idea of enthroning the Sacred Heart as an image in households and places of work was taken up and promoted around this time in the context of a more general move away from Marian worship and toward making Christ a more central figure in the church (Christian 1992: 114–15). The image of the Sacred Heart was presumably similarly promoted among Indian Catholics at around this time. Its centrality among the Mukkuvar, then, is owed in part to a development within the wider Catholic Church, one that had its origins in particular historical and political circumstances outside India.

But the reasons for the continuing importance of this image must be sought also in the local circumstances of its incorporation and in the specific meanings with which the image is imbued. As an image consecrated within the household, in a context where Hindu consecration of images implies the installation of very specific sorts of localized power, the Sacred Heart emerges as an important source/site of religious blessing and power for people in the fishing community. It is also, as Christian has noted (1989: 85), one of the few Catholic images of Christ that emphasize the mature, whole man, rather than the suffering victim of the crucifixion or the Christ child. For the fishing community, the central Christian deity is Christ himself rather than God the Father. It is perhaps not surprising then that this image of the adult Christ, a Christ who moreover promises them blessings and power rather than his own self-sacrifice, occupies a central part in their worship.

Christianity in Marianad, then, is recognizably Christianity and specifically Catholicism, but, as with Christianity in other contexts, it is imbued with themes, beliefs and practices that are essentially local, in this case often shared with local Hindus. While we could, with Mosse, see this as primarily a matter of Catholic accommodation to Hindu idioms, we could also see both Hinduism and Catholicism in the region as local religions, both with a long history, and both understood through local cultural idioms and practices, particularly relating to notions of people, substance, and power. However, it should not be forgotten that though it is possible to see the continuities between Mukkuvar Catholicism and local Hinduism, for the Mukkuvar, their religion is importantly part of an oppositional discourse of identity and of separation from the Hindu majority. As people say in the village, "Jesus Christ is *our* God," and, for their part it is clear that they are therefore, quite firmly, Christians.

Notes

This chapter is based on fieldwork carried out between October 1991 and January 1993 in Marianad, Kerala. The fieldwork was supported by a postgraduate award from the Economic and Social Research Council and supervised by Chris Fuller and Henrietta Moore. An earlier version of this chapter was given at a seminar series on Christianity at School of Oriental and African Studies (May 1994). I am grateful to the participants, and also to all those who participated in the workshop *Words and Things* at Manchester in June 1996 and at the London School of Economics in September 1998. Particular thanks go to Fenella Cannell and Philip Thomas for their careful reading of the text and helpful suggestions for revision.

1 For example, see Fuller 1976; Bayly 1989; Mosse in this volume and 1994b; and Visvanathan 1993.
2 This point has also been made by Kalpana Ram (1991, chap. 1), writing of the Mukkuvar community in Kanyakumari, just south of Trivandrum District.
3 Further details of gender, kinship, economy, and household organization can be found in Busby 2000.
4 It should be noted that the idea that husbands and wives come to share substance is widespread across India. In Hinduism, however, the more common formulation of this idea is that the wife becomes a "half-body" of her husband, and he remains, by default, one body that incorporates hers. This formulation is more in accordance with the hierarchical nature of the husband-wife relationship in Hinduism, particularly in north India.
5 This is extremely unusual in the context of India, where wives generally eat after their husbands, symbolically enacting their inferiority. It marks a much greater equality between husband and wife in the fishing community, which

I would relate less to their Christianity (Christianity is in the main as patriarchal as Hinduism, if not more so) than to the particular economic division of labor, which gives women a much greater freedom and autonomy than in most agricultural communities and makes male-female exchange and cooperation central to the household economy (see Busby 2000).

6 A small booklet explaining the history of the shrine to Our Lady at Vailankanni also articulates this sense in which Mary is the mother of all and emphasizes her crucial importance as the mother of Jesus: under a particularly sentimental picture of Mary holding a small baby, the inscription reads "Without Mary, no Jesus, and without Jesus, no Mary."

7 The idea that different deities are at one level simply manifestations or forms of the same God is also strikingly similar to the Hindu conception of deities; in this sense there is a blurring between the apparent monotheism of Christianity and the apparent polytheism of Hinduism, and certainly understandings of Catholicism in Marianad come close to the Hindu model at times.

8 In contrast, the church clearly has no truck with Kadalamma, considering her non-Christian, and the more pious among the people I spoke to in Marianad about these things were also defensive about her existence or worship, arguing, for example, "When you pray to the Lord, why do you need to pray to the sea? It's enough, you pray to him." Most, however, see no real incompatibility between the two.

9 Ram (1991: 61–73) describes a situation further down the coast, in Kanyakumari, where the figure of Kadalamma seems to have been totally eclipsed by Mary, who is seen as wholly benevolent, serene, and placid, while the dangerous destructive forces of female sexuality are projected onto a local Hindu goddess, Eseki. Ram sees these two as split versions of the Hindu mother goddess, the one completely good, and associated by the local Mukkuvar with Christianity, the other completely evil and associated with Hinduism. The antagonistic (antisyncretic) form of the relationship here may be related to a recent history of violence and conflict between local Catholics and Hindus.

10 See, for example, Gilligan 1982 for an articulation of an alternative, relational view.

11 See, for example, Parry 1980, 1986, 1994; Raheja 1998; and Osella and Osella 1996.

12 Mosse (1994), making a similar point, has categorized these as form and content.

13 For example, one describes Christ as having "six qualities," a characteristic of Vishnu; there is mention of the "eight corners," which are important points of reference in Hindu architecture / cosmological space; there are said in another mantra to be thirty-three crore angels, the exact number usually quoted of Hindu deities. But at the same time, there is constant reference to Christ and to Christian imagery, especially the power of the cross.

14 Ram (1991: 56), discussing similar healing mantras, also notes the impor-

tance of the contact with the body: the talisman "derives its full efficacy not merely from the prayer [written on it] but from actually being worn on the body."

15 The confession here is not specific but general, uttered by all, although those who feel they have something specific weighing on their conscience will presumably give a particular significance to the words they utter.

16 As I have said, there are a number of other Christian groups in Kerala, but because they are none of them Latin Catholic, it is possible for people to elide the difference between faith and denomination and to see these groups also as "not *our* Christian."

···Three···

Possession and Confession

Affliction and Sacred Power in Colonial and Contemporary Catholic South India

David Mosse

This chapter concerns the interpretation and management of misfortune in Roman Catholic communities in a region of Tamil South India, and the notions of person and agency these entail. In particular it examines practices of spirit possession and exorcism that have persisted (in various forms) alongside the sacraments of confession and communion established by Jesuit missionaries from the early seventeenth century. I will suggest that the central confession-communion discourse of the church and the peripheral possession-exorcism discourse of certain saint cults present contrasting—indeed, opposed—discourses of misfortune and different conceptions of person and agency. While church teaching in the region has long laid emphasis on the autonomous, responsible moral Christian person whose eternal future is shaped by the internal struggle with sin (see Mauss [1938] 1985), cults of exorcism at the shrines of Catholic saints give expression to South Indian cultural conceptions of the person-body as fluid, having permeable boundaries, invaded (and produced) by social, spiritual, and environmental forces that come to be objectified within the body (Osella and Osella 1996, 1999; Daniel 1984). In contrasting "possession" and "confession" in this way a number of questions are raised: can the existence of vibrant spirit-exorcism cults be viewed as commentary on the success or otherwise with which Christian missionaries communicated a new notion of interiority cross-culturally (see the introduction to this volume); are peripheral "possession" cults a response to external assertions of power and the imposition of a certain kind of religious discipline and ritualism; and, if so, do possession-exorcism cults imply resistance to official interpretations of suffering and a priestly monopoly of the sacred, or are they rather an indication of the inability of an otherworldly pious missionary religion to satisfy the range of religious needs of the laity? (See Hofer 1974 for similar questions asked of possession in South Asian religion, and see Leach [1972] 1983.) These are historical questions requiring more work. For the moment I can only suggest some patterns and coincidences, tensions and contradictions that emerge from archival and fieldwork in southern Tamil Nadu.[1]

Possession and Confession

Let me begin with an account taken verbatim from August 1896 diary entries of the Jesuit missionary and parish priest in the village of Alapuram,[2] Father Gnanaprakasam.[3]

> SUNDAY 16 AUGUST: Before mass I hear that Jeronym's wife, who had come to confession yesterday was struck with a sort of frenzy. She began to see certain beings in the eastern nook of her room. They appeared with sword, sickle and lances and threatened to stab her. The whole night she was crying, "there they come, to stab me, to cut my throat." The holy water was thrown and St Benedict's medal attached to her neck. But she tore away the crucifix, the medal, her own jewels, her clothes. Her eyes were looking to the eastern nook. The strangers called her away and she wanted to follow them. Except once or twice she refused to pronounce the Holy name of Jesus. She even uttered blasphemies and impure words when they suggested the holy names.
>
> The girl was married some three months ago. [I am told that] a certain man at Odaykal disputed [desired] the girl, and when he couldn't succeed he threatened vengeance. He told the girl that one day she would tear her own clothes. This man has a sorcerer for his friend at Odaykal. The sorcerer is ever engaged in doing mischief.
>
> At 4.30 I went to the house. When she cried out I asked who is it? "I don't know" was her uniform reply. I suggested the holy name. She said the apparition does not let her pronounce those words. When I told her to think of Jesus, Mary and Joseph, she kept quiet. Apparently she did think of them in her heart. Her constant groan was, "There he comes, to cut my throat. He breaks me, twists me." She pointed to the eastern nook. I caused a picture of the crucified saviour to be brought in and hung in the eastern nook. She

prayed all to put it out of sight. She consented to wear the crucifix and the medal of St Benedict.

MONDAY 17 AUGUST: I bless the girl with "In Principio exit" then with "Sanctu Michael" and some other prayers of the church. She said that 4 persons were coming to torture her. "Who is it?," asked I. She refused to say. What village? "He is my village" was her reply. She refused to give his name. At 4.30 P.M. again I went to bless her. I noted that the apparition now actually tormented her by seeming to bruise her. When I was hearing confession a man came to tell me that the apparition tears her breasts with a hook and she was opening her mouth and breathing hard. I told them to apply the medal of St Benedict to the stomach and invoke the saint. They did so and placed before her a statue of St. Michael. She grew calm and slept.

TUESDAY 18 AUGUST: After mass I was surprised to see her coming to church led by several persons. She said she had her own prayers which she would recite. So she did and recited [in] an act of contrition. Then I made her come to confession. She refused first, but at last consented and made her confession very sincerely. Then she swept the exterior part of the church and talked to bystanders. Even then she said in a low voice "Look there he comes." Then again at home she became victim of the apparitions, being bruised, stabbed and cut. I entered when she was writhing and crying aloud unable to bear her pain. Two persons were obliged to hold her. I blessed her and threw holy water and caused the sign of the cross to be made on her forehead every time the pain was excessive. I repeated the holy name and threw holy water. Finding however, that nothing brought her relief, I caused all the bystanders to say aloud the Our Father and Hail Mary to St. Benedict. She got calm at once. Seeing this I caused another five decades to be recited. She wanted to sleep. I went again to bless her at 5.30 P.M. I was surprised to find her kneeling and looking like one in perfect health. She kept swaying when I blessed her, then I recited 5 decades along with the bystanders. She also kept an attitude of prayer and turned her face to the statue of St Michael. She came for evening prayers.

WEDNESDAY 19TH AUGUST: As I said that she could communicate today, she came to confession before mass and received communion with others and returned home quietly. Later she walked out and stayed under a vembu [neem] tree. She was brought straight to church. Then I blessed her and caused 5 decades to be recited at church. She went home where she insulted her husband because he had beaten her a few days ago.

THURSDAY 20TH AUGUST: This morning she confessed [in] a most sensible manner. She received communion. Between 7 and 9.30 some symptoms of folly—two or three times she said "look he comes" but the phantom produced no other effects. I called her to church, blessed her and she was calm. I asked her who appeared and troubled her. Her mother was present. The girl said 4 persons of whom three were *catai* ["matted hair," here referring to *munis*, inferior Hindu deities] the fourth was the man that ill-treated her the most. The mother asked if it was Santiago Pillai. She said no. Who then? She was apparently ashamed to give his name. "Was it his son?" She nodded assent. The mother said, "but the son Arogyam is an innocent boy." *Avan̠tan̠ eviṭṭarkal* ["him only, they incited (him)"] was her reply. This man had no *catai*. Then I caused 5 decades to be recited and sent her home. The previous night she had a dream. St Mickel [Michael] appeared to her and said that she should already have met her death if he had not prevented it. But still she would die next Sunday [the feast of the Pure Heart of Mary]. I told her she should leave it into God's hands, but that she should not fully believe a dream of this kind.

These events raise some themes of general interest to an anthropology of Christianity—for example, the power of sacred words and things and the antipathy of the Christian sacred to spirit agents. But my present concern is primarily with a tension this episode marks between two approaches to suffering and affliction and two conceptions of personhood and agency. On the one hand this is an instance of spirit possession remarkably similar, in its broad context (that is, relating to desire and involving a young recently married woman), to accounts recently given for South India and Sri Lanka (Nabokov 1997; Ram 1991; Spencer 1997; Stirrat 1977, 1992; Caplan 1985). As I will explore later, this kind of possession episode displaces the person as autonomous moral agent and "exteriorizes" affliction onto spirit agents. But, on the other hand, this is also an account of the way in which a missionary priest subordinates this popular interpretation of affliction and demonic agency to the church's emphasis on confession and communion, showing how affliction is resolved through a reaffirmation (through confession) of the woman as a Christian person—a stable responsible moral agent—and a displacement of the reality of external demonic agents. Personal affliction comes ultimately to be inseparable from personal sin in an interiorization of guilt (D. Taylor 1985). In the transition from possession to confession, Christian sacred objects and words are applied to the woman as an afflicted individual; they serve as an analgesic to quiet, to alleviate pain, and to bring sleep. But they are not the means to battle with spirits; rather, they prepare the way for sincere and contrite confession and communion, which are the ritual means by which the woman takes possession of herself and returns to ordinary social behavior (in, for example, the domestic act of sweeping the floor). Indeed, the episode ends as the "symptoms of folly" subside, the demon becomes an "innocent boy," and the woman is ashamed.

The tension between the central confession-communion discourse and the peripheral discourse of exorcism has a broader historical context, which I want to explore. Father Gnanaprakasam's diary entries can be seen as a commentary on the position of the Catholic church in the late nineteenth century in the Tamil countryside, exhibiting its uncertain relation to indigenous conceptions of evil, its efforts to discipline local ritual practices, and its struggle to provide authoritative Christian interpretations of subjective experience within a predominantly Hindu cultural setting. These concerns of late-nineteenth-century Jesuit priests are contained within a longer mission history—beginning in the early seventeenth century and extending to the present—which has grappled with the tension between Christian religion, understood as universal, and its Indian culture form. While my story starts by considering the point of view of the missionary embattled with unruly parishioners and unruly manifestations of divine power, it will later shift to consider the manner in which Tamil villagers themselves seek to resolve the tension between the universal and absolutist claims of Christianity and their own experience as inheritors of particular cultural practices. My focus throughout will be the exploration of questions of personhood and agency in religious conceptions of misfortune. But let me begin with a description of further events in nineteenth-century rural Ramnad that appear to present the possession-confession tension writ large.

Unruly Saints: Independent Saint Cults in the Nineteenth Century

In July 1873, twenty-three years before Father Gnanaprakasam's diary entry, his forbear in Alapuram parish, the French Jesuit Father Favreux, was dismayed that people were abandoning the important festival of St. James (Cantiyakappa) in the parish and were "taking themselves in immense majority" to a shrine at Oriyur, the place of execution of the Portuguese Jesuit missionary John de Britto, martyred in 1693. What troubled Father Favreux was that his parishioners were flocking not to an authorized pilgrimage with the sacred rites of the church but to an unauthorized exorcism cult of St. John de Britto (known as Arulanandar but not canonized until 1947), and in particular to the power of the martyr invoked by an Utaiyar caste exorcist named Mandalacotei Odean, who

> installed in a chair in front of the *kallarai* [martyr's tomb] without troubling himself to hear Mass receives numberless so-called possessed . . . the majority of low caste, hair disarranged, breasts uncovered, on their knees submitting to an interrogation on the name, the number and quality of the demons, to the blows of a whip. Having cut a bunch of hair [they were sent] to the tank to bathe and other indecencies practiced by this man and in view of all the world and the [Goan schismatic][4] priest approving, and this not only at the festival but again all Wednesdays. Possesseds come more in number than ever. A practice until this day unheard of in the church and at festivals even under the Goanese and which carries away by misfortune many of our Christians. Is there not need to refer to the Bishop? (Favreux, diary entry, September 8, 1872, my translation from the French)

By the 1870s the shrine of Arulanandar was a well established regional pilgrimage center attracting thousands of pilgrims "Christian and pagan" to receive the blessing (*āsīrvātam*) and grace (*aruḷ*) of the saint, especially on Wednesdays (the day of the martyrdom).[5] But above all Oriyur was a center for exorcism and the chasing of demons. The possessed would shake and "dance" as they approached the shrine or touched the festival flagpole (*koṭimaram*), to which childless women tied pieces of cloth containing coins.[6] Several late-nineteenth-century accounts confirm the exorcists' procedures. The demons possessing the women confronted the power of the saint at the site of his death, a power that was concentrated materially in dust from the tomb sprinkled on their heads. In their discomfort the possessing spirits would shake and scream, but they were disciplined and forced to reveal their identity through the violent blows of the exorcist's whip, such that "the true miracle," another French priest, Darrieutort, noted in 1876, "is to see this head transformed into an anvil, not split itself." "The day when I sent a person of confidence to make known of that which happened at Oriyur," he continues, "more than 60 heads turned to the queue one after the other, waiting stupidly." At last knots were made in the women's hair, one for each spirit, and in the tank these were cut so that they sank into the water.

Oriyur was in fact only the most striking of a number of independent saint cults documented in late-nineteenth-century Ramnad. Many were local and short-lived, attracting large crowds for a brief period, then disappearing. Broadly speaking, these cults divide into two categories. First there were shrines that focused on the "good dead" as a source of benevolent power—the tombs of marginal women and especially of young girls who died before puberty (*kaṉṉi*) in a state of absolute sexual purity and who were more or less identified with the Virgin Mary. In 1873, for example, Father Favreux writes of a tomb of a low-caste Cakkilyar woman on the Salaigramam road at which miraculous powers attracted large crowds. In April 1874 a new pilgrimage "started to be made to Caroumbcoutam at the tomb of I know not which mad woman, said to be baptized at death," and in the same year two more tomb-shrines were described, one at the tomb of "a mendicant of very low caste, passing as the Virgin and half man," and the other an "ill-famed woman dead without ever having received the sacraments."[7] However, it is not these but a second category of shrines that concerns me here. These focused on the male saints and their charismatic intermediaries and, like Arulanandaiyar (St. John de Britto) at Oriyur, gave special focus to possession and exorcism.

The French Jesuit Father Fasenille described one such cult in 1877. I summarize: a Catholic Pallar (untouchable caste) man brought a miraculous crucifix from Colombo, which had been found in the forest of Vannatu Cinnapar (St. Paul the First Hermit). Miracles began to occur, and crowds came to where the crucifix had been placed—on the altar of a "pagoda" to St. Xavier, built by the man's father. Not wishing to share the same building with St. Xavier, the crucifix appeared to the man's father in a dream and demanded to be moved outside. A huge cross was therefore constructed and the crucifix nailed to it. Here it received offerings of ghee, oil, and so forth and was "all running with butter, oil like the Poulliers [Ganesh statues]." "The Pallen has above all an unbelievable power for chasing the devil," Fasenille explains. "For this he obliged those possessed to stay for a long time in front of the crucifix. All at once, the poor devil uttered some great cries. He complained that he was being consumed by flames inside and out, and implored that he be left to leave." The Pallen [Pallar] exorcist then ordered the demon to the end of a tuft of hair on the head and cutting this the demon departed.[8]

This and other independent cults of exorcism focusing on powerful male saints continued and thrived as Jesuit missionaries sought to consolidate their ecclesiastical domains in the late nineteenth century.[9]

Jesuit Missionaries and the Catholic Religious Domain in Maravarnadu

Catholic communities in the southern Tamil district of Ramnad (also known as Maravarnadu, the country of the Maravar caste) were mostly converted during the seventeenth and eighteenth centuries by missionaries of the Jesuit Madurai mission founded by the Italian Roberto de Nobili. In his pioneering project of "accommodation," de Nobili sought to embrace Indian cultural traditions and to distance himself and his mission in the Tamil cultural heartland of Madurai from the Portuguese trading powers of the Coromandal coast, whose missionaries, by merging Christian faith and European culture, had associated Christianity with impurity, inferiority, and the status of *parangis* (aliens or Westerners). De Nobili urged that the Gospel should take Indian civil (social and cultural) form and that converts need not abandon cultural identities or rules of caste, since these were social rather than religious institutions (Cronin 1959; Neill 1984; Chandler 1909). Departing from established Jesuit understandings, de Nobili presented Hinduism as a natural and social order to which Christianity would graft and provide the light of true religion (Zupanov 1996: 1203). In other words, de Nobili replaced a theological articulation with a sociological articulation. His was an ethnographic perception: where superstition and paganism had hitherto been seen, he discovered Hinduism as a universe of social practice, and caste as a matter of social honor and rank (1205).

While de Nobili, as an "upper caste teacher-renouncer" (or *sannyāsin*), engaged with Brahman enquirers and their literate philosophical traditions, a second class (or caste) of missionaries—*pandaraswamis*—worked among non-Brahmans, including the ruling Maravar warrior caste of the marginal plains area of Ramnad. The Portuguese Jesuit John de Britto was foremost among them. Here Christian teaching, sectarian identity, and churches were actively incorporated into a seventeenth-century political system in which religious shrines and their patronage by warrior chiefs provided the means to secure and extend political constituencies. In these warrior polities, Jesuit *pandaraswamis* received protection from local rulers in return for the granting at Christian festivals of ritual public honors, which symbolized chiefly political power (see Mosse 1986, 1997;

Bayly 1989; Stein 1980; Appadurai and Breckenridge 1976). Equally, caught up in the tensions of a fissiparous political system, missionaries could find themselves viewed as instigators of political intrigue or cession and consequently victims of antipatronage. This indeed was what led to the execution of John de Britto in February 1693 on the orders of the head of Ramnad's ruling Maravar caste—the Cetupati, or the king of Ramnad.[10]

The religious domains of the pioneer Jesuits in precolonial Ramnad were diffuse and unbounded. Judging from the seventeenth and early-eighteenth-century letters, they provided a distinctively spiritual leadership as renouncer-teachers, administering the sacraments, presiding over ceremonies, and recruiting through conversion as well as providing a Christian ritual means for the articulation of local systems of caste rank (Mosse 1994a, 1997; Correia-Afonso 1997). While Hindu idolatry was condemned, cults growing around Catholic saints were encouraged. Indeed, Jesuits consolidated mission centers around syncretic saint cults that had filtered inland, following networks of trade and pilgrimage from the established Catholic communities of the Coromandal coast (for example, Mosse 1997; and see Bayly 1989: 379–84). The thaumaturgical power of early missionary saint heroes was celebrated as a sign (to the unconverted) of the power of Christian faith and divinity. Prominent here was the site where John de Britto had been executed and impaled on a wooden stake (a two-foot fragment of which is still preserved) at which a shrine was built in 1770. In the 1730s (when the sacred place received patronage from a Ramnad king), Jesuit missionaries write enthusiastically about the shrine, to which "every Wednesday Christians and Gentiles come in ever increasing numbers. . . . the unbroken series of prodigies increases from day to day the devotion of the faithful."[11] The Jesuit letters note the fame of the shrine increasing with reports of many miraculous occurrences—healing the blind and paralyzed and making the barren fertile through ingestion of the red sand[12]—correcting many strange abnormalities, among them a baby boy born with the face of a monkey and a goat born with a huge udder that issued both milk and blood.

De Nobili's accommodation method permitted a molding of Christian shrines and ritual practices to a Hindu cultural form. Indeed, political circumstances made this a necessity, since missionaries had limited authoritarian control over their congregations and churches. The latter often remained under the control of Maravar caste regional chiefs, or local headmen. Accommodation was premised on a sharp dichotomy between the spiritual and the temporal. In effect, the early Jesuits presented Christianity as, in Dumont's terms, a "religion of choice," a "Christian path" (*kiristu mārkkam*) superimposed upon the obligations of caste. But while de Nobili preached an abstract soteriology in Madurai, the missionary movement in Ramnad built on popular acknowledgment of the miraculous power of Christian divinity. In practice this most likely merged with a pragmatically oriented religion involving not only the saints and the "good dead," but also village deities and malevolent demons and ghosts. While maintaining a distinct salvation-oriented religious practice focusing on the priest and sacraments, Christians were integrated into social systems of caste and participated in a shared popular religious culture with their Hindu neighbors (Mosse 1994a, 1997). In other words, the religion of confession and the sacraments also left room for mediation of a more pragmatic kind through diviners, astrologers, exorcists, and the like—by means of which new Christians could continue to manage misfortune understood in indigenous terms (including possession). Being Christian did not necessarily preclude the need to interact with non-Christian divinity, especially to avert or manage misfortune. One new convert made the point to the Jesuit Darrieutort in 1876. Convinced of the truth of Christian teaching, she had decided to convert. She continued: "Here I am ready Swami; I have arranged everything to be baptized this morning. You see, all my life I have been a strong devotee of Subramanium [Murugan]. In order not to irritate him too much by my desertion, I have these past days bought a quantity of fine cocks. While you baptize me they will be immolated. I hope that he will be content" (Darrieutort 1876: 5–6).

The Jesuit Madurai mission's experiment in accommodation to Hindu society was from the start a marked departure from the post–Council of Trent standardization of Catholic missionary practice and the centralization of authority in Rome (Fernandes 1991). The mission generated a complex controversy surrounding, in particular, caste practices known as the "Malabar Rites." Disagreements with Rome eventually led to the suppression of the Society of Jesus by papal bull in 1773, and the Jesuits were expelled from India (Neill 1984). After the suppression of the Society of Jesus, the missions were handed over to the Paris Foreign Missionaries or fell under the ecclesiastical jurisdiction of the See of Goa, and it was Portuguese and Syro-Malabar priests from Cochin, Mylapore, or Goa—all referred to as "Goanese" (being under the Padraodo, or patronage of the king of Portugal), who administered the churches of Maravarnadu. However, missionary resources were scarce (and made scarcer by the French Revolution) and scattered, and pastoral care was irregular in remote rural parishes (*Jesuit in India* 1852).

The Society of Jesus was reconstituted by Pope Pius VII, and French Jesuits returned to Maḍurai (created as a separate vicarate) in 1838. When they returned, they did so in a spirit of *restoration* rather than experimentation, in an effort to put everything "back to the point it was before the disasters of the late-eighteenth century fell on the church" (Neill 1984: 306). Influenced by a post-Napoleonic feudal-monarchical reaction to the Revolution, missionary societies were conservative, evangelical, and under a supervision and control from Europe that was "detailed and harassing" (Neill 1984: 306; Fernandes 1991). Parish administration, liturgy, and worship were to be carried out in Roman fashion.

But in fact the French Jesuits did not restore bounded Roman Catholic domains in nineteenth-century rural Ramnad, they created them.[13] They were able to do so not least because of the changed political context of British colonial rule, which allowed missionaries a new profile and "a distinctly European conception of religion as a domain separate from politics over which bureaucratic control could be imposed" (Mosse 1994a: 93). The infiltration of indigenous religion that had occurred under older missionary accommodations seemed increasingly out of place. Indeed, the missionary priests of the colonial nineteenth century set themselves the primary task of defining and defending religious and ecclesiastical domains.[14] In doing so, they conceived a very paternalistic role for themselves. As the visiting father superior exhorted the Alapuram parishioners in January 1895, "the priest is father, teacher, judge and doctor."[15] Priests did indeed view themselves in terms of such roles, preaching, arbitrating disputes, dispensing medicines (or, more often, extreme unction) at times of cholera and smallpox.[16] Most importantly, priests were entrusted with the religious care of their spiritual children. More often than not this was a question of setting rules and boundaries of conduct, listening to confession and punishing transgressions. In particular it was the priest's task to impress on his parishioners the exclusive nature of Christian creed and sacraments, to set up a barrier against the seepage of pagan idolatry. The failure to respect the categorical distinctions that separated true religion from pagan practice brought the priests' scorn down on their disobedient children—characteristically described as weak, foolish, ignorant, lacking in faith, stupid, "a buffalo with a human face."[17]

Parishioners discovered attending pagan dramas, removing "sorcery" (*cuniyam*), observing astrological impediments (*cūlam*), or engaging in

Hindu practices or "witchcraft" of other kinds were publicly humiliated, having to wear a crown of thorns during Mass, or to go around the church on their knees; they paid fines, were whipped, or faced exclusion from the sacraments. They were made to swear an oath, touching a crucifix or standing before a statue of the saint, that they would "not attend pagan worship or secure things offered to the devil."[18] When misfortune struck, priests were ready to explain this as retribution for engagement in the "abominable villainy and deceit" of witchcraft—broadly taken as any non-Christian mediation.[19]

But not only did the "new" Jesuits enforce a clear distinction between the realm of Christian religion and that of pagan idolatry, they also dismantled de Nobili's divide between the religious and the secular by expanding the religious sphere. By degrees, the social hierarchy of caste, segregation in seating arrangements, the social order of communion, and festival honors were removed from the church domain (see Mosse 1994a, 1997). At the same time, there was a progressive exclusion of those non-Christians (for example, Hindu village headmen) who earlier claimed rights and honors in Christian shrines and festivals. Nineteenth-century Catholic religion became newly institutionalized as the domain of church authority. Expressions of religiosity beyond the ordered hierarchy of the church were negatively characterized as "diableries."

In the late nineteenth century, these "diableries" included the independent saint cults of exorcism, often at the same centers where an earlier generation of Jesuits had celebrated miracles of sacred power. It is not that the efficacy of sacred objects and words was denied, but that sacred power manifest outside of the delegated authority of the church hierarchy was at best suspect foolery and at worst diabolical. Its manifestation in the name of the saints was mere blasphemy and insolence.[20]

There was, however, another factor influencing Jesuit perceptions of saint cult centers, and another dimension to the forging of a Jesuit "spiritual polity." When they arrived to take over the parishes of the old Madurai mission in the 1850s and 1860s, the new Jesuits found that their jurisdictional claims met strong resistance from the resident Goan priests under *padroado*.[21] In the 1850s, competition between these rival Catholic mission agencies came to a head in direct and aggressive confrontation at major regional festivals and shrines (see Mosse 1997: 92–96). Valid claims to jurisdiction depended upon the demonstration of local support. In consequence the rival missions arranged profligate display of ritual, ceremony, and social honors at their shrines in order to win and secure popular allegiance, until a concordat signed between Rome and Portugal in 1857 established a system of double jurisdiction that left some shrines with the Portuguese of Goa. Among them was the de Britto shrine at Oriyur, which was overseen by Goan priests under the bishop of Mylapore until 1929 (Archdiocese of Madurai 1983: 143–45). The activities and shrines of the Goan schism became, in the eyes of the Jesuits, centers of ecclesiastical corruption, particularly clearly illustrated by toleration of the exorcist Mandalacotei Odean at Oriyur. Invariably Jesuit priests concluded their shocked descriptions of cults at shrines or tombs by noting that these were the places at which inadequately educated Goan priests conducted Mass.

Jesuit priests faced competition not only from Goan centers but also from American Protestants active in the area from the 1850s to whom parishioners threatened to turn. Moreover, village Catholics readily manipulated competition between Jesuit "intruders," the Goan "schismatics," and Protestant "heretics" (not to mention the Independent Catholic Church of Ceylon, Goa, and India, a breakaway sect led by the excommunicated renegade Father Soarez) in order to obtain intervention from their priests and to secure the ritual markers of caste power and status—that is, festival honors at major Christian churches (see Mosse 1997).[22] While the diableries of which the Jesuits so disapproved were, then, a way of placing the practices and parishes of mission rivals beyond the pale, the success of these regional centers was evidence that the capacity of the Jesuit missionaries to discipline their flocks was itself limited.

Piety and Confession

The parish diaries, letters, articles, and contemporary writings not only describe the "boundary work" of the French Jesuit missionaries (and their Tamil recruits), but also throw light on an underlying theology. If one emphasis of the nineteenth- and early-twentieth-century Jesuit preaching was on the exclusivity of their brand of Catholic practice and the evil of pagan religion, another, more primary, was on the fate of the eternal soul. The French Jesuits presented a distinctly Roman and very pietistic otherworldly form of religion to their parishioners. Holding to the principles of the order's sixteenth-century founder Ignatius Loyola, they considered (to quote from his "Spiritual Exercises") that

> Man was created for this end, that he might praise and revere the Lord his God and serving Him, at length be saved. But the other things which are

> placed on the earth were created for man's sake, that they might assist him in pursuing the end of his creation; where it follows that they are to be used or abstained from in proportion as they profit or hinder him pursuing that end. Wherefore we ought to be indifferent towards all created things, in so far as they are subject to the liberty of our will, and not prohibition, so that to the best of our power, we seek not health more than sickness, nor prefer riches to poverty, honour to contempt, a long life to a short one. But it is fitting, out of all, to choose or desire those things only which lead to the end. (Quoted in I. Taylor 1849: 197)

The diaries make it clear that these priests were less concerned to avert suffering and misfortune in this world—which after all were the result of the Fall—than to bring to mind their consequences for the condition of the eternal soul, by way of prayer, confession, and a clear conscience. They redirected anxiety about the present to an anxiety about future eternity, portraying life as a constant struggle against the passions of fallen human nature. At times of crisis (famine, drought, or epidemics), villagers were advised to fast and make their confession. One priest noted that "nearly all the villagers confess in the morning in the hope of getting some showers of rain" (Mahé diary, August 14, 1936), another that "cholera is a good preacher" (Sarukani diary, July 9–10, 1926). Special masses could be held as well for a good harvest as for the souls in purgatory. Moreover, the focus was the individual. Religion was a private and spiritual affair of the individual. Personal spiritual development was to be achieved through disciplined prayer and a moral personal and family life (Parish diaries). And this above all involved constant struggle against the passions and our fallen nature (*Jesuit in India* 1852: 177).

The focus on salvation mediated by the sacrificial cross and ensured through confession, communion, and submission to the authority of the church (priest, bishop, and Pope) also implied an essential separation of humans from God. Immediate manifestations of the divine were treated with deep suspicion, at best diversions from proper concern with the everlasting fate of the soul, at worst devilry.

These missionaries, however, accepted the value of judicious use of exterior means of awakening piety in the soul (*Jesuit in India* 1852: 178), including devotion to the saints among faithful villagers having "minds too rude and weak to do without material and palpable objects of adoration" (4). A large number of devotions were linked to special needs and occasions, or the festival calendar. During epidemics, for example, a novena for St. Sebastian, the Virgin, or some other saint was inaugurated with processions and blessings with the statue, or a Way of the Cross undertaken. In 1898, the Catholics of one village were advised "to pray to the Sacred Heart and St Joseph" as a means to overcome the tyranny of a Hindu headman.[23] More especially, attention was drawn to the immediacy of divine power in punishing the unrepentant. But despite the implied belief in the power of the saints to intervene in the world on behalf of Catholic villagers, individually and collectively, the emphasis was on saints as intercessors, who would bring strength and moral fortitude to the suffering faithful. In general, in the preaching of the missionaries, the saints were not power divinities who would do battle with evil and affliction manifest in the form of malevolent demons and spirits.

As for the demonic itself, Jesuit attitudes were complex and ambivalent. Crudely, villagers' belief in spirits was either derided as foolery or viewed as the work of the devil, diverting Christians from true religion. On the one hand, demonic agency as a source of misfortune was largely dismissed, since the struggle against evil was internalized as a matter of individual responsibility and personal guilt (see Caplan 1989: 61 on Protestant missionaries). On the other hand, pagan India itself was viewed as being in the grip of the devil. As one Jesuit commentator wrote in relation to the prevalence of spirit possession, "if Christianity has diminished the power of the devil in Christian countries, we may naturally suppose that his power remains unbroken where the cross has never been planted" (*Jesuit in India* 1852: 35).

To sum up, the saint cults of exorcism of the 1870s through 1890s can be seen as thriving at a time of transition. Jesuit missionaries, intent on "restoring" Roman Catholic practices in rural churches, were imposing a new discipline over the activities of their parishioners. The boundary between Christian religion and pagan idolatry and caste society was newly drawn and rigorously imposed. A strong prohibition on participation in non-Catholic cults combined with active encouragement of devotions to the saints, and demonstration of a superior and punitive Catholic sacred power. But the mission politics of the time meant that the ability of priests to discipline the laity was compromised. At the same time, missionary preaching stressed the internal battle against sin, the need to struggle against the passions, and gave firm emphasis to the eternal fate of the individual soul. Only through ritual action authorized by the church could Christians find salvation, solace from personal affliction, forgiveness for the sins of passions, and protection from pagan evil. The saints might be invoked, but ultimately only moral action, humble confession, and communion of the contrite individual would secure true benefits in this life and the next.

Judging from the record provided by Jesuit parish diaries, such teaching remained in force throughout the first half of the twentieth century, and the lay Catholic religious thought of the villagers with whom I stayed in the mid-1980s bore the impress of this Jesuit teaching. In particular, confession retained a central place in interpreting misfortune. While my Catholic informants explained that affliction could have external causes—astrological "bad time" (*keṭṭa kirakam*) or attack by demonic agents—fundamentally it was inseparable from the moral state of the individual person. While suffering might be sent by God to test individuals (demons might even be deployed to this end), explanations of misfortune more commonly related to sin and confession. However, these concepts were often also given a distinctively immediate, material, and embodied interpretation. For example, some spoke as if unconfessed sin could accumulate, bringing bodily sickness and affliction, usually to an individual. Occasionally collective sin might be punished by drought or disease. Others spoke of how the Virgin appeared in their dreams to warn them of the perils of unpardoned sin. Regular monthly confession, penance, and pardon averted the dangers of accumulating sin, removed it, and prepared a person to receive sacred power through the sacrament. To go to Mass, however, without confession, while harboring hatred, guilt, or secret crimes, was to invite the punishment of God.[24]

But while the church and the laity have for long laid stress on the internal drama of confession, this has always coexisted with the "externalized" drama of possession in cults of exorcism, where the laity reject the exclusive mediation of the Catholic hierarchy. While new boundaries made exorcism cults more visible and more diabolical to the Jesuit commentators, other factors encouraged people to give new focus to the power of saints in the management of misfortune. Arguably, a teaching on sin and suffering—the logic of confession—itself opened up a space for the expansion of saint-exorcism cults, giving focus to the contrary logic of possession so dramatically manifest at places such as Oriyur in the late nineteenth century. It is to this logic that I now turn. But before doing so, I should also point out that Hindus (always a significant proportion of pilgrims to these centers of exorcism) also found new mediation to divine power with which to contend with spirit agents of misfortune in the power of the Catholic saints. Commonly the response to malevolent attack was to initiate a propitiating cult and turn the demon or deity into a protecting force for an individual or kin group (see Reiniche 1979: 183–86, 193). The dangerous exterior demon is transformed into a benign deity of one's own (*conta cāmi*) in what, following I. M. Lewis (1966), one may speak of a shift from "peripheral" to "central" possession (cited in Gellner 1994: 28). At Catholic shrines, however, Hindus sought a superior Christian power to defeat and exorcise malevolent demon-gods in a quite different way.

Battling with Demons: The Drama of Possession

Under the influence of closer ecclesiastical regulation, the Arulanandar shrine at Oriyur had by the 1960s ceased to be a center of demonic exorcism and possession. However, such practices persist today in ecclesiastical backwaters. One such place is the small shrine to St. Anthony the Hermit (Vannan Antoniar, Anthony of the Forest) in the village of Muttupatanam, to which a steady stream of pilgrims and victims of possession journey. Here the practices I witnessed in 1983–84 throw light on persisting themes in Catholic possession and exorcism.

The possessed stay at the shrine for days, weeks, or even months at a time, during which the demonic agents—either inferior Hindu deities or malevolent spirits of the dead (both *pēy-picācu*)[25]—are forced to reveal themselves. Exposure to the purity and holiness of the shrine, prayer, holy water, incense, candles, and the power of the saint focused on his statue torture the demon-ghosts and make their victims' bodies "dance" (*atu*)—a more or less dramatic shaking, rolling, leaping, and shouting characteristic of spirit possession. In fact, the more violent the "dance," the weaker the hold on the possessed victim.[26] The drama culminates as the catechist-exorcist interrogates the possessing spirits, subjecting the possessed to escalating verbal abuse and physical violence until the spirits (often several in one person) reveal their names, origin, and the reason they are troubling their victims. For the witnesses this is often an entertaining drama, rather than a scene of terror, since, faced with the real power of the saint, the demons' claims to identity and power are ridiculed and shown to be illusory. The exorcism concludes as the *pēy-picācu* swear in Jesus's name to leave, a lock of hair is cut, and the victim returns to worship in a stilled posture after a purifying bath. The whole event is, in a formal sense, a rite of passage (Stirrat 1977). Possession (the entry of disorder) creates a heated and impure condition of abnormality, which is dealt with in a series of rites of separation (the pilgrimage, the ritual bath, a change of clothes, the cutting of hair), which are also "cooling" and facilitate the reincorporation of the victim into ordinary social life. She is separated from her abnormality, and the temporarily disturbed categorical distinctions (the living and the dead, humans and deities) are reestablished. But further (and perhaps rather obviously), these transformations are bodily; they take place in the body, involve a heightened awareness of self as body, and require a powerful engagement of the senses (touch, sound, smell). As will be clear when discussing the entry and effects of demonic agents, possession is a process that is eminently embodied (cf. Stoller 1995).

What happens at the saint's shrine is only the final moment of a longer diagnostic process in which the subjective experience of the afflicted (predominantly young women)[27] becomes objectified as demonic. In essence, the possessed person discovers that feelings and desires they thought were their own are in reality the responsibility of malevolent demons (Stirrat 1992: 107). Moreover, this is a public process that draws on conventional idioms of the demonic (see Kapferer 1983; Stirrat 1992: 107). Autonomous people become, temporarily, public spaces in which accounts of how and why an individual became possessed draw in various actors—other family members (alive and dead), Hindu demons, gods and goddesses, and ritual specialists. That is to say, the state of possession is not defined by the victim herself; rather, it is a group representation of a problem or set of problems. In striking contrast to the logic of Catholic confession, the account of misfortune involves not only a large cast of actors, but also a range of motivations and issues, including disrupted and unsatisfactory relationships and frustrated desires, rather than narrowing down on the personal sin of an individual. In possession, the self as bounded moral agent is replaced by a more fluid person, constituted and acted upon by the desires of others (alive and dead) and their spirit agents (Spencer 1997). While in possession the responsibility of action is shifted onto others, human or demonic, in confession behavioral (or bodily) anomalies are interiorized as personal guilt.

An individual instance of demonic possession acquires an objectivity through the deployment of shared notions of human susceptibility and demonic agency and its external signs. In this sense, each exorcism involves a possession story, which provides an ex post facto account of how an individual became afflicted. The story begins by explaining how people noticed characteristic signs of changed behavior (refusal to dress or speak properly) or bodily function (pain, sudden fits, fainting, irregular menstrual bleeding, sudden changes in face or voice). A condition of vulnerability to demonic attack is then sought, for example: going or being alone (*taṉiyākappōkam*) in marginal/transitional places (wasteland, forests, boundary stones, cemeteries, irrigation sluices, roadside places) at marginal times (twilight, midday) or moments of bodily transition (or unguarded openness; see Osella and Osella 1999), such as childbirth, puberty, or menses; being under harmful planetary constellations or experiencing imbalances of the bodily humors. The vulnerability may equally be social in the sense of ruptured relationships or conflicts arousing the suspicion of sorcery. Then a frightening incident or a sudden shock (the appearance of localized whirlwinds, animals of unusual proportions) is identified that caused or allowed the demon to enter the victim's body (perhaps through a sudden intake of breath). In short, the possession story affirms an individual's exposure to points where the structure is weak and vulnerable to disorder (Kapferer 1983: 106) and emotional states—especially fear, a dangerous, hot emotion (Osella and Osella 1999)—that create corresponding personal weakness and permeability.

Idioms of possession also define women as intrinsically vulnerable to demonic attack, and the female body (being more permeable) as the point of entry for demonic disorder (see Kapferer 1983: 100–101, 105). Women, typified as weak and fearful, are also seen as more involved in emotional human relations, and occasionally more "sinful," the latter euphemistically referring to women's putative greater sexual desire and (following Eve) susceptibility to temptation. Indeed, sexuality provides a pervasive idiom of demonic possession. A woman's unguarded sexuality attracts demons, and any beautification—flowers adorning hair, turmeric on the face—increases vulnerability.[28] The signs of possession—unbound clothing, bodily movements and especially hair—are all signifiers of passion and abandoned sexual containment (Ram 1991: 88). This draws attention not to individual sinfulness so much as the demonic nature of the forces' sexuality, and the lust (ācai) of the demons (especially inferior Hindu deities or *muṉis*) who afflict women by sleeping with them in their dreams, bringing sterility reproductive disorders—miscarriages, irregular bleeding, or death.[29]

Missionary Catholicism certainly retained an indigenous notion of the ambivalence of female power—fertility and life dependent upon dangerous and destructive sexuality—but rather than resolving the paradox through the bivalent Hindu goddess, split into her dangerous erotic and benign married forms,[30] Catholic logic isolated the positive pole (health, life giving, fertility, and motherhood) in the form of the Virgin Mary from its negative underpinnings (dangerous sexuality, violence, and death) (Mosse 1986: 443–53, 1994a: 316–17).[31] While the Virgin represents fertility without sexuality—she is often viewed as a perpetual prepubescent *kanni* who "never flowered"—the forces of sexuality are demonized (sterile sexuality), or, as Ram argues (1991: 63) projected onto the Hindu goddess. If sexuality is demonized, demons can take the place of sin and guilt.

Possession then involves the collective manipulation of shared representations in which personal suffering comes to be explained in terms of external conditions and the objective dangers of passions and places. As one woman put it to me, "We know the *pēy*, where they are, as we know which parts of the tank are deep." Clearly this involves a shift away from a dominant anthropological model that has viewed spirit possession as a product of women's marginal position in society and an outlet for protest and resistance (I. M. Lewis 1971; see debate in Stirrat 1977; Kapferer 1983; Boddy 1994; Stoller 1995). Such a model privileges one (the victim) of the many actors involved (Kapferer 1983: 96). As Isabelle Nabokov (1997) points out (drawing on Hindu Tamil material), women do not express and manage personal problems through episodes of possession but rather find their problems (and their persons) refigured in public idioms of possession, idioms which, as Ram reminds us (1991: 48), clearly connect "to rules and practices of physical containment and discipline which help to create the sexually appropriate gendered body."[32]

But although a focus on public idioms of possession avoids the problems of naive psychologizing, it also diverts attention from the sort of personal history of possession that has been the focus of Gananath Obeyesekere's work (1981). While no longer conventional subjects of their own actions, as Stirrat 1992 and Nabokov 1997 show, the possessed nonetheless use public representations of demonic agency to act out their problems, either in movement (as detailed by Stirrat) or narrative (as detailed by Nabokov), whether those issues are sexual passion, frustrated desire, romantic fantasy, or violent and erratic behavior. In her aptly titled 1997 article "Expel the Lover, Recover the Wife," Nabokov interprets the possession narrative as being about extramarital sexual fantasy and the control over marital sexuality. My field notes and the Jesuit missionary diaries quoted above certainly give evidence of possession episodes among Catholics linked to romantic failure and sexual control.[33] But my evidence suggests that possession refers to desires and passions wider than sexual longing, and a nexus of relationships of power and authority beyond marital ties. Indeed, at St. Anthony's shrine *peys* are not in the main "spirits of young men craving intimacy" (Nabokov 1997: 300) but the spirits of those who in *different* ways (sexual longing among them) remain dangerously attached to the world. It is true that *pēy* are attracted to their victims by love (*aṉpu*) more often than anger, but this is explicitly the fondness (*piriyam*) or jealousy of relatives, the "bond of blood" (*irrattappācam*) as much as lust (*ācai*). The possessed have close relations or bonds (*pācam*) with their spirits; they are their intimates.

However you look at it, possession by *pēy-picācu* is "about" unbridled desire and attachment, passion, and the dangerous (destabilizing, heating) but "infinite capacity of human beings to want what cannot be had, a capacity which turns rancid with frustration" and which lingers perilously after death (Ram 1991: 84).[34]

Here the identities of the spirit agents and their victims appear to converge in a way which (in the drama of exorcism) allows the afflicted to put their own history and distress into their spirit counterparts, as "women find themselves in their demons" (Nabokov 1997: 306). These are not isolated roles; the drama of possession is a drama of the social, the experience and frustrations of family relations, of intimacy and jealousy, of power and authority, imposed and resisted. But ultimately, passions, desires, and attachments and their power have to be trivialized in the face of the saint and removed. Just before being cut from the victim's body as knotted strands of hair, the possessing ghosts and demon-deities make requests—usually for trivial items indicative of the hold that desire has over them, the items requested corresponding to the type of demon-ghost involved: a cup of tea, a *beedi*, a comb, mirror or "old rice" (for *kuratti* gypsy ghosts), a hen with an egg (*muṭṭaikōḻi*—for Kali), a toddy or a cock (for a Muni demon-god).

Power of the Saint

Possession, we begin to see, brings together, makes manifest, and embodies the missionaries' twin dangers to the soul—pagan religion and human passions. But the power of demons of passion is only one aspect of the drama of possession; the other is the power of the Catholic-saint exorcists to expel them. I want therefore to turn to the cultural construction of the saints at the center of the drama of exorcism. While the person of the possessed is unstable, changeable, and multiply invaded by passion and paganism, the saint himself is, by contrast, a paragon of the unassailable core and enduring moral Christian person. But let me first examine the conception of the saints' power.

The first thing to note is that it is male Catholic saints—St. John de Britto (Arulanandar), St. Anthony the Hermit (Vanatantoniar), or St. Paul the First Hermit (Vannatu Cinnappar)—rather than the Virgin, who chase demons. In doing so they manifest a power that is dangerous and violent in contrast to the Virgin's, which is nonviolent, benevolent, strongly associated with healing, fertility, and a marked absence of punishment or demonic exorcism.[35] The power that tortures evil spirits can also punish the wicked and perjurers. Early Jesuit accounts of the exercise of such power by Arulanandar (de Britto) at the site of his martyrdom can be illustrated by a letter of 1735, which records how "a gentile" committed the sin of perjury at Oriyur: "All at once his legs and arms became horribly swollen. He became blind and within 8 days was dead. Nobody dare now take false oath . . . that is why the gentile judge declared guilty a pagan who refused to swear in this place that he was innocent of a crime of which he was accused, whilst he declared that he was ready to do it in the temples of idols."[36] At the time of fieldwork, St. Anthony's shrine at Muttupattanam was among other centers of saintly power where disputes were regularly settled or oaths sworn.[37]

The potency of the saints and their power to defeat the forces of evil derives in particular from their own ascetic austerity, self-control, and detachment from the world of desire. Their regenerative abstinence fittingly contrasts the barren eroticism of the demons they defeat. Recall that the miraculous crucifix brought from the forest of Vannatu Cinnappar refused the shelter of the St. Xavier chapel in which it was first placed. This saint is indeed commonly worshipped outside the settlement in the paddy fields, which he protects from pests and where he is represented by a simple cross. In Alapuram, a Cinnappar cult initiated by a migrant returning from Malaysia focused on a shrine built in a tract of wasteland beside the cemetery, and even the tree under which the saint was once worshipped fell down since it compromised his extreme asceticism.

The ascetic power of both Vannan Antoniar (Forest St. Anthony) and Vannatu Cinnappar (Forest St. Paul) is signified in their location in the forest, which, in Tamil conceptions, is the place of the transcendent values of renunciation, as well as of the terrible powers of demons (see Reiniche 1979). Elsewhere I have explored the local conception of "forest saints," or forest dimensions of local saints (see Mosse 1994a: 317–18). For the moment it is sufficient to note that the "forest" (*kāṭu*)—the open space set in contrast to the social space of the village—is the symbolic location of the wild and dangerous power of the saints, in particular that which confronts demonic power. In addition to marginal places, St. Anthony is associated with transitional times. The saint is worshipped at the festival of *poṅkal*, a major Tamil festival of socioeconomic transition in the month of Tai that marks the move from one agricultural cycle to the next, from the season of water and fertility to that of sun and heat (Reiniche 1979: 43, 65; Good 1983).

The connection between renunciation, the saintly endurance of suffering, and power directed against demonic forces is most clearly seen in the figure of St. John de Britto, the great martyr and exorcist of nineteenth-century Maravarnadu. The hagiography and cult of St. John de Britto bears all the markings of those of the martyrs of Christian antiquity (Brown 1981). For the devotee, de Britto's life, passion, and death marked him as having a special relationship with God. During his life (now represented in a popular religious folk drama), de Britto's suffering at the hands of his Hindu persecutors was a source of regenerative power, revealed in miracles of healing and endurance. But it was the saint's violent death that provided the imaginative focus for his power, and the site and instruments of death that became the focus of the martyr's sacred power over demonic forces.[38] The impaling stake was a locus of violent power directed against possessing demons, and the executioner's sword, according to legend, became attributed with the power to drive out demons (Saulière 1947: 477). Indeed, at his shrine de Britto is represented not only as a holy ascetic (with wooden staff and crucifix) and tortured martyr (being beheaded), but also as an embattled warrior with raised sword. The power of the saint is rooted in violence and symbolized in the spilling of blood (Oriyur's red sand)—an ambivalent symbol of divine power and danger.[39] As I have argued elsewhere, "in Tamil conceptions divine power having its source in violence is itself violent," and honored with the violence of sacrifice and meat offerings. Attempting to explain the practice (discontinued in recent years) of slaughtering animals (goats and cocks) at his festival, one villager told me, "by blood sacrifice they killed [him]; by blood sacrifice they give [to him] [*irratappaliyil koṉṟārkaḷ irattappali kotuttārkaḷ*]" (Mosse 1994a: 312). There is a pervasive connection between the saints' receipt of animal sacrifice and the chasing of demons. The pain and torture of the saint's violent (but sacrificial) death and its instruments (the word and the stake) are turned on the possessing demons.

As I suggest in Mosse 1994a, Catholics share with Hindus the notion that divine power which is violent and associated with the chasing of demons (and which receives sacrifice) is also inferior. It is the attribute of lower forms of divinity and exercised only within a hierarchical order in which circumscribed powers—of punishment or exorcism—are delegated from superior beings to inferior ones (312–13). From this perspective, the (male) saints have a lower-order power delegated from Christ and the Virgin, exercised as their ministers and warriors in a delimited domain. Indeed, the saints take on the very characteristics of the inferior demon-gods they exorcise—linked to marginal places, receiving animal offerings and even (in the case of St. Anthony at Muttupatanam) incarnating themselves in possessing their devotees.[40] But, just as the more universal power of superior Catholic divinity (Christ and the Virgin) is separated from the violent and dangerous power, so too the male saints are (in certain instances) understood as delegating their own inferior attributes and violent power to inferior beings, this time Hindu deities who carry out the violent punishments on their behalf (313–15).

In this conceptual universe—which is essentially Hindu—the attributes of the Catholic saints are fluid and relational, that is defined by a set of hierarchical relationships—at one moment the saints are dangerous and punitive, at another isolated from the "contamination of power." From this perspective, Hindu deities are not contrary to Catholic saints but controlled and incorporated into their domains, just as at the social level Hindus are (or were) incorporated into the festivals of the saints in the village (such as St. James's at Alapuram until 1938) in their ritual division of labor and in the hierarchy of caste honors they involved (Mosse 1994a, 1997). The relationship between the Catholic and Hindu groups or deities is, to adopt Dumont's apt phrase, one of "encompassing the contrary" (1980: 239–45).

But this construction of the saintly power makes no sense at the centers of exorcism. These are exterior places of the forest[41] where Hindu deities have no legitimate subordinate place, no delegated role. They manifest themselves only as demonic intrusions. Indeed, de Britto and St. Anthony are figures in which the missionary opposition to the darkness of all "Hindu idolatry" comes to be represented. De Britto's life is represented as a struggle against Hindu power. He not only expelled evil spirits but also neutralized the "sorcery of Brahmans" directed against him. According to one nineteenth-century legend, a Hindu temple in which he once spent a night was "miraculously cleft asunder" (Favreux diary, January 2, 1855; Besse 1912: 296). After his death de Britto became a warrior king and protector of the Christians of Maravarnadu. But since the historical and legendary conflict between the saint and Hindu power (the Hindu king)—that is, the battle over pagan religion—was also conceived as a battle against a generalized demonic disorder, Hindus as well as Christians were able to participate in the benefits of the saint's blessing.

At their shrines in the notional forest, and for the visiting pilgrims and possessed, St. Anthony or St. John de Britto were figures of absolute sanctity and power. The identity of the saint was not fluid and relational (as in the village) but defined by essential characteristics of holiness and power. The saint of the exorcism cult is a superperson, a figure who, like Christ, demonstrates personhood enduring beyond death and dismemberment. Indeed, through the extremity of bodily torture the enduring and unassailed Christian person is manifest; the more disfigured and divisible the body, the more resilient and impermeable the sinless saintly inner person and soul. The saint, whole person in divided body, becomes a fitting figure to reestablish the self of the possessed, whole in body but divided in person. Ultimately this is done by exposing the illegitimate and false and illusory nature of the demonic power—returning the possessed to their Christian selves.

We have, then, two contrasting polarities. For the possessed victim, in moving from the home and village to the saint's shrine there is a transition from the stable moral person of everyday life to the unstable multiple person controlled by externalized desires and beings most clearly evident when exposed to the power of the saint (and then back again following exorcism). In the conception of the saints, there is a polarity between the saint in the village, defined by hierarchical sets of relations in which Catholic saints and Hindu deities exist as unequal but complementary powers, and the saint in the forest, where he is conceived of in singular, absolutist terms and opposed to Hindu deities that can exist only as demons or illusions.

It is now time to try to link this cultural logic to the broader historical themes of the chapter. The central point is that (ironically, perhaps) these centers of diableries dramatized the very absolutist and universalistic teachings of the Catholic mission itself. First, at the saint's shrine in the forest, Christian truth was uncompromised, and Hindu deities were exposed (by the power of the Christian saint) as either absolutely evil or absolutely illusory. Second, exorcism cults spoke directly of the struggle against human appetites and passions. These cults gave symbolic expression to the same confrontation of Hindu divinity with the superior Christian sacred power, and the exposure and removal of sin which the missionaries preached, but which they singularly failed to put into practice in the form of power deployed against demonic agents of misfortune. The saints' shrines were places where the struggle between good and evil could be dramatically enacted, where sin and suffering could be objectified as demonic and be visibly defeated. Indeed, in a sense, possession and exorcism can be seen as a parallel rather than a contrast to confession. If, borrowing from Foucault (1976: 61–79), we see confession as bringing something hidden to light and removing it as a form of offering, then possession is a "mode of confession," both are "techniques of truth." The saints do directly and dramatically what priests achieve only imperfectly —the purging of inner sin, desire, and passion from body and soul. One could go even further and, following Taussig 1993, suggest that possession cults involve a type of mimesis.[42] Perhaps the saints mimic the preaching and practices of the missionaries (whose deified persons they sometimes are) and reproduce in vivid color the Christian struggle against evil passion and pagan religion. And this mimesis might be or might have been a popular means to understand and reformulate the Christian religious experience in a more immediate, this-worldly, and embodied form among local Catholics.

In any case, the stark Manichean opposition of good and evil beings and the struggle between Christian and Hindu divinity implied was far removed from the everyday life where Christians and Hindus participated in the same social and ritual world. The Catholics in Ramnad in the late nineteenth century (and to a degree today also) had to reconcile an uncompromising universalist missionary teaching with the social reality of coexistence with their Hindu co–caste members. Arguably, the cults of exorcism focusing on the Catholic saints helped in this reconciliation. The gods of their Hindu neighbors could be demonized, but only "in the forest." In the world of the village, however, they could not allow the everyday battle between good and evil to be conceptualized as a battle between Christians and Hindu divinity. They could not (as coastal communities of Catholics in South India and Sri Lanka had) "posit Hinduism as an evil and invasive force responsible for sickness, misfortune and suffering" (Ram 1991: 62, 71; see Stirrat 1992). Catholics in the villages of Ramnad, as I have argued before, occupy a dual moral world that accommodates both the relativist world of caste and village deities and saints and the absolutist truth claims of Christianity. What I am suggesting now is that this may also be the product of a particular historical moment when the absolutist teachings of the church most strikingly contradicted social life as lived.[43]

During the second half of the twentieth century, centers of exorcism focusing on the shrines of Catholic saints in rural Ramnad declined in popularity. At important churches such as Oriyur, the Catholic hierarchy effectively suppressed activities which it came to view as uncouth, backward, and uncivilized (*aciṅkam*) more than diabolical, relegating them to relatively obscure substations such as St. Anthony's church at Muttupatanam. A new generation of parish priests deemphasized the cult of saints in favor of a focus on Christ and the sacraments as the sole mediators between God and humans (Mosse 1994b: 99). No longer viewed as intercessors and still less as sources of supernatural power, the saints were presented as exemplars of the Christian life (Houtart n.d.: 299), and devotions and saints' festivals were encouraged only because they brought people to confession (Houtart et al. n.d.; Stirrat 1979). The postindependence and post–Vatican II church has also replaced its denunciation of Hinduism with programs of interfaith dialogue and inculturation. At the same time, its commitment to the preaching of a "social gospel" of justice and equality has renewed criticism of the church's accommodations to caste (see Mosse 1994b for discussion of these broad changes). Thus at Catholic festivals an implicit focus on the saint's power and protection is replaced by explicit focus on social and moral education and on social justice and anticaste equality through scripted dramas, slide shows, or festival banners.

The strong emphasis of the orthodox church on social and salvation-oriented aspects of religion as against the pragmatic concern with power to heal has, many argue, tended to go along with another upsurge of independent saint cults. Stirrat 1992, for example, gives an account of the postcolonial rise of thaumaturgical power at Catholic shrines in Sri Lanka. In South India, such a model might make sense of nineteenth-century saint cults as a reaction to the new discipline of the Jesuit mission, but it would not make sense in the late twentieth century. In Ramnad, there is no revival of independent saint cults. However, misfortune continues to be conceived in demonic terms, and exorcism remains a sign of sacred power (Ackerman 1981: 94; Caplan 1985, 1987a, 1991). It is in this context that Pentecostalism rather than a pietistic devotion to the saints has a new ascendancy within the Catholic as well as the Protestant churches (Caplan 1987a, 1989) in Tamil Nadu.

Let me close with an illustration summarized from my field notes of 1984.

Every Tuesday and Friday a crowd of several hundred come to a chapel of St. John de Britto in a small Pallar-caste village. The leaders of this Pentecostal gathering direct attention not to the saint, but to Jesus, who will drive away Satan. The gathered crowd are told to remove all amulets or other protection against demons, to open small bottles of coconut oil, and holding these in their right hands to tell Jesus of their suffering. Intermittently speaking in tongues, the prayer leader states that God will change the oil into his own blood and that on hearing Jesus's name the *picācus* (demons) will run. As the devotional chorus gains momentum, many women in the crowd begin to sway arhythmically, shrieking with hair loosened. Male Pentecostal leaders move through the crowd, grabbing the possessed women by their hair and pressing crosses onto their foreheads, or aspersing holy water, threatening the demons, saying that it is not water but the blood of Jesus. Over several hours the session moves from ordered preaching and prayer to a frenzied climax before order returns and many *pēy-picācu* have been driven out.

This particular exorcism cult grew up around a Pallar-caste healer-exorcist, Rajendran, a charismatic man who presents himself as a *san-nyāsin*. The parish priest, however, keen to discourage a cultic focus on an unordained individual, successfully diverted attention away from Ra-jendran, initially by requiring that individuals wishing to exorcise spirits first obtain a letter of permission from him, then by forming ten to twelve laymen into a "society" (*kulu*) to oversee the center.

By 1999 this cult itself had virtually disappeared, but a few kilometers away, in 1990, an ex–Roman Catholic priest established a prayer garden of the Church of Truth and the Spirit, which reportedly attracts as many as five thousand to prayer and healing events. While a radical assertion of Christian fundamentalism and individualistic spirituality erases all signs of Catholic or Hindu ritualism, the message of Christian healing and power over the evil causes of affliction provides a vehicle for persisting popular modes of explaining misfortune where the established church is increasingly unable to do so (see Caplan 1983: 30).

Conclusions

In focusing on concepts and practices dealing with misfortune, I hope to have thrown light on elements of a complex popular Catholic conception of personhood and interiority in one South Indian context. Placing ideas of person and agency in the context of mission history begins to raise important questions about the culturally and historically specific processes of communicating or appropriating ideas of self, soul, and sin. I have tried to show that nineteenth-century missionary concerns often focused on defining and protecting exclusive Christian religious domains, and that the particular pietism of nineteenth-century Jesuit missions and the demonizing of pagan religion could be mapped onto a conception of demonic passion and divine power focusing on Christian saints at shrines of exorcism. In other words, nineteenth-century saint-exorcism cults provided not just a contrary to the sacraments of confession and communion, but a mimetic version of the universalist missionary teaching on the evil of both pagan religion and human passion, as well as a dramatic means of dealing with both. While forged in the particular context of the late nineteenth century, exorcism cults draw on a popular culture of evil that continues to indicate and articulate the transformative power of Christian religion understood in new ways. Finally, this should not be read as the story of a tension between Western (Christian) and Eastern modes of personhood. Rather, it draws attention to different therapeutic movements present in many societies, which are to degrees either centripetal (confessional), focusing on the individual moral agent, or centrifugal (possession-oriented), expanding and dispersing agency; and of course as well as confession, European society has its own centrifugal religious or psychoanalytic therapeutic traditions that objectify subjective experience and disperse responsibility (Spencer 1997 and personal communication).

......

Notes

I am particularly indebted to Fenella Cannell for very helpful editorial comments on an earlier draft of this chapter. Thanks also to Caroline Osella and participants at *Words and Things*, the workshop in the anthropology of Christianity where the chapter was first discussed, as well as at seminars in Edinburgh and the School of Oriental and African Studies, London.

1 The primary concern of this chapter is historical—accounting for the dra-

matic appearance of popular spirit possession and exorcism cults in a regional Jesuit archive in the late nineteenth century—but I make liberal use of my anthropological fieldwork in developing an interpretation of these cults. In doing so I do not wish to imply an interface between a historicized mission Christianity and an ahistorical, separate, and coherent popular "local culture." While I do believe that fieldwork can enrich historical analysis, the reverse is also true. A sense of history helps us understand cultural practice as variable, constructed, and contested in the context of specific social and political configurations. Exorcism cults in the 1890s and the 1980s have their own different contexts, being shaped and reshaped by changing relations of power and the global context of the Christian church (see Stirrat 1992; Caplan 1987a; and my forthcoming work, *The saint in the banyan tree*, for a more explicitly diachronic perspective).

2 "Alapuram" (a pseudonym) is a mixed Hindu-Christian village in (old) Ramnad District in a region where some 15 percent of the population is Christian and in which I undertook fieldwork during the period 1982–84 (and intermittently, although on other subjects, from 1993 to 1996 and again in 2004).

3 The original text in English and Tamil was written by Father Gnanaprakasam, whom I judge to have been one of a handful of Tamil Jesuits serving the French Jesuit mission at this time. This entry and that of other diaries (1854–1948), which I reference by author and date, were from the Jesuit Madurai Mission Archives at Shembaganur, Kodaikanal, Tamil Nadu (henceforth JMMA). Two diaries in Latin covering the period 1854–65 are summarized in French in *Résumé du Diarium Maravae* written by Father Favreux (ca. 1865–66) and cited as *Résumé*.

4 See below for comments on the nineteenth-century sectarian divide between Jesuit and Goan priests.

5 In fulfillment of vows, individuals would (and do) perform various acts—including tonsure (*motai*), or *karumpu toṭṭi* (carrying a prayed-for child around the church in the woman's wedding sari slung from sticks of sugarcane)—and make offerings of various kinds, including grain, vegetables, candles, and money, but especially sprouted coconuts for fertility, goats, and cocks (never hens) sacrificed especially on Wednesdays (*Résumé*, 281–82).

6 I have discussed the significance of the festival flagpole in relation to saintly power and demonic possession in Mosse 1994: 318–19.

7 Favreux diary, December 23, 1872, April 27, 1874, and May 1874. In the same years, Favreux reported "extraordinary crowds" and offerings not far from Tiruouvalour at the tomb of a Sanar- (Nadar-) caste infant named the Infant Jesus, and at Tokanendel at the tomb of a vagabond. Then in 1894 Salentamata (the spirit of a dead woman or manifestation of the Virgin) told a returning migrant from Rangoon to plant a cross for her. A Brahman who objected was threatened in a dream. Miraculous cures came from water placed at the foot of the cross (Gnanaprakasam, November 18, 1894). In each case cults focused on the tombs of people (children, vagrants, women,

mendicants) whose marginality to Tamil society equated with the renunciatory good death (see Mosse 1994: 308).

8 Extracted from the letter from Father Fasenille (1896).

9 In 1873, Father Favreux received reports of a "hybrid" cult from the village of Arudakulam focusing on a sacred tamarind tree of Arulanandar (de Britto), where a Shanar (Nadar) man having visions and claiming the power of Arulanandar *sami* performed miracles with holy water at the tomb shrine of "une mauvaise" Christian under a sacred tamarind tree from which she had hung. Hindu and Christian pilgrims came from as far away as Madurai (over three hundred on a Friday) and a large amount of money was collected, *poṅkaḷ* rice cooked, and goats sacrificed. A cross was erected in the tree and a *kōvil* (shrine) constructed under the management of a Hindu *kanakupiḷḷai* (accountant). In the 1890s exorcisms were also described at St. Sebastian's shrine at Kokkurani village (Gnanaprakasam November 24, 1896). Further examples of exorcism cults are given in the published letters of Father Pouget (1890), Father Lacombe (1892), and Father Larmey (1876).

10 For an account of these events, see Kadhirvel 1977; Mosse 1986: 35–42; Bayly 1989; Nelson [1868] 1989; Nevett 1980; Saulière 1947.

11 See, for example, the Annual Letters (A.L.) of the Madurai Mission from 1734: A.L. Father J. Vieyra, 1734 (July 14, 1735); A.L. Father Salvador dos Reys, 1735 (June 26, 1736); A.L. Father F. M. Orti, 1743 (September 4, 1744), all in *Lettres annuelles du Madure*, no. 17 (1708–56) (trans. F. L. Besse), Jesuit Archives, Shembaganur.

12 The sand at Oriyur, turned red by the blood of the martyr, possesses healing powers.

13 This was a gradual process. In the early years of the new Jesuit mission, foreign priests covered large areas, traveled frequently between scattered congregations to preach, hear confessions, and administer sacraments. Conditions were so harsh that in the first ten years, twenty-one out of sixty-four priests died, most before the age of thirty-five (*The Jesuit in India*, 1852).

14 Indeed, in the eyes of certain nineteenth-century Protestant critics, Jesuitism was itself defined by an impulse to "absolute domination over the spirits of men" and an idea of centralized power and uniformity "crystallized and shining on its surface and mathematical in its figure," which was the nearest thing to a "spiritual polity" the church had produced (Taylor 1849).

15 Gnanaprakasam, parish diary entry, January 24, 1895.

16 Cholera epidemics were an almost yearly occurrence in Alapuram village, including outbreaks in 1895, 1898, 1900, 1903, and 1904; the village was visited by smallpox in 1906.

17 In February 1907, the priest was particularly incensed by "quelques imbeciles du village" who had planned to form a bank and had printed a notice in which the names of the Immaculate Conception and Shiva were brought together (Gamon, February 5, 1907).

18 Gnanaprakasam, parish diaries, February 28, April 4, March 6, August 4, and August 28, 1896.

19 When one Santiago caused certain ceremonies and sacrifices to be made in his house for his sick son, the missionary noted that "God punished witchcraft by sending a double death." The recourse of a Christian family to a *pattunūḷ* (spirit intermediary) resulted in three deaths.

20 A not insignificant factor here was the loss of church revenue implied in the appropriation of offerings at saint's shrines by exorcist impostors: at Oriyur in the 1870s, the exorcist Mandalacotei Odean was taking for himself and local Utaiyar caste leaders over a quarter of all offerings (Favreux diary, September 8, 1872, July 25, 1873).

21 The papal bull of 1514 conferred on the crown of Portugal the privilege of appointing bishops in countries conquered by Portugal in the East. Interpreted rather loosely, this was taken to apply to the southern Maravar kingdom of Ramnad.

22 The Oriyur shrine was a religious center in which, in particular, Catholic Utaiyar caste cultivators who migrated into Ramnad at the end of the seventeenth century gained a ritual and political preeminence. Not only did the popular de Britto cult focus on an Utaiyar exorcist, but the caste was able to secure festival honors at the shrine, which gave dramatic expression to the rising land-based power of this caste that had come to match and challenge the older dominance of the Maravar caste, based as it was on royal kinship and political office (Mosse 2003). In order to retain these privileges, in the 1850s the Utaiyar chiefs of Oriyur and neighboring villagers raised funds to help the Goanese priests fight court cases against the Jesuits over rights to patronage of their churches (*Résumé*, 50). Lower-caste Christians (Pallar and Nadar) sought protection from the oppression of high-caste Hindus, while all castes sought missionary support in protracted caste honors disputes at major saints' festivals. Of course, missionaries also exploited their role as arbitrators of dispute and holders of ritual privileges to secure support of one group or another.

23 Gnanaprakasam, parish diary, February 11 and May 6, 1896.

24 I was given several instances that paralleled the eighteenth-century Jesuit account of a woman at Oriyur "who went for mass without confessing her hatred against another was unable to swallow the sacred host, which stuck in her throat so that she choked to death" (September 4, 1744; F. Orti, *Lettres annuelles du Madure*, 17.90).

25 Out of 153 cases recorded at St Anthony's shrine in 1984, 80 percent of the exorcised spirits were ghosts and 20 percent Hindu deities. The deities—mostly the goddess Kali, and the gods Madan, Karruppan, Conai, and Muni—are in fact often conceived of as relatively abstract entities taking indefinitely more concrete manifestations in the form of one of a large number of location-specific guardian deities. I was able to list forty-seven separately named Munis. Women tended to be possessed by Munis of their own village (true of 24 percent of cases), although a few, such as Pandi Muni—Muni of the Pandiyan Kingdom—had an influence throughout Madurai and Ramnad districts.

26 While a person possessed by a ghost leaps around, one possessed by a Hindu deity may sit motionless or, adopting a yogic posture, pretend to the status of the ascetic Shiva. Correspondingly, when possessing their victims, the stronger the demon-ghost, the less physical force is implied: ghosts "catch," "seize" or "grasp" (*piṭi*) their victims, while Hindu demon-gods (*muṉis*), or "higher deities" (for example, Aiyanar, Kali) "hit" (*aṭi*), or "touch" (*toṭu*) their victims.

27 Of the 153 cases of possession recorded at St. Anthony's shrine in 1983–84, 90 percent were women, and of these 65.7 percent were between the ages of sixteen and twenty-five.

28 Correspondingly, to be surrounded by ugliness—iron, old chappals, a broom—affords protection against demonic agents.

29 Case: While her husband was working in Malaysia for four years a woman renowned for her beauty was "kept" by a Muni, who brought her flowers and *poṭṭu* (vermilion). On returning, her husband found that each time he approached her, she would start heavy menstrual bleeding. A *kōṭaṅki* (exorcist) was called to get the Muni to leave, but while he was beating his *uṭukku* drum to invoke his deity, the Muni took the woman onto the roof of the house, where she hanged herself.

30 There is a large literature on the way in which Tamil mythology and village festivals bifurcate the goddess into her two aspects. See, for example, Shulman 1980; Beck 1981; Moffatt 1979; Reiniche 1979; Good 1985; Bradford 1983.

31 See Mosse 1986 and 1994 for details. The missionary priests implied the sinfulness of sexuality generally, as well as its association with the Fall and with death. The link between sex (especially illicit female sexuality) and death was sometimes explicit. Women caught in adultery had to wear black saris and a crown of thorns (*muḷmuṭi*, the emblem of Christ's humiliation and death) and circumambulate the church.

32 Putting the point the other way around, Ram (1991: 90–91) points to a "demonological interpretation of the ordinary female reproductive cycle" among Catholic Mukkuvars (a Tamil fishing caste), which finds striking parallels in early modern European associations between womb disorders and the supernatural.

33 Case: Rosamma was brought to St. Anthony at Muttupattanam after her mind "changed." She refused to talk or dress properly and had run away from home. A while before she became ill, her family had arranged her marriage to her *māmārmakaṉ* (her prescribed marriage partner), who was serving in the military, a highly prestigious job. A very large dowry had been raised involving the sale of family assets (cattle, etc.). A day had been fixed for the wedding and invitations sent out. At the last moment, however, the bridegroom withdrew. He had the wedding clothes made to fit his sixteen-year-old brother, who was obliged to take his place. For several months the marriage remained unconsummated. Rosamma tried to avoid her young husband and return to her natal home. People began to talk about

the youth's inability to "keep" his wife. Then he began to beat her, and from then her "mind changed." When she came to St. Anthony's shrine, three *pēy-picācu* were made to identify themselves. The first was the ghost of her father; the second, a *muṉi* (inferior Hindu deity), and third a *kuratti*—the ghost of a gypsy woman.

34 Desire is often typified as the craving for trivia, which is a characteristic of possessing spirits. Even the possession of a trivial luxury item (such as a piece of meat) may arouse the envy of lurking ghosts. The spirits of Kuruvar gypsies (who live by begging and the collection and selling of trivia) only exemplify the dangerous craving for trivia of all *pēy*.

35 See Mosse 1994 for further elaboration of this contrast between the male saints and the Virgin. It is not always true that in this region the Virgin does not punish the wicked or do battle with demons (see Deliège 1997: 293). After all, she is also portrayed as stamping the serpent underfoot. But the Virgin is conceived of as having a superior power and therefore able to command other saints to do battle on her behalf, as, for example, when St. James (locally, Cantiyakkappa) was sent to defeat the Moors of Spain.

36 Father J. Vieyra, July 14, 1735, *Lettres annuelles du Madure*, 17.26. Another letter wrote of a shepherd boy, who "consumed with fever and intending to destroy the chapel was paralyzed, but restored to health after he confessed and promised to repair the church"; and of a "young prince" who nearly died when, with failing faith, he took medicine for his intestinal pains after visiting the shrine at Oriyur. Father Salvador dos Reys, June 27, 1736, *Lettres annuelles du Madure*, 17.44.

37 Often members of the shrine's "management committee" were involved in attempts to resolve disputes before it came to this. The church received a payment known as *paṭikācu* or *paṭikāṭṭi*—"cut the money"—from all disputants who came to the shrine. Reconciled parties also sought to bind their agreement on oath in front of the saint's statue. Some believed that the saint's judgment could be invoked against one who had wronged another, as punishment, or at least to force reconciliation at the shrine. For example, a brother and sister had refused to speak to one another for ten years following dispute over the inheritance of family land. The sister, who believed that she had been denied her rightful share, came to plead to St. Anthony to intervene and put an end to the injustice. Her brother's son them became very sick, vomiting blood. Interpreting this as the justice of St. Anthony, they made a pilgrimage to Muttupatanam to resolve the dispute. At the shrine they prepared pots of *poṅkaḷ* rice (associated with the saint), offering these along with cloth at the altar. The disputing parties exchanged candles and holy water and marked the sign of the cross on each other's foreheads.

38 The martyrdom itself is believed to have been accompanied by unnatural and regenerative events. The body leapt backward on decapitation and it radiated a great light. A drop of the saint's blood entered and healed the blind eye of the Pallar executioner, and as the saint's blood soaked into the earth it turned it red, giving it healing powers. Eight unseasonable days of

rain followed the execution (Nevett 1980: 228). De Britto's body was dismembered, his limbs nailed to the execution post or scattered as he had himself foretold (Mosse 1994).

39 The Virgin, who "by contrast, was never wounded [and never menstruated] and her power has no implication of violence . . . is associated with the spilling or overflowing of [cooling, purifying] milk" (Mosse 1994: 311).

40 Roughly on one Friday a month the catechist and exorcist at Muttupatanam was assisted by a Hindu woman, through whom St. Anthony identified demons or sorcery, foretold the future, or advised on corrective ritual action. Interestingly, the catechist believed her to be possessed not by St. Anthony but by a particular Hindu muni.

41 This notion of the forest is strictly metaphoric, conveying the sense of the "out there" to which the pilgrim journeys, set apart and opposed to home and village.

42 I am grateful to Caroline Osella for raising the issue of mimesis in possession for me.

43 It is tempting to find a parallel here with Dumont's thesis (1982: 3) that in "holistic society," absolute universalism and individualism, such as that contained in the fundamental conception of man that flowed from the teachings of Christ, can exist only outside the social order (that is, in the forest): "As Troeltsch said, man is an individual-in-relation-to-God . . . in essence an 'outworldly individual.'" If through Mass and confession (and later social action) the Jesuit priests strove to engender Dumont's "inworldly individualism," for nineteenth-century Catholics true power was to be found in the figure of the forest saint or martyr as "outworldly individual."

···Four···

Reading as Gift and Writing as Theft

Fenella Cannell

"Reading" the *Pasion*

All over the region of Bicol, and elsewhere in the Philippines, the rhythm of Lent is marked out in two activities. By day, one notices pairs of men or women, sitting in the shadiest corner of the house, with a cheap paper book open in their hands, as they practice chanting from the text and debate disputed passages among themselves. By night, each Friday, the dark and quiet are disturbed by music and light from at least one house in the *barangay*;[1] periods of a plaintive two-voice song—a kind of ornamented chant—continue into the small hours, interrupted now and then by bursts of richer, poignant, hymnlike melody for several voices. Inside the houses, pairs of singers each take their turn in front of a makeshift altar, one pair replacing another as the first grows tired. The performances end only at dawn.

The text that people sing with such dedication is the Bicol-language Passion (*Pasion Bicol*); that is, the story of the creation of the world, the coming of Christ, his preaching, suffering, and death, and the foundation of the Catholic Church, translated into 230 pages of verse in the local language and printed by local religious publishers. Most people in rural Bicol consider it the responsibility of the proper adult to be able to contribute to these vigils, even if they do not regularly stage one in their own home, and great pride is taken in skillful performances and in closely coordinated work by pairs of singing partners.[2] Even when the *Pasion* is staged as a Passion play (*tanggal*) in Holy Week, the actors who sing it are still local people, drawn from a squatter's area of the nearby town, neither professionals nor officers of the church.

The striking—and often very beautiful—Passion performances are, however, never referred to in Bicol as "singing"; instead the phrase that is always used to describe them is "*reading* the Passion text" (*magbasang Pasion*). The Bicol word for reading, used on its own, is often taken to refer to this kind of religious devotional practice.[3]

This usage should serve to remind us of the fact—obvious, but somehow often lost sight of in anthropological discussion—that reading and writing, far from being neutral technologies with a self-evident and universal set of effects in the world, are ethnographically shifting categories.[4] While the Philippines has often figured in international statistics as the country at the top of the regional literacy tables, little attention is paid to what this might mean, not for the national elite, but for the rural majority.

Most, though not all, people in Bicol can read and write a letter. But while the educational achievements of the hard-pressed state primary schools and their pupils are in many ways remarkable, it would be a mistake to imagine that farming and fishing communities experience the fluent, private, individualized literacy of university-educated anthropologists and statisticians. Both reading and writing are locally considered to be very hard work in Bicol barangays, and—in excess—likely to damage your health. Letters and telegrams are usually written only for serious purposes (a family death; news from a relative who has migrant work abroad; a request to borrow money that could not be put in person) and are often, to outsiders' eyes, formulaic in composition even when they are between intimate kin.[5] Most letters are also designed to be read by numbers of people, not just an individual recipient. Writing materials are a serious expense and these among other costs often force parents, however unwillingly, to interrupt or truncate their children's schooling; children may also volunteer to lose a year in order to help their parents by working during a family crisis. In homes where all kinds of equipment may be in short supply, printed books and pamphlets are few and are often stored with other valuables, while painstaking handwritten copies of texts—for instance, the words to the hymn sung annually for the fiesta of the barangay patron saint—are folded and put away with equal care, and are lent, borrowed, and shared when the need arises. Very little about "reading," in fact, is conducted casually.

The significance of these observations should become clearer with some explanation of the wider significance of the Passion texts.

The Bicol *Pasion* whose readings I witnessed, is in fact only one of the large number of Filipino Passions in different local languages. Of these the oldest, from which the Bicol *Pasion* and many other versions originate, is a text also often called *Pasyon*, but referred to here to avoid confusion as the *Casaysayan*,[6] which is written in Tagalog, the language of the national capital and its surrounding provinces. This Tagalog text is an 1826 reworking of an original produced in 1703 by a member of the early Spanish colonial–period Tagalog elite, Gaspar Aquino de Belen—a man who worked in the print houses of the Jesuit order in Manila and was closely associated with the Jesuits. Aquino de Belen himself presented his *Casaysayan* as a translation from the Spanish and clearly based it on popular Spanish religious texts dating back to at least the sixteenth century, or earlier.[7] The stated aim of the translation—and of the backing it received from the Catholic Church in the Philippines—was to hasten and perfect the knowledge of right Christian doctrine among new Filipino converts, and to familiarize laypeople with the story of Christ's death and resurrection, and all its implications for Christian salvation.

Much has been made in the literature of the significance of the *Casaysayan*, and in particular two outstanding historical works (Ileto 1979 and Rafael 1988) have focused on its role in Philippine conversion and its historical implications and preconditions. Reynaldo Ileto has identified the text as the source of idioms of popular revolutionary uprising in the last days of the Spanish colonial period, and the first days of the American one. While it had been recognized that some parts of the islands, notably the Visayas, conducted local uprisings against the Spanish in what might be called a "shamanic" idiom, Ileto demonstrated (1979: 14) that the apparently more assimilated Tagalog areas of the archipelago also made use of supernatural concepts during the revolution, although in this case they drew them from the indigenized Passion story. As Ileto has pointed out, a text that was, after all, part of the apparatus of colonial rule therefore evolved toward very different political ends. The Tagalog Passion had become a fund of antihierarchical idioms of Christian social justice, recast within a distinctively local form of understanding.

The Tagalog *Casaysayan* is also central to the work of Vicente Rafael, writing on the earlier end of the Spanish period. Rafael's work extends Ileto's insight into the indigenization of a formerly colonial language of power, by showing how in the processes of translation from Spanish to

Tagalog terminology there arose a number of untranslatable "gaps" in meaning. As a consequence seventeenth-Century Tagalogs "translated" Christianity into terms that more closely approximated an adapted form of their own understandings of social reciprocity and exchange.

Rafael argues that the *Casaysayan* was in fact only a supplement to a much longer work by Aquino de Belen concerned with the art of Christian death and the fate of the soul (Rafael 1988: 196–209).[8] Such works were intended to assist the conversion process in the Philippines by bringing home to new Christians the crucial importance of placing the value of the afterlife unequivocally above the value of the life of this world, and managing both moral behavior and the processes of confession, absolution, and penance, so as to be saved and not damned. They were thus welcomed by Spanish priests wrestling with the sometimes disconcerting viewpoints of their new parishioners. Rafael shows us (1988: 166) that such texts also became the special preserve of Tagalog lay catechists, usually drawn from the local elite, on whom the Spanish church (chronically short of manpower) was obliged to rely, and who thus inserted themselves into the new regime of power.[9] Such instructors were often entrusted with the physical possession of the religious books themselves (Schumacher 1981: 86) and therefore became both the literal and the metaphorical brokers of Christian meaning. This position was even more crucial because throughout the Spanish period there was very little Spanish-language education available for most Filipinos, and only the wealthy elite were able to bring their children up speaking the language of their colonizers and therefore able to deal with them on their own terms.

However, the appeal of Christian conversion for the mass of ordinary people, for whom the rewards of participation in the material and symbolic order of colonialism could never be as great, remained to be explained. Here, and centrally for the argument of the present chapter, Rafael stresses the attraction of the Catholic notion of salvation for Filipino converts. Rafael accepts (together with myself and many other writers on the Philippines) the historian W. H. Scott's argument (1983) that the basic structure of precolonial society was defined by variations on debt bondage; social relationships were therefore constructed through idioms of exchange, either benevolent or predatory. One particularly haunting image was of the fate of the dead, who were exposed to the possibility of endless postmortem predation by spirits; while the elite might buy their way out of this threat by providing sacrificial substitutes (usually slaves) and ritual protection for their people at death, the poor went into the next world as they had lived in this—undefended. Citing contemporary Tagalog poetry describing the joy of the soul in heaven, Rafael argues (1988: 174) that Christianity, on the other hand, offered—to Tagalog eyes—a Paradise in which bliss consisted in freedom from this specter of social predation. The *Casaysayan* therefore formed part of an instruction manual on how to reach this Tagalog version of heaven, and its language, addressing Christianity's central proposition yet subtly reformulating its meaning by retaining its store of untranslatable local resonances, offered a bridge for the colonized to the world of the colonizer, even for those who could not speak Spanish. The irony of the situation was thus that, as the new Tagalog Christians appeared to be learning to deal for the first time in the terms of Christian theology, they were simultaneously and subtly transforming it, thus retaining areas of thought which their colonizers could not invade.

Rafael, then, is convinced that a crucial factor in attracting Tagalogs to Christianity was the notion of Paradise, but he also emphasizes how great was the effort involved in translating (even partially) such a new idea. In this focus on salvationism as the defining feature of the Christian religion, from which the social dynamics of its adherents must follow, his argument falls within an area of agreement in the literature that is, broadly speaking, descended from Hegel's characterization of Christianity.[10]

For Hegel, the historical development of religions from the time of the ancient Greeks onward produced certain kinds of problems that were expressed most intensely in Christianity. In particular, the attribution of divine power to a single, transcendent God, and the corresponding loss of belief in a power immanent in the world, left men with a melancholy sense of being orphaned, or painfully distanced from contact with the divine, which Hegel sometimes referred to as the "unhappy consciousness." Christians would continually face the question of how to relate to a God who, generally speaking, was not present in this world, but in the world beyond to which normal consciousness did not have access, and the parallel problem that the life after death was to be valued more highly than the life of this world, establishing what others have called an "economy of salvation." Anthropologists have generally interpreted this line of thinking to mean that a key focus in the study of Christianity should be the constant attempts Christians make to mediate between themselves and this too-distant deity, while always being pressured to remain within the boundaries of what the Church regards as the doctrinally permissible.

Above all, Christian theology sets up hierarchies, often dualistic in form, which are disturbed only at peril to the innovator,[11] and in which the key contrast is the supervaluation of the transcendent and the devaluation of the ordinary life of the world.

Rafael's account of the logic of early Filipino conversion is not written in these terms, but is partly identifiable with them. For the Spanish of the early modern period, as he reminds us, the unanswerable superiority of God's order over the earthly order was properly to be reflected in the supremacy of the church over souls, and of the Spanish king (also the Holy Roman Emperor) over his subjects, native and colonial. At this level, the new Spanish hierarchies were to some extent reconfigured, for Rafael stresses that the Tagalogs made use of the "gaps" afforded by translation difficulties to retain much of their own notion of exchange within the Christianity to which they converted.[12] Rafael also explains the motivation of (respectively) elite and commoner Tagalogs for conversion, however, in terms which reflect his view that each group for its own reasons had accepted a version of the Christian teaching which placed heaven and hell as incommensurables to this world, and which focused the Christian mind on those destinations. Both groups accepted the idea of a morally transcendent world beyond, and in that sense, both were integrated into an innovatory form of hierarchy.[13]

In this essay, I will argue that in the case of Bicol, both the picture Rafael paints of the centrality of translation to conversion and the generally accepted notion of the universality of the salvationist mode of thought in Christianity need to be taken further and approached from other angles. I will make this argument by looking in more detail at the ways in which popular sacred texts such as the Bicol *Pasion* were appropriated, and by looking not only at the content of such texts, but also at the ways in which the activities of "reading" and "writing," as they figured specifically in the lowland Philippines, might have altered textual meaning.

In order to make these arguments, it is crucial to recognize that the issues surrounding translation in the conversion of the Philippines were even more complex than Rafael shows us, for the languages attempting to speak to each other were not only two (Spanish and Tagalog) but many more than two.

Spanish missionaries in the Philippines had determined from the outset on a policy of evangelizing in native languages only, in order to promote a faster and more unequivocal understanding of Christian teaching among potential converts. Despite this commitment, however, it was quite impossible until this century for Catholicism to be monolingual. Spanish (technically, Castilian) prayers and devotional works were sourcebooks for priests and missionaries, and they clearly attracted the keen interest of members of the local elite who, like Aquino de Belen, wished to be able to speak not only Christian doctrine but also fluent Castilian. Moreover, the central office of the Catholic faith, the Mass, could not be conducted in any tongue but Latin until the Second Vatican Council (1962–65) ruled that henceforward it should be celebrated in local languages. The office to which missionaries pointed as the central mystery of the faith, and as the crucial meeting between God and man, was therefore spoken in a Castilian version of a language that virtually no Filipino would be taught. Two largely mysterious languages containing secrets of the new religion were therefore in circulation during the early Spanish period, and it is my consistent observation that, despite Vatican II, prayers and texts in Spanish or Latin are still greatly prized by Bicolanos today, although they are rarely if ever able to tell the difference between the two. In addition, one has to recognize an internal economy of translation from one Filipino language to another, which has accompanied the historical development of Filipino Christianity, as the original Tagalog *Casaysayan* was produced in Bicol-language and other versions around the archipelago.

Reading as a Gift

If the Tagalog *Casaysayan* was the means by which the colonial elite of the early-eighteenth-century Philippines inserted themselves into the modified economy of salvation, one might wonder what the status of the Bicol translation of that document was, and what the implications are of its enormous popularity with ordinary Bicolano farmers and barangay people. Was the Bicol *Pasion*, produced in the mid–nineteenth century, intended in any sense as a token of submission to the logic of the Catholic Church, as the Tagalog *Casaysayan* had been in the early eighteenth century?

While the detailed local history of the region is still being written, any interpretation must remain slightly speculative. The circumstances of the *Pasion*'s translation, however, suggest that in some ways this may have been the case. The *Pasion* was translated from the Tagalog at the instigation of the Archbishop Fransisco Gainza, a reforming figure who dedicated his time in Naga to producing a renaissance in texts in the Bicol language, all of which had religious subjects.[14] His aim was, that these texts should become widely available so as to increase Bicolanos' understanding of their religion (Abella 1954: 171–82), thus renewing and replicating the intention of the first missionaries.

There is an unexplained ambiguity in the literature over the authorship of the Bicol *Pasion*, some citing Gainza himself, while others give the author as Hernandez. This ambiguity appears to arise from the preamble to the book, in which a dedicatory letter by Gainza is followed by a second letter by one Tranquilino Hernandez, signing himself in October 1866 as "former captain of Polangui" (a small town in Camarines Sur):

> To the most holy and most respected and venerable Dr. D. Fransisco Gainza, rightful Archbishop of this Nueva Carceres:
>
> Excellent Sir,
>
> I have only recently really come to know the travails and sufferings of our most beloved Father, because of the good deed that one owes the blessed God, and thus you see indeed that your inner feelings did not turn until this dear Passion of Our Lord Jesus Christ was put into the Bicol language so that it might illuminate our cloudy understandings, for the truth is, Excellency, and I will make it known so that no one can any longer conceal it, that *we Bicolanos up until now, the most part of us, were just mouthing the Passion in Tagalog, getting some information from it if we got some information from it, and not if not, and otherwise just reading only. . . .*
>
> To you, my beloved Father, I was constantly making appeals that you should examine and look deeply into this translation into Bicol for yea, indeed, this is what is truly called "the vulgar tongue," for you know indeed my miserable failures in these tasks. For indeed moreover my mouth would indeed have been heavy in giving my "yes sirs" to you, due as they say to the miserableness and lowness of my understanding, but however I strengthened my spirits in the reliance and hope of the help of the dear God in these same tasks. For why, my Father, because if you had anything to forbid or to command in this work, I was given the hint . . . and I was made to know it, for your heart and breast are full of these extra blessings [*cadugdugan*, literally, something added on]. *Accordingly, my Father, this little fatigue of mine that has been worried over and watched over long into the night, will perhaps be counted as something more, o [thou who art] full of feeling*, as I count on the help of my beloved Father . . . and accordingly indeed *my hope of your precious blessing*

here in the passing world and your miserable servant [literally, sheep / flock animal] always kisses your sacred hand.

At the foot of the letter is a note, apparently addressed to the future "readers" of the *Pasion*: "The author asks for his due from anyone who reads this: of one 'Our father.' "[15]

This letter suggests, although not with absolute certainty, that Hernandez was responsible for the translation, and for Gainza commissioning it, and that just as the Tagalog *Casaysayan* was translated as a Catholic conversion text but by a Filipino person, so the Bicol version of that text was translated at the instigation of a reformist Spanish Archbishop but by a Bicolano member of the provincial elite.

This letter is a rather strange document. It seems to hover between a respectful address to the archbishop, and a prayer to the Christ of the Passion, and at times, it is unclear which of them is being addressed; who is it, for instance, who was beseeched to examine and guide the author's translation, the "father" bishop, or the "father" Christ? The two seem almost to be conflated, perhaps not inappropriately for one who has accepted the authority of the church. The author of this letter seems indeed to be perfectly clear about the orthodox interpretation of such religious devotions; in the first paragraph he emphasizes the importance of really understanding the deeds and sufferings of Christ, by having them revealed in the Bicol language, while in the second paragraph he makes very proper references to this life as the "passing world" and asks for the reader to pray for him, which implies that he believes in Purgatory and official Catholic doctrine on the afterlife. Nevertheless, there remains something strangely fervent and elliptical about the phrasing, which suggests that he was not entirely at ease.[16]

If the Bicol *Pasion* was seen by its translator as a declaration of enthusiastic submission to the authority of the church, that same submission to the church and its interpretations was no doubt expected of his readers. In fact, wider evidence seems to suggest that the act of reading itself was for rural people inextricably associated with religious submission throughout the Spanish period.

Spanish period rural education was in the hands of the religious.[17] There is no doubt that the standard of education for those who could not reach the major towns was highly uneven and sometimes extremely low. The priest was nominally in charge of most village schools, while very young children might be taught their letters by a lay catechist, sometimes a woman. The traveler Feodor Jagor, who journeyed through Bicol sometime between 1857 and 1873, recorded some brief—and unfavorable—impressions of the schooling of Bicol children at that period, adding that: "a kind of religious horn book is the first thing that is read in the language of the country, and after that comes the Christian Doctrine, the reading-book called CASAYSAYAN" (Jagor [1875] 1965: 118).

Whether Jagor actually meant to indicate the Bicol version of the *Doctrina Christiana*—the book that contains what children needed to know in order to be confirmed[18] or whether there was also some other book of Biblical stories to which he was referring—or whether the schoolchildren of Bicol were actually being asked to read the Passion-story "Casaysayan" itself in either Tagalog or Bicol, is difficult to determine. It is certain, however, that until the inception of the radical primary school system of the American colonial regime, reading—even at the simplest level of the learning of the alphabet from a hornbook—must have been inseparably linked for ordinary Bicol children to the reading of prayers and other texts, to the questions of the priest, and to the authority of the church.

What, then, does it mean for present-day Bicolanos to insist that what they are doing, during Lenten vigils, is "reading" the *Pasion*? First, we know from Hernandez's letter (and this is borne out by statements made by troupes of specialist Passion players I knew in Bicol) that the Bicol text replaced as a "clarification" the Tagalog text that had been used (read) before. According to the Passion-players, the Tagalog text was not just read privately, but was also read in performance. Since Tagalog is fairly readily but incompletely understood by Bicolanos, one can imagine a phase in which the Passion (i.e., the *Casaysayan*) constituted yet another layer of the polylingual, half-understood, half-recognized religious texts with which Bicolanos were surrounded.

The Archbishop's intentions have to some extent been realized. Bicolano *Pasion* singers are perfectly capable of explaining many of the episodes given in the text they "read," as well as of rhetorically quoting a number of passages from it, and they themselves emphasize their skill in producing the words clearly, a statement that would no doubt have gladdened the heart of the local priest. Yet at the same time, they stress the "matching," "harmony," and "pairing" of their two voices, concepts that refer to ideas of balance, testing, and blending in Bicol rhetorical techniques in quite different contexts (such as formal riddling contests and courtship ritual). The extent to which Bicolano people literally "read" in our sense when they perform the *Pasion* is, therefore, debatable. Actual performances often depart to some extent from what is printed on the page, and my observation over many readings is that singers rely on memory as much as on the text, despite the length of the piece. Semi-memorized, the reproduction of the *Pasion* occupies a space between the exclusively oral and the exclusively literate.

The technology of performance also goes far beyond what we mean by *reading*. In singing pairs, one person always leads, while the second harmonizes and ornaments the line. The way in which this is organized musically actually cuts across the structure of what is printed on the page. Thus while the *Pasion* is arranged in stanzas of five lines throughout, the musical ornamentation occurs principally at the ends of the first, second, and fifth lines and runs together the others in rhythms determined by the chant more than by the meter of the printed line. To know where to ornament, as well as to learn the wide repertoire of possible musical variations appropriate for particular points in the text, requires complex knowledge and experience, none of which can be read from the book itself. The performance of the *Pasion* by singing pairs in some respects actually seems to replicate a common pattern in Bicol religious performances generally. Rather as one member of the pair leads each verse (with ornamental interruptions) and the other joins in, so in many other circumstances (such as the performance of hymns to the patron saint of the barangay sung while carrying his statue on procession) a prompter will read out the lines from a single text slightly ahead of the moment when the group of performers needs to sing it; often, the prompter will start reading while the singers are still completing the line before, producing a slightly syncopated effect in the performance. Bicolano reading often has this quality of interruption, of something extra being interjected. The line is not produced on a direct path from eye to mouth.

What is even more important is that, although the words that the singers read are perfectly orthodox and are intended for their enlightenment, and although they may reproduce these words with some attention to clarity, the relationship of exchange into which they insert them is not the one intended by the church.

To be more precise, the evidence from my own fieldwork is that Filipinos such as the poor and rural people with whom I lived are relatively uninterested in the classic Christian "economy of salvation."[19] People in Bicol rarely spontaneously mention the ideas of heaven or hell, and I have never once heard them mention the notion of Purgatory.

Although they have a keen sense of moral behavior, they are also unlikely to refer to the possibility of damnation when talking about wrongdoers; instead, those who transgress in Bicol are said to have a very difficult time dying at all, lingering in their final illness until they have "paid back their debts," or visiting the living as ghosts. While Bicolanos are keen Catholics, they also attend Mass rather infrequently (preferring to sponsor novenas, say prayers at home, or visit a shrine), and they make confession and receive communion still less often. Moreover, they seem to feel no particularly pressing need to receive extreme unction before death. While the Catholic Church regards access to the offices of a priest as essential for salvation, therefore, ordinary Bicolanos are not especially priest-centered, nor are they deeply invested in a morality within the economy of salvation, which is centered on sin, repentance, and justice in the next life.

I am not trying here to claim that rural Bicolanos are unfamiliar with the basic teachings of the church or incapable of understanding the messages of the *hulit* (little sermons) that punctuate the *Pasion* text. It is simply that, although a very great deal of talk in Bicol concerns saints, death, and the supernatural, the topics of sin and the fate of the soul are very rarely to the forefront of anyone's mind.

Death practices in Bicol outwardly conform to the requirements of the church, in that these days even the poor feel a requiem mass is desirable. But the real concerns of the bereaved are not phrased as a question about whether the departed is suffering in hell or enjoying heaven. Instead the focus is on a complex and gradual process of separation of the living and the dead, in which the "pity" of the dead must be deflected before it causes harm to their surviving relatives, and of which the end point is a state in which the dead are in some ways deliberately "forgotten," being "remembered" only once a year, on All Soul's Day, when they have the right to eat and sleep with the living.

The domain to which souls vanish, moreover, is a somewhat ominous but extremely indistinct destination called the *kadikloman* (literally, dark place), which is blurred in Bicol talk and practice with the world of the nonhuman spirits (or "people we cannot see"), from whom indeed the dead are not entirely distinguished.

Far from being a guarantor of a hierarchical order within which personhood is constructed, therefore, the Bicolano idea of the afterlife seems designed to evade categorization and judgment and to refuse to separate out one thing from another. I never knew a single person to mention the note from Archbishop Gainza at the front of the *Pasion*, which promises forty days' indulgences from suffering in Purgatory to "whatever Christian reads this with true feeling and in remembrance of the sufferings of Jesus Christ Almighty." Many, if not all, however, read the *Pasion* in the expectation of healing from sickness for themselves or others, which would be granted by a contract not with a universal Christ, but with a very particular one, the local cult figure of the *Amang Hinulid*, or "dead Christ." This figure—a painfully realistic image of Christ laid out for burial—is from the church's point of view meant to dramatize the passage from Good Friday to Easter Sunday, and it was the theme of the Resurrection and the church triumphant on which Bicolano missionaries took care to place the greatest emphasis. From the local point of view, however, the figure is always the "*dead* Christ," and the culmination of the religious year is Good Friday, not Easter day. The *Ama* does not so much mediate between a transcendent and an earthly reality as constantly travel backward and forward between the "visible world" and the *kadikloman*, which, although certainly supernatural, is not morally superior to ordinary life as the Christian heaven is meant to be. In this, he acts like the most accomplished of the shamans, for whom his shrine is a focal point.

"Reading" the *Pasion*, therefore, probably does in some senses constitute a subordination of the reader to the church's meanings, but the readers themselves are somehow capable of directing the gift not to the church (whose officiants are, after all, nowhere present during these household devotions) but to their own idea of the *Ama*, the Father, whose primary concern with them is, from their point of view, not to subject them to the disciplines of the Christian economy of salvation but to provide them with shamanistic gifts of healing power.

Writing as Theft

According to the Franciscan chronicler Ribadeneira, the Bicolanos of the early seventeenth century were enthusiastic to use writing to record the words of the missionaries:

> The desire which they have to hear the Word of God causes many to make their own little books, like Books of Hours, in which they write with their own characters or letters what the Father preaches to them, in order not to forget it. They ordinarily ask the ministers to tell and recount to them the lives of the saints, and particularly like to hear the life and miracles of our

> Lady and of women saints who were penitents. They are careful to write it all down and they read it frequently with great delight for their souls, and try to do works which are in conformity with the examples that they hear from the friars. (Ribadeneira, quoted in Schumacher, ed., 1987: 84)

This passage is one of several by the same chronicler that stress the pliant and penitentially inclined temperament of the new Bicolano converts, stressing their thirst to attend mass and confession, their ready understanding of sin, and their penitential fervor, all of which were read as signs of their newly awakened fear of hell.

The religious dictation sessions Ribadeneira describes are intriguing for a number of reasons. First, there is the issue of language; the chronicler seems to be stressing those occasions on which the missionaries were preaching (therefore in Bicol); yet, though he also mentions the enthusiasm of the Bicolanos for the Mass, there is no mention of words (which would of course have been in Latin) being taken down in that context. For the Spanish religious, their converts engaged in writing simply as an act of receptivity to the clear and unequivocal messages of the Christian God and his agents. Second, Ribadeneira, writing at this early date, notes that the Bicolanos took their notes in their own script.

Indigenous Filipino scripts (which are quite closely related to each other) are mentioned by several other of the early chroniclers, many of whom learned the script and who give examples written in it. As Scott (1984: 52–61) and other historians have noted, the scripts were more ambiguous than those using the roman alphabet. In Filipino script, there are characters for all the consonants of the language, but vowel markers did not distinguish between *e* and *i*, or between *o* and *u* (*a* has a marker to itself), while the endings of words were also ambiguous.[20] Thus in a famous passage Gaspar de San Augustin complains that a certain two letters of the syllabary "can be read in eight ways, which are *lili* (side), *lilim* (shade), *lilip* (border), *lilis* (to raise), *lilit* (?), *lilim* (the act of shading something), *liclic* (to deviate), *liglig* (to drop something), and with all these they are understood" (San Augustin, *Compendio*, quoted in Rafael 1988: 45–47).

To read a Filipino script thus required both an intimate familiarity with the language and a pleasure and skill in guessing, which in certain contexts such as in the writing of love-verses was probably a deliberately cultivated art form akin to riddling, and which was called in Tagalog *baybayin* (to coast). The apparent scene of religious dictation, therefore, actually contained at least two potential sources of ambiguity: there was the question of what the Filipino listeners would have made of (or written down of) the Latin liturgy rather than the Bicol exegesis when they heard it, and there was the question of the possible ambiguities arising from the script.

Ribadeneira notes that at the same period, Bicolanos were already putting on dramatic performances that represented the lives of the saints and were also already "begging" to be taught novenas and to be given items such as rosaries and pictures of Christ and the saints, which they kept on small altars in their houses (Schumacher 1987: 86). They were also themselves carving circular medallions with images of the saints, which they wore as protective amulets, a practice that seems to be a direct continuation of the carving of such medals of especially powerful *anitos* (ancestors / spirits), which were also worn in the same way. In fact, while to missionary eyes all this activity looked highly orthodox—and the Bicolanos themselves no doubt felt they were celebrating a conversion of significance and the acquisition of new deities—from the outside, it looks like a range of directly appropriative activities, of which I would suggest the religious dictation formed a part.

Indigenous Filipino scripts were thought unsuitable and inaccurate by the missionaries, and Filipino lowlanders were rapidly brought to abandon them in favor of the roman alphabet and the Spanish style of writing. Nevertheless, I would argue that writing remained an important instrument of Filipino appropriation, and rather as Rafael has argued that Filipinos continued to enjoy an aesthetic in which the unambiguous meaning of words was temporarily suspended, and to deploy this attitude to language in resistance to colonial norms, I would argue that Filipinos also continued to enjoy forms of writing that reveled in ambiguity and both opposed those forms of ambiguity to Spanish priorities and parodied ambiguities they found in Spanish texts.

Throughout contemporary Bicol, as in much of the rest of the lowlands, spirit mediums and ordinary people alike make frequent use of a written form called *orasion*, which I would translate as prayer spells, since the word conveys both meanings; in fact, the use of orasion is part of a deliberate resistance to the attempt to separate "legitimate" Christian power from "illegitimate" forms of power derived from the spirits, in Bicol healing practice. The more prayer spells one has, the more likely one is also to have mastery of a range of other broadly shamanic powers. The greatest adepts collected their many prayer spells together into a volume known as a "little book" or *librito*.

A Bicolano *pamontra* (from the author's field notes)

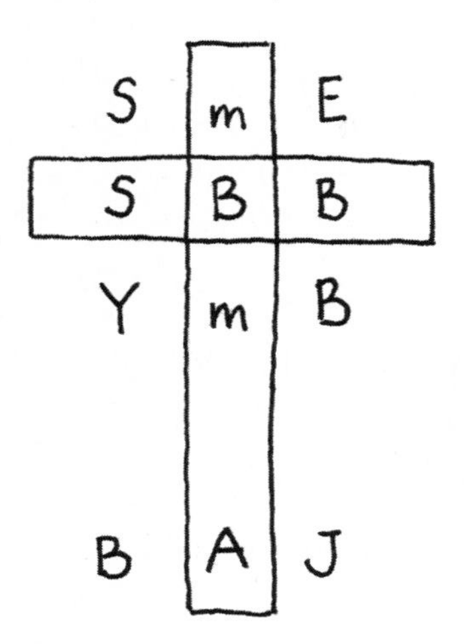

The libritos contain a range of prayer spells that fall within a fairly standard repertoire. One common form, for instance, is the pamontra, or protective prayer spell to stop harm befalling one, especially harm caused by the spirits. The form of such an orasion is usually a drawing or diagram with some religious allusion, surrounded by arrangements of letters that appear to be abbreviations, and an accompanying text.

In the case of the pamontra I was kindly taught in Bicol, the text runs:

Sa marumpot na Espiritu
sara Be Bolo me
Yoto divan some
me dios me Bolo
mia Beduara Amen
Jesus.

The text clearly combines Bicol words (*marumpot*, wicked, for example) and Spanish and Latin terms, which, as I mentioned earlier, most Bicolano people cannot distinguish.

Such texts clearly combine together many elements taken from heard

Catholic liturgy, but they also draw on written or printed models. Although I was never able to photocopy a Bicolano librito (their owners understandably do not lend them out), I can illustrate some of their characteristics by using an example from archives, which as far as I know has not been discussed in the literature. This is the text published by the bibliophile Wenceslao Retana in 1894 as *Supersticiones de los indios filipinos: Un libro de aniterias*. Retana, introducing his rare find, explains that he had it copied in 1892 from an original in a Dominican monastery in Avila, where it had been brought back by a priest, Lafuente, who had been formerly stationed in Santa Barbara, Pangasinan, in the Philippines. The text was thought to have been written in about 1845–55, and had been confiscated by a tribunal from a Filipino "bandit"—that is, from someone engaged in anti-Spanish guerrilla activities. Such books of prayer spells were often used by rebels against the state, and this special purpose marks the librito, which contains many suited to this purpose; prayer spells against firearms, small arms, and hand arms, against the system of justice (i.e., the courts), those for winning in wrestling and in struggles, for escaping when captured, those against traitors who might give one away, and so on. However, all such libritos (certainly all those I have heard of in Bicol) probably contained at least some of these kinds of spells, and its militaristic tone therefore does not make it entirely untypical, though it made it of special interest to the Spanish.

The original book, Retana tells us, was handwritten on cheap blue commercial paper and bound by its owner, who carried it hidden in a scapular. When he had it copied, Retana asked the priest Lafuente to add notes on each page, explaining what he understood of their meaning, for the librito is written in a mixture of Latin, Spanish, and Pangasineno (the local language). The book as published is therefore also an interesting guide to what the priest thought of his "bandit" parishioners' collection of prayer spells, and their style of presentation.

Besides the military prayers, the librito contained some which are typical of a Filipino "shamanic" repertoire, such as prayer spells against snakes, witchcraft, and lightning (9); to seduce women (16); to propitiate crocodiles (associated with spirits) (34); against snakes, against malintentioned people, to stop them carrying out those intentions (74); to become invisible (85); to protect the body from disease; to protect against malign and predatory spirits, especially the dreaded *aswang* (a form of viscera-sucking witch); to be protected on journeys and when entering and leaving the barangay (23) and so on (a Bicolano collection would also include an orasion to travel swiftly by land and water, and another to be able to keep the bones of your ancestors in the house and harness their supernatural power as guardians without coming to any harm).

The logic of such spells informs other aspects of lowland, at least Bicolano, magical practice. One is in a world of supernatural forces pitted against each other, and what matters is both to acquire the assistance of those who are more powerful than oneself and to acquire a range of patrons (human and supernatural) who can act as protectors. Thus the book repeatedly makes appeals to a whole series of Catholic saints; Saint John is to fight with the guerrillas on the battlefield (36), and the Virgin, Christ, and local patrons such as Santa Barbara are also invoked. This appropriative logic goes further, however, for it attempts to redefine the nature of the saints and holy figures, claiming an origin for them which is different to that given by the church. On page 33, for example, the author recommends that three paternosters should be recited to Santa Barbara, who is then referred to as "the grandmother of Jesus Christ." Lafuente explains (in Spanish), "the first part is indecipherable; what follows seems to mean; that when (the grandmother of Christ) was a heathen, she was called as is indicated in the symbolic letter which precedes this [spell]. But since she has been baptized, they impose on her the name of Siontisia;—there follows a recommendation that 3 Paternosters, a Credo and a Salve should be recited."

Again, on page 61, we have more of this alternative version of origins. The librito mentions the *troncalis na mundo* (a Spanish-Pangasineno phrase, meaning "trunk or origin of the world," which was also the title of a famous popular book of religion). Lafuente comments:

> We can deduce from the context, that here one is dealing with the principal or origin of the created world, and that introduces god the father, the son and the holy spirit, which are referred to as *insimi santo*. . . . there follows, the name of the grandmother of the aforesaid tres personas, when she was still a pagan, and before they were all baptized by themselves, which was *Itate*, and the name of the Son *Miset*, *Sin Cristno*, because when they baptized themselves they released themselves, and they were at the mountain which is called Burney . . . and the name of the grandfather was *Sordoban*. (Retana 1894: 65)

Now, in more fragmentary form (for after all, contemporary Bicol is not the site of millenial revolution), alternative views about the creation are

An illustration of Spanish-style Filipino prayer book typography (after the 1963 edition of the Bicol *Pasion*)

MAGNA PAGNADIEON

GABOS NA SUCAT MANODAN

NIN TAUONG CRISTIANO

AN PAGNURUS

Sa pag tadaan ✠ nin Santa Cruz, Cagurangnan ✠ niamong Dios, agauon mo cami ✠ sa samong magna caiual, sa pangnaran nin Dios Ama, asin nin Dios Aqui, ✠ patin nin Dios Espiritu. Amen Jesus.

✞

AN PAGSOLSOL NIN CASALAN

Cagurangnan cong Jesucristo, Dios na totoo, asin tauo naman na totoo, Cagguibo, asin Cagtubos sacuya, nagsosolsol acong gayo nin todoc na pagsosolsol ninsi pagcasala co sa saimo, huli can sinanglitan na

✠

also current in Bicol and the Visayas,[21] while the use of numinous appellations for spirits, and claims that they are simultaneously Christian divine figures, are very common. While the guerrillas' librito is obviously making a claim to an alternative supernatural genealogy in a more extreme and deliberately antihierarchical form, it is not radically divorced from ordinary day-to-day lowland practices.

The librito's written appearance is very close to the Bicolano orasion. There are several types of text. Some involve largely comprehensible and sequential (though always idiosyncratic) passages of Latin prayer, on which Lafuente comments with tolerance if not approval. Some mix Latin fragments with passages of Castilian and Pangasineno. It is important to note how the librito is studded with instructions like those that would be given by a priest or catechist (or in the text of the Passion story): "Say 3 Paternosters: say a Credo" and so on. These recommendations, tapping into the power of the church, are meant to give efficacy and legitimacy to the spells, to activate them, as it were. Some prayer spells are in more diagrammatic or pictorial form, although again it is important to note that throughout the text, the author frequently inserts an imitation of the printed sign of the cross, +, which was constantly used to punctuate Spanish Catholic religious documents, and Lafuente notes that the captured guerrilla (who was no doubt also a healer) had explained in jail that at these signs, the user should make the sign of the cross over a patient, as the priest makes the sign of the cross over his congregation in blessing. Again, this gesture (called *santiguar* from the Spanish) is constantly used in Bicolano healing and mediumship.

Where the prayer spells are most diagrammatic, they are marked not by representationality (as, for instance, a Filipino sorcerer might make a wax image of an intended victim), but by a play with the arrangement of letters on the page, which obviously refers to and models itself on Spanish printed religious texts. But what is also very striking is the use of formally arranged letters, which appear to be word markers with some of the letters, especially the vowels, taken out (as one might write in English m—th—r as for *mother*). On page 12, for example, is a sequence of letters:

N g m
M t m
L t m
N t m
— — —.

A page from Lafuente's *librito* (Retana 1894: 12–13). Reproduced with the kind permission of Cornell University, from their Kroch (Asia) Collections.

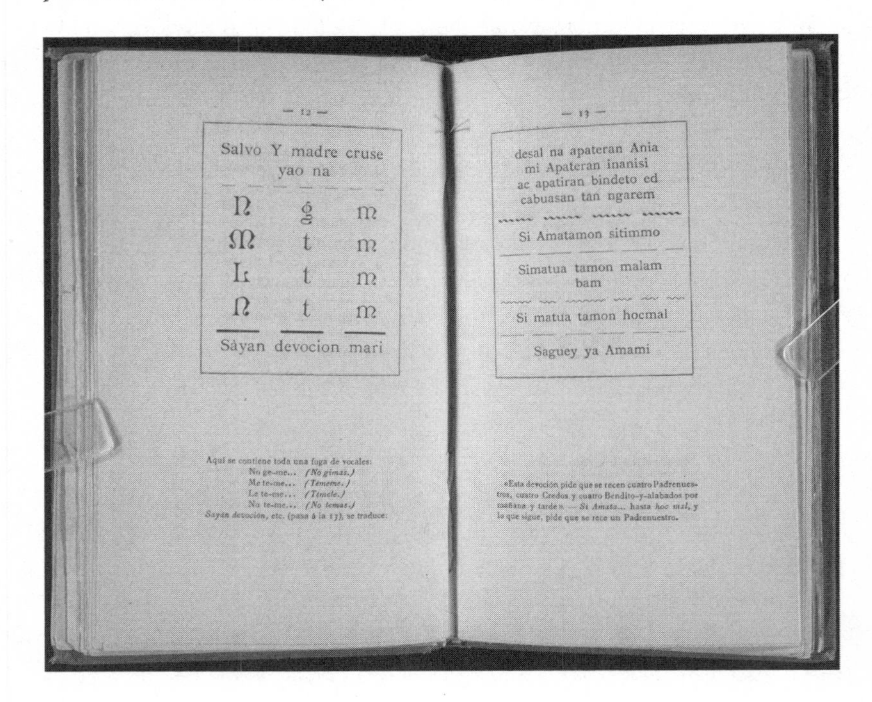

— 12 —

Salvo Y madre cruse
yao na

N g m
M t m
L t m
N t m

Sàyan devocion mari

Aquí se contiene toda una fuga de vocales:
No ge-me... *(No gimas.)*
Me te-me... *(Téme me.)*
Le te-me... *(Témele.)*
No te-me... *(No temas.)*
Sayan devocion, etc. (pasa á la 13), se traduce:

— 13 —

desal na apateran Ania
mi Apateran inanisi
ac apatiran bindeto ed
cabuasan tan ngarem

Si Amatamon sitimmo

Simatua tamon malam
bam

Si matua tamon hocmal

Saguey ya Amami

«Esta devoción pide que se recen cuatro Padrenuestros, cuatro Credos y cuatro Bendito-y-alabados por mañana y tarde» — *Si Amata...* hasta *hoc mal*, y lo que sigue, pide que se rece un Padrenuestro.

Under these, Lafuente comments, "Here one finds a whole fugue of vowels: No-ge-me (Don't groan) Me te-me (Fear me) Le-te-me (Fear him) No te-me (don't fear) . . ."

While the capitalization, and the painstaking formation of the letters in the original, are clearly references both to the insistent (and to the non-Spanish reader, mysterious) use of capitals and abbreviations in Spanish religious books (letters standing for the religious orders, for titles, for statuses in the church, Latin Scriptural tags such as I.N.R.I., etc.). They also seem to recall the arrangement of letters in the alphabets of Filipino Spanish-period hornbooks (which were of course always religious and always taught by the church's officers or delegates). Third, however, one might wish to reflect on the reactions to such spells of the Spanish priest Lafuente. Although relatively tolerant and curious in tone at the outset, his remarks degenerate into near-fury through the hundred-odd pages of the book, and the more distant the orasion is from "comprehensible" Latin (as well as the more subversive the intention of the spell against the state), the more irritated he becomes. On page 23, for instance, he re-

A page from Lafuente's *librito* (Retana 1894: 28–29). Reproduced with the kind permission of Cornell University Library, from their Kroch (Asia) Collections.

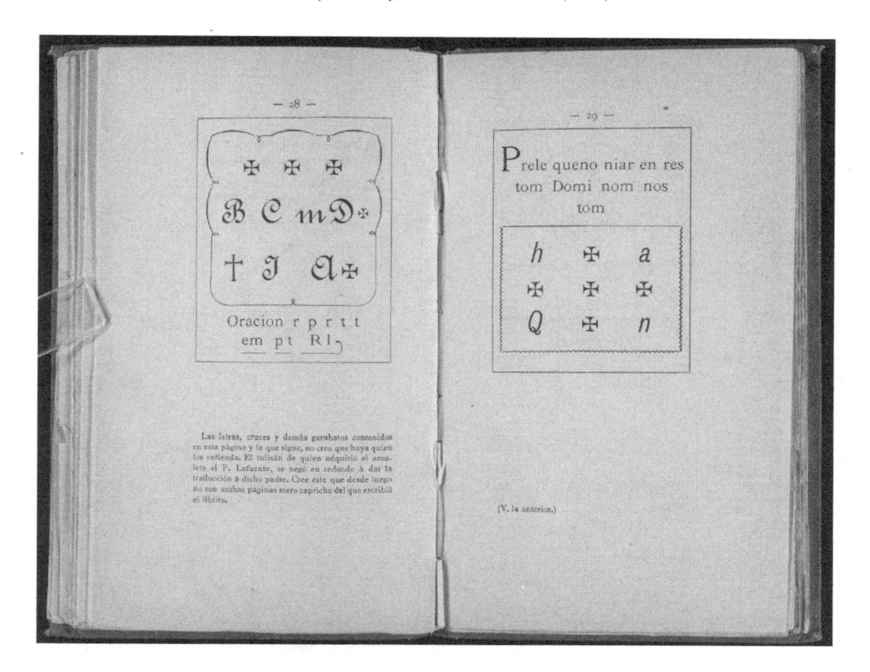

— 28 —

Oracion r p r t t
em pt RI

Las letras, cruces y demás garabatos contenidos en esta página y la que sigue, no creo que haya quien los entienda. El tulisán de quien adquirió el amuleto el P. Lafuente, se negó en redondo á dar la traducción á dicho padre. Cree éste que desde luego no son ambas páginas mero capricho del que escribió el librito.

— 29 —

Prele queno niar en res
tom Domi nom nos
tom

(V. la anterior.)

marks, "These symbolic letters only the privileged in this 'occult science' of the bandits know how to interpret"; on page 49, "More incomprehensible letters"; on page 71, "A prayer to Saint John, even although he is a saint, he will find himself in difficulties to decipher it," and on page 100, "It is difficult to annotate these bits and pieces; from page 95 to the end of this little work, there is a complete lack of sense."

The model from which some of the content of the Latin parts of the librito is taken is suddenly suggested to us by Lafuente right at the end of the book. "We know," he says, "that the *author* kept at hand at one time an old *Breviary* which he later lost, and remembering certain words through his readings, he arranged them—adulterating them at the same time—whence he turned them into this kind of object" (Retana 1894: 100). The breviary (in Latin) was intended, of course, for the use of the Spanish and especially the priests, and not for the Filipinos, who had their own native-language versions of "Christian doctrine," and it was probably this distinction that made it attractive to the guerrilla shaman. Whether he knew that the words he was copying were in Latin or whether he thought they were some more obscure reaches of Castilian

A page from Lafuente's *librito* (Retana 1894: 60–61). Reproduced with the kind permission of Cornell University Library, from their Kroch (Asia) Collections.

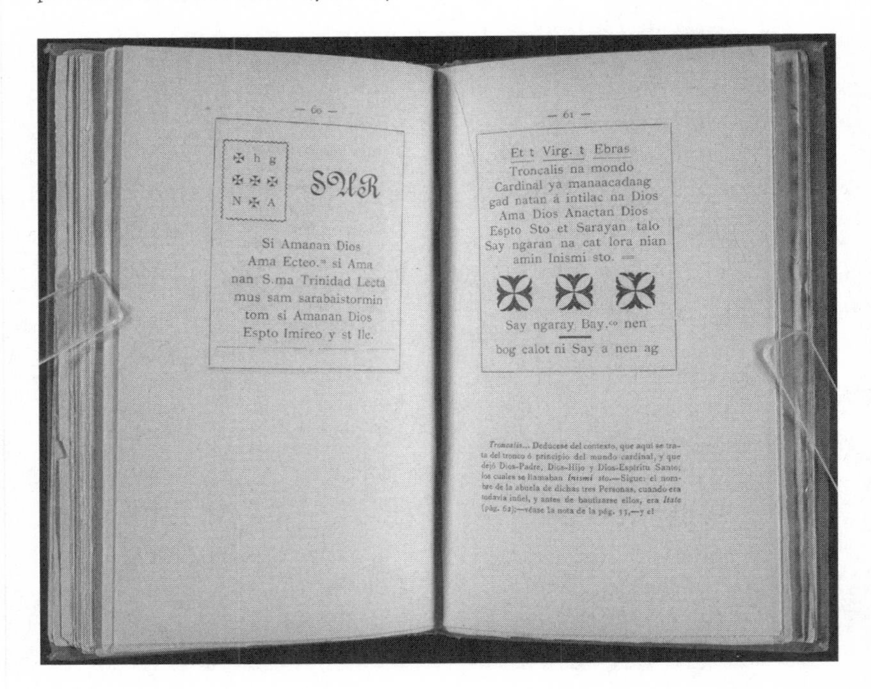

— 60 —

SMR

Si Amanan Dios
Ama Ecteo.[a] si Ama
nan S.ma Trinidad Lecta
mus sam sarabaistormin
tom si Amanan Dios
Espto Imireo y st Ile.

— 61 —

Et t Virg. t Ebras
Troncalis na mondo
Cardinal ya manaacadaag
gad natan á intilac na Dios
Ama Dios Anactan Dios
Espto Sto et Sarayan talo
Say ngaran na cat lora nian
amin Inismi sto. =

Say ngaray Bay.[co] nen
bog calot ni Say a nen ag

Troncalis... Dedúcese del contexto, que aquí se trata del tronco ó principio del mundo cardinal, y que dejó Dios-Padre, Dios-Hijo y Dios-Espíritu Santo; los cuales se llamaban *Inismi* sto.—Sigue: el nombre de la abuela de dichas tres Personas, cuando era todavía infiel, y antes de bautizarse ellos, era *Itate* (pág. 62);—véase la nota de la pág. 33,—y el

would be interesting to know; it is likely that few Filipinos made this distinction clearly. On the other hand, the words of the Latin Mass (albeit pronounced by Spanish priests, so probably sounding very much like Spanish)[22] may have intrigued many Filipinos, not only because of the obvious centrality of the ritual, but also because even for those who knew some Castilian, they would have remained at further remove from comprehension, powerful and familiar, yet inaccessible. Access could be provided only through memory and imagination, or through the half-comprehending examination of printed books in Latin.

I wonder, however, whether the "fugue of vowels" isn't also indicative of something more than a desire to imitate the layout of these Latin models. The play with sound and suspended meaning which the librito often invokes seems strangely reminiscent of the *baybayin* style of reading-as-riddling that belonged to the old Filipino scripts. Although I am not of course suggesting that the script itself (almost extinct by the 1630s) was somehow preserved into the nineteenth century, perhaps part of its aesthetic was; in a context in which power and magic often seem to reside in ambiguity and ambivalence, it would be extremely appropriate to perpetuate an attitude to writing that constantly evoked the ideas of mystery, hidden meaning, and the possibility of alternative interpretations by the skillful. If so, this would make the use of Latin (rather than just Castilian) by the librito writers even easier to understand, for the meaning of Latin for most Filipinos would almost inevitably be partially suspended and evasive. The librito is, from the Spanish point of view, a total inversion of the objectives of clear hierarchy of meaning and the transmission of orthodoxy to which the Passion (including the Bicol and other native-language Passions translated from the Tagalog at just the time this librito was written) dedicated itself. The book was politically subversive not just because of its association with guerrillas, but in its approach to knowledge, however scornfully this might be regarded by the priesthood. Perhaps the act of writing, as well as the act of reading invoked by Rafael's Derridean approach, was equally important in the transformation of relations of power in the colonial Philippines.

Books as Objects and the Circulation of Arcana

There is clear evidence that throughout the nineteenth century and the first two-thirds of the twentieth, there was a keen interest in the production, translation, and exchange of popular religious texts in provincial life, at the amateur level. This interest is probably in fact far older, since manuscripts of such texts and handwritten copies of hymns, stories, prayers, outlines of religious choreography for special performances, and so on have for a long time been (and still are) in intensive circulation in towns and villages. It seems clear, however, that the volume of cheap printed texts of Bible stories and homilies from local presses expanded greatly in the nineteenth century. The demand for and supply of these texts in Bicol was no doubt boosted by the activities of Archbishop Gainza. Despite the deficiencies of friar education, a degree of functional literacy always seems to have been comparatively high in Philippine rural areas. Moreover, insofar as many of the pieces (such as wedding addresses and other homilies) were probably written by Bicolano authors, the expansion of printing may have represented a crossover with the oral culture of the period, and with its rhetorical set pieces and styles.

While I was conducting fieldwork, I was haunted by the constant mention of two particular texts that were cited as additional sources for the construction of the Passion play and as objects of supernatural virtue.

These two texts, the *Tronco del Mundo* and the *Martir de Golgota*, were, however, never actually produced for me to see, as everyone always claimed to have lost them. Subsequent research revealed conflicting claims about these titles. The Tagalog-language *Tronco* is said to be a version of the Passion commissioned by the rebellious and heterodox Colorum movement (Javellena 1983: 288), while the *Pasyon Kandaba, martir sa Golgota*, again in Tagalog, is said to be a "translation of a Spanish fictionalised account of the life of Christ, from which are taken . . . colorful and beloved apocryphal characters" for the Passion plays (D. Fernandez 1996: 12). However, these sensible explanations misrepresent the fact that these titles are given vague and contradictory descriptions and variant titles in most of the references to them I have been able to find. The only Bicol-language *Tronco* I could find is a tame-looking collection of Old Testament stories in verse form, issued under Pope Pius VI (1939–51).[23] The only *Martir* I have found is a Tagalog extract, again in verse, whose title can be translated as *The Rejoicing of Heaven and Earth at the Most Holy Childbed of the Dear Virgin in the Blessed Cave or Stable of Bethlehem; Adapted from the Martir De Golgota.*[24] However, schoolteachers in the early 1950s in Camaligan, Camarines Sur (near to my fieldwork site), recorded a local resident, one Don Mariano Nicomedes, as the translator of both the *Tronco* and the *Martir* into Bicol as well as a *Pasion de Santa Cruz* and Rizal's anticlerical and patriotic *Filibusterismo*.[25]

The conclusion to draw from this proliferation of texts and virtual texts is that it was not only the content of a particular text which defined its arcane power, but also the context in which that translation was made and the book used. The *Tronco*, it will be recalled, refers to the origin of the world and the process of creation, and we saw that the writer of the librito produced an explicitly unorthodox version of these events. Bicolanos, however, treasure the idea of the *Tronco* text and retain its arcane associations, without necessarily altering or even producing the text itself. It is associated with power because of the stories and hints mentioned around the idea of the creation, and because of its use in the Passion-play cycle, which is part of an exchange with divine power not controlled by the church. Religious books may be valued in part in Bicol because of the arcane associations of religious writings—that is, they may be valued as objects, and not only with reference to the content or message of the text. If so, we may be seeing the remains of a curious economy of circulation of books as arcana in Bicol, in which elite people such as the (possibly very respectable) Don Mariano dedicated themselves to translating books into the Bicol language for the sake of pious clarity, but these texts themselves took on a life of their own and became repositories of power despite themselves when they entered into the hands of other users.

Conclusion

Rafael seems to be right in talking of a way of understanding—an aesthetic perhaps—that relies on ambiguity and hesitation in meaning. In the history of the Philippines, in which colonial powers have constantly told people to discard relationships with supernaturals that they themselves wish to retain, ambiguity seems to provide a holding ground, in which such matters reach a very broad number of temporary or individual solutions. But uncertainty goes deeper than that—and deeper than Rafael's study of the textual evidence from the sixteenth to eighteenth centuries indicates, for contemporary Bicolanos refuse in many contexts to disambiguate the world of the spirits and the realm of the *Ama*, both of which are usually referred to as belonging to the *kadikloman*. If Rafael is correct, therefore, and the mass conversion of the Philippines did take place through the mechanisms of attraction exerted by the idea of heaven, the economy of salvation and the specific (though translated) hierarchy of afterlife above this life which attaches to it, then at some point, that mechanism must have swung back in the other direction, at least for the poorer Filipinos among whom I did my fieldwork. Even in the case of the elites, however, there is room to doubt the importance of notions of morality linked to the afterlife, since according to Neils Mulder's article "All Filipinos Go to Heaven" (1987) the urban middle and upper classes of metropolitan Manila place little importance on the notion of judgment in the life to come. This is not to say that the ideas of heaven and hell have had no impact on the Filipino imagination, but they seem not to have had that impact which the missionaries confidently expected.

The second conclusion to be drawn is that while Rafael builds his conclusions around a subtle analysis of texts, arguing that the failures inherent in the process of translation itself ensured that indigenous Filipino meanings, especially notions of power and exchange, continued to be thinkable and to condition converts' understandings of Catholic doctrines "against the grain" of Spanish intentions, this focus on the words of the text may not be sufficient. In the case of the Bicol *Pasion*, we saw that a text which promises submission both to the clarity of orthodox meaning and to the hierarchy of the church, and whose readers may have identified the act of reading in some fundamental sense with that submission, was nonetheless performed in ways that potentially modified its message and was moreover inserted within a symbolic exchange with the *Ama* that was distant from the church's intended message. But readers did not simply draw these associations out of the words of the Passion text itself; they were also potential in the style of its singing, which recalled other valued aspects of social interaction, such as notions of balance and contestation between matched players.[26] The text can itself become not only a location of meaning that resides in the untranslatability of indigenous terms but also an object that is itself an occasion of desire and of exchange,[27] and which can enter into an economy of arcane knowledge even while reproducing apparently orthodox meaning.

......

Notes

A significant part of the historical research on this chapter was carried out with the assistance of a British Academy Small Research Grant, which is gratefully acknowledged. Earlier versions of this chapter were presented to the *Words and Things* workshops from which this volume originated, in Manchester and at the London School of Economics, and I would like to thank all the participants, including Maia Green and our discussants at the LSE, William A. Christian Jr. and Patricia Spyer. A later version of this chapter was presented in the Brown Bag series at Cornell University's Southeast Asia Program, where many colleagues, including John Wolff, Jim Siegel, Jane Fajans, Smita Lahiri, and Andrew Wilford, made most valuable comments. I would also like to thank Tak Chaloemtiarana; Nancy Stage Loncto and others at the Kahin Center at Cornell; the Cornell librarians; and, for providing lasting sources of inspiration and roads of inquiry, Ben Anderson and Vince Rafael.

1 This is the smallest administrative unit of Philippine government; therefore it means "village" in rural areas and "neighborhood" in towns and cities.

2 Most *Pasion* singers, and all who stage a reading in their own homes, have made a vow (*promesa*) to the local cult saint.

3 The second main shaping context of Bicolano literacy is that of the state primary school system, inherited from the guiding project of the American colonial era. See Cannell 2005a.

4 Much of the most interesting work on literacy has been done by historians. In anthropology, Jack Goody (1986 and 1987) proposed universal effects for writing technology that continue to be influential, although also widely critiqued.

5 An exception is love notes passed between young people; there are a large

number of pattern books for love letters and letters of proposal on sale in Naga bookshops.

6 This is the first word of the text's long title in Tagalog (and it has cognates in other Filipino languages); literally, it means "a relation of events, a story."

7 The exact models he used are the subject of vigorous debate. On the genealogy of the Tagalog Passion, see Tiongson 1976; Javellena 1983, 1984, 1988, 1990; Santiago 1988; and Lumbera 1986.

8 In accepting Rafael's argument, we should note that this would place it within a long tradition of European *artes moriendi* texts and illustrations (Ariès 1981: 605–8; Cannell 1995).

9 The Spanish refused to allow Filipinos to be made priests at this period.

10 Although few anthropologists may have read Hegel directly, his influence has been profound. See the introduction to this volume for further discussion.

11 The greatest danger is of being defined and punished as a heretic.

12 For a discussion of the contrast with European Catholicisms treated in recent ethnographies, see Cannell 1999, especially 193–99.

13 The nuance of Rafael's argument is better appreciated by reading the original than by the overly condensed summary offered here.

14 The exception is the printing Gainza ordered of the early missionary Marcos de Lisboa's pioneering sixteenth-century Bicol dictionary (1582–87), a work that could also be considered both pious and scholarly. Gainza made it clear that de Lisboa was in many ways his inspiration.

15 My translation and emphases. I have tried to preserve what seems to me to be the genuine strangeness of the writers' expressions, even at the expense of producing slightly contorted English prose.

16 The interpretation offered here is necessarily somewhat speculative, given the number of topics in Philippine local history on which detailed work is still to be done. However, the argument is not untested, since it conforms both with the evidence offered in my 1999 monograph and with the experience and knowledge of other Philippinists and Southeast Asian scholars (John Wolff and Jim Siegel, personal communications).

17 This is the notorious "friar education" system that was the cause of much controversy within Spain itself in the late nineteenth century and was derided by the Americans in the early twentieth century as part of their propaganda against the previous regime.

18 There is a thirteenth edition of *D.C., Catecismo de la Doctrina Cristiana en idioma Bicol*, by Father Martinez, printed in 1905, which may be what is referred to, but this is not titled "Casaysayan."

19 For a more extensive treatment of this argument, see Cannell 1999: 137–62.

20 For printed examples of Filipino scripts, see Scott 1994: 214.

21 These included, for example, the belief that the Virgin Mary existed as a kind of ancestress before the creation and watched it happen (because she is portrayed in the Bicol *Pasion* before the story of the Creation), and alternative versions of the story of Adam and Eve.

22 Although it was standard practice to use Latin, it is clear that the Spanish did also say common prayers such as the paternoster in Castilian from an early date, also printing them in this form. This may have made the Spanish-Latin distinction even less clear.

23 This is the book published in Naga City in 1971 as *Tronco del Mundo: An aguiagui kan kinaban bago pagabot si Jesucristo sa ipag-awit*, by Manuel B. Salazar.

24 This book was published in 1922, and Nemesio Magboo is given as its author.

25 This information is found in the documents relating to the folklore project in which primary school teachers were asked in the early 1950s to gather and record information on local folkways. Particular authors' names are not usually recorded, and the documents are filed under the name of the Philippine Bureau of Education (1953); for these references see the section on the town of Camaligan, page 15.

26 These appear as well as in the text's woodcut illustrations, which serve as models for the performance of the Passion plays (*tanggal*) of the area. There has not been space to develop this material at length here.

27 On the importance of the circulation of apocrypha to the spread and acceptance of early Christianity, see Cameron 1991: 89–119.

···Five···

Materializing the Self

Words and Gifts in the Construction of Charismatic Protestant Identity

Simon Coleman

Conservative Protestants perceive sacred words as key to their faith. They often argue against the idea of worshipping material things rather than maintaining a living faith embodied in the person, the Spirit, and the Word (Harding 1987). This stance of apparent suspicion toward the incorporation of objects into religious practices has seemed somewhat hypocritical to many outsiders, given the willingness of some believers—especially those in the United States—to accumulate considerable material possessions in their daily lives (Barron 1987; Brandon 1987; Hellberg 1987). Statues of the Virgin Mary may not be worshipped, but it has sometimes appeared as though Mammon certainly is.

James Davison Hunter notes (1983: 7) that the contemporary conservative Protestant worldview (to the extent that a single view exists) has many roots: a German Pietist emphasis on spiritual perfectibility on earth combines with a Methodist stress on experiential conversion and Baptist doctrines of personal salvation. The Second Great Awakening in nineteenth-century America played a key role in replacing Puritan notions of predestination with Arminian notions of the individual's responsibility in attaining personal salvation (Austin-Broos 1997: 55). Later, the holiness movement, grounded in notions of perfectionism, came to cultivate the idea of the profound transformative experience following from conversion and the consequent "in-filling" of the individual with spiritual power. Subsequently, Pentecostals argued that the ability to speak in tongues could be seen as an outward sign of inner sanctification. (Thus, Austin-Broos [1997: 265] refers to Pentecostalism's idea of "God in me.") At the same time, nineteenth- and twentieth-century urban revivals frequently involved the deployment of rationalized, quantified approaches to soul-saving (Hunter 1983: 12; Frankl 1987): as the Spirit flowed over the masses, its precise effects were monitored and cultivated with care.

Over the last thirty years, conservative Protestantism has seen a revival in its fortunes and increase in its visibility in the United States and beyond. Factors contributing to such growth (see Marsden 1984) include the growing wealth of believers themselves, support from a public increasingly outraged by the permissiveness of post-1960s society, widespread loss of faith in secular, scientific models of reality, and the willingness of such Christians to use all modern technological means to get their message across to anybody prepared to listen.

The origins of the Faith movement, the branch of conservative Protestantism with which this chapter is concerned, lie in part within North American revivals that emerged after the Second World War. In the years following the conflict, many preachers found their voice in emphasizing themes of healing and material plenty.[1] A young pastor who cut his teeth in such revivals was Kenneth Hagin, who in 1974 founded his Rhema Bible Training Center in Tulsa, Oklahoma. Hagin succeeded in attracting preachers from around the world to take his courses and thereby participate in increasingly global networks of Faith Christians. Having completed their studies, students of the training center often returned to their home countries in order to start up their own ministries. Followings for Faith teachings, often promulgated by Rhema graduates, can be found in large urban areas with middle-class constituencies, such as South Africa, South Korea, Singapore, parts of South America, and certain areas of Europe (Martin 2002), but the prosperity message has also appealed to less advantaged groups who have maintained aspirations for personal (and sometimes wider) forms of transformation and empowerment.

Within Protestant denominations, the Faith movement is well known if not notorious for placing particular stress on the relationship between the possession of correct faith and the cultivation of physical, material, and social well-being. Invoking but also transforming Calvinist themes, members argue that prosperity is the right of the true believer (Hollinger 1991). Older notions that success might be associated with grace through predestination are therefore democratized to embrace all who have chosen to enter the New Covenant by becoming born again. Barnhart (1990:

159–60) describes such beliefs as a form of "folk theology," a set of motivational propositions designed to appeal to a lay audience: "Its principal 20th-century roots trace back to the swashbuckling faith healers of the big tent and to popular God-wants-you-to-get-to-the top sermons that reflect the theme of Norman Vincent Peale's best seller, *The Power of Positive Thinking*." Certainly, parallels with Peale's "psychoanalytic gospel" (Cawelti 1965: 215) are drawn by a number of authors (Hellberg 1987: 23; Schultze 1990: 41), and common intellectual roots can also be found with Christian Science and the teachings of Mary Baker Eddy (Hollinger 1991). Faith Christianity shares with these other moral systems a concern with the discovery of systematic principles for success that are both measurable and related to the interface between mind and the deployment of language.[2]

In the United States and the country where I have carried out most of my fieldwork, Sweden, such Christians are characterized by opponents as propagating a "Health and Wealth" Gospel, implying a naive belief in the power of faith to provide the person with perfect health and abundant worldly goods (see Barron 1987). I hope to show how the ideology and practice of these believers posit the existence of a complex set of connections and even affinities between language and the material world. Among Faith Christians—and in practice, among many other conservative Protestants—words are objectified in their complex relations to physical media, whether these are human bodies, mass media, or even aspects of the built environment.

When sacred words are regarded as thinglike in their autonomous force and their production of tangible results, the identity of the born-again person appears to be pervaded and even constituted by such language. To read and listen to inspired language is seen as a means of filling the self with objectified language, even in a physical sense. However, in examining such deployment of language we have to consider the implications of *producing* words as well as consuming them. I hope to show that to "speak out" sacred words that have been stored in the self is not merely to communicate to others in a semantic sense; it is also to recreate and extend one's persona in the act of giving an aspect of the self to others—an aspect that is never truly alienated from the giver. Such a view has implications for the development of ideas of spiritual hierarchy and empowerment within the movement. More broadly, it encourages a consideration of the idea of speaking inspired language in relation to Maussian notions of the gift. I conclude by looking at how the deployment of language by Faith Christians has parallels with other forms of more obviously material giving in the movement.

The Word of Life

The Christian organization I will describe is located in the ancient university town of Uppsala, a little to the north of Stockholm. It has been set up in an industrial estate on the eastern border of the urban area. At first sight, it is almost impossible to distinguish the group's premises from the huge warehouses and offices of the rest of the industrial estate, but one can soon find a distinctive logo—an open Bible, a sword, and a rainbow[3] —fixed to the side of a building, as well as a large sign that indicates that the visitor has arrived at the Word of Life (Livets Ord) Bible Center.[4]

The somewhat out-of-the-way location of the Word of Life in Uppsala expresses a more general peripherality in relation to mainstream religious practices in Sweden. Even other Protestant churches regard it with considerable suspicion and have shown concern that it has been poaching some of their members, a hardly surprising reaction given that most of the original supporters of the ministry were Christians disillusioned with the apparent staidness and traditionalism of their former churches. A large proportion of those who become involved in the group are between eighteen and the middle thirties. No obvious trends are currently discernible regarding the class affiliation of adherents, while the group has only recently begun to target the increasing numbers of Catholics and Muslim immigrants in contemporary Sweden.

The Word of Life has been characterized in popular and semiacademic works as a youth-snatching, foreign-inspired, fascist, yuppie, money-grabbing, heretical, and deeply un-Swedish organization, peddling the worst aspects of American culture to a nation whose identity in a globalizing world is already under threat (see Coleman 1989). Yet it cannot be seen as without supporters if viewed from a wider perspective. Apart from being linked up to a global and national network of similar organizations,[5] it claims to run the largest Bible school in Europe (and this in a country renowned for its apparent degree of secularization). As well as the Bible school, which attracts hundreds of students a year from Scandinavia and many other countries in the world, the group maintains a congregation of over 2,000 people, a series of schools for younger children and teenagers, a university, and a media business producing satellite television, books, videos, cassettes, and other goods. Indeed, the Christian identity of many Word of Life members is bound up precisely with the thought that they are able to transcend locality in having an influence on others—producing, as a book written by the group's head pastor puts it, *Faith Which Conquers the World* (Ekman 1985).

To think of the Word of Life as representing a merely "local," Swedish form of Christianity is clearly problematic. The group's head pastor, Ulf Ekman, was a priest in the Swedish Church until the early 1980s, when he went to train at Kenneth Hagin's training center, and on his return started up the Word of Life on the model of entrepreneurial ministries such as Hagin's. Ekman's ministry has become the de facto leader of a new Faith denomination in Sweden, consisting of perhaps 20,000–30,000 Christians marked by their emphasis on "positive confession" and prosperity. Summer conferences held at the group's facility now attract some 8,000 people a year. During the Swedish organization's steady expansion, it has maintained constant contacts with similar groups in the United States, inviting North American preachers over to Uppsala to speak at monthly conferences. Although the United States (along with Israel) is still located at the top of the perceived hierarchy of spiritually powerful nations, geographically and evangelically marginal groups such as the Word of Life can gain spiritual symbolic capital within the Faith network by attracting international delegates to its meetings and foreign buyers for its goods.

Words as Things

Susan Harding (1987: 167–69) points to the significance of language among conservative Protestants in her contention that rhetoric, not ritual, is the prime vehicle of conversion, and that spiritual realities are communicated through nonsensuous, linguistic means. To her, the language of Baptists is made up of a bundle of strategies for confronting the listener or reader, stripping them of their cultural assumptions and investing them with a fundamentalist mode of organizing and interpreting experience. Witnessing therefore attempts to reconstitute the listener as he or she becomes alienated from previous assumptions.

Harding's account is itself a wonderfully gripping and involving anthropological narrative, engaging the reader in her version of ethnographic reality. Nevertheless, she excludes two important elements of conservative Protestant use of language, at least as they are manifested among Word of Life adherents. The first concerns the way the deployment of language can reconstitute not merely the listener, but also the speaker (see Stromberg 1993). The second relates to the way language cannot simply be divorced from sensual forms in the way that she suggests, since the power of words is so often demonstrated in their effects on and constitution of the material world as well as the born-again person.[6]

These claims require some explanation and expansion in relation to my own ethnography. Among Word of Life adherents, not only is the Bible seen as a source of objective truth, but the words of an inspired speaker can also be regarded as truth incarnate. A Pentecostal faith in the power of oral communication combines with a form of spiritually oriented positive thinking to produce what adherents call "positive confession," the notion that inspired words gain a form of performative efficacy whereby that which one speaks is manifested in the material world.

Beliefs concerning prosperity and the efficacy of language are combined in Faith practice. It is sometimes argued that sufficient repetition of a word or phrase accumulates the force of the word, for instance *joy* or *success*. The words of a preacher recorded on videotape lose none of their power to heal or save when played back in the believer's living room. The Word is perceived as an independent power rather than a collection of signs in need of socially determined interpretation. Here, for instance, are words of one believer, who had been injured in a car accident, and whose health had apparently been despaired of by medical doctors:

> I was so conscious of my inner person that I saw the body as a house that needed to be repaired. And . . . I said to one part of the body after the other to begin to function: "Leg, in the name of Jesus, walk! . . . Hand, in Jesus' name, function! You are under God's blood! You are healed in the name of Jesus . . ."
>
> We rule from the inside. We are in a position of rule over our body.[7]

In this statement, we see a distant echo of the Pauline notion of the body as temple. The healed woman places her physical self under the control of supernatural authority, manifested in Jesus's name and other spiritually charged language (see Coleman 1996). The healing words she uses are made living by being uttered rather than merely read. Significantly, the words are spoken by her alone: she is able to perceive one part of her self—her body—as objectified and made subject to the language emerging from her Spirit.

The cultivation of orality in an otherwise literate context implies a self-conscious reaction against the fixity of the written word while retaining the textualist's concern for reliable, unchanging "knowledge." During services or in more personal devotions, spoken language can be directed at an unknown other, a friend, an object, or indeed oneself. In this case, the woman concerned was a relatively important functionary within the Word of Life hierarchy. Her being involved in a car crash was interpreted by some adherents as an indication that her work was sufficiently powerful to attract attention from the devil, but her triumphant deployment of healing words (converted into a narrative relating such linguistic facility) indicates her ability to defeat even apparently hopeless situations.

Glossolalia takes even further the notion of language as pure, autonomous force bereft of semantic baggage. Restrictions of grammar and meaning itself are removed, allowing the act of giving voice to become a purely bodily act (see Csordas 1995). Tongues is the verbal equivalent of physically and visually articulated ecstasy such as dancing in the spirit: both signify an embodied spontaneity and the possibility of a communion with others untroubled by parochial conventions of expression. Through its performative functions of healing and conversion it acts as a concentrated, particularly focused, exemplar of all sanctified language.

Given that the body indicates and exemplifies divine favor, illness generally—any state of bodily imperfection—is a problem of faith as well as a physical condition. Such a view amplifies conventional Pentecostal dualities in which the collectively sanctioned Spirit and Word control the individual and egotistical flesh (see Wilson and Clow 1981: 242–45). The experience of ecstasy and speaking in tongues becomes both a loss of self and a gaining of access to a language from God that, in its physical effects, transcends the need for interpretation. As one former Bible school pupil put it to me, she came to see herself as a kind of receptacle for the divine: "One has God's nature so totally, that everybody is a small Jesus, almost." The Word, whether contained in language or Jesus—Himself the Word made flesh—represents a collectively sanctioned but often individually consumed principle of empowerment to which the believer has to submit, transforming the self into a living icon.

Such emptying out of the self in favor of an idealized other, reminiscent of Diane Austin-Broos's "God in me," is also expressed in the way ordinary adherents model themselves on powerful, "Word-filled" preachers who appear particularly to address their situation. For instance, two women told me they were identified by others, and indeed perceived themselves, as being Swedish versions of a popular American preacher. An identificatory logic exists whereby the spiritually powerful can influence others through words that are perceived as coming directly from one Spirit to another, bypassing the distorting influences of the mind or culture.[8] By identifying themselves with foreign preachers, in particular, Swedish charismatics can come to see themselves as embodying spiritual forces that render irrelevant their state (in the world's eyes) of politico-religious peripherality.

Faith mistrust of symbolic language does not mean that recurring metaphors are absent in Faith discourse: rather, it implies that their perceived status *as* metaphors is somewhat ambiguous (see Forstorp 1992). Thus, a youth pastor has argued in a sermon that the reception of God's word is like the eating of spiritual breakfast, an exercise that is necessary if one is to become, as he put it, the equivalent of a spiritual bodybuilder.[9] This was not a straightforwardly metaphorical statement: the Word is genuinely seen by many believers as accumulating within the self as if it were a physical entity, producing a more powerful and mature Christian. At times, an even more direct connection between the internal self and the external body is suggested. Here are the words of an American preacher during a sermon, describing a "visit" he paid to Jesus:[10] "And there Jesus stood. . . . His hair came down to about here. And one thing that I noticed: it was that he had muscles! Isn't that great!" This vision illustrates the continually living nature of Christ as well as the authority of the person granted an audience with Him. The encounter is presented not as a symbolic meeting with divinity, but as one that is to be taken as literally as any biblical text. I have also seen a painting of Christ, placed for a time in an office corridor at the Word of Life, that depicted him as a kind of bodybuilder in motion, appearing almost to burst out of the confines of the picture frame (see Coleman 1996).

A view of Christ or the Christian as a kind of Mr. Universe (in more senses than one) is not in itself new (see Moore 1994: 211). The image of Jesus as muscle-bound has, however, particular significance within the context of movement ideology. Important to bodybuilding culture is the so-called exaggeration principle (Coleman 1996), according to which limitation—in terms of vitamins ingested, repetitions completed, or size obtained—is seen as an enemy to be overcome. The docile body in such a culture is one that has submitted to the possibility of endless expansion as well as to the constant monitoring of progress through anatomizing the body and reducing its parts to measurements that compare the fragmented person with his or her previous incarnations as well as to the body parts of others.

Adherence to Faith principles does not necessarily involve subscribing to a gym, although there are some evangelists who interpret the phrase "power evangelism" to involve the act of missionizing by those strong in body. Self-identification with Christ involves a particular form of mimesis through the appropriation of the performative force contained within biblical texts and the in-filling of the Spirit. The Word can be made flesh not only in the body of the Savior but also in that of the believer. In practice, the person can attempt to learn by heart as many Bible verses as possible so as to "store" them in the Spirit, can use language spoken in Jesus's name to heal the self as well as others, and can see the body as a temple of the Spirit whose healthy external features directly mirror an internal spiritual well-being.[11]

These Faith notions both echo and transform conventional Protestant views of corporeality. Philip Mellor and Chris Shilling (1997: 6–9) link current Western tendencies to conflate seeing and knowing with earlier influences from the Reformation. Reformers' emphasis on the mind's ability to receive the Word of God implied that the eye and ear were valued more than touch and smell in the Protestant body. Combined with this, a disciplined, privatized, inner-directed habitus prioritized cognitive dimensions of belief (10–16). In Faith contexts, the body is no longer denied spiritual status in the sense that it becomes an index of the spiritual state of the believer. The Christian engaged in a process of "spiritual bodybuilding" learns not only to glean the truth from biblical and other inspired writings, but also to read the body as a text that can give inductive proof of the power of the ingested Word.

Bodily practices and disciplines among these believers call for an analytic synthesis of Goffman and Foucault. "Positive Confession" can be extended beyond the realm of spoken language into forms of self-presentation that demonstrate the empowerment of the physically and spiritually healthy person, ranging from dancing, raising the hands, and even quaking during services to employing an enthusiastic demeanor in ostensibly everyday circumstances. The audience for such presentations is not only fellow believers or nonbelievers, but also the self. Just as language can be applied to one's objectified body to produce healing, so according to some adherents can the acting out of a joyful state produce the desired effect. Self-actualization and proof of the presence of internalized divinity are achieved through deploying a body language that is specifically

Faith-oriented. Such language is to be understood as a form of visual, indeed corporeal, literalism, since as with sanctified words the translation from original, physical manifestation to effect in the world is ideally direct, without distortion. One former Bible school student at the Word of Life expressed well this sense of attempting to become one's own icon: "You should have faith in your self, or you should have faith in your own faith. . . . It means that if you stand sufficiently long in faith the invisible will become visible."

Per-Anders Forstorp (1992: 96), who has studied another Faith congregation in Sweden, talks of being told by an informant that we are a mirror of what is inside us. In a ritualized echo of this sentiment (103), older children at the Faith school he examined are given as homework the task of saying Bible verses as they look at themselves (or one might say subject themselves to the conservative Protestant gaze) in the mirror.

The sense of internal as well as mutual disciplining that these practices imply demonstrates some of the complexities of attempting to locate sources of authority among Faith Christians. Edmund Leach ([1972] 1983) runs through classic themes concerning mediation and hierarchy in his binary presentation of "icons of subversion" versus those of "orthodoxy." The icon of orthodoxy involves the priest as mediator between person and God—superior to fellow humans, suppliant to God, but also guardian of access to divine authority. In the opposed model, grace is given directly to the inspired individual—a nonhierarchical context not dependent on ritual mediation of a priest. Where the incarnation is not seen as a once-and-for-all-event, says Leach, its divine authority is perpetually realizable in the present, with potentially revolutionary effects.

In practice, it would be difficult to know which of these models to apply to Word of Life adherents. Divinity is clearly democratized in the sense that it becomes located in the Spirits of all who are born-again. Yet the believer learns to subject the self to an internalized disciplinary apparatus whose form is derived from other members of the group.[12] Admittedly, the influence of an organization like the Word of Life is unlikely to be totalizing for most of its supporters: many combine attendance at the group's services with membership of another church. The authority of preachers comes from the fact that they are able to persuade others to listen to their messages in a competitive marketplace of spiritual consumption. The lack of a fully established priesthood with exclusive access to the divine does not remove the ordinary believer from being inserted into an apparatus of charismatic inequality, where all are winners but some win more than others, and according to which many means exist to measure the spiritual successes of the self and others.

Words as Gifts

Webb Keane (1994: 605), referring to the Anakalang of eastern Indonesia, describes the objectlike qualities of ritual words and their ability to become detached from the particularities of speakers and events (620). In this context, the power of ritual speaking derives from appearing to repeat verbal types grounded in an ancestral past, so that ancestral agency is echoed and evoked. Word of Life sacred language is equally objectlike but derives its power and protection against the contingencies of the present not so much from ancestors as from a notion of the living influence of God, embodied within and rendered active by the believer's practices of reading, listening, and speaking.

Keane's piece argues that the successful conjoining of words and things in his case study helps portray transactors of exchange as bearing an agency that transcends physical individuals. He states this in the context of arguing that assumptions concerning the boundaries between people and things have, since Mauss, been challenged by theories of exchange. It is this last issue I wish to discuss in more detail—specifically, the notion that speaking in an evangelical context can be considered in the light of the Maussian notion of the gift.

Let me summarize Mauss (see Parry 1986: 453–58) as arguing that the gift contains some part of the spiritual essence of the donor, and that this situation compels the recipient to make a return. Because the thing contains an aspect of the person, it is not truly alienated from the giver, and because of the participation of the person in the object, the gift creates enduring bonds between people. Such a view has been both critiqued and developed by later writers. For Chris Gregory (1982), gifts are opposed to commodities since they are inalienable; he follows Mauss in proposing that the giver acquires superiority over receiver since indebtedness is established (Thomas 1991: 14).

Word of Life members' deployment of sacred words has parallels to and differences from themes raised by Mauss. Words, like gifts, must be activated to take effect, put into a kind of verbal circulation, and speaking is the most common way to convert language from its latent to its active form. As with the gift, words have objectlike qualities that allow them to be removed from the person and retain a semiautonomous existence;

such existence is *semi*-autonomous not only because words are directed at a recipient but also because they retain an objectified element of the charismatic identity of the speaker. Clearly, the recipient of language is not expected to reply with an equal or greater number of words, and is not "in debt" to the speaker in an obvious way. However, one who deploys sacred language expects a return on his or her linguistic investment. That return involves a belief that the words have taken effect, have made a difference to the world in a way that can be measured or at least imagined. Such a difference then becomes a constitutive part of the speaker's persona, a test of spiritual efficacy that they have passed.

Where an expected result does not occur, disappointment and disillusion may result, but many means exist, Azande-like, to explain away failure: one's faith may be in need of a boost, or one is being "attacked" by forces scared of evangelical power. In addition, we must consider the very particular role played by recipients of sacred language. Harding notes how the audience for the evangelizing narrative she describes is turned into a passive object whose assumptions are to be replaced. Similarly, at the Word of Life, receivers of linguistic "gifts" are often placed in a position where a stereotypical response is required. During a sermon, the congregation is required to do little other than reply "Hallelujah" when prompted by the speaker. This sense of producing relatively predictable responses also permeates more intimate, person-to-person discourse, where people are aware of the need to maintain a positive habitus at all times. Thus believers are likely to feel much more comfortable exchanging testimonies of personal empowerment and pronouncing mutual blessings over each other than engaging in so-called negative confession, such as criticizing others or expressing self-doubt. However, even when a person evangelized in the street seems aggressive or mocking, there is always the possibility that they will see the light in private. Significantly, also, Faith evangelism is designed to use communications technology: radio, television, and videos, as well as books and magazines. Each of these media contains and transmits objectified words of speakers (or writers) but divorces the giver from immediate interaction or dialogue with the receiver. At times, the broadcaster can even imagine an audience or set of receivers where none exists: Quentin Schultze (1996: 64) notes that most missionizing media have small audiences, largely made up of believers themselves.

According to such a communication system, the idea of a recipient is necessary but such a person/set of people often does not need to be interacted with on an idiosyncratic level. Ekman (1989: 106) describes other people as channels through which God provides bounty to the believer. In broadcasting words—an action often compared, using biblical imagery, to the sowing of seeds in the knowledge that a bountiful harvest will result[13]—these evangelicals are opening themselves up to criticism from a secular world that regards such actions as highly aggressive. Yet from the viewpoint of the speaker, an attempt to convert the other through linguistic means is not merely an attempt to save a soul; it is also an attempt to convince, or even constitute, the spiritual persona of the self.

Words and Money

Broadcasting of the self through objectified vehicles is not confined to the use of language. Other forms of activity, like speaking, involve the notion of "reaching out," attempting to affect the world while not necessarily risking being in dialogue with it. The most obvious example involves Faith practices in relation to material objects, and in particular money.

Let me make the point by recounting an incident from my fieldwork. One evening, around sixteen years ago, I turned up early to a midweek meeting at the Word of Life. At first, I hardly noticed the elderly woman sitting next to me, but then she touched me on the shoulder and smiled. She explained that she was very short of money but that God had blessed her by giving her a sum of kronor the day before (about twenty pounds). God had also told her, apparently, that she should give half of the money to someone else whom she would meet at the service. That person was me—not somebody she had ever met previously, but the person who happened to sit next to her. She opened a purse containing nothing but two notes, and handed me one, worth about ten pounds. After some internal debate, I decided to accept the money and rather sheepishly put the note into my back pocket.

I found this incident rather embarrassing when it occurred. But as time went on, I found that certain elements of the event—the giving of money after having just received some, and moreover the giving of it to an unknown other, as well as the careful specification of the amount—began to make sense. I realized that what I had taken at the time to be a pure gift was not quite as simple as I had thought. In fact, the woman was practicing a form of giving that *did* expect a very specific return, and I was a somewhat unwitting vehicle toward achieving the desired payback.

Some further discussion of Faith teachings and practices is necessary here (see Barron 1987). Faith preachers argue that the promise God gave to Abraham in Genesis 17 included the blessing of prosperity. They connect this world-affirming doctrine with Paul's words in Galatians 3:13–14, 29 about the blessings given to Abraham coming to the Gentiles through Christ. Blessings can also be related to specific acts of the believer, including giving away money. Kenneth Copeland, an American preacher, claims the following in his book *The Laws of Prosperity*: "Invest heavily in God; the returns are staggering, 100 to 1!" (quoted in Barron 1987: 89). Giving to God, through tithes and offerings, is a condition for financial prosperity.

Ulf Ekman also defines prosperity as key to Christian faith: "Financial prosperity is not just another subject. It is a part of the character of God" (1989: 11). Moreover, the giving manifested by humans is merely an earthly replica of God's actions: as Ekman puts it, encouraged by John 3:16, God is a giver by nature (13). The result of all this giving, according to the law of return, is that resources accrue with interest to the donor. Faith Christians should ideally be equipped not merely to live comfortable lives, but also to evangelize with sufficient resources. Anathema to the ideology is the stockpiling of money. Ekman states: "Wealthy people who are not saved are reservoirs for the devil. They pile up possessions and gather wealth to themselves, thus restricting resources which could be put to much better, active use" (58). Christians are encouraged to think big, to consider investing in sowing out gifts that appear on a profane level of understanding to be unwise: "If you want to get somewhere with God, you need to reach beyond your present financial limitations" (67).

Much though certainly not all of Word of Life practice echoes these injunctions. Bible School students have told me how many of them worked part-time to support their studies, but others just "stood in faith," "believing funds forward" and trusting in God's beneficence. The sense of breaking everyday limitations in order to demonstrate the powers of faith is taken by some to have direct entrepreneurial implications, and quite a few members have started up businesses as a means of building a career combining, and not merely juxtaposing, spirituality and material success. A member of the congregation described to me his decision to move into a larger house, even though he knew he could not really afford it, since a bigger home would represent both his ideal aspirations and a measure of his ambitions for him and his family. Such an act—a form of positive confession in bricks and mortar—was replicated on a larger scale in the mid-1980s when the congregation decided to move to larger and expensive premises: although the new hall of the building was far too big for the congregation at the time, each empty seat was said to represent a convert already claimed for Christ.

Outside the main hall of the new premises is a large shop in which videos, audiocassettes, books, and specific consumer items like jacket pins with the Word of Life logo can be bought. The extensive literature the groups produces in the form of newsletters and magazines is full of advertisements giving reduced prices on goods, as well as testimonies by members concerning the economic miracles they have experienced. The Word of Life and fellow Faith organizations around the world are creating a global yet internally oriented charismatic economy whereby goods as well as people are transferred between congregations, and markets for spiritual consumer items are extended. To some extent, also, congregations support each other by sending donations from collections to special projects: for instance, Ulf Ekman has talked of sowing $10,000 into an American pastor's television work in the hope of a greater personal return.[14]

How are we to interpret the Faith attitude to money? One theory, put forward by outraged outsiders, is that it is just a moneymaking business operating fraudulently under the name of religion (see Coleman 1989). If this were true, it would, however, be strange for the leading members of the group to spend so much of their time investing, if not overinvesting, in extremely ambitious projects such as radio stations, satellite broadcasts, and donations to other preachers' ministries. Another, more reasonable hypothesis (see Barron 1987) connects prosperity preaching with high demands for funds. The creation of the need for constant expansion as a marker of identity and the perceived participation in an economy of evangelization creates a circle that could easily move from being benign to being vicious: more funds are generated all the time, but more money simultaneously needs to be generated to keep the system going.

Such a hypothesis might explain something of the urgency of requests for money that are made by group leaders, but it says little of the meanings of money for those involved at mere membership level in the movement. Thus, it is important to remember that fundamental to the workings of Faith ideology is the notion that effects of faith and correct practice can be measured objectively: the numbers of souls saved, money collected, and churches started in this missionizing economy are the subject of constant appraisal and are located within narratives of constant progress and growth. These narratives are also applied to the self. One is not only born-again but also has to grow in faith. A Foucauldian technology of the self is created whereby inner and outer states are objectified and monitored to maintain socially derived ideals of happiness and prosperity.

Given such preconditions, money acts as an ideal index of faith. Results can be measured, and of course money gathered through whatever means can be seen as indicating future possibilities of action. Let me give the example of the collection that is taken up every meeting. When an exceptionally large amount is raised, this is announced with some glee. A report on the 1986 Faith Conference[15] talks of how an American preacher, Lester Sumrall, spoke in support of an offering to the Word of Life's new building and how the next evening the amount collected for the building was announced: around 100,000 pounds. On such occasions, a multi-layered form of assessment seems to be going on. The amount collected represents a collective achievement of the group in support of a shared project. It also acts as an index of the charismatic drawing power of Sumrall himself.

Key to such a system is the idea that the person cannot rest on his or her laurels. Sumrall is only as good as his last collection, just as the Christian entrepreneur is only as good as his or her last deal. In this context, giving more than one can afford makes perfect sense: it keeps money in circulation, it allows one to assess the effects of one's action on the world, and it helps to render material one's inner state of faith. Ideas concerning the workings of money link with wider attempts to seek systematic principles that both describe and control divine force immanent within the self.

Let me take this reasoning a step further. We have seen how much Faith practice involves forms of linguistic objectification of experience—the speaking of inspired words that gain power when they are uttered, the taping of services on video so that they can be played back to have exactly the same effects as if they were live, the creation of generic narratives of conversion, and so on. Such forms of objectification involve, as Danny Miller (1987), influenced by Hegel (see Coleman 1996), has noted, two acts: externalization of something from the self, and then the reabsorption of that which has been externalized.

In a similar way, the giving of money by Faith Christians is an externalization of the self, and of course it is expected that reabsorption will take place: if words when reabsorbed come back in living and inspired form, the sign and measure of money's inspiration is the interest it has acquired. The speaking out of words and the giving away of money provide means of reaching out into a world of both threat and opportunity. Just as money (capital) is to be kept flowing, so words can become living and gain power only when spoken and thereby tested against the contingencies of the present. An aesthetic of constant movement is common to both, as the giving of money and the broadcasting of the self in language extract the spiritual "essence" of the person and render it available to and open to scrutiny by others and oneself. In both linguistic and monetary forms of externalization, the act of exchange is fertile (see Parry 1986: 465) in the sense that it constitutes a sanctification of the self objectified and rendered accessible to the recipient.[16] We can therefore return here to the image of the spiritual bodybuilder, seeking for a perfection that can never be complete. Although not conjuring up the idea of exchange as such, it echoes the notion of accumulation of capital to the self as an index of spiritual success. Muscles and money come to signify the same fruits of a search for unlimited expansion.

The manner in which the self is externalized in both words and money tells us much about the nature of social relations articulated in this religious culture. Simmel and Marx associated money with the growth of individualism and destruction of solidary communities (see Carrier 1995: 9). Olivia Harris agrees (1989: 234) that a romantic European view of money has regarded it as a sign of alienation and individualism. In Western circles, money frequently signifies the interests of individuals as opposed to that of the community (238), so that it is often perceived as the antithesis of the holy—indeed, the concept of religious community in Judeo-Christian traditions has often been defined in opposition to money. Harris also notes, however (234), that liberal philosophy sees in money the advent of rationality in human behavior and the freeing of humans from the shackles of dependency. Such a view is echoed by Simmel's notion that money could promote a wider and more diffuse sort of social integration—an enormously expanded social universe. Anonymous and impersonal, money for him measured everything by the same yardstick and so could act as an instrument of freedom, a condition for the extension of the individual personality and expansion of the circle of trust (see Bloch and Parry 1989).

Parallels with the Faith movement are clear: in the putative global charismatic economy, the deployment of both language and material resources such as money ideally provides individual members with the means to assess themselves according to apparently neutral, universal criteria. The sacred and the material become not antithetical but mutually dependent in the sense that the religious "community" of faith is also an internal market of striving individuals, each keen to further what some call their "spiritual careers," and each keen to use whatever resources are available to extend into an anonymous world whose transformation implies that investments of the self in the world are never truly alienated. Words, as with money, provide the possibility of self-abstraction and circulation, away from a sharply defined, limiting social fabric (see Comaroff 1985: 144). This stance is rather more complex than a simple equation of Protestantism with "individualism," since it implies that the spiritual self is realized in reaching out to others, and that what can be transferred between people is that which is generic, or shared, by believers.[17] The apparently contending (from a conventional Western viewpoint) elements of personhood that are implied here are highlighted in a criticism regularly made of the Word of Life: that it simultaneously encourages selfishness and hyperindividualism among its adherents, and yet also brainwashes them into religious submission.

Thus I came to realize that the elderly woman described above who handed me money was not engaging in an act of pure giving. She was engaging in a form of donation both similar to and distinct from Mauss's famous notion of the gift in non-Western contexts. The participation of the person in the Maussian gift is supposed to create an enduring bond between people (see Parry 1986: 453–57). The woman, however, was not expressing or creating an enduring bond between her and me; rather, she was extending her gift into a world where the unknown other could be the apparent recipient of the donation, but where the greatest beneficiary would be herself. A commodification of the self in one respect was an attempt to reappropriate her objectified spiritual force in another. In this way, if the gift contained some of her spiritual essence, she was also extending herself, her ambitions, and her religious imagination into a much wider sphere, that of the global Faith economy.

Conclusion

I have stressed the need for Word of Life members to reach out into the world in the very act of constituting a spiritual self. In a certain sense, however, Faith methods of reaching into the world are rather parochial in form and implication. Much investment of money takes place *within* the internal Faith economy of ministries, even if such ministries are spread throughout the world. Stereotypical language, movement, and decor displayed on such globally exchanged products as videos and magazines help to frame the multiple and dispersed contexts of Faith preaching as reassuringly similar to that of Sweden. Yet such reaching out with the Word and other resources at least provides a sense of keying into and transforming a world beyond the self. As Alfred Gell (1988) has remarked in a different context, magical thinking in our society can be efficacious not only because it is imaginatively compelling, but also because it opens up ideal realms of possibility toward which people can strive using prescribed action. Faith teachings for many believers have the attraction of implying that mediating structures or hurdles between the self and success can be removed, made irrelevant, since faith conquers everything, although lack of success must be explained away if it is not to rebound on self-image.

Some anthropological work would seem to imply that Faith teaching is decidedly peripheral in Christian contexts. Johnny Parry notes (1986: 467) that all major world religions stress the merits of gifts and alms, ideally given in secrecy and without expectation of worldly return. Unreciprocated gifts become seen as the means to a liberation from bondage to the world, a denial of the profane self, atonement from sin, and a means to salvation. He adds: "To a greater extent than in the Indian religions, Christianity—with its notion that all men are fashioned equally in the image of God—has developed a *universalistic* conception of purely disinterested giving" (468).[18] What I have been describing, however, is the establishment of forms of giving, considered vitally important to spiritual identity, in which self-interest and benefit to (even unknown) others are not seen as mutually exclusive, indeed are made dependent upon each other. In Parry's argument (46) the world religions and capitalism produce an ideological split between the notion of the free gift and the notion of interested exchange: as the economy becomes disembedded from society, transactions appropriate to each become more polarized in symbolism and ideology. Faith doctrine denies the possibility of creating an unbridgeable split between spheres of existence—all are united by being under the thrall of and therefore reflective of divine power. Free gifts to others are not wrong, but they miss the central point of Christian action: ultimately, the individual person must cultivate a spiritual contract with God. The recipient of a linguistic or monetary gift is made a potentially (though not always) anonymous part of an economy of salvation that seeks for the believer the best of both this world and the next.

I do not want to give the impression that such giving pervades every single moment of existence: a believer will give a pint of milk to a friend without necessarily expecting a dairy herd to arrive in their back garden the next day. Some supporters are perfectly capable of contextualizing and compartmentalizing the movement's practices within their own lives. A former missionary and current member of the local Pentecostal church told me, for instance, that he went to his own church to help others, but to the Word of Life to help himself. My point, however, is that practices of giving, combined with the idea of simultaneous accumulation and circulation of spiritual capital, provide powerful means of subjecting the believing person to constant (self-)scrutiny. Such giving indicates how Faith ideology dissolves or transcends old divisions between the linguistic and the material in Protestant worship. The charismatic self is constituted by becoming a materialized self through the agency of words and things.

......

Notes

I'd like to thank other participants in our "Words and Things" workshops for their comments on this chapter, and in particular Fenella Cannell and Patsy Spyer, who provided many carefully considered and insightful remarks. Shortage of space has prevented me from responding properly to the issues raised by others; they will have to be considered more fully in future work. Although resonances with other chapters have not been made explicit, I hope the reader might be able to perceive parallels regarding such issues as the relationship between words and objects; connections between ideas of personhood, substance, and power; and the mutually reinforcing processes of conversion and consumption. I develop a parallel argument to this chapter in an essay called "The Charismatic Gift" in the *Journal of the Royal Anthropological Institute* (2004), but that essay is more explicitly concerned with the attempt to link the notion of a "charismatic gift" in the Christian (and Weberian) sense of a quality of authoritative inspiration to a Maussian concept of the gift as breaking down distinctions between people as well as between people and objects.

1 For a much more detailed history of the Faith movement, see Coleman 2000.

2 The first nationally known preacher to promulgate prosperity ideas was probably Oral Roberts. According to Barron 1987, Roberts says that in 1947 his eyes fell on 3 John 2: "Beloved, I wish above all things that thou mayest prosper and be in health, even as thy soul prospereth," with life-changing results. The central figure of the movement is, however, still Kenneth Hagin, whose Bible school in Tulsa has trained many of the current leading prosperity preachers.

3 The rainbow represents the notion of covenant, as revealed in Genesis; the

sword alludes to Paul's letter to the Ephesians (6, 11), calling on them to "Put on the whole armour of God" and take up (17) "the sword of the spirit, which is the word of God."

4 The phrase "Word of Life" derives from 1 John 1 and is a reference to Jesus.

5 Skog 1993 estimates that perhaps 10,000 sympathizers of such groups as the Word of Life exist in Sweden, located in some ninety congregations.

6 Indeed, this latter point might be expanded in relation to Harding's later work, *The Book of Jerry Falwell* (2000), which contains a modified version of her 1987 paper. Harding's analysis of Falwell's religious persona sees him as constituted fundamentally through narrative. Yet, even Falwell, a Bible-toting fundamentalist preacher, can and perhaps should be viewed through an analytical lens that takes in the material and visual as well as the linguistic dimensions of his ministry.

7 *Word of Life Newsletter*, April 1985, 6.

8 There may be parallels here with Kenneth Burke's (1969) notion of "identification," developed in the context of a theory of rhetoric, wherein the resonances between identification and actual consubstantiality are explored. For Burke (46), identification and persuasion come close to each other when an act of persuasion may be committed for the purpose of causing the audience to identify itself with the speaker's interests, and when the speaker draws on identification of interests to establish rapport between him or herself and the audience. Moreover (57–59), an audience may feel as though it is not merely receiving but also creatively participating in the speaker's assertion.

9 Recorded on Word of Life cassette LOS10.

10 In Swartling, "Trosrörelsen—En Personlig Erfarenhet" (The Faith movement—A personal experience), ms. archived at Kyrkans Hus, Uppsala.

11 Parry's description of Hindu body builders in Banares (1994: 170–73) emphasizes the connections between bodily perfection, salvation, and asceticism. While the Faith depiction of building the body is more metaphorical in implication, and indeed apparently nonascetic, it retains the sense of disciplining the self in order to achieve self-transformation. Austin-Broos (1997: 146) refers to the way "in-filling" of the Spirit among Jamaican Pentecostal women involves valorizing body mass as representing a plenitude of divine force. Faith practice presents, in place of a female vision of spiritual cornucopia, a much more masculine image of a hard-bodied, invulnerable Jesus.

12 Faith doctrines share with Quakerism an emphasis on spontaneity. See Bauman 1989.

13 Such imagery is also used to describe the action of giving money to Faith causes.

14 Talk at the Word of Life, March 4, 1987.

15 *Word of Life Newsletter*, August 1986, 10–11.

16 Parallels are evident with Jean Comaroff's (1985: 235) discussion of holy collection as a central Protestant legitimation of the role of money, and with the Zionist understanding of the term as an accumulation to the self, a means

of regaining control of the self in the gift, not an alienation from the self implied by the Christian ideal.

17 For a consideration of this stance in relation to Western notions of the person, see my forthcoming article, "The Charismatic Gift."

18 Compare with Parry 1986: 468: "Since the things of this world are seen as antithetical to the person's true self, his soul, an ethical salvation religion is I think likely to encourage that separation of persons from things which is an ideological precondition of market exchange."

···Six···

The Effectiveness of Ritual

Christina Toren

Despite the many profound changes wrought by colonization, war, and conversion to one world religion or another, different peoples retain their historically differentiated collective uniqueness as Fijians, for example, or English, or Samburu, or Inuit, or Australian Aborigine, or French. Relations between people within any given collectivity continue over time to be characterized by historically particular forms of kinship, particular forms of political economy, and informed by particular ideas of self and person, body-mind, gender, and sociality. In "Cannibalism and Compassion" (1998) I discussed, for example, historical transformations resulting from conversion to Christianity in the nineteenth century in Fijian ideas of the person—that is to say, in how Fijians conceived of the subject/object relation between the self and lived experience. I showed how, in doing away with cannibalism and other sacrificial practices, conversion deprived chiefs of their power to demonstrate their own *mana* (effectiveness) in annihilation of the mana of others and revealed that the consumptive processes informing personhood and chiefship could find their locus in *veilomani*, the mutual compassion or pitying love that defines kinship. The ideas and practices that inform Fijian social relations, like any other aspect of human being, are conserved as a function of the selfsame process through which they are transformed. How can this be so? This chapter provides an answer through an analysis of the ontogenetic process that renders contemporary Fijian Christianity at once orthodox and distinctively Fijian.[1] Its broader intention is to show the effectiveness of ritual and ritualized behaviors for the at once transforming and conservative processes that make us what we are. At the end of the chapter I return to the articulation between radical historical change that alters the conditions of everyday life and the microhistorical process of human ontogeny.

Ritualized activities pervade daily life in the villages of central Fiji, such as the eight villages that make up the country (*vanua*) of Sawaieke on the island of Gau where I did fieldwork.[2] Specifically Christian rituals include prayer before every meal (including morning or afternoon tea, taken on special occasions) and numerous church services throughout the week; the Wesleyan church in Sawaieke held early morning prayer every day, at least three evening services during the week, two full Sunday services (morning and evening), and Sunday school. Moreover, all the many traditional ceremonies, such as *sevusevu* (the offering of *yaqona* root that requests permission to be in a place and accompanies all yaqona drinking) and the elaborate ceremonies of welcome to any official visitor, include Christian formulas at the end of speeches of presentation, and often a long prayer of Christian blessing. It is, however, in the ceremonies occasioned by death that Sawaieke people reveal most clearly how their commitment to Christianity and to what is traditional (*vakavanua*, literally, according to the land) inform one another in such a way as to define what it is to be Fijian. This chapter focuses on showing both how important are these ritualized activities and ceremonies—Christian and traditional—for Sawaieke children's constitution of the ideas that inform a specifically Fijian Christianity, and how orthodox Christian practice is by no means bound to produce orthodox Christians. As will become apparent, there is no need here to posit any explicit or implicit attempt at either syncretism or resistance; explanation enough is to be found in the process through which, over time, people make sense of ritual practice—a process that is here uncovered by means of an analysis of transformations in certain ideas held by Sawaieke girls and boys aged between seven years, ten months (7/10) and thirteen years (13/0).[3]

My argument turns on the idea that the conserving and transforming properties of what humans say and do are aspects of the microhistorical process through which we become ourselves. In this process mind is continuously brought into being as a function of the whole person in intersubjective relations with others in the environing world.[4] It is not a process in which people considered as individuals interact with one another and in so doing create (or express) a social situation and a social relationship—it is not social construction. Intersubjectivity is always and inevitably historically prior because, whenever we encounter one another, we do so as carriers of our own, always unique, history, and whenever we speak to one another we speak out of the past that we have lived. We do not, therefore, negotiate meaning in interaction with one another, as cultural constructionists would have it. Rather, I make sense of what you are doing and saying in terms of what I already know: any new information is assimilated to my existing structures of knowing. This process at once transforms that information in the course of its assimilation (and to this extent conserves what I already know) and transforms my existing structures of knowing in the course of their inevitable accommodation to the new information (and to this extent changes what I know).

In other words, our structures of knowing are differentiated through functioning and thus evince a kind of inertial property as a function of age. The longer they've been functioning to assimilate information, the more highly differentiated they already are, and the less they can transform as a function of accommodation to new situations. The corollary of this is that mature people who encounter new ideas and practices willy-nilly substantially transform those same ideas and practices in assimilating them to their own. It follows that the developmental process in which, over time, I constitute my ideas of self and other, of relationship, of the world, is one that in effect conserves (even while it transforms) the ideas and practices I encountered early on and made my own in the course of the day-to-day, many and manifold, intersubjective relations in which I was nurtured, neglected, loved, rejected, made much of, instructed, played with, ignored, or left to my own devices. Our engagement in the peopled world is always an emotional one, and all our long-held ideas and practices are imbued with a feeling of rightness that goes well beyond any mere rationalization—an observation that holds as much for what we consider it proper to reject as for what we maintain.

Here, as elsewhere, my argument is that ethnographic studies of how children constitute the ideas that adults take to be self-evident enable us to achieve analytical insight into historically specific social processes. Thus it makes sense to me that children (including infants) should be included in anthropological fieldwork on precisely the same basis as any of our other informants—because only they can give us access to what they know about the peopled world, and what they know can provide us with analytical insights that cannot be obtained any other way.[5]

The children's data analyzed here were obtained in 1990. The majority of my adult informants are Sawaieke villagers, including some who were brought up in the village, educated in high schools on the mainland, and now live in the capital, Suva, where they are employed as teachers, nurses, security guards, and government officials. Several have traveled overseas. Every one of my child and adult informants has his or her own ideas about religious practice and doctrine, about the ancestors and what is *vakavanua* (according to the land), but I would argue that where I make generalized observations, adults would be likely to agree with them. My use of the ethnographic present is intended to suggest the continuity that resides in transformation such that the ideas and practices I discuss here are likely still to prevail in Sawaieke and indeed among Fijian Methodists at large as a function of the processes through which meaning is constituted over time.

How Lived Experience Becomes Meaningful

The systematic data analyzed here are derived from what Sawaieke children had to say and write about God, about Sunday school (*wilivola*, literally, reading), and about death ceremonies. Death ceremonies—*somate*—are highly salient in Fijian village life; they occur relatively often[6] and induce a pervasively heavy and portentous atmosphere that lasts from the moment the death is announced until the fourth night of ceremonial observance, when the initial mourning period is lifted and light-heartedness is explicitly encouraged; the next day, the normal daily round is resumed. Death ceremonies combine Christian observance with Fijian traditional practices, and while children are forbidden to attend them, they cannot avoid knowing how they are conducted.

In each case, where the children produced written accounts their task was to write a story about God, about Sunday school, or about death ceremonies. They were given no other guidance as to content and wrote their accounts in their school class groups, each child sufficiently separated from his or her neighbors to prevent copying.[7]

A content analysis of the essays that looked strictly at the words used by children showed that, except for differences informed by gender or by age, what they had written about God and Sunday school was remarkably uniform and orthodox. I include both raw numbers and percentages here to give the reader an idea of the uniformity of children's observations.[8] To begin with *na kalou*—God. Twenty-six girls between the ages of 7/10 and 11/9 and twenty-two boys aged between 8/2 and 13/0 produced stories about God. Girls mentioned twenty-six different aspects of God in all; one-third or more said that:

God loves us (18, or 69 percent), God made everything (14, or 54 percent), God has many admirable qualities (14, or 54 percent), God saves us (13, or 50 percent), God protects us (12, or 46 percent), God approves or disapproves of certain acts (10, or 38 percent), God gives us good qualities (10, or 38 percent), God helps us (10, or 38 percent), God gives us food, drink, and other material things (9, or 35 percent).

Boys mentioned in all twenty-one different aspects of God, and one-third or more said that:

God loves us (14, or 64 percent), God made everything (14, or 64 percent), God has many admirable qualities (11, or 50 percent), God's child is Jesus or God was born into the world as Jesus (9, or 41 percent), God saves us (8, or 36 percent), God helps us (7, or 32 percent), God gives us food, drink, and other material things (7, or 32 percent) and does miracles (7, or 32 percent).

While the children's accounts of God were remarkably similar, there was some suggestion that gender informed their ideas in that boys were only minimally concerned with the good qualities God gives to humans, and in their account of God's own qualities boys were likely to focus on God's not being always angry and not fighting, while girls focused on qualities such as God's good temper and forgiveness. Girls in the middle age range and older (those aged nine and over) were also more likely to remark on what behaviors God approves or disapproves of (10, or 48 percent of girls over nine). Increasing age discriminated the inclusion of more arcane details. Thus seven girls and nine boys aged nine and over (33 percent of girls and 53 percent of boys over nine) referred to the relation between God and Jesus, or between the Father, Son, and Holy Spirit, or between God and other Gods.

Concealed in the idea of God's primary attribute being that of loving or having compassion for humans is a shift whereby, from age 9/10 onward for both girls and boys, the nature of God's love is commented on as either unconditional and enduring in the face of humans' bad behavior, or conditional on a person's pitiable state, on good behavior, or on Christian observance. Both ideas (antithetical as they appear) inform the hierarchical aspect of compassion as definitive of kin relations within household and clan.[9]

Here I should note that adults' views—as derived from participant observation—make ritual Christian observance the crucial sign of belief in God; God's love for humans depends on their attendance on him and this in turn governs whether or not a person will be saved. One must be seen to say grace before meals, to bow one's head and close one's eyes while praying, to attend church services twice on Sundays and at least once during the week, to give money to the church and to support church organizations and church projects. This matter of the visibility and frequency of Christian observance connects with the traditional and still prevailing Fijian idea that it is attendance on a God or chief that actually empowers him. So, while all the old Fijian gods and ancestors continue to exist, their power is greatly diminished because those people who do attend on them can do so only in secret; since conversion to Christianity, attendance on the old gods and ancestors constitutes witchcraft.

Children are well aware of the importance of Christian ritual observance because their attendance at church is mandatory: they are expected to be present at at least two out of the three Sunday services, at Sunday school, and at any service held for them during the week. In Fijian, Sunday is *na siga tabu*, literally the forbidden day, also translated as "the sacred" or "the holy day"; women and girls have to prepare meals, but apart from this one should not do any work and should confine one's activities to churchgoing, reading religious texts, and rest. So, on Sundays, children are forbidden to play sport, to go swimming, to run about on the village green, or to play in any obvious way. Each school day begins with prayer and each school week with a special religious assembly taken by a church elder.

The importance of ritual observance is apparent in what children wrote about Sunday school, wilivola. Again their accounts were remarkably uniform, with twenty-three out of twenty-five girls and all twenty-two boys providing a more or less elaborate account of the procedural aspects of Sunday school from the sounding of the drum after lunch until the children were dismissed to come home; younger children's essays were less detailed than those of older children but nevertheless the vast majority followed the same pattern. Boys and girls tended, however, to emphasize somewhat different aspects. One-third or more of the girls gave a more or less detailed procedural account (23, or 92 percent), told what they learned at wilivola (15, or 60 percent), noted that reading occurs every Sunday (12, or 48 percent), explained why we attend church or wilivola (12, or 48 percent), referred specifically to the numbers of children or named their teachers (11, or 44 percent), remarked on what is forbidden on Sunday (8, or 32 percent), and said that Sunday reading is good and enjoyable (8, or 32 percent).

Over one-third or more of boys gave a more or less detailed procedural account (22, or 100 percent), told what they learned at wilivola (9, or 41 percent), and remarked on what is forbidden on Sunday (8, or 36 percent).

Of the nine boys who told what they learned, two of the youngest referred to virtues such as obedience and piety, one to being taught not to swear, and the remaining six to learning songs and stories. The sixteen girls who told what they learned also emphasized stories but tended to be more explicit about their content; twelve girls further remarked that its purpose is to reveal what is written in the Bible, while the five oldest of these girls (aged 10/4 to 11/6) said also that its purpose is to come to know God or Jesus. Only one boy (aged 11/6) made this same remark.

Children's accounts of *somate* (death ceremonies—twenty-five essays by girls, twenty-two by boys), like those for Sunday school, exhibit a distinct bias toward the procedural, with increasingly rich detail with age about what happens from the time the death is notified to the ceremonies for the fourth, tenth, and one hundredth night. One-third or more of 25 girls gave a more or less detailed procedural account (24, or 96 percent); remarked on women's weeping (23, or 92 percent), communal meals (18, or 72 percent), the burial of the body (18, or 72 percent), the church service or blessings, hymns and so on at the grave (17, or 68 percent), the grave itself (13, or 52 percent), the coffin (12, or 48 percent), people coming from other villages for the ceremonies (11, or 44 percent), the bringing of mats, bark cloth, and other valuables for presentation (10, or 40 percent), the bringing of feast food for presentation (9, or 36 percent), and women's preparation and cooking of food (9, or 36 percent).

One-third or more of twenty-two boys gave a more or less detailed procedural account (21, or 95 percent); remarked on the burial of the body (17, or 77 percent), on the church service or blessings and hymns at the grave (15, or 68 percent), the grave itself (14, or 64 percent), women's weeping (13, or 59 percent), communal meals (12, or 55 percent), the coffin (9, or 41 percent), the particular kin who weep, dress the corpse, and so on (9, or 41 percent), the fourth, tenth, or one-hundredth-night ceremonies (8, or 36 percent), and men's killing of a cow and pig (8, or 36 percent).

This procedural bias is accompanied by a definite shift with age whereby children older than 9/0 included personal references in their accounts, or described ceremonies for specific named kin or in which they had been personally involved; this shift is found in the essays of thirteen out of twenty girls (65 percent) and seven out of seventeen boys (41 percent) over nine years old. These personal references are further distinguished, in the case of girls, by a shift from goal-oriented to actor-oriented verbal constructions along with the use of first-person pronouns (I, we), which itself suggests a shift in their orientation to the activity being written about—one that is apparently informed by gender.

In their essays about God and about Sunday school, children seem more concerned with doctrine and procedure than with their personal involvement; the following three examples (by a girl aged 9/4) demonstrate the shift in tone that may be found in essays about death ceremonies written by children over nine years old; the first essay is about God, the second about Sunday school, and the third about death ceremonies. Note how this child, even while she gives a generalized account of what is done for a death, injects a distinctly personal note.

> "A story about God." We perform church services to God. Church services to God are really very useful. For we may sing hymns, for we read the Bible. God orders our lives. God alone. He helps us in all our activities. God is good. He helps us and looks after us wherever we go. God also formed the parts of our bodies. God takes care of us a great deal. God also loves/pities us. God has power. We always pray to God. We always ask God to give us wisdom.
>
> "Reading on Sunday." We always read on Sundays. We children learn some stories about our reading on Sunday. We read the sacred book. We sing during Sunday reading. Some are bad children on Sunday. We learn a lot of stories in the sacred book. Our teacher reads very clearly to us some stories about Sunday reading. After lunch the drum sounds, we go at once to church so that we may attend to our duty or reading. If every single day we read no trouble will come to us. Our teachers always help us.
>
> "The Somate." The somate is truly a terrifying thing because someone is dead, the ladies cry. The somate is held in the place where somate are held if a gentleman or lady dies they are at once carried here to their house. There are also communal meals according to clan. We eat together if there is a death. For myself, if someone died in our house I should be absolutely overwhelmed. If there is a somate a cow is killed and chickens and a pig. After that the coffin of the dead gentleman or lady is carried away for burial. Beautiful mats are spread below [the coffin], after that a little earth is put on top, then it's buried completely.

Unlike a number of much younger children, this little girl does not, in her account of the somate, mention the church service for the death or prayers and hymn-singing at the graveside; most salient for her are the weeping, the communal meals, the burial, and the grave itself. Weeping and the preparation and cooking of food for communal meals are women's duties, and the frequency of their mention in girls' essays implicates the gendered nature not only of the activities themselves, but of the way that gender is intrinsic to the learning process itself. Weeping also features in boys' essays, but even so boys refer more often to predominantly male activities such as the burial and the church service at the graveside—both of which are dominated by men, who are also implicated in references to the grave, which is dug and prepared by men.

Boys are much less likely than girls to inject a personal note into their stories (41 percent of the boys, compared with 65 percent of the girls over nine years old) and when they do so, these personal references have a qualitatively less engaged tone to them. Thus boys by and large continue to make use of goal-oriented verbal constructions, and when they do use actor-oriented constructions, they tend overwhelmingly to use third-person plural pronouns (they) where girls make greater use of the first person (I, we). Only one boy, aged 11/10, produced an essay about the somate that approached the tone found in girls' essays (an extract is to be found in the appendix).

The following essay, by a boy aged 11/9, is more typical of the tone of essays on the somate by boys over nine years old:

> When someone dies the somate is done, children are forbidden to be there, or meet together or play or shout or laugh, the [people in] the somate are silent, when someone appears with valuables they weep, if some guests come those in the somate may be happy or crying. . . . When those who are kin of the dead do the burial they will cry in the village. The grave diggers are ready, they wait to carry the coffin there. The coffin carriers carry it on their shoulders to church for the service, then there is the service, after that [the coffin] is carried to the grave for burial, when they arrive there at the grave they do the church service, then the minister speaks: earth to earth, sand to sand, after that the burial is done at once, after the burial they come [home] here, after that there is the ceremony for the fourth night, after that the kin of the one who is eating stones disperse, they will go home and it will not be long before there is the [ceremony for] the hundredth night.

Nevertheless, that some boys over nine do inject a personal note in their stories shows that at this age they, like the girls, are beginning consciously to assimilate mandatory collective activities to their sense of themselves as particular children, in particular kinds of relations with particular kin. Death at once disrupts the relation between the child as ego and his or her dead kinsperson and is an occasion for the elaboration of other relations with other kinspeople.[10]

This developmental shift suggests too that around age 9/0 to 10/0 children are beginning deliberately to reflect on what they know and, in so doing, to assimilate their understanding of Christian doctrine to their knowledge of Christian ritual, in such a way that the doctrine becomes explanatory of the ritualized behavior that had earlier had no particular meaning beyond the performance of it. Thus what I have called above a procedural bias is the foundation of the child's knowledge.

This procedural bias is apparent too in, for example, any Fijian village adult's account of his or her attendance at a wedding, funeral, or other occasion elsewhere. This is a casual observation derived from listening to adults relate their experiences abroad to their kin who had remained at home; these accounts routinely give a blow-by-blow description of each day spent at the festivities, including such mundane details as the fact that the teller got up in the morning, bathed, dressed, went for breakfast, what precisely he or she ate, how afterward they made their way to the village hall, entered, sat down there in such and such a place, and so on—apparently conforming to an idea of narrative structure that places weight on temporal and procedural aspects. In other words, the children's written style of "telling a story about Sunday school" or "telling a story about funeral ceremonies" is very similar to adults' oral style when they tell others about what happened at the Methodist Conference or Provincial Council or other meeting or festivity or ceremony.

What interests me in the case of both children and adults is that this procedural bias is evidently related to ritual, which itself tends to be talked about not in terms of meaning, but in terms of who should do what, when, and how. In anthropological texts "ritual" refers usually to discrete ceremonies; I use "ritualized behavior" here to refer more widely to behaviors that are pervasive in daily life, so taken for granted that their ritual quality is rarely recognized. I would argue that most, if not all, behaviors have a ritualized aspect—that is to say, an aspect that can be rendered explicit as "a rule." Here I am following Gilbert Lewis's (1980: 11) formulation that "in all those instances where we would feel no doubt that we had observed ritual we could have noticed and shall notice whether the people who perform it have explicit rules to guide them in what they do. . . . What is always explicit about ritual, and recognized by those who perform it, is that aspect of it which states who should do what and when."

Adults are usually capable of ascribing a meaning to ritualized behaviors, but from the child's point of view that meaning cannot be obvious; it does not declare itself. For the child, the significance of the behavior may be simply that this is how you do *X*. In my previous work I have shown how this childhood experience of embodying a ritual behavior or series of behaviors is crucial for the process in which, over time, meaning comes to be ascribed to that behavior such that its performance becomes symbolic of that meaning.[11]

The developmental process through which a Sawaieke child makes Wesleyan doctrine meaningful for him- or herself has to be such that "the Christian way" comes to be at one with "the way of the land" and "the chiefly way," which are generally explicitly held by Sawaieke adults to be in perfect accord. With apparent ease, they can reconcile their devout, and in most respects apparently orthodox, Methodism and their acceptance of the word of God as written in the Bible, with their equal certainty that the old Fijian Gods and ancestors still exist and in their benign aspect come under the Christian God's aegis and do his will, punishing for example those who willfully abjure the obligations of kinship or attendance on a properly installed chief; the ancestors' malign power is also routinely unleashed in witchcraft. The question is, how can this reconciliation be achieved when there is no explicit acknowledgment in any church service or Christian prayer or Bible story or Sunday school teaching of the continuing existence of the ancestors? The answer lies, I think, in the day-to-day pervasiveness of ritualized behavior in Fijian village life, in the dominance of ritual performance over doctrine in villagers' ideas of what it is to be Christian (which is not to deny the many explicitly and implicitly syncretic statements to be found in both the historical archive and in contemporary Fijian media), in the connected idea that it is attendance on the Christian God, or ancestor or living chief that actually empowers him, and in the idea that the ancestors' power is immanent in the world, while that of the Christian God is transcendent.

In the child's lived experience, the ritual quality of daily life is learned through obedience to endless injunctions from their elders to do certain things in certain ways and not to do other things. For the young child, bowing one's head and closing one's eyes for prayer and not playing or making a noise on Sunday is thus of the same order as adopting a respectful body posture in the company of adults and not playing on the village green when a chiefly ceremony is being performed in the village hall. Doctrine is not unimportant here; nevertheless the child has embodied an array of ritualized behaviors to the point where they are automatic, long before it arrives at an understanding of the doctrinal orthodoxies that are held by adults to render their ritualized behaviors mandatory.[12] From the adults' point of view, their injunctions to children about how to behave all bear on aspects of *veiqaravi*, "mutual attendance," in its most general sense; so, for example, when children are asked (as they often are) to give out an impromptu prayer before meals, they are explicitly implicated in an act of recognition paradigmatic of Fijian ritual interaction. In such mundane ritualized practices children may come to recognize veiqaravi as a pervasive form of recognition that unites different domains of Fijian social life.[13]

Elsewhere I have shown how, in respect of Fijian hierarchy, this process of constituting the meaning of ritualized behavior results in conforming behavior that suggests a complementary consensus about its meaning, whereas in fact people hold significantly different ideas of hierarchy as a function of both age and gender.[14] This is likely too in respect of the articulation of specifically Methodist ritual and doctrine, though it is a difficult thing to get at since the doctrine appears at first sight to be as thoroughly assimilated as the ritualized behaviors. Note, however, that the various forms of Fijian Christian practice and doctrinal differences (between Seventh Day Adventism and Methodism, for example) may be a topic of conversation when people are drinking yaqona, and also a topic of debate.[15]

Fijians I know are all Christians (mostly Wesleyans); all are assiduous in their Christian practice and all assert beliefs that accord with the Bible and the Methodist hymn and prayer book. Mostly such assertions seem not to be merely conventional and to be characterized by an emotional tone that shows the beliefs to be considered unassailable and personally relevant. The emotional tone of this commitment is especially apparent in the mourning ceremonies that accompany a death.

The Ceremonies for Death

The announcement of a death precipitates immediately the impassioned weeping of those women who are close kin to the dead and members of his or her house: wife, mother, daughter, sister. Their shrill wailing can be heard far across the village interspersed with tearful appeals to the dead: *Isa, Watiqu!*—Alas, my spouse! *Isa, Tamaqu!*—Alas, my father! Very soon these female mourners who are immediate kin are joined by other, especially elderly, women (many of whom wear black) who have come to perform their duty in the *bikabika*, the house where the corpse, dressed in its best clothes, is laid out—usually for not more than one night—before it is buried.[16] The ladies who are close kin sit on the floor nearby the coffin, which is placed on a pile of fine new mats in the honored part of the house that is called above, and they weep. Other mourning kin come in groups, men and women together; they enter by the common entrance below, seat themselves on the floor below the *tanoa* (the large wooden vessel in which yaqona is mixed and from which it is served), and present on behalf of their clan, their *yavusa* (group of clans related by ritual obligations and intermarriage), or their village, the valuables they have brought with them for *na reguregu* (literally, the kissing)—rolls of mats, bark cloth, whale teeth.[17] During the speeches of presentation the weeping subsides, only to begin again when the speeches are over and one or two of the visiting ladies who are close kin to the mourners and the deceased proceed up the room to embrace the immediate female kin of the dead and weep with them for a while beside the coffin before retiring to a more humble seating position. The sound of weeping and wailing rises and falls as each new group of visitors enters and more and more ladies join the bikabika; during this first night, until the body is buried, they will join in the periodic wailing of the closest kin.

Meanwhile the men have gone to join their male kin who are drinking yaqona for the death in another house nearby belonging to the same clan. As the bikabika becomes more crowded, the presentations of valuables and feast food are conducted there in the house where the men are gathered; the sound of the men's repeated thanks expressed in the formulas of speeches and ceremonial clapping (*cobo*, a soft clapping with cupped hands) can be heard in the bikabika. Younger men and women have also their duties to perform. Young men have to go to the gardens and bring back bundles of taro and cassava, to butcher a cow and a pig or two, and to pound yaqona root to maintain a constant supply to those of their peers who are looking after the mixing and serving of yaqona in the bikabika and the house where the men are gathered. The young married women and girls together prepare the food, lay the cloth, and wash the dishes for each of the communal meals (breakfast, lunch, and dinner) that over the next few days will be served to scores of mourners who have come to attend on the death.

The name for the ceremony of presenting valuables (*reguregu*, literally, sniff-kissing) refers to the final good-byes of the living to the dead. Just before the coffin is closed, a whale tooth is placed on the chest of the corpse,[18] and the close kin of the dead come one by one to press their noses against the cheek or forehead of the corpse and sniff deeply, taking into themselves its sweet rotting smell.[19] The coffin is then taken up and removed from the house via "the land door" (*darava e vanua*), which is closed after it.[20] There follows the church service and the procession to the grave, which is usually situated on land belonging to the clan of the dead; it is lined with a layer of mats—the coarsest next to the earth and the finest nearest the coffin. There is a further brief service of prayer and hymns for the burial. Then those mourners who have accompanied the coffin to the grave return to the village—the ladies to the bikabika and the men to the other house—and, soon after their return, there is the ceremony of "the opening of the door" (*na idola ni katuba*). A *tanoa* is brought into the bikabika via the land door through which the coffin had exited and yaqona is solemnly prepared and served; the first bowl is poured out on the ground through that same door and only then are bowls served in due order to the highest-status men present and thereafter to the mourning ladies, who will remain there until the fourth night. On the day of the fourth night the ladies of the bikabika employ themselves in making intricately beautiful and sweet-smelling garlands, which, along with bark cloth, they take in procession to decorate the grave. For the fourth night the men join the ladies in the bikabika and there is a presentation of feast food and yaqona drinking. The singing of secular songs and joking resumes. After this, the mourners disperse to their own houses, only to regroup for the ceremonies of the tenth night after the death, when there are further presentations of feast food, and the hundredth night when, with the ceremony of *vakataraisulu* (permitting clothes), the final mourning restrictions are lifted and valuables are presented to those who have taken on themselves the various *tabu* that are a sign of mourning (e.g., ladies' wearing of black dresses, men's not shaving and so on).

Death is explicitly a sacrifice to the Christian God; this is apparent in the following extract from the sermon made by the Wesleyan lay preacher at the funeral service in church for an elderly Sawaieke man in 1990:

> This evening my kinspeople, we who are able to be here this evening, it is right that we should look at the path followed by this kinsman of ours. No one of us will be excepted from the same course. Today in Sawaieke there are two gentlemen [who have died]. Just one household, just one clan from which yesterday their two lives were removed. One died in Suva, one was stricken here.
>
> We shall ask, Who, perhaps, is to follow? We made a joke about it during our making of the new road that we should buy a cart for ourselves. So those who are stricken here, their coffin would be loaded onto a cart then taken up to the grave. We were making a question of who might be the first fruits offering for it. And [who that might be] is understood today. The day that was appointed by God for this elder to be made the first offering. He will turn toward this path, incline at once toward the land into which his body will dissolve, so that he may sleep eternally.
>
> Gentlemen and ladies, if we are saying much this evening, it is because we are speaking of our lives. It is right that we should confirm today what Jesus says in the lesson we have already read: I am the path. The holy book tells us that the end of all the paths that are proper to us people is death. But the path Jesus spoke about to his disciple, to Thomas, was this, I am the path, and the truth, and the life. If we follow it, or we rely on it, or we raise our eyes toward it, or we look at it, we will discover comfort there every day of our lives. At the time when we are called, as yesterday this gentleman was called, we shall accept the call in a contented and resigned spirit.

The idea of death as a sacrifice pervades all the speeches that are made for a death. The Christian God is said to appoint the day of death, just as he appoints that of birth, but it is still the land—*na vanua*—which reclaims its own, for people are *na lewe ni vanua*, lit. "the substance of the land" and this is why people who die in Suva or elsewhere are usually brought home by ferry or plane to be buried on land belonging to their clan. The ancestors are implicitly invoked in all the speeches for reguregu and the other traditional ceremonies; these are addressed to the mourners using their honorific titles, which themselves name the *yavu tabu*, "forbidden house foundations" situated on clan land and sacred to the founding ancestors of each clan (*na kalou vu*, literally, origin gods) who are their owners and guardians.

In cases where witchcraft is suspected, death is a sacrifice to the ancestors in their malign guise as *tevoro*, devils. One who wishes evil toward his or her kin drinks yaqona alone, pouring out a libation to the ancestors and requesting that they strike down a named kinsperson. By contrast, God takes us in the spirit of love—for God's loving compassion for us people is held by Fijians, as by other Christians, to be his primary attribute. Even so, God is said to allow the ancestors to strike down one who offends against the land, for example, a corrupt politician who defrauds the people; and it is the ancestors who, under God's aegis, implicitly demand the performance of all proper traditional ceremonies for the dead, for it is these ceremonies that placate the ancestors in the person of the newly dead who has joined them.

The power of the ancestors is immanent in the fertility of *na vanua*, the land, and this fertile power is acknowledged when, on the occasion of a death, the land's products are given back: in the body of the dead, the coarse and fine pandanus mats in which the coffin is swathed, the bark cloth and garlands that go to decorate the grave, the bowl of yaqona that is poured out on the ground as a libation. The whale tooth laid on the chest of the corpse is a product of the sea, but it is also that supreme valuable (*ka liu*, literally, leading thing) with which, in life, chiefs reciprocate the tributary offerings of landspeople. All these valuables are sacrificed along with the dead person, who takes up his or her place alongside ancestors whose continued presence demands proper acknowledgment. Until these ceremonies are performed, the newly dead will not rest in the grave and is likely to appear in the village and terrify the living who, for at least the first four nights, and even up to the tenth, do not walk alone in the dark across the village green or from house to house, but go in groups, while those who are accustomed to sleep alone—young men, for instance—make sure of their safety by sleeping together in one house. Only with the performance of the hundredth-night ceremonies can one be sure that the dead will rest—especially those dead who died an untimely death or who were installed chiefs of their *yavusa* or country.[21]

I have to emphasize here that while the ritual speeches for these ceremonies implicitly invoke the ancestors, they always explicitly refer to the Christian God and his church. The ancestors have their rightful claim on their descendants (*nodra kawa*) as kin, and God enjoins the ancestors' compassion for the living insofar as the living fulfill their kinship obligations to the dead and to one another. Death ceremonies make these obligations take material form in the ritual services performed and in the valuables and feast food given by each household, whose members together carry them to the leading house of their clan so that the amassed valuables and food may be taken in procession and presented to mourning kin, *vakamataqali*, according to clan. Similar ritual services and presentations are a feature of all life-cycle ceremonies—birth, circumcision, marriage, death—and of the festivals at Christmas and New Year and the ceremonies that welcome honored visitors or install a chief, and so are communal meals, but death ceremonies are distinguished by the rupture that occasions them and the sorrow and fear that are intrinsic to them.

Children and Death

Children are forbidden to attend somate, though they may indeed be present at the funeral service in church or at the graveside, but they cannot avoid knowing about them. I want to argue here that somate are peculiarly important for how Fijian village children learn to be Christians —in particular the process through which Wesleyan ritual and doctrine become personally relevant to them. I begin with an edited extract from my field notes for 1982. It concerns the members of a family I know well. Their real names are not used here.

Adi Mere [a married woman in her early thirties, separated from her husband and living in her natal house] tells me that *sa leqa ko Ratu* ["Father is dead," *Ratu* being an honorific term used for a father of chiefly rank, in this case the speaker's Father's Younger Brother]. They had heard that afternoon. A message had come over the radio that her younger brother should go to Qarani [the village on Gau where the post office and other government services are located] to await a telephone call. About 7 P.M. she comes to my house, wants to hear the radio. The death of her Father's Younger Brother [a man in his seventies] is announced and at once she jumps up from where she is sitting on the doorstep to the side entrance and rushes off into the darkness. I get up, look out, see that several old ladies are loitering outside the kitchen under the lemon trees, awaiting the official announcement and the performance of their duty on this occasion. Within a few moments they and Adi Mere are in [the other house belonging to this clan] where her Younger Brother and some of the men are already drinking *yaqona*, and a great wailing and moaning begins. . . . Every twenty minutes or so a new contingent of old ladies (and some younger ones) come to join in.

It is the dinner hour and the food is already prepared and laid out ready in the kitchen where I join the children who have nearly finished eating. Alisi [a girl aged 11 / 1] tells me that in the night Adi Mere had seen the cat jumping

> about in a particular manner and had known thereby that someone was about to die. Suddenly, without warning, Alisi and Tu Kini [a boy aged 11/3] and Tu Peni [aged 6/3] jump up and rush outside. They are crying too now. They stand under the lemon trees wailing, go over to the house where the adults are drinking *yaqona* and peer through the cracks in the bamboo lattice that forms its walls. They cry and cry. Alisi has already told me that on her way to buy benzine [at the village store] she had been crying because her grandfather was dead. Little Tu Peni is crying loudest of all. I have the impression that he is frightened. The children look very lonely outside the house there in the dark, they would not dare to enter the house and no adult comes out to take any notice of them. I have finished eating, return to my house, but hearing Tu Peni's shrill crying I call him into my house, get him a bowl of tea and some biscuits.

Village children are often left to their own devices; in this case the mother knew that no obvious harm would come to her youngest son because she could rely on the older girl and boy to look after him; the children's being afraid was simply to be accepted as an aspect of everyone's lived experience. It is worth noting that the older boy, usually a stoical child, also cried even though boys are not supposed to cry for the dead—this being explicitly a female duty—and that none of these children were especially close to their dead grandfather whom they had rarely seen. It seems likely therefore that what children in such a situation identify with is the impassioned weeping of their mother (in the case of the older boy his Mother's Younger Sister); her weeping makes them afraid and confused and so they weep too, but no adult—all of whom have other, more pressing duties to perform—comes to console them.

It seems probable that this experience, which is both predictable and relatively frequent in the life of a village child, is crucial to the child's constitution over time in intersubjective relations with others of his or her ideas of self—ideas that are invested with obligation as a function of veilomani, mutual compassion or pitying love, which ideally describes all relations between kin.

What Sawaieke children wrote in their essays on somate about the weeping that accompanies a death is contained in an appendix to this chapter. Ninety-two percent of girls (23 out of 25) made reference to weeping in their essays compared with only 59 percent of boys (13 out of 22) and, as may be seen, girls' and boys' essays differ somewhat in tone—boys' references to weeping tending, with a few exceptions, to be more removed, less empathetic. Even so, it would seem likely that the dramatic weeping for death ceremonies is important in boys' lived experience; indeed it is suggestive that one boy (aged 10/6) insists on promiscuous weeping by everyone: "All his or her kin will cry, his or her siblings and household. . . . Also the gentlemen will cry and his or her cross-cousins, siblings, grandfathers, grandmothers, they will cry. . . . The gentlemen, young men, girls, will also cry." Note also the boy (aged 9/10) who remarks somewhat testily: "Yes, those who are still in the village are tired out with all the crying in the village."

It is also worth noting here that 64 percent of girls (16 out of 25) and 64 percent of boys (14 out of 22) made use of specific kinship terms in their essays—referring either to a named kinsperson as dying, or to the particular kin who weep, dress the corpse, or perform other duties incumbent upon them as kin. These references implicate the idea that the fundamental conditions of social life are given by kinship, which ideally encompasses all relations between people, including marriage, and which ordains, as it were, for any particular kinship relation, the precise nature of the duties that are entailed by veilomani, caring for each other or loving each other.

The Effectiveness of Ritual

Sawaieke people's ritual practice is all about veiqaravi, attendance on one another, and in every case, from the least to the most elaborate, it implicates at once relations that are *vakaveiwekani* (according to kinship), *vakavanua* (according to the land), *vakaturaga* (according to chiefs), and *vakalotu* (according to the church);[22] veiqaravi in all its various forms implicates the mana of the ancestors, whose continued effectiveness continues to be immanent in the world, even if it is ultimately referable to the transcendent Christian God. My argument here has been that these social relations manifest in veiqaravi, especially those "according to kinship," mediate Sawaieke children's constitution of ideas of the peopled world and what is in it, and that the process of constituting over time an understanding of the meaning of ritual practice is itself the very process of the fixation of belief. And given that this is so, it follows that Christian practice is, for anyone who grows up in a predominantly Wesleyan Fijian village, bound to become invested with the emotional force of early and repeated experiences of death ceremonies, which themselves are all about the obligations occasioned by the mutual love of kinship and the sacrifice and grief it can entail. The incidental triumph of this Fijian ritual practice is that, without the utterance of a single unorthodox word, it assimilates God's power to the mana of ancestors and installed chiefs and makes it go to work in the world in such a way as to validate an idea of the person and social relations that is always about mutuality.

This chapter has shown that what may appear to an observer to be a coercive power that is intrinsic to ritual and religious doctrine is the constituted end product of a long process through which, over time, people render their early lived experience meaningful. It follows that for the overwhelming majority of those contemporary adults and young adults whom I knew as children in 1990, it is still the case that the power of the ancestors is immanent in the world and that belief in God refers to the necessity for at once acknowledging God's preeminence and augmenting God's power through attendance at church services, rather than to the matter of God's existence, which is simply not an issue. The immanence of ancestral mana renders it knowable even if capricious; it is always a function of the nature of the being it informs, whether animal or human, and where that being is human it is always human passions that drive its manifestation.[23] And in the Fijian idea of the person[24] as a locus of relations with others, human passions are always informed by, and take their form through, relations with other humans.

Conservation and transformation are, as shown in this chapter, twin aspects of the process in which meaning is constituted over time. The corollary of this is that, considered as a spatiotemporal location, the lived present contains its own past and its potential future; it is our artifact, an emergent aspect of the way that, as living systems that are human, we function at once to constitute and incorporate our own history—that is, the history of our relations with others in the peopled world. Transformation is an aspect of how living systems, including humans, function to develop and maintain themselves over time, but while this kind of change is continuous and inevitable, it is not radical in the sense of the kinds of historical changes precipitated, for example, among Pacific peoples by European expansion, colonization, and conversion to Christianity. To the extent that the conditions of our existence are radically changed by major historical events, so our ideas and practices change in accommodating to them; at the same time we transform exogenous ideas in making them our own.

Appendix

Girl, 7/10. They cry. Some of them cry. When someone dies they weep. . . . Some of those who gather for the somate cry a great deal . . .

Girl, 8/9A. If one of our kin dies they will weep for him or her . . . If another elderly man [literally, grandfather] dies, the children of that elder will weep for him.

Girl, 8/9B. There is crying.

Girl, 8/10A. They cry.

Girl, 9/0. At the somate the ladies cry. . . . Some of the ladies weep sorrowfully —most of all the wife of the one who has died. Her eyes are all swollen with the crying she does. All her sorrowful crying might also kill her. The rest of the ladies keep on crying until the wife's crying is almost over.

Girl, 9/1A. For the somate there is crying when a lady or gentleman dies in a village or house.

Girl, 9/1B. One day my grandmother died. I cried all that day. My mother cried sorrowfully a very great deal when my grandmother died. . . . My mother [Mother's Elder Sister?] and my mum and aunt [Father's Sister?] were really overcome. . . . The sorrow felt by my aunt and my big mother [Mother's Elder Sister] was something else. The two of them cried every day.

Girl, 9/3A. Someone dies in a village. The cry about it together in the somate.

Girl, 9/3C. This somate was truly miserable for me. For this somate the guests cried or the ladies here in the village. They went crying to the grave because a gentleman died, many gentlemen are dead, many more than I remain.

Girl, 9/4. The somate is truly a terrifying thing because someone is dead, the ladies cry . . . for myself, if someone died in our house I should be absolutely overwhelmed.

Girl, 9/6. Those attending the somate weep. . . . When the coffin is taken to the church for the blessing, during the service some of them are crying because they won't see each other again. When it is carried to the grave. Some of them are crying when they arrive from the house, some of them are not crying.

Girl, 9/10. One of my little fathers [Father's Younger Brother] had died. My little mother [Father's Younger Brother's wife] cried. There was mourning because of it. At the time when Little Father was buried, I cried a great deal and my Little Mother cried a lot too. . . . Little Mother had taken photographs of the crying. When we arrived home here Little Mother photographed the crying. We went at once to one of our Big Uncles [momolevu, Mother's Elder Brother]. Big Uncle asked, "Is your little father dead?" I at once answered him, "Yes." Then the crying was photographed.

Girl, 10/3. If someone dies the kin of the dead person will cry.

Girl, 10/4B. All the ladies cry. His wife is crying a very great deal.

Girl, 10/6. A long time ago my grandfather died. We who are siblings to one another cried. Likewise those who are my cross-cousins. . . . All my father's siblings cried. . . . After lunch we noticed the ladies weeping noisily because of going to bury my grandfather. A little while after that they stopped crying.

Girl, 10/8. My mother replied in a tearful voice that her older [male] sibling had died. My sorrow was something else because he was one of my uncles [*vugoqu*, here mother's brother] whom I loved. . . . Our kin went to the place of the somate and we who are siblings to one another cried together there in our house.

Girl, 11/0A. The couple's children cried and so did their mother. When they were weeping about it the people of Sawaieke heard them. . . . His children cried. The coffin where their father lay was open. They then kissed their father and said good-bye. . . . After the burial the gentlemen and ladies returned crying to the village.

Girl, 11/0B. The ladies cry. The gentlemen do not cry. It is disgusting for gentlemen to weep. But when a high chief dies, or an installed chief, crying is forbidden. Only the conch shell cries. . . . The mournful weeping of the dead one's siblings or children or other relatives is pitiful.

Girl, 11/5A. Last week my *momo* [Mother's Brother, Father's Sister's Husband] died. My sorrow was something else. . . . The ladies came to weep. . . . I called his children and grandchildren to come and kiss him. . . . The ladies cried.

Girl, 11/5B. When he died his children and grandchildren cried. It was a pitiful death ceremony. . . . Just at that time we noticed that inside the house his children were crying because their father was going to be buried. Their mother was crying.

Girl, 11/6. Then a big death ceremony was performed, they were crying, the boy's mother was weeping dreadfully. All the people of the village were very sorry.

Girl, 11/7. When they hear they are really very sorry. . . . We hear the weeping.

Girl, 12/2. When he died the people of his house cried. . . . When they went to kiss their grandfather they were crying. . . . His grandchildren wept mournfully. . . . When we arrived here in the village we had lunch, those who were with his daughter went on crying and so did some of her remaining siblings. The Minister told them not to mourn.

Boy, 8/2. There is crying.

Boy, 8/6. There is weeping. The [dead man's] wife weeps.

Boy, 8/9B. For the somate we (inc.) weep. . . . For the somate we weep.

Boy, 8/10. For the somate we cry. For the somate we cry sorrowfully. For the somate we cry a great deal . . . For the somate there is weeping.

Boy, 9/1A. For the somate there is weeping.

Boy, 9/1C. For the somate there is weeping. . . . When someone dies the ladies go to the place where the somate is so that they may weep.

Boy, 9/8. His spouse and children will cry. When someone dies the women weep.

Boy, 9/10. Every time that someone dies the very first thing that is done is the weeping. The crying goes on for a long time, after the crying the dead body is taken to church to have a service done for it. . . . When the preaching is over there is again a great deal of crying and the Minister's children and the children of the dead person are very sorry [about the death]. Also the people who are there for the burial are also very sorry. Yes, those who are still in the village are tired out with all the crying in the village. After the preaching they bury the dead person, the burial takes a little while and those who are doing the burial are crying.

Boy, 9/0–10/0. At the somate those who remain cry. The somate is really admirable. Because they pity the person who has died. . . . Every single day the truck brings [people for] the somate. When the truck comes like this the ladies and the gentlemen of the village weep. Especially those who remain at their house [i.e., at the dead person's house]. At their house they weep for the person who died. The somate is sorrowful for the gentlemen and ladies in that house.

Boy, 10/6. When someone dies all his or her kin will cry, his or her siblings and household. . . . Many people cry. . . . When someone dies they will cry loudly. Also the gentlemen will cry and his or her cross-cousins, siblings, grandfathers, grandmothers, they will cry. The somate is a chiefs' thing. The gentlemen, young men, girls, will also cry.

Boy, 10/7. Then the ladies will cry, then one of the ladies will say "Earth to earth, sand to sand."

Boy, 11/9. When someone dies the somate is done, children are forbidden to be there, or meet together or play or shout or laugh, the [people in] the somate are silent, when someone appears with valuables they weep, if some guests come those in the somate may be happy or crying, they will slowly fan the corpse, when we who are kin of the dead do the burial they will cry in the village.

Boy, 11/10. My sorrow that our cross-cousin had died was really something else. . . . All the elderly women [literally, grandmothers] burst out weeping again when the box in which lay the body of my cross-cousin was brought in. . . . When we arrived home our mother was crying mournfully in the window. It was a bad day for us when my cross-cousin died because my mother was just weeping sorrowfully. The death of my cross-cousin was announced on the radio, when my mother heard what was being said on the radio again her tears began again to flow, just because that is the way of it, it was a bad and heavy day for us.

......

Notes

1 For an analysis of the specifically Fijian nature of Fijian Wesleyanism, see Toren 1988 and 1995a. Others have written ably on various aspects of Fijian Christianity, including its history, the articulation (or not) between church and *vanua*, and its significance for Fijian politics from the early 1830s (when the first missionaries began their work) to the present day, when it is taking new forms such as Pentecostalism. See, for example, Kaplan 1990 and 1995; Miyazaki 2000; Rutz and Balkan 1992; Ryle 2001; Thornley 1979; Tomlinson 2002.

2 Fieldwork in Fiji occupied twenty months in 1981–83, four months in 1990, and two months in 1993. In 1990, the chiefly village of Sawaieke had a shifting population of around 270 and Sawaieke country (*vanua ko Sawaieke* —all eight villages) had a population of about 1,500. The economy is mixed subsistence (gardening, small numbers of pigs, cows, and poultry) and cash cropping, yaqona being the most lucrative crop. Fiji Indians make up almost half the population of Fiji, but on smaller islands like Gau, the population is often almost entirely Fijian.

3 The children who attended Sawaieke District School came from two of the eight villages of Sawaieke vanua (country), Somosomo and Sawaieke; the present study includes all those children who in 1990 were pupils in classes 3–6. The abbreviated form for years and months is used hereafter.

4 For a full explanation of this process, see the introduction to Toren 1999a and see Toren 2002b.

5 For examples of what we can learn from child-focused ethnography, see for example Toren 1990, part 2 of 1999a, 1999b, 2002a, and 2002b. For an interesting ethnographic comparison of the way that ideas about children

inform the day-to-day material relations between people that constitute a particular subsistence economy, see Gow 1989. Other works by Gow (2000 and 2001) make use of data about children and from children to illuminate the ideas and practices through which people make sense of themselves and their relations with one another in the environing world.

6 I attended at least six such ceremonies in Sawaieke village itself during my first eighteen months there, and many others in other villages of the vanua.

7 In two cases the topic might have been interpreted in more than one way. *Kalou*, meaning God or spirit, denotes the ancestors as well as the Christian God, though if one wishes to be unambiguous the ancestors are *kalou vu* (literally, origin gods); *wilivola*, which denotes Sunday school, translates literally as reading. Thus it was open to children to write a story about either God or the Gods, and about either reading in general or Sunday school. In writing about na kalou, children confined themselves to the Christian God; in writing about wilivola, a few children who did a second essay interpreted the term to mean reading in the general sense, but the primary meaning for children (at least when asked by myself to produce essays on the subject) was the reading that denotes Sunday school. Somate, meaning death ceremony or funeral, contains no obvious ambiguity.

8 I am not here attempting experimentally to test a hypothesis, so I have not used statistical tests to gauge the significance of the results. Compare Toren 1990: 196–216, where, in the course of analyzing how Sawaieke children constitute the idea that hierarchy is to be taken for granted as a principle of social organization, I test the hypothesis that hierarchy is more evident to a child in the depiction of the ritualized activities of meals and yaqona drinking than in depictions of meetings.

9 Except for the equal relation between cross-cousins, which typically obtains across houses and across clan, all Fijian kinship relations are hierarchical and marked by a greater or less degree of respect and avoidance, with the obligation devolving on the junior party.

10 It is also at this age—around 9/0 or so—that Fijian children begin to focus explicitly on relations with peers and the reciprocal competitive equality that characterizes these relations and differentiates them from others (see Toren 1999b).

11 See Toren 1990, 1993a, and 1993b.

12 See Toren 1995b. Provided one supposes that it is *meant to mean*, ritual can always be rendered meaningful and thus communicative. Even so, ritual and ritualized behavior are not *primarily* "a form of communication," as Robbins 2001a, following Rappaport 1999, would have it, because the meaning that can be made of ritual is necessarily secondary to its performance.

13 I am indebted for this insight to Hiro Miyazaki (personal communication).

14 See Toren 1990: 198–247.

15 For a debate, see Miyazaki 2000.

16 The term *bikabika* is used to refer to any house where ladies have gathered to observe the four nights for a death or first birth.

17 The valuables presented in *reguregu* are of two kinds: *na i yau tabu*—forbidden valuables, and *na i yau tara*—permitted valuables; the former are put to one side *me nona isole ko koya ka mate*—as the wrappings for the one who is dead, and the latter are divided up when the four nights are over among his or her close kin.

18 *Vatu ni balawa. Na tabua ka dau biu e na dela ni kisi ni mate me nona i curucuru ki Naicabecabe ko koya ka sa mate.* (Stone of the pandanus. The whale tooth that is placed on top of the coffin as the dead one's entrance fee to Naicabecabe [literally, the steep place].) This description is found under the heading "The Uses of Whale Teeth" in a booklet given out to students at Gau Secondary School in the late 1970s. Note, however, that in pre- and early colonial times the *vatu ni balawa* was to be thrown at the pandanus at Naicobocobo, the northern point of Bua Bay, Vanua Levu that was "the jumping-off place" for the spirit on its way to Bulu (see T. Williams [1858] 1982: 243 and compare Thomson [1908] 1968: 118). It seems likely that in the booklet Naicabecabe is a deliberately chosen substitute for Naicobocobo since, wherever it is possible, Fijians find in their traditional practices a prefiguring of Christian ideas (see for example Toren 1988, which shows how Leonardo da Vinci's "Last Supper"—a copy of which in the 1980s and 1990s used to be found in nearly all village churches and houses—may be taken to suggest an analogy between Christian and chiefly ritual).

19 This ceremony implies that, in the past and even today, death as a radical conversion of substance is pivotal to the cycles of consumption and exchange between the people and the land. The intangible substance of the dead is consumed by their living kin, and their tangible substance is buried on ancestral land (or, in the past, in the foundations of houses). See Toren 1998.

20 The land door was used to remove the coffin in each case that I witnessed a funeral, but since I never asked whether this is always so, I cannot be sure if only this door may be used—as opposed to the sea door on the facing wall or the common entrance below. Given the sacrificial logic of the death ceremonies, however, it follows that the coffin should, on its final journey, exit the house via the land door.

21 For comparative accounts of Fijian death ceremonies, see T. Williams [1858] 1982: 187–200 and Waterhouse [1866] 1978: 324–27 for the nineteenth century; Hocart [1912] 1929: 177–84 for early-twentieth-century Lau; Hooper 1982: 101–8 for contemporary Lau; and Ravuvu 1987: 179–202 for contemporary Waimaro.

22 For the aesthetics of *veiqaravi*, see Miyazaki 2000.

23 Where mana is manifest in animal form, it takes the characteristics of that animal—a shark, for instance.

24 See Toren 1998.

···Seven···

Forgetting Conversion

The Summer Institute of Linguistics Mission in the Piro Lived World

Peter Gow

In this chapter I address a curious feature of my ethnography of the Piro people of Peruvian Amazonia. Many Piro people converted to evangelical Christianity in the late 1940s and 1950s, due to the activities of missionaries of the Summer Institute of Linguistics (SIL), and clearly experienced this conversion, at the time, as an important event in their lives. By the 1980s, when I began fieldwork with Piro people, however, no mention was made of this conversion by its participants or their younger relatives, or even of the specifically religious dimension to SIL activities. The SIL period remained important for them, for they described it as the origin of their contemporary "civilized" life, but its specifically religious features were seldom discussed, and conversion never. By the 1980s, Piro people described themselves as Christians and talked as if they always had been: the idiom of conversion played no role in their elaborated narrative accounts of their own history. Why should such an event as conversion both be so important to Piro people, and so eminently forgettable by them?

The questions I address here, why Piro people should have converted to evangelical Christianity and subsequently forgotten about it, and why they asserted to me that they had always been Christians, are clearly not Piro questions. They are the sorts of questions that anthropologists ask, and they contain a hidden danger. Most anthropologists have historically come from societies in which Christianity has been the dominant religion, and the discipline of anthropology has been formulated within intellectual traditions strongly marked by Christian thought. Because of this, anthropologists are likely to find themselves asking questions that are far closer to the questions asked by Christian missionaries than to those asked by the people the former study and the latter seek to convert. Indeed, the sorts of things that interest missionaries and anthropologists about Christianity are quite similar, or at least are much closer to each other than they are to what Piro people find interesting in Christianity. I return to this issue in the conclusion.

Stephen Hugh-Jones (1994) has recently suggested that the activities of Christian missionary organizations among indigenous Amazonian societies might be profitably interpreted in relationship to indigenous practices of shamanism. In particular, he chides Christopher Crocker (1985) for his analysis of the disappearance of one kind of Bororo shaman, "the master of the soul's way," while totally ignoring how Salesian missionaries have themselves historically taken on this shaman's functions through their obsessional regard for the "soul" aspect of Bororo life. Hugh-Jones is here suggesting that historical transformations of different kinds of shamanism in indigenous Amazonian societies provides one of the points of insertion for Christianity in indigenous Amazonia, and that indigenous Amazonian Christianities are therefore likely to be inflected by modes of shamanism.

I think that Hugh-Jones's suggestion provides an important strategic route for the analysis of Christianity in indigenous Amazonian societies, and I follow out some of its implications for the Piro case here. But I think that his suggestion further raises the question of what indigenous Amazonian shamanism is, and in particular how shamanism is connected to the cosmologies and sociologies of the societies in which it is practiced. These issues have been raised recently by a number of anthropologists, such as Joanna Overing (1993), Eduardo Viveiros de Castro (1998), Fernando Santos Granero (1993), and Phillippe Descola (1992), and there is a growing consensus that to abstract the social logics of indigenous Amazonian societies from their cosmologies does not make much sense. In particular, Overing and Viveiros de Castro have focused on the ways in which shamanry, what shamans do, provides a key switchpoint between the immediate social world and the wider cosmic frames in which it takes place.[1] If, as Hugh-Jones suggests, Christian missionaries are kinds of shamans in indigenous Amazonian societies, and if shamanry is the mode by which the social is connected to the cosmic and vice versa, then we can ask of indigenous Amazonian Christianities how they present novel solutions to the problem of this relationship between the social and the cosmological, and why that novelty would matter.

Two further points must be made before proceeding to the analysis. First, the data analyzed here must be considered in a wider spatial and temporal system. Peru is an overwhelmingly Christian country; conversion to Christianity had played a key role in its early colonial history and continues to figure in the nationalist representation of that history. Piro people would have to travel far indeed to find a country where Christianity is simply one religion among many, and religious differences, as opposed to sectarian differences between Christian traditions, play little role in Peruvian life. Second, the community in which I did most of my fieldwork, Santa Clara, was nominally Catholic and contained a Dominican mission center. However, the primary religious experience of Christianity for most adults in this community was with evangelical Protestant Christianity and more remotely with Seventh Day Adventism, and most of my data refer to those experiences. For Dominicans in the 1980s, conversion was viewed as a very long process, to be preceded, following their own brand of liberation theology, by the growth of communities (Alvarez 1984). Religion did not, therefore, loom very large in local daily life.

The SIL Mission among the Piro

In early 1947, Esther Matteson began her work as an SIL missionary among the Piro people of the Urubamba river in southern Peruvian Amazonia. This project, along with one among the Ticuna people along the Amazon mainstream far to the north, was the first SIL evangelization outside of Mexico, where the Wycliffe Bible Translators/SIL had been first established. For over thirty years, the SIL missionaries were an important feature of the lives of most Piro people, to the extent that, in the 1980s, they would talk about *cuando han llegado los gringos*, when the gringos arrived, as a defining moment in their recent history. It was, they told me, through the arrival of the American missionaries that they "liberated themselves from slavery," in the local sense of living in debt bondage on the haciendas of their bosses, and "became civilized," in the local sense of living in their own villages with schools and legal title to their land. So, the SIL missionaries had been a dramatically important influence in their lives, but what Piro people did not talk about much was the religious aspect of their action. At most, in the 1980s, I would be told that the SIL missionaries were "good people," who therefore "wanted to help us": their religious faith made them good, and hence compassionate to the condition of Piro people.[2]

Piro people's accounts of their relations to the SIL missionaries were remote from what I had been led to expect of the relations between North American evangelical missionaries and indigenous Amazonian peoples. The extant literature was largely concerned with the malign nature and ethnocidal potential of such missionization: the 1960s and 1970s were a period when few of the ethnographers whose work influenced me had worked with heavily missionized peoples, and usually missionaries of various stripe appeared in their work as the coming death-knell of the cultures they sought to describe. So alien were Piro people's accounts of their relations with the SIL missionaries that I essentially ignored the problems they presented in my earlier work. Only through a later concern with trying to reconstruct what is known of the recent history of Piro people, and how that history could have been lived by them, did I begin to wonder why the religious aspects of the SIL mission had so little continuing resonance for them (Gow 2001).

This point is important, since the religious dimension of the SIL mission had clearly been important to many Piro people at the time. Esther Matteson herself described the situation in the early 1950s as follows, from an ethnographic monograph published in the scholarly journal, the *Kroeber Anthropological Society Papers*,

> The Roman Catholic religion, first introduced to the Piro in the seventeenth century, has never been very fully accepted. Samanez y Ocampo, 1885, reported that in extreme cases the medicine man resorted to "holding mass" in the woods, mixing a little ritual with the smoking and sucking usually practised.[3] There is no indication that such "mass" is held anywhere on the Urubamba today. Apart from the group living on the premises of the Dominican Mission on the Sepahua River, there is practically no apparent influence of Roman Catholicism on the beliefs and culture of the Piro. Practices of witchcraft are unaffected. Neither pictures or figures of saints are found in the homes, nor is the baptism of children common practice.
>
> The Seventh Day Adventist missionaries have exerted considerably more influence. Their abstinence from certain meats, and observances of a period of inactivity, fit in well with the taboos of the Piro. The chief contributions of this group to the tribe have been a definite decrease in drunkenness, and instruction in Spanish in the mission schools. A few years ago a group of Piro

> were visited by a representative of the indigenous Evangelical Church of Peru and some sort of affiliation was initiated.
>
> Since 1949, translations of portions of the Bible without sectarian teaching have been supplied them. This has met with enthusiastic reception on the part of some 300. In fact, most of the Piro of the Urubamba relate their recent marked advance in education to this source. Without question it has had far more effect on the Piro culture than the superficial religious influences previously mentioned. (1954: 72–73)

Matteson's account is a reasonable summary of the history of contacts between missionaries and Urubamba Piro people up until the early 1950s. Admittedly, three centuries of missionization by Jesuits and later Franciscans may seem like an awful lot of contact with Roman Catholic missionaries. However, none of these missions lasted very long; they often ended when the missionaries were killed by their Piro neophytes; and they were always separated by long periods of time during which contact with missionaries was slight or nonexistent. Indeed, the Franciscans seem to have abandoned their long evangelization of the Piro following the collapse of Alemany's mission in the 1880s. Heras summarized the situation in the late nineteenth century: "The Piro in Cuzco, in Miariya, in Santa Rosa de Lima, in Buepoano and in the many other places he frequents is always the same, that is, self-interested, miscreant, shrewd and hypocritical" (quoted in Amich 1975: 427).

If the Jesuits and Franciscans failed to convert the Piro after so many centuries of trying, why did the SIL succeed? There is some doubt that they really fared any better. David Stoll, author of a major study of the SIL, summarizes SIL accounts of their work among Piro people:

> Matteson found the Piro sunk in such an appalling moral condition that she could not include their folk tales in her primers for Piro children. Yet within a few years Piro headmen were asking her to reform their *patron*-dominated villages in a burst of enthusiasm for the Protestant Ethic. A government official was amazed by the sudden change. He needed food supplies for the penal colony at Sepa, but the Piro never had anything to sell because they were usually drunk. Soon he was shocked to see sobriety, new houses and gardens. The Piro had surplus food to sell and wanted to produce more. They were going to school and reading the Bible.
>
> In only eight years Matteson finished the New Testament and "witnessed the complete transformation" of the tribe. After 15 years, in 1962, the *Peru-*

> *vian Times* reported that "the Linguists expect to be able to withdraw soon, leaving observers to keep the tribe on the right lines for a few years." In the 20th year of the Piro work, Matteson reported that, despite many weaknesses, which seemed overwhelming, the Piro church was prospering and God's Word prevailing against fear of evil spirits. And as the Piro work approached its 30th year, Matteson's successors faced the same problems she had: except perhaps when a missionary was in the village, congregations and Christian leaders carried on as they had prior to salvation. (1982: 125–26)

By the time of my fieldwork, in the 1980s, the SIL missionaries had become a relatively minor presence in the lives of Piro people. By then, their evangelical work was in the hands of the Swiss Mission, who maintained a much lower profile than had the SIL in the nominally Protestant communities. Their work as teachers was taken over by Piro teachers themselves in the SIL-affiliated communities, or by other local people in some cases (see Gow 1991). Their most significant role for Piro people in the 1980s was running courses for bilingual teachers in their base in Yarinacocha, especially during the long rainy season school holidays. The SIL missionaries themselves, however, seldom appeared on the Bajo Urubamba.

Missionaries

What was the mission of the SIL workers among Piro people? Founded by Cameron Townsend in 1934, the Wycliffe Bible Translators / Summer Institute of Linguistics is an interfaith Protestant missionary organization, dedicated to translating the Bible into all spoken human languages, in fulfillment of the command of Jesus, "Go ye therefore, and teach all nations, baptizing them in the name of the Father, and of the Son, and of the Holy Ghost" (Matthew 28:19). As Stoll [1982] points out, the SIL also has a distinctively millenarian cast, in the form of a marked concern with the Second Coming, in tune with its social origins in the American Midwest and its project of bearing the Good News to the last unreached people in the uttermost parts of the earth.

Throughout its history, the SIL has operated a dual strategy, which explains its two names. The SIL is concerned with the technicalities of translation work, and with the entailed project of literacy education among the communities they work with: it is not a missionary organization, nor are its linguists missionaries. The Wycliffe Bible Translators is a missionary organization, concerned with fund-raising and recruitment. Of course, the personnel are identical in the two cases, but the fiction of separation was strategically important to the SIL: through this separation, the organization was able to gain official recognition and support for its work from Latin American governments without drawing too much attention from the Catholic Church. This strategy was especially effective in Peru, where the SIL gained official sanction from the Ministry of Education and ended up in effective control over almost all education in indigenous Amazonian communities. The Peruvian government was concerned to find a way of turning the indigenous peoples of the Amazon region into Peruvian citizens, through education, and the SIL project seemed to be both a simple and a cheap way forward.

Because the SIL is not officially a missionary organization in Peru, it is quite difficult to know exactly how they set about their evangelical work. Most of their publications are pervaded by the artfulness of their official status, and I did not find it easy to either meet or discuss these issues with SIL missionaries themselves. There is, however, a body of literature produced outside of Peru on specific SIL missions, such as Emily Wallis's account of the conversion of a Shapra chief in *Tariri, My Story* (Wallis 1966), and the very extensive literature on the SIL mission among the Huaorani people of Ecuador, by missionaries, former missionaries, and others (see, for example, Wallis 1961). There is, unfortunately, no such corresponding accounts of the Piro project, but, if this available literature can be used to model the experiences of those SIL missionaries working among Piro people, it is clear that conversion was central to their work. Central to that conversion process is Scripture and its inerrancy: the Bible is God's Word (in Piro, *Goyakalu Tokanu Steno*, God's collected words), and it must be followed. Conversion, like faith, is in this case a highly interiorized relationship to God, of the sort perhaps overly familiar to us from the work of Weber.

Conversion

In 1968, Juan Sebastián, Matteson's major male Piro language informant, dictated his own account of Piro history for a school reader titled *Gwacha Ginkakle/Historia de los Piros* (*History/Story of the Piro People*) (Sebastián, Zumaeta, and Nies 1974). One chapter is devoted to the changes initiated among Piro people by the SIL missionaries. This chapter is titled "Genshinikanrewlu," and it is there translated as "La Vida Nueva," "The

New Life." Unfortunately, I do not know what exactly Sebastián had to say about "The New Life" (see afterword in this essay), for that chapter was torn out of my copy by an SIL functionary before I was given it. I had paid for the book, and taken aback by this violence, I asked why I was receiving such a damaged copy. I was told that the Ministry of Education had strong objections to its sectarian religious bias. Whether anyone in this ministry had ever bothered to read this book, I do not know, and perhaps the SIL merely suspected that the complete text could provide further ammunition for those who attacked their work from either an anti-imperialist or a Catholic position.

In the *Diccionario Piro* (Nies 1986), also prepared by the SIL, the term *genshinikanru* is translated as "conversion, change in attitude." *Genshinikanrewlu* would mean something like "caused to have a new way of thinking, memory, love, respect." The root of these words is *gishinika*, "to think, to remember, to love, to respect," and thus has the same root as the word *nshinikanchi*, "thinking, memory, love, respect." As I have discussed at length elsewhere (Gow 1991), this is a core faculty of the Piro person, and the basis of their supreme social value of "living well": it is because people develop nshinikanchi through responding to acts of care during childhood that Piro people seek to manifest this "thinking, memory, love, respect" to each other by living together in the same village, and by sharing game with each other. This is the definition of "living well," which is thus both the product of and producer of nshinikanchi. It should be pointed out here that Piro people do not construe nshinikanchi as a bodily interior state. It is immediately perceptible in another person, for the supreme manifestation of nshinikanchi is coresidence, in the sense of one's willingness to be visually present to the other. Nor do Piro people link this faculty strongly to the soul (*samenchi*): if nshinikanchi is one's conscious experience of self as related to others, and in the ongoing regard of others, the *samenchi* is one's unconscious experience of radical personal uniqueness, in illness and in dreaming.[4] I return to this issue later, but note here that the decision to translate "conversion" as genshinikanrewlu had some important and very Piro consequences.

In the Protestant tradition, conversion and faith are radically interiorized states. Conversion is being born again, coming to experience salvation as an exclusively personal transformation in relationship to the world and to God. In his account of his own conversion, the Shapra chief Tariri reports, "Jesus came into my heart," and the SIL missionary Doris Cox reported joyfully, "So he was born again!" (Wallis 1966: 72–73).[5] As a description of such a transformation, the Piro term *genshinikanrewlu* both is and is not particularly appropriate. It alludes to the new way of thinking implied by conversion, but not to the radical interiority implied by the English phrase "Jesus came into my heart." As I noted, nshinikanchi is not a bodily interior state, but rather the intersubjectively available grounding of sociality in a Piro person. As such, nshinikanchi always refers to ongoing social life, to a collective "living well," as opposed to radically individual experiences.

Even in the absence of Sebastián's account of "conversion," there is good reason to believe that Piro people, at the time, thought of "conversion, the new life" as a primarily collective experience, rather than a primarily individual one. Sebastián, describing the contemporary lives of Piro people in 1968, states, "The Piro people of my generation did not know about books; also, we didn't live in villages. We used to live scattered about in temporary shelters, and after a couple of years we moved off to another place. In the dry season we lived on the beaches, and in the rainy season in the forest. We always returned to the beach when the river fell. Now we have schools and we live in villages" (Sebastián, Zumaeta, and Nies 1974).

"Living scattered about," living without villages, is the focus of strong moral opprobrium from Piro people (see Gow 1991). Correspondingly, living in villages is a requirement for "living well." The headman of Santa Clara village, Artemio Fasabi, who was born the year Matteson arrived and had trained as both a bilingual schoolteacher and a pastor, told me, "To be an *evangelista*, you have to live in a village of Piro *evangelista* people. When I lived in [the Swiss mission base], I liked the way of life, having services every day, praising the Lord, and everyone preaching. But here it is impossible, there are too many distractions." He had already specified these "distractions" to be "dancing and drinking and women." I will discuss the nature of these distractions further, but it is clear that Piro people thought of conversion primarily as a collective act, and as the precondition for a new form of living well, rather than an individual, interiorized act.

Conversion as a Religious Experience

How did conversion, as a collective act and as a new mode of social life, connect up to Protestant notions of faith? Sebastián is quite specific here,

> The spiritual life of the Piro people has also changed. Before, the shamans were feared and to children it was said, "Watch out! Don't talk or laugh. Don't make fun of the shaman or he will ensorcell you, and you will die!" But now it isn't the shaman, but God who is feared and loved. Now only a few people fear shamans. Neither are the demons feared, because we know God looks after us. He is great and made everything that exists. Thus have our lives been changing, since we know God. We praise him and thank him, hoping that everything that we ask him for he will give to us, if that is his will. (Sebastián, Zumaeta, and Nies 1974)

Conversion, therefore, involved a transformation away from fear of shamans (*kagonchi*) and demons (*kamchi*), to the fear and love of *Goyakalu*, God.

Matteson, in her ethnography of the Piro, represents this conversion as a shift in religions. She writes,

> The tribal religion is a polytheism of innumerable gods and goddesses living in heaven. The words "heaven" and sky are synonymous, meaning "the upper expanse." Tsla, the creator god so prominent in the mythology, receives neither homage nor petition. Rather, invocations are addressed to the general name goyakalu (from the adjective goyaka, "lasting") "an eternal one." . . . Any individual whose sins are comparatively few, and all powerful witchdoctors, go to heaven and become gods. They receive their "goyaknu," which carries the added thought of splendour and majesty. . . . The ghost of any witch doctor is dreaded, because the witch doctor is supposed to go back and forth at will from heaven to earth, embodying himself in whatever form he chooses. [1954: 72]

By Protestant standards, this is a fairly horrifying religion and would justify Matteson's report, quoted above from Stoll, that she found the Piro in "an appalling moral condition." Clearly, to replace this belief system with Protestant Christianity was an important task, even if key aspects of it, such as the words for divinity, *goyakalu*, eternity, *goyaknu*, and heaven, *tengogne*, could be retained.

It is, however, far from clear that Piro people experienced Christianity as a new religion at all. Artemio Fasabi assured me that his old-time Piro ancestors had always worshipped God, saying,

> My mother told me that long ago when the old people took *ayahuasca* (a hallucinogen), they said it was their God who sent them visions. Those who

> took a lot of *ayahuasca* knew a lot about God, they were good and went to heaven. Those who knew nothing did not.

Similarly, Sebastián states,

> Long ago the ancient people did not know much about God, although they had heard of him. But they wanted to see him. So, many took hallucinogens. They drank hallucinogens wanting to see God. They drank *ayahuasca*. They saw God, it is said, they called him "Father" (*Patutachri*). They drank *toé* (a hallucinogen) and other plants, trying to see God. But they never got there.
>
> My father told us that he had heard that God existed, but he wanted to know him and learn who he was and where he lived. Then, the shamans told him that by drinking *toé* and *ayahuasca*, he would see God.
>
> Therefore he too wanted to see God. He drank *toé* for five days in the forest. But he told us that he did not see him and went on asking, "Where does God live, under the earth or in the sky?"
>
> Then one day after the time of rubber there arrived those who explained to us about God. They told us that he exists and that he had created all that can be seen and all that cannot be seen. Then we also understood that Jesus lived in this world, and that he died for our sins. (Sebastián, Zumaeta, and Nies 1974)

If "conversion" led to a loss of fear of shamans, at no point does Sebastián suggest that shamans did not have the remarkable powers they were credited with. The problem was that shamanry was inadequate as a technique for finding God. For that, the "white people," "those who explained to us about God," were necessary.

It is hardly surprising that Piro people knew about the Christian God, after three and a half centuries of attempted evangelization by Jesuits and Franciscans, and in constant contact with more fully missionized peoples. It seems to me unquestionable that *Patutachri*, "Father," the being for whom Sebastián's father searched through hallucinogens, was the God of the Catholic missionaries: *patu* is an old vocative kin term for "father," and *Patutachri* means "the one who is habitually addressed as 'father.' " It is clear that there had been considerable interest in this being among Piro people, and for a long time.

This has a number of interesting implications. First, it would seem that Piro people did not experience Evangelical Christianity to be a new religion, in the sense of a new set of beliefs or as a cosmology. Evangelical

Christianity was simply their own cosmology better explained by people who knew more about it. They were already believing Christians when they converted, and conversion was not a radically interior spiritual or mental transformation, but a new way of living out an already extant cosmology.

Second, Piro people could think of themselves as already Christians because what Matteson described as the Piro "tribal religion" was not a religion as the term is clearly intended here to be understood: it was not a system of beliefs. As Vilaça has described for the Wari' (1997), indigenous Amazonian cosmologies are based not on belief, but on experiential knowledge. What Matteson called the Piro tribal religion was in fact a complex and highly unstable mixture of modes of knowledge, varying in source from mythic narratives to the assertions of living shamans to reports from neighboring peoples. There was no canon of any kind, and cosmological propositions would be constantly subjected to scrutiny for their fit with personal experience and hence potential plausibility.

Goyaknu, "eternity," is central to Piro cosmology because of a fact central to Piro experience, mortality. Humans—Piro people—do not endure; they are born, grow up, grow old, and die. Human life is marked by mortality and a corresponding set of desires, both sexual and oral (Gow 1989, 1991). The satisfaction of these desires is ultimately lethal, but when orchestrated by nshinikanchi, and its consequent direction toward social others, is productive of new generations of Piro people. Piro collective ritual action, in festivals and in particular in *kigimawlo*, girl's initiation ritual, uses people's desire for manioc beer drunkenness to transform relations of distant kinship into affinity. Kigimawlo celebrates the prolonged seclusion of a pubescent girl and provides her with a long life. Longevity is a deferral of mortality for a period sufficient to allow social life to continue as an extended project (Gow 2001).

Piro collective ritual action uses the power of manioc beer drunkenness to subvert nshinikanchi, "memory, love, respect, thinking," in order to generate new sexual and hence affinal relations. This corresponds to a parallel subversion in shamanry, where hallucinogens are ingested to stimulate another form of "drunkenness," the sensory-motor transformations of these potently psychotropic plant extracts. Here the subversion of nshinikanchi is more profound, for those who take these hallucinogens seek to transform their perceptual apparatus into that of powerful spirit beings, the "mother spirits" of the hallucinogenic plants, in order "to see as" these beings, to see from their point of view (Viveiros de Castro

1998). When in this transformed state, people see entities and places that are normally hidden from view, either because their normal visual appearance is deceptive, or because they are invisible. Such entities are revealed to be people, for they appear to the drinker in human form, and the places are villages and cities where these people live. Shamanry (*kagonchiwata*), as a technique, involves increasing familiarity with these places and beings, and their identification as people, with whom shamans can then interact. In particular, shamanic potency consists in learning and then singing the songs of these people: shamans are able to act because they transform their selves from ordinary humans into more powerful humans. This potency is a form of doubling, being simultaneously two kinds of human, both ordinary and spirit beings.

The importance of these spirit people for shamans is both that they can see, and that they are immortal. By transforming in hallucinatory experience into such spirit beings, shamans are able to cure ordinary people of illness, by setting up a temporary switch point between their cohumanity with the patient and their cohumanity with the spirit people. They do this because of their compassion for their patients (Gow 2001), but in the process, shamans cease to experience the central problem of humanity, mortality. Through constant identification with spirit people, shamans become immortal. As Matteson noted of the situation in the 1940s and 1950s, "All powerful witchdoctors . . . go to heaven and become gods."

Resolving Dynamic Instability

The centrality of mortality to the human condition, and its resolution through shamanry, has a much larger role in the wider temporal frames of the Piro lived world. In Piro mythology, the culture hero Tsla is consistently identified as *kgiyaklewakleru*, "a miraculous creator, a transformer of things." This epithet establishes Tsla as a hypershaman, for his ability "to create miraculously" is the most intensified mode of shamanry imaginable. But, in Piro mythology, Tsla left the Bajo Urubamba River precisely because of mortality. On hearing a particular bird of ill omen calling, Tsla told his younger brothers, the Muchkajine, "This is a land of death," and he set off downriver with them. In doing so, Tsla left the Piro lived world marked by mortality, and removed the action of *giyaklewata*, "to create miraculously," from that world. Today, only powerful shamans can hope to dodge the condition of mortality, through diligent application to the consumption of hallucinogens.

If Tsla's departure from the Piro lived world left Piro people with the problem of mortality, it also set up a key dynamic imbalance: "miraculous creation" was now located downriver, where Tsla went with his younger brothers the Muchkajine. These brothers are literally the "Long Ago White People."[6] For Piro people, *kajine*, "white people," originate in that same downriver world and are marked by their possession of "miraculous creations," the *gejnu*, "wealth objects, fine things." It is to get hold of these items that Piro people enter into various forms of exchange relations with various kinds of white people (see Gow 1990, 1991, 2001). This relationship is cosmologically central to the Piro lived world, insofar as "white people" are considered logically necessary for Piro social life.[7]

The SIL turned up on the Bajo Urubamba during a period of radical turmoil for these people, and in particular in their relations with white people. Since the 1880s, Piro people had been living in debt slavery to the local white bosses, a condition that was becoming increasingly unviable for them. Since the late 1930s, an alternative existed, in the form of Seventh-Day Adventist missionaries, but this presented several serious cosmological problems for Piro people, for it was institutionally tied to the cosmology and sociology of the neighboring Asháninka people. The SIL fortuitously arrived in the middle of this crisis and presented Piro people with an attractive alternative.[8]

Until the 1940s, virtually all Urubamba Piro people were living as debt slaves on the haciendas of their *patrones*, "bosses," and in particular the three big haciendas of Francisco Vargas, the "big boss of the Piro people." Vargas had inherited the relations of indebtedness between Piro people and his own boss, Carlos Scharf, who had in turn inherited them from the infamous rubber boss Carlos Fermin Fitzcarrald. These debt relations originated in the massive increase in the velocity of exchange relations between Piro people and white traders during the 1880s, and rapidly transformed, through the chaos inspired by the expansion of the rubber industry, into Piro people's almost total economic, political, and military dependence on white people. By the time of the collapse in rubber prices in 1912, all alternative sources of wealth had effectively disappeared, as had the trade networks on which they depended, and Piro people had no alternative but to depend on Vargas (Gow 1991).

By all accounts, life with Vargas was not attractive. As Virgilio Gavino, an old Piro man, tersely put it, "The bosses treated us very badly. They beat us with sticks when we didn't work. We were their slaves." However, working for Vargas was the only way to obtain the "wealth items" crucial to ongoing social life, and Vargas also orchestrated Piro ritual action, by taking the lead in the most important form of that action, girl's initiation ritual. As Sebastián puts it, "the old dead Piro people . . . lived in the white man's places. They depended on the white man. He protected them. Whatever dangers they feared, only he helped them" (Sebastián, Zumaeta, and Nies 1974: 171–73).

Throughout the 1920s and 1930s, however, a potential alternative to the bosses was increasingly present to Piro people. As John Bodley (1970) and Michael Brown and Eduardo Fernandez (1991) have discussed, the North American Adventist Stahl had been evangelizing Campa people in the Perené area to the east, with considerable success, since the 1920s. Urubamba Piro people would have known of these developments, given the extensive network of intermarriages, kin ties, and other relationships covering the area and linking Asháninka and Piro people together. By the 1930s, the message of Adventism had been brought into the Alto Ucayali by an Asháninka man from the Perené, in response to local enthusiasm, and led Adventist missionaries to found a mission as Unini, on the Alto Ucayali River just below Atalaya / Santa Rosa, and following the death of Vargas in 1940, they established a new mission on the Urubamba at Huau village.

What was the nature of Piro interest in Adventism, which, as discussed above, Matteson saw as having had a profound impact on them? Space prevents a detailed account, but it seems that Piro people responded with a milder version of Asháninka messianism. They thought that the world was going to end, and that, if they followed the prescriptions of Adventism correctly, they would be taken into the sky. Such a possibility corresponds to a feature of Piro cosmology expressed in a mythic narrative: that, through rigorous consumption of hallucinogens, people could collectively enter the sky and become divinities (Alvarez 1960, Matteson 1965, Gow 2001). This, it seems, is how Piro people interpreted Adventism, and it would suggest that Piro people understood the Adventist message as a potential collective shaman-becoming, and the Adventists as powerful shamans. If Adventism lacked the use of hallucinogens, it did provide Piro people with something as potent, *Goyakalu tokanu*, "God's Word," brought to them by a new kind of "white people."

Evidence for this comes from a remarkable fact. Most Piro people, at this period, abandoned the production of fermented manioc beer. As I noted, fermented manioc beer, and its consequent drunkenness, is central to Piro collective ritual action, which in turn is central to the ongoing production of affinal relations (Gow 1997). Fermented manioc beer was abandoned at this time as a consequence of the abandonment of ritual life, and in particular *kigimawlo*, the girl's initiation ritual. This is additional confirmation that Piro people had, at this period, a radical messianic expectation, for they abandoned precisely those actions associated with the projection of their lived world into the future as an ongoing project of making and unmaking social relationships. These changes undoubtedly reflected Adventist preaching against alcohol but also reflected Piro people's own understanding of these practices. As Matteson noted, Adventist influence here was enduring, and even in the 1980s and 1990s, some Piro people would tell me that fermented manioc beer, like girl's initiation ritual and its musical forms, were things of the *kamchi*, "demons."

Following the analyses of Bodley (1970), Brown and Fernandez (1991) and Karen Jacobs (detailed to me in a personal communication), Seventh-Day Adventism corresponded closely to an important feature of Ash-áninka cosmological thought: the possible appearance of *itomi pava*, "the sons of the Sun," to restore the cosmic imbalance caused by the increasing powers of the *viracocha*, "white people." As I have noted, this hope would have corresponded to one feature of Piro cosmology, the sky-entry myth, but it would also have conflicted with a more important one, instantiated in Tsla mythology, whereby transforming relationships with *kajine*, white people, are key to the ongoing possibility of Piro social life. If the Ash-áninka Adventists liked Adventism because they thought that the Adventist missionaries were not white people, but sky beings, Piro Adventists must have been troubled by those missionaries' refusal to act as a new kind of white people.

The world-transformational nature of the Adventist message seems to have appealed to some Piro people, but I think that the responsiveness to Adventism more powerfully reflected a specifically Piro project: the desire to become Christians in the local sense of *cristianos*, "humans, people." Throughout the period from the early 1880s, Piro people had been excluded from contact with the Franciscan missionaries by the rubber bosses and their successors. The hostility between missionaries and bosses in Peruvian Amazonia had complex historical roots (Gow 1991), but it essentially concerned control over indigenous people's labor, and this led the bosses to prevent contacts between the Franciscans and their workers. However, the status of *cristiano*, "Christian," was an important one in the local socioeconomic system, since it served to unite the class of white bosses and the mestizos or *moza gente*, "mixed-blood people," against the fully enslaved *indios*, "Indians," like Piro people. The racial hierarchy was mapped onto one of religious faith: white people and mixed-blood people were Christians, Indians were pagans.

During my fieldwork, in the 1980s and 1990s, the Ucayali Spanish term *cristiano* was used by speakers of Ucayali Spanish to mean "human." It connoted the specific positive moral qualities of the potential relationship that was possible with such an entity, and its primary contrast was to the category *animal*, "animal." *Cristianos*, "people," were those entities with which it is possible to have ongoing and moral social relationship, and it was perfectly correct to describe the forest spirit *sacha supay* as both a *diablo*, "demon," and as a *cristiano*, "Christian, human": this spirit is a "demon" when he attacks people with illness, and a "Christian" when he helps shamans in curing. By contrast, to give an example close to my own heart, dogs are not "Christians," because they do not understand when you try to treat them well: Piro people were bemused by my excessive solicitude for my own dog. Similarly, *indios bravos*, "wild Indians," were not *cristianos* because it was impossible to have peaceful exchange relations with them.

These late-twentieth-century formulations are probably marked by only one important shift from the situation of the 1930s and 1940s: Piro people now self-identify as *cristianos*, "Christians," in a way that would not have been the case in the earlier period. What would wanting to be Christian have meant to Piro people then? Fundamentally, I think, it meant wanting to be seen as humans by white people, kajine, and so to be included within a domain of appropriate moral relationships. It meant, in the phrase of Virgilio Gavino quoted above, not being made to suffer by the white bosses. The Adventists, by opening up the missions at Unini and Huau and preaching about God, held out this possibility to Piro people, and they were initially very responsive to it.

If the Adventist missionaries allowed Piro people to be "Christians" in this sense, there was a contradiction here from a Piro perspective. Adventists stressed separation from nonbelievers, and hence from local white people and mestizos. This exclusiveness has proved popular among Asháninka Adventists, but it must have seemed a difficulty to Piro people: what is the point of becoming *cristianos* like the white people and mestizos and then having nothing to do with them? The arrival of the SIL provided a way out, for the SIL were committed by the nature of their contract with the Peruvian government to transforming the Piro into citizens—that is, from the Piro point of view, "fellow humans" of the white people and mestizos.

Living as Evangelical Christians

When the SIL missionaries arrived on the Bajo Urubamba in 1947, they rapidly established themselves among Piro people and quickly ousted the Adventists from Huau. The SIL missionaries were able to supplant the Adventists, I suggest, because their project provided what Piro people saw as a better solution to the serious problem of the period of social chaos and messianic expectation. The greater merit of the SIL project, in the eyes of Piro people, would seem to have been its explicit direction toward them, as Piro people. Central to this merit was the core of the SIL project, translating the Bible into Piro. As Sebastián put it, following on from his account of the coming of the teaching about God, "The year in which Esther Matteson arrived among us was 1947. After she had come, they said about her, 'She wants to learn our language, and translate the Word of God into our language.' Later, she told me about the Piro language, and explained that we could have books and learn in our own language. 'It would be good and we could do it,' she said" (Sebastián, Zumaeta, and Nies 1974).

In Sebastián's account, "our language," "the Piro language," and "the Word of God" are very close in form: *wtokanu*, "our language / word," *yineru tokanu*, "Piro people's language / word," *Goyakalu tokanu*, "God's language / word." The translation of the New Testament into vernacular languages is central to the SIL project, but I think that Piro people probably understood it in a quite different sense. Language is a major marker of the difference between Piro and Asháninka peoples, and this is true even though many of the former and some of the latter can speak both languages. Matteson's project, formulated as Sebastián understood it, held out the prospect of a solution to the crisis they were experiencing directed specifically at them, as Piro people, rather than received at secondhand from Asháninka people, as with Adventism.

In the 1980s and 1990s, learning the Piro language had a specific meaning for Piro people: the desire for extended coresidence with them. Since all Piro people are multilingual, social life can proceed without the need for the coresident other to understand or speak Piro. However, *gwashata*, "living well," depends on the ability of this other to understand

Piro, for only then can that person be truly human. To understand Piro is to enter a condition of expanded moral possibilities. Vargas spoke Piro, I was told, but the Adventists had made no attempt to learn this language. By wanting to learn the Piro language, Esther Matteson signaled to Piro people her desire for a deeper and more profound relationship with them.

Matteson's project of translating the Bible into Piro would have held out to Piro people a solution to a problem inherent in Adventism and of the messianic crisis in which that message took hold. If, as the Adventists undoubtedly preached, the solution to the serious chaos in which Piro people found themselves lay in "The Word of God," then that solution was couched in a language, Spanish, and a form, writing, that had potent meanings for Piro people at the time. Writing was a symbol of the power that the white bosses had over their Piro slaves (Gow 1990), while Spanish was, and remained, *kajitu tokanu*, "white people's language." The Adventists had opened schools in Unini and in Huau, but instruction was exclusively in Spanish. This would have presented insuperable difficulties for Piro people learning the truth about *Goyakalu tokanu*, "God's Words": learning a technique of which they were institutionally ignorant in a language that they felt themselves to understand and speak badly.[9] Matteson (1954: 65) noted that many made heroic efforts to overcome these difficulties. To have God's Words translated into Piro, and to be taught to read in Piro, would greatly reduce the effort required, but more importantly it would assert the exclusivity of the new relationship between Piro people and this new kind of white people. The center of gravity of Adventism had been among Asháninka people. The SIL missionaries who set up in Huau were clearly primarily interested in Piro people themselves.[10]

One consequence of the SIL project was the centrality of schools. Schools were there to teach children and adults to read and write in Piro, and then Spanish, in order that they have access to the Word of God, the Bible (in Piro, *Goyakalu tokanu steno*). The sorts of community forms entailed by this project were, however, interpreted by Piro people as the primary purpose of the SIL project. Sebastián's "conversion, new life," as we have seen, was primarily a new mode of "living well," through a relationship with the SIL missionaries, and through them, with the cosmos.

The school, and its stress on reading and writing, would have had a potent meaning for Piro people. As I have discussed elsewhere in detail (Gow 1990), at least one Piro man, Sangama, had formulated the key to the power of the bosses as lying in their technique of writing, *kajitu yona*, "white people's designs," and *kiruka*, "books, papers." The identification of writing as an important attribute of white people was general to Piro people, and their illiteracy was a powerful image of their ignorance. But, as I also discussed there, the importance of writing for Piro people was also connected to their understandings of *yonchi*, "designs," and to the role of design in ongoing social life. The SIL project held out the promise of inserting "white people's designs" into the heart of Piro social life, in the specifically Piro form of the written Piro language.

The SIL project solved another aspect of the dilemmas presented by messianic enthusiasm for Adventism. Most Piro people had abandoned performance of the girl's initiation ritual. In this ritual, *yonchi*, "design," played a key role, for through covering the girl's entire body with designs, she was rendered as the hypostasis of *giglenchi*, "beauty," as a key Piro value and provided with the longevity necessary for the ongoing transformation of social relations to proceed (Gow 1991). By abandoning that ritual, the role of *yonchi*, "design," in controlling the process of transforming social relations had been lost. By translating the "Word of God" into Piro, and by opening schools in which Piro people could learn to read and to write, Matteson provided a means by which Piro people could reinsert design at the center of their social world and its ongoing transformation. Now, however, the design was to be the powerful technique of "white people's design," writing, rather than the technique of "Piro design."

In some senses, conversion can be seen as a transformed girl's initiation ritual. The initiation ritual united all the Piro people scattered along the Urubamba into one place to celebrate the successful seclusion of a pubescent girl, and through the ritual, to project that transformation into the future. As such, the girl's initiation ritual celebrates the success of the girl's seclusion from dangerous others and provides her with longevity. This ritual was abandoned during the chaotic period following the death of Vargas, who had indeed been its great sponsor. The vacuum left by the abandonment of this ritual in the messianic period of Adventism was then filled by the founding of schools. Indeed, my informants, recalling this period, insisted that all Piro people lived with the gringas in Huau. While this was probably never literally true, the image of united residence in a single village is close to the uniting of "all the Piro people from along the river," which is central to the imagery of girl's initiation ritual.

Life in SIL-dominated communities also had its own form of ritual life, which were intimately linked to the issue of writing. These were religious services (in Piro, *gapatjeru*; in Ucayali Spanish, *culto*). These rituals were characterized by prayers, readings from the Bible, and song. These songs were a new musical genre generated by the SIL missionaries themselves, *Goyakalu shikale*, "God's songs," hymns. These were written by the SIL, and are on the whole adaptations of North American hymns, with Piro words fitted to the original melodies. When I heard them sung in Bufeo Pozo in 1988, considerable effort was made to sing them from the hymnbook, rather than from memory, and it seemed that this reading was crucial to their performance. Julia Laureano, from Santa Clara, bemoaned the fact that she had lost her hymnbook, even though she seemed to remember the words of these hymns well enough.[11] The collective singing of these songs was, I was told, a key feature of being evangelical Christians, along with reading the Bible and praying.

The *Goyakalu shikale*, "God's songs," have an interesting feature, as sung discourse. All the major genres of Piro sung discourse are characterized by a shifted subject position, such that the singer never sings from his or her own subject position: in love songs, the singer sings from the position of both the desired target and from the position of a mythic animal, while in shamanic songs, the singer sings from the position of a powerful spirit being. Given the generality of such shifted subject position in Piro sung discourse, the same is likely to be true of hymns. It seems entirely probable that Piro people considered, and consider, themselves to be evangelical Christians only when they are actively singing Goyakalu shikale. That is, it is in the very act of singing these Goyakalu shikale that Piro people came to occupy the subject positions referred to within them. The model here would be shamans' songs, the "drug songs," where the singer seeks identification with a specific other subject position. Take the following example, that of *Kigler-Pagognepa Shikale*, sung for me by Julia Laureano,

Kigler-pagognepa,
Kigler-pagognepa,
Gerotu nopji netanu wane,
Gita chinanu rugletkatka.
Kigler-pagognepa,
Kigler-pagognepa,
Ruknokatkana wa Satanasyo
Kigler-pagognepa.

In the good world to come,
In the good world to come,
I will see my new house
I will say everything has been made good.
In the good world to come,
In the good world to come,
Satan will have been overcome,
In the good world to come.

In singing this song, I suggest, the singers come to be the people for whom the proposition it contains is true: rather than merely celebrating the faith of an evangelical Christian, this is the moment of being an evangelical Christian. Just as the singer of drug songs seeks an identification with a powerful being, so to the singers of God's songs seek such an identification. Certainly, singing was mentioned far more often to me than prayer in accounts of evangelical Christianity. One old man remembered Huau in this way: "It was beautiful when the gringas held their religious services there, and the people sang."

Conversion Lived Out

The activities of the SIL missionaries would, from the perspective of Piro people, have had a certain ambiguity. If my analysis of Adventism is correct, the nature of the SIL project must have struck Piro people as slightly odd: why establish the whole extended project of schools and so on simply to teach knowledge that would render social life unnecessary? Piro people would have been faced with a choice between the educational dimension of the SIL project and its specifically religious aspect, as two radically opposed solutions to the problem of how to "live well."

For the SIL missionaries themselves, these two projects were of course the same: schooling gave access to reading skills, which in turn gave access to the Bible, which in turn would lead Piro people to be believing Christians. And there is good evidence that the SIL missionaries were bemused by the reactions of Piro people to their work over the years, as I noted in the quotation from Stoll above. Stoll captures well the strange mixture of radical transformation and of futility that characterized the SIL mission among Piro people, but he is wrong to say that they "carried on as they had prior to salvation." This may be true with regard to certain aspects of religious life, but it was certainly not true with regard to ongoing social life. Piro people had radically transformed the basis of community organization over this period.

By the 1980s, at least in the communities I knew best, there was relatively little interest in the specifically religious dimension of SIL activities. Santa Clara was by then a formally Catholic community, but even in the neighboring communities that retained a nominal Protestant affiliation, there was some collective religious activity, but not very much.[12] There were sporadic revivals of enthusiasm, such that people would occasionally seek to live, temporarily, without drinking, and two brothers-in-law from Nueva Italia suddenly set off for the Swiss Mission base at Cashibococha, to learn, it was said, "to be preachers." In general, however, there was little interest in following what Sebastián had called the "New Life." Indeed, many Piro people were openly defiant of evangelical Christian missionaries: in 1988, I was attending a festival in the new Asháninka community of Centro Pucani, when the Swiss Mission preacher turned up and ordered the people to throw away their manioc beer. Many did so, but Celia Mosombite, the Piro schoolteacher, refused and led a substantial portion of the population in a beer-drinking festival that competed with the missionary's service throughout the afternoon. As she said, "What right have the gringos to tell us what to do?"

One important change had happened in the intervening period. Piro people had acquired a new relationship with a new kind of white people. This was *el gobierno de Lima*, "the government in Lima," the Peruvian state. Since the left-wing military coup of Velasco in 1968, Piro people had come into direct and, for probably the first time, benign, contact with state officials due to that government's commitment to the social inclusion of all Peruvians. By the mid-1970s, Piro communities were being registered for land titles, and there was increasingly direct state control over local schools. In terms of what interested Piro people, the SIL had become increasingly marginal to their lives, and consequently, what interested SIL missionaries had ceased to matter to them.

What Piro people did not give up as time passed, however, was the centrality of schools and of school education in their social lives. It seems that they chose subsequently to deemphasize the specifically religious aspects of the SIL work, while concentrating on its educational aspects. The reason for this undoubtedly lies in the manner in which school education is a transformation of the older systems of *yonchi*, "design," and the girl's initiation ritual: both provide a means by which social life can be projected into the future. This was not true of the period of messianic enthusiasm for Adventism, or for Sebastián's conversion: those were short-term solutions to periods of extreme crisis in living well. Within Sebastián's own narrative of 1968, discussed above, we see a shift from the New Life to the present-day lives of Piro people, as a solution was found to the problem of living well. By the 1980s, my informants, such as Artemio, had reformulated the nature of those transformations, eliding the New Life and its religious dimensions, and stressing the importance of schools and the consequent liberation from slavery.

Of major significance in the decline and "forgetting" of the religious dimension to the transformations of the 1940s and 1950s must have been the return to the use of fermented manioc beer. Abandoned in the face of an extreme crisis, and with the sanction of Adventist missionaries, fermented manioc beer returned to the scene, to collectivize and generalize the new knowledge being acquired. By the 1980s, Piro people had developed new forms of ritual life, the *fiestas de la Comunidad Nativa* (festivals of the Native Community), which focused on the collective appropriation of acquired knowledge for the generation of communal viability (see Gow 1991). As in the case of the fiesta in Centro Pucani, many Piro people were now openly hostile to missionaries' attempts to prevent the consumption of fermented manioc beer.

Some confirmation of this analysis can be drawn from Sebastián's term for the conversion, *genshinikanrewlu*. The term, translated as "conversion, new life," clearly implies a profound change in ways of thinking, but not necessarily of the highly interiorized kind valued by the evangelical missionaries themselves (see Vilaça 1997 on missionary work among the Wari' of Western Brazil). As I have discussed, the root word nshinikanchi, "mind, thinking, love, memory, respect," is profoundly relational and depends on the other people toward whom it is manifested. As such, genshinikanrewlu, "new mind, new thinking, new love" would require a collective transformation in ways of thinking. It would therefore have been extremely vulnerable to any mass defections from it. This point may also explain the forgetting of the period of messianic enthusiasm in the 1980s. Genshinikanrewlu, conversion, was important to Piro people while it lasted, as a "new way of thinking, living with other people," but it became unmemorable as Piro people achieved what they would later term "the liberation from slavery": villages centered on schools, rather than on the bosses.

Conclusion

I want to return to the conclusions of Heras and Stoll quoted before, to the effect that Piro people have remained unchanged by evangelization. There is, I think, something profound in the conclusions of these writers, as they summarize the accumulated wisdom of the Franciscans and the SIL respectively. I am attracted to this vision of Piro people's plucky intellectual resistance to centuries of Franciscan, and decades of SIL, attempted indoctrination. But this leads easily into the intellectual danger I discussed at the start, that of the proximity of the intellectual worlds of missionaries and anthropologists, and their mutual distance from that of Piro people. From Piro people's point of view, both the Franciscans and the SIL were wrong, for both sets of missionaries changed their lives in quite remarkable ways. The problem is that the changes the missionaries effected were not the ones the missionaries wanted. For anthropologists, the problem then becomes that of moving away from the missionaries' question, "Did they convert?," to a more ethnographic one, "What did Piro people find interesting about the missionaries' work?"

This issue has been raised by Viveiros de Castro (1993), in his discussion of the same historical reaction of the ancient Tupinambá of the Brazilian coast to early European missionaries. Noting the frustration of the Jesuits at the Tupinambá's mix of enthusiasm and indifference to their message, Viveiros de Castro raises the analytical problems presented to anthropology of cultures marked by a profound "desire to be the other, but on their own terms." What can we make of Piro people's avid desire to be evangelical Christians in the 1940s and 1950s, their apparent receptivity to the SIL religious message, and their indifference to this same message and to their own prior conditions in the 1980s?

Viveiros de Castro, following the Jesuits themselves, has termed this problem the "inconstancy of the savage soul." His concern is not with the historical processes of conversion among the Tupinambá, but with the very adequacy of anthropological theory to address such issues at all. As he notes, the anthropological concept of "culture" is a direct descendant of the Jesuits' notions of faith and belief, and retains those older concerns with highly interiorized states of being and with mental representations. As such, anthropologists become forced to ask questions about Christianity in a language already steeped in Christian concerns. Drawing on his own fieldwork among the Araweté, speakers of a language closely related to Tupinambá, Viveiros de Castro renders the reactions of the

Tupinambá to the Jesuits more comprehensible: if, as was almost certainly the case, the Tupinambá shared with the Araweté the tendency to locate certainty with the other, not with the self, and hence to have enacted ongoing social life as a process of other-becoming, rather than the reproduction of an already existent self-being, then their enthusiasm for Christianity is at once more easy to understand and more paradoxical. They wanted to believe the Christian message because it was what the Jesuits believed, but they wanted this highly interiorized state of being, Christian faith, precisely because it was proper to the other, not to themselves.

For the Piro case, this point can be clarified by reference to shamanry. If Piro people have historically thought of Christianity and Christian missionaries by analogy to shamanry and shamans, this is not because shamanism was Piro people's traditional religion. As I showed above, Piro people did not possess a religion in the sense of a set of beliefs, nor is shamanry a religion. Shamanry is what shamans do, and shamans do what they do on the basis of their special personal experiences and consequent knowledge. Belief plays no part here. Shamans lay claim to specialist and counterevidential knowledge, which they manifest as potent efficacity in the world through sorcery and curing. They therefore serve Piro people as the privileged model for thinking about all arcane and counterevidential knowledge, such as that claimed by Christian missionaries. And they continue to do so, for the everyday lived experiences of sorcery and curing necessarily loom much larger in the lives of Piro people than do the words and actions of the missionaries.

Hugh-Jones's suggestion that we think of missionization in indigenous Amazonia through the lens of shamanry is therefore a fertile one. My argument here, following on from the discussions of Viveiros de Castro (1993) and Vilaça (1997), helps us to understand how radical that insight might be. Because indigenous Amazonian peoples take the spiritual message of Christianity to be a new form of shamanry, that specific message is subjected to all the radical instability of shamanic knowledge in general, instantiated as it is in the particularities of particular shamans, their unique personal experiences, idiosyncrasies, and forms of knowledge. A growing ethnographic literature deals with precisely the radical instability of indigenous Amazonian Christianities: see Pollock 1993 on the Kraho and Kulina, Vilaça 1997 on the Wari', Journet 1995 on the Curripaco, and Wright 1998 on the Baniwa.[13] All paint a similar portrait of indigenous Amazonian people responding to missionaries with the same bizarre mix of fervent enthusiasm and total indifference. It is not that indigenous Amazonian peoples cannot understand Christianity, for they clearly can and do. What they do not seem willing to accept is why that understanding is supposed to matter so much. That, of course, is the missionaries' problem, but it is also one that should be of interest to anthropologists.

When I consider what exactly it is that puzzles me about the way in which Piro people forgot about their conversion, I think the answer lies with their failure to use it as a very powerful conceptual tool for thinking about their past. Other peoples in the world, including my own, have found it a handy metaphor for linking lived experience to grand historical frames. Pondering why Piro people should not choose to do so suggests to me that Viveiros de Castro is right to urge anthropologists to ponder more deeply the Christian roots of so many of their concepts. I think that Piro people converted to evangelical Christianity primarily because they wanted the SIL missionaries as a new kind of white people, and they wanted to be evangelical Christians because the SIL missionaries wanted them to be so. But, because they did not think of their cosmology as a religion parallel to evangelical Christianity, they could not see that the missionaries were trying to bring them a new religion. Conversion, therefore, made sense to them as a historical action, but not as a historical event. Conversion could occur in a given existential predicament, but once achieved, it lost its historical purchase and was forgotten. If, as the SIL missionaries preached, following Sebastián's account, God "exists and . . . he had created all that can be seen and all that cannot be seen," then this was the nature of the cosmos, and Piro people had hence always been Christians. And this strange conclusion makes me wonder what on earth an anthropological theory adequate to explicate it would look like.

Afterword

I have recently gained access to what appears to be the original of "The New Life," which I downloaded from the SIL Peru website at http://www.sil.org/americas/peru/. This is a new edition (1998), and this text differs subtly from the first edition in a number of ways, but I assume that Sebastián's original Piro text is unchanged. The following is my translation of the Piro original. Sebastián said, "Then with my mouth I invited Jesus to live in my heart. When I received Jesus, I saw nothing. And I did not receive anything. Therefore I trusted God and asked him to teach me and to show things to me" [1998: 160]. Sebastián also states that conversion is not about our bodies, but about how we act toward others. Sebastián's account of his conversion is certainly fascinating, and I hope to analyze it further in the future, but my initial reading of it essentially confirms my analysis in the present essay, as well as my basic sense that censorship never really works.

......

Notes

Fieldwork on the Bajo Urubamba between 1980 and 2001 was funded by the Social Science Research Council, the British Museum, the Nuffield Foundation, the British Council, and the London School of Economics. I would like to thank Fenella Cannell, Bill Christian, Karen Jacobs, Andrew Holding, Cecilia McCallum, Alan Passes, Christina Toren, Aparecida Vilaça, Eduardo Viveiros de Castro, and the participants in the workshop for their help with the formulation of the ideas presented here.

1 My use of the term *shamanry* reflects a growing usage (Viveiros de Castro 1992; Descola 1996) that felicitously emphasizes the specific action features of what matters about shamans over the generalized cosmological systems within which these actions occur, as implied by "shamanism." The problem of the latter term is that it implies that the cosmological system is specific to the shamans, rather than general to the societies within which they operate.

2 See Gow 2000 on compassion in the Piro lived world.

3 The reference would seem actually to be to Sabaté 1925, not to Samanez y Ocampo 1980.

4 *Samenchi* is the absolute form of the root *-samenu*. Technically, my usage here is incorrect, for *samenchi* always means "dead soul": a living person's soul is an obligatorily possessed part of that person.

5 One would want, of course, to know exactly what this phrase would mean to a Shapra man.

6 See Lévi-Strauss 1995 for a discussion of the place of white people in indigenous Amazonian mythology and its relation to dynamic instability.

7 Alvarez 1984 suggests that the pre-Columbian kajine of the Piro were Inca state officials who traded at the Pongo de Mainique.

8 The SIL arrival was fortuitous in the sense of contingent to the immediate Piro situation. I do not know why the SIL chose the Piro for one of their first projects.

9 Obviously, many Piro people at the time would have spoken Spanish, but only the local dialect of Ucayali Spanish. Teaching in the Adventist schools would have been in the unfamiliar form of erudite coastal Peruvian Spanish.

10 This was not a concern to exclude Asháninka, but to assert Piro centrality. Many Asháninka people remained living in Piro SIL-sponsored communities, and many Asháninka children learned to read and write in Piro. See Gow 1991 on this.

11 When Julia Laureano sang SIL hymns in Piro, I was always amazed by her exact imitation of an American Midwest vocal style reminiscent of country-and-western music, quite unlike her singing in Piro, Asháninka, or Andean styles. This was presumably an exact imitation of SIL missionary women's voices. It was as if this style, the way the SIL woman missionaries themselves sang, was the correct one for the genre of God's songs.

12 I saw more such activity in the large upriver communities of Miaría and Bufeo Pozo in 1988.

13 It should be noted that there are, to my knowledge, no detailed studies of the meanings of Christianity among those long missionized indigenous Amazonian peoples of western Amazonia or northern Bolivia, where the situation is likely to be rather different.

···Eight···

The Bible Meets the Idol

Writing and Conversion in Biak, Irian Jaya, Indonesia

Danilyn Rutherford

In this is furnished a sign for those who wish to establish that Christianity is still but a veneer here—that no sooner do they see something that awakens a memory of the old than they lapse back into the old. No, the latter is not correct; all that remains is a memory that has not yet worn away.—Rauws 1919: 111

In his 1919 guide to western New Guinea, the Utrecht Mission Society's most important field, Director J. Rauws described the incident that heralded the dawn of Christianity on Biak, an island in the furthest reaches of the Netherlands Indies (see Rauws 1919: 141–43; see also Kamma 1977: 2:617–22). In 1908, at the mission post at Mansinam, a three-day paddle from the notorious "nest of pirates," Brother F. J. F. van Hasselt received an unexpected invitation. The people of Maundori were burning their idols, the messenger told him. Would he like to come and see the fire with his own eyes? The son of one of the first missionaries to serve in darkest New Guinea—a place where the seeds of piety fell on very rocky soil—van Hasselt had reason to take the request seriously. For over fifty years, the "Papuans" in general—and the Biaks in particular—had tested the faith and fortitude of the Protestant evangelists with their apparent indifference to the Gospel. But now their message was finally finding a place in the hardest of Papuan hearts. Tales of a miraculous dream and vision had led communities throughout the region to destroy their idols and amulets (see Rauws 1919: 123; Kamma 1977: 2:615). Van

Hasselt and his colleagues were being flooded with requests for native evangelists from heathens who had finally seen the light.

The request from Biak was delivered by the brother of Petrus Kafiar, one of the missionaries' most promising "foster sons," a former slave who had just returned from the native seminary in Java. Accompanied by Petrus, who was to become Biak's first native teacher, van Hasselt accepted the invitation. He was not disappointed. At Maundori, the village where Petrus was born, a clan head, a shaman, and a warrior—"formerly a notorious ringleader of headhunts and drunken sprees"—all orated on the excellence of the Gospel. When the speeches were over, the villagers rose en masse to collect their *korwar*, the carved wooden reliquaries that housed the spirits of recently deceased relatives. Along with countless smaller figures, van Hasselt consigned seventy-two korwar to the flames. During visits to other villages, undertaken later, similar scenes transpired.[1] Following the destruction of these signs of heathendom came the construction of signs of Christendom: the schools, churches, and teacher's residences that each community had to provide before the mission would send them a native teacher. For the missionaries and their supporters in Holland, burning and building served the same divine purpose: they gave the new Christians' "inner life" an "outer form" (Rauws 1919: 171).

Writing in hindsight, Director Rauws acknowledged the importance of historical factors in prompting the mass conversions that swept Dutch New Guinea at the turn of this century. The opening of steamship lines and the enforcement of colonial law and order gave the coastal Papuans a taste for the novel and a need to learn Malay, the archipelago's lingua franca and language of rule. What happened in New Guinea was a primitive variant of what was happening throughout the Indies: a "native awakening" that swept the colony as policies changed, technologies improved, and distances collapsed (see Shiraishi 1990: 27). But while these structural changes presented the Utrecht Mission Society with new opportunities, according to Rauws, they could not account for why the Papuans turned to the Gospel to guide them into modernity. Something else had led the heathens to forsake heathen ways: it was the power of the Word.

Eighty-seven years have passed since Director Rauws ended his guide to New Guinea on this uplifting note. To all appearances, today's Biaks have not let him down. The Christian Word bears a power over the fate of people and groups, while heathen objects are little more than souvenirs. Biaks once placed korwar in their clan houses and canoes, decorated their boats, buildings, and furnishings with korwar-shaped figures, and wore korwar-shaped amulets around their necks. Fashioned of soft wood and sometimes equipped with a skull, a korwar protected its owners from illness, death, and misfortune, until it stopped working and they threw it away. Sold in tourist shops in Biak City—and even on the Internet—today's korwar are made of ironwood, for improved durability. They are meant to serve as lasting mementoes of Biak culture, not as ephemeral receptacles of the spirits of the dead. What was once a magical object has become a minor commodity. And yet, the victory of the Gospel over the power of the ancestors may not be as complete as it seems. As I hope to show below, in Biak, the Word has not simply replaced the korwar; one might say it has become the heathen thing.

There is no question that the events recounted by Rauws signaled an important transition in Biak society. The island's current residents share Rauws's perspective: by converting, their forebears ended the age of heathen darkness and took their first steps into the modern world. With close to 100,000 inhabitants, living on three small islands, Biak-Numfor is the most densely populated regency in the Indonesian province of Irian Jaya, now known as Papua, which covers the western half of New Guinea (see Biak Numfor dalam Angka 1992). Biak City, the multiethnic capital of the regency, features an airport, hotels, department stores, a ply mill, several military bases, and dozens of government offices and schools. The islanders, who speak an Austronesian language, profited from their early exposure to mission education, and rates of literacy in Biak's villages have long been high (see de Bruyn 1948). While many Biaks depend for their livelihood on gardening and fishing, others have joined the ranks of the provincial bureaucracy or found positions in private industry or the church.

Today's Biaks reside throughout Papua and further afield, reflecting the value of sojourns in *sup amber* (the land of the foreigners). Their seafaring ancestors had a long history of contact with powerful outsiders, including the Spice Islands Sultans of Tidore, who sporadically received tribute from their distant Papuan subjects (see Andaya 1993). With the Dutch colonial state strengthening its grip in New Guinea, the twentieth century clearly introduced Biaks to new forms of hegemony (see à Campo 1985; Locher-Scholten 1994). My goal in this chapter is not to discredit local views of the past, but to bring to light a more elusive kind of history. In the case of Biak, it seems possible to imagine continuities in the very ways in which people embrace change.

In this chapter, I attempt to make sense of what happened in Maundori on that day in 1908 by analyzing the interplay between words, things, and memory in Biak. I explore the connections between contemporary accounts of conversion and the conditions that shaped Biak's colonial past. By approaching the korwar and the Gospel from both a mission and a Papuan point of view, I suggest an interpretation of the burning of the idols as something other than the symptom of an inner transformation. Linking a comparison of ideologies to an analysis of the conjunction of practices, this chapter brings to light a form of social memory that has failed to simply wear away.

My argument is based on a pair of assumptions: on the one hand, that words must be considered as things in the world, and, on the other, that things are conceivable only in symbolically mediated forms (see Keane 1997a; Munn 1986: 7; Said 1983). These assumptions add up to an insistence on the "textuality" of discourse, a focus on its pragmatic and material properties, as opposed to an interest exclusively in what it means (see Bauman and Briggs 1990; Keane 1997a; 8; Silverstein and Urban 1997; Rutherford 2000). Key to my analysis of the overlap between Biak and mission interests is the written quality of the Word. One finds two distinct yet interrelated attitudes toward writing in the dominant tradition of Western philosophy (see Derrida 1976, 1981). On the one hand, the text extends living memory, giving an author's words and thoughts a lasting presence. On the other hand, writing replaces memory with a threatening substitute, a supplement that supplants what it is supposed to preserve. In an exaggerated form, writing embodies the structure of delay and distancing inherent in every form of representation. Writing brings out the dilemma posed by all forms of discourse: with expression always dependent on a collectively shared code, the speaking subject is never really "there."

Although my analysis is informed by broader perspectives on the dilemmas of social discourse, in this chapter I stress the specificity of local practices. While the missionaries and their Papuan converts shared a belief in the potency of the Word, they had very different notions of its power. For the missionaries, the Gospel represented the salvation of the "deeply sunken" Papuans. "The same for all peoples, in all places and at all times," the Word would bring New Guinea's natives into a universal congregation of souls touched by an omnipresent God (Rauws 1919: 171). For Biaks, the Bible, like the korwar of the past, serves to mediate between local communities and a dangerous and alluring outside world. Where the missionaries envisioned the Gospel as transcending distances and differences, Biak practices use the Scriptures to reproduce boundaries. The Bible, like the idol, provides an experience of haunting, an encounter with the powers of alien lands.

The different conceptions of the Scriptures discussed in this chapter arose in the context of particular histories. Just as the Pietists who brought the Gospel to New Guinea were the product of a distinct social order, so too are the Biaks who seek power by way of the Word. My exploration of the conjunction between these orders breaks into four parts. The first considers the power of the Word as seen by the Dutch and German Protestants who founded the New Guinea mission. The second explores the relationship between the "idol" and the Bible from a Biak point of view. The third delves the roots of contemporary Biak conceptions by examining the constraints imposed on mission practice by local conditions on this "unpacified" colonial frontier.

The conclusion moves between myth and history to reach a new understanding of Biak's Christian awakening. Contemporary analysts, like the missionaries before them, have taken Christian conversion as signaling an emergence among the colonized of "modern" forms of consciousness (see Comaroff and Comaroff 1991; Steedly 1996).[2] Suddenly imagining themselves from the perspective of an otherworldly God, believers embrace new notions of space, time, and self (see Durkheim [1893] 1984: 230–31; Derrida 1995; Kierkegaard [1843] 1985). But my examination of current practices and the events of the past suggests how one might imagine the burning of the korwar as a moment of expansion in a repertoire of strategies for incorporating the new. Transformations have clearly occurred in Biak conceptions of Christian writing, but these changes have less to do with the "colonization" of Biak consciousness than with Biaks' evolving means of engaging with coveted foreign things. Before attempting this rereading of Biak's awakening, we must consider how the missionaries viewed the Word.

The Power of the Word I: The Christian Workman

The founders of the New Guinea mission were not unique in making speech the pathway to the soul. In a range of evangelical traditions, the power of the Word rests on its being heard, preferably in the language that is closest to the heathen listener's heart (see Utrechtsche Zendingsvereeniging 1920; Renck 1990; Rafael 1993; Derrida 1981). But the Protestants who worked in New Guinea complicated this model of divine communication by stressing the role of labor in the process of conversion. To understand the evangelical project undertaken in the territory, one must grasp the tangled connections that mission leaders traced between the Word, revival, and work.

For the men who recruited and trained the first evangelists sent to New Guinea, what the Gospel did was as important as what it said. Ottho Gerhard Heldring, a Dutch pastor, and Johannes Gossner, a defrocked German priest, adhered to the Pietist strand of Protestant thought that emerged in Germany in the late seventeenth century (see Pelikan 1989: 118–73; Weber [1930] 1992: 128–39; see also Armstrong 1993: 293–345). Pietism can be seen as the correlate of the philosophy of the Enlightenment, a philosophy that Kant is said to have argued "destroyed dogma to make room for faith" (Armstrong 1993: 318). The truth of religion no longer lay in the logic of its postulates or the authority of its traditions, but in its psychological effect on the individual believer. As Weber argued most famously, the Protestant ethic created a double bind for the faithful, who could never be sure if they were doomed or saved ([1930] 1992). The Pietists responded to what could not be known by the intellect by focusing on the movements of the emotions (Weber [1930] 1992: 137).[3] The spreading of a word "intended to shine 'not before our eyes, but in our heart' " (Pelikan 1989: 128), evangelism, like asceticism, offered a source of reassurance. Allowing believers to participate in the moment of conversion, the mission appealed not only to the dream of a universal congregation but also to the needs of the evangelists and their audiences back home.

Gossner's and Heldring's concern with the spiritual effects of the Word arose against the backdrop of difficult times. Heldring became involved in the growing social welfare movement in Holland in the mid-nineteenth century, following the potato famine, as an outspoken proponent of "internal and external colonization" (see L. Heldring 1882; Gouda 1995).[4] At home, Heldring supported communities in the newly reclaimed polders, where he preached against the "superstitions" that held poor farmers in their sway. Abroad, he envisioned a partnership between the "serious dissident" and the "unthinking poor." The former would gain "nourishment for his soul"—and preach the Gospel to the latter, who would provide the labor needed to sustain new settlements. Undertaken in the Indies, the partnership would benefit a third party, the "deeply sunken heathen" who would come to understand true faith through his exposure to the colonists. As time went by, the figures of faith and industry merged in Heldring's imagination, strengthening his conviction that colonization could kill two birds with one stone.

Heldring's dream of sending unpaid "Christian Workmen" to bring the Gospel to the heathens, laid out in a tract published in 1847, brought him into partnership with Gossner, who was already training unemployed youths for this purpose. In 1836, Gossner was approached by a small group of lower-class young men, who had failed to qualify for evangelical training (see Kamma 1981: 1:15–18).[5] Gossner took the young men into his home and began to prepare them to preach the Word. For Gossner, all a missionary needed to know, by way of formal training, lay in the hymnal and the Holy Book. When faced by tropical diseases—and the temptations of indolence—the trainees were exhorted to work and pray.[6] In all, Gossner managed to train over a hundred artisans, "privates in the great army of Christendom," who served without pay in Australia, India, and the Netherlands Indies in cooperation with preexisting missions (L. Heldring 1882: 224). Gossner resisted establishing a formal organization for his own enterprise; only over his objections did one come into existence late in his life (Kamma 1981: 1:27).

As candidates for the project, Gossner and Heldring sought individuals who had "really and truly experienced a spiritual awakening" (Kamma 1981: 1:23). Heldring's writings provide a portrait of the role of the Word in such awakenings, which revealed the truth in the outer world of appearances and the inner world of the self. Heldring's account of the life and work of J. van Dijken, a Christian Workman sent by the pastor and his friends to serve in Halmahera, provides a striking example of this process of recognition and rebirth.[7] During his "rash youth," van Dijken had avoided public worship—that is, until the day he was caught up in the revival sweeping the Netherlands (L. Heldring 1882: 225). Fearing the mockery of his comrades, he began to sneak to church to attend Thursday evening meetings. At first, "out of false shame," he refused to enter the chapel; instead he stood outside the door and listened in. Eventually, however, the words did their trick, and van Dijken began worshipping openly: "The uplifting preaching of Ds. van Lingen, in Zetten, brought him still closer to the Savior and to the memory of a dream, which had haunted him for years. In it he had seen himself standing in the midst of heathens, preaching the Gospel, something that then had in no small part provoked him to laughter and that now was so distinctly and seriously present to his mind that his heart was filled with love for the heathens"

(225). For the aspiring missionary, the Word worked by motivating a haunting, if inscrutable memory. Under the influence of "uplifting preaching," "love for the heathens" emerged as the proper meaning of the once laughable dream.

Among the heathens, the Word worked by giving meaning to labor. Taking his cue from the Apostles, Heldring envisioned the Christian Workman as someone who would gain entry to the heathen community by diligently and virtuously plying a trade that was "needed in the place he is going." "Gradually he learns the language and shows by his conduct the nature of the Christianity he professes, and slowly he earns the trust of the natives. And when he believes that the time has come to speak of the Christ who lives within him, then shall not the heathen, whom he has loved as a fellow man, be willing as well to lend him an ear for the preaching of God's Word?" (1882: 215). But if labor set the stage for the preaching of the Word, the Word also allowed the heathens to recognize the nature of what they had witnessed, as we learn from Heldring's account of van Dijken's experiences in Halmahera. The evangelist settled in a lakeside village and got down to work. First, he felled a patch of trees to make a house site in the thick forest, then he carved eighty-two steps in the steep cliff that led to the water hole, then he cut a permanent path through the dense undergrowth to encourage the local Alfoeren to visit him at home. The natives were impressed. "As if at a work of art, the Alfoeren stared at the finished work and admired the lovely road. But it was not this admiration that van Dijken desired, but interaction with the inhabitants of the area, and in this he saw his trouble amply rewarded, for the curious population now turned up from all directions" (226). The visitors were impressed by van Dijken's crops—his coffee, his cotton—"but many prejudices still remained in the way of common intercourse" (227). When van Dijken's clock struck, the Alfoeren fled; "even the ticking for a long time remained an abomination in their eyes, for the continual motion betrayed an evil spirit, such as they saw in everything"—including van Dijken's new well. Only after van Dijken learned the local language could he begin to reveal to the natives the nature of the forces they had witnessed in his handiwork. Before long, the natives had given up their "Death feasts"—"a horrid idolatry"—and had established their own congregation, which celebrated Sunday and Thursday services. One should note the progress made in the consciousness of the Alfoeren: from surprise grew admiration, then belief. The Alfoerens' fear of the evil spirits within things gave way to a recognition of the divinity in souls, first van

Dijken's and then their own. Labor expressed a message that could be read, after the fact, when the Word of the Lord had done its work.

Like the Protestant ascetics described by Weber ([1930] 1992), Gossner and Heldring combined a belief in the power of the Gospel with a conviction that work signified at the same time it produced. Heldring's script depended on the heathens tracing the missionary's startling industriousness to a transcendent source—a God whose power illuminated the inner life of the believer. "Joy in the Lord has to constitute his strength, and a happy heart must radiate from his eyes, so the heathens see him and ask, 'How can a person become this way?' " (Kamma 1981: 1:24). Crucial to this move from the world of production to the invisible core of the self were van Dijken's vernacular sermons, which linked material progress to labor undertaken to glorify an omnipotent, omnipresent God. With the recognition of such a God, idolatry becomes impossible, since power no longer can shelter in things (see Durkheim [1883] 1984: 230–31; see also Derrida 1995: 100). The surprise that leads to conversion should be the heathen's last. This perspective on power is very different from that found in Biak, where, as we shall see, the source of potency must always come as a shock.

In 1897, over forty years after the Christian Workmen began their labors in New Guinea, one of their successors pointed out that he had learned to take care in expressing himself to the primitive Papuans. "Our speech has to be filled with images and comparisons if we want the spoken word to be interesting," Brother Metz noted. "But then we must be careful that the image is not taken for the thing itself" (Kamma 1977: 2:514). While Metz may have been right about the effects of the Papuans' consumption of mission rhetoric, he may not have been right about the cause. In the following section, I consider Biak perspectives on conversion in the context of a longstanding valorization of the foreign. One might say that Biaks have taken an "antimetaphorical" approach to the Bible (see Abraham and Torok 1994: 131–32). Instead of adopting the perspective of foreign evangelists, Biaks seem to have incorporated their signs.

The Power of the Word II: The Idol and the Bible

I have described elsewhere how Biaks reproduce the cultural values that orient social action through their attempts to appropriate the power of outsiders (Rutherford 1996, 2000, 2003). This dynamic appears most dramatically in the sphere of Biak kinship, where outmarried women elicit alien gifts from their brothers in an attempt to transform their children into valued people. Transactions between cross-siblings are crucial to the reproduction of Biak's exogamous, patrilineal kin groups and of relations between Biak and the outside world. In the past, mother's brothers performed ritual services and gave special gifts for the benefit of their sisters' children. Consisting of clothing, porcelain, coins, and other items acquired by Biak adventurers, a brother's gifts were seen as embuing a sister's children with the qualities that define an *amber* (foreigner), a person of exceptional prowess. With the bride wealth given for a woman returned in the form of alien gifts for her children, this mode of exchange sparked an inflationary dynamic that constituted distant places as a crucial source of surplus. To this day, a woman's value, her children's status, and her brother's prestige rest on her family's ability to exceed a local economy through ongoing raids on foreign lands.

By transforming the foreign into a source of identity, Biaks undermine the emergence of inherited hierarchies.[8] The affection that prevails between cross-siblings finds its flip side in the aggression that divides clan brothers, who compete for the gifts of their mother's brothers and the resources of the patrilineal group. Continually supplemented with value from afar, what descends through the patriline cannot constitute stable differences. Because the patriline is not a source of stable differences, Biaks continually look elsewhere for what will set them—and their descendants—apart. In coping with this dilemma, Biaks reproduce a cosmography that identifies the ancestral and the alien (compare Helms 1988; 1993). Foreigners present an ambivalent face to Biaks: dangerous and unpredictable, yet uncannily familiar. Ancestors, as well, are both threatening and protective, prone to sudden interventions in daily life.

The dynamics of Biak kinship provide a perspective for understanding the meanings attributed to Bibles and idols. While mission documents reflected a limited agenda, they do provide a relatively detailed portrait of the production and use of korwar by Biaks and other coastal Papuans (see Geissler 1857; Rauws 1919; Feuilletau de Bruyn 1920; Kamma 1939–41; van Baaren 1968, 1992). Made of wood, bone, beads, and cloth—with some models incorporating the deceased's skull as the figure's head—korwar were carved following the burial of particularly influential men and women.[9] They were meant to serve as a sort of telephone to the supernatural and to protect the bereaved from a jealous ghost. According to Biak belief, the dead left two spirits, the *nin*, or shadow, and the *rur*, or soul. The former loitered in the corpse's vicinity following the person's demise; the latter joined the anonymous souls in the land of the dead.[10] Summoned by a shaman, the *nin* entered the korwar, endowing it with the power to forecast the future and to protect its owners from the hazards of travel, warfare, and disease. A hybrid composed of the body and shadow of the dead, a korwar mediated between the living and the threatening spirits that lurked in caves and streams, around tall trees, at treacherous capes and in the ocean, with its unpredictable waves and wind.

During the period of its use, a korwar's owners made small offerings of tobacco and betel to the figure and had the shaman consult it in times of need. Here is how one missionary described such a consultation:

> The speaker bows low before the image, in the same way as a Papuan is accustomed to bow before a superior, say the sultan of Tidore or his envoy. In bowing, both hands are stretched out in front of the forehead. If nothing particular happens at such a consultation, it is a sign of the korwar's approval: should the consultant begin to tremble, however, then that is a sign of the contrary, and he goes forth unsatisfied. Favourable wind, a lucrative journey or voyage, everything is managed by the dead. (van Baaren 1968: 27)

Placed near a sick bed or stowed in the hull of a canoe, korwar seem to have offered a sense of comfort. But when a korwar failed to forecast a calamity, its owners got rid of the figure. Eventually, all korwars met the same fate and were smashed, sold to traders, placed on a grave or simply thrown in the sea.[11]

The korwars' abandonment bore witness to the difficulty of maintaining a stable link to the ancestors, when their powers keep reappearing in foreign lands. The members of each generation sought out their own sources of recognition, erasing the legacy of their forebears as they inscribed their own. That the korwars' power was only temporary appeared to the missionaries as a mark of the Papuans' lack of authentic religious feeling (Rauws 1919: 37).[12] But in the context of what we know about Biak kinship, this impetuous-seeming practice made a certain sense.

"It is naturally not the korwar that people worship, but the spirit of the dead that resides in it. It goes without saying that the Papuan does not always sense the difference and identifies the one with the other" (Rauws 1919: 44): for Rauws, this ambivalence reflected the primitive state of Papuan religion. But for our purposes, this observation provides a point of connection between what we know of the korwar and contemporary conceptions of the Bible. The korwar's power to intervene in the world of the spirits lay in its ability to manifest difference as difference. Its magic lay in its placement on the cusp of death and life, on the border between a person and a thing. Serving as both an image and a receptacle of the dead, the korwar at once recuperated what was absent and reminded the bereaved of their loss. It is this fetishistic, uncanny, alien quality that writing, like the korwar, conveys for Biaks. It is this quality that one must suppress in order to read the korwar as a symbol of tradition and the Bible as a vehicle for the message contained within.

Elsewhere, I have recounted how the Bible, much like the korwar of old, serves as a medium of identity and a magical possession (Rutherford 2000). In addition to these formal resemblances, Biaks explicitly link the Bible and ancestral objects, including the korwar. When Biak elders describe their community's Christian "awakening," they stress the seductive materiality of the Bible. Conversion is recounted as a tale of capture, carried out by the boldest of warriors: they did not know what they were getting, but they knew it would be good.[13] But while the leaders who told me these stories smiled at their ancestors' ignorance, they were just as likely to describe the Bible as a treasured object.[14] "We no longer need the old heirlooms," village friends often told me. "Now we have the Gospel instead!"

Inserting the Bible's arrival into the history of three clans from the same village, the following myth presents the Gospel as the replacement of the korwar. The tale begins as a love story set deep in the island's interior, where an Apiem woman developed a passion for a young Kaumfu man. Every day, while she was gardening, Young Woman Apiem saw Young Man Kaumfu returning from the forest with game. Born into a clan that subsisted only on "empty taro," she longed for the young hunter's meat. Finally, she could bear it no longer. She followed the hunter home and begged to be his wife.

Young Man tried to send the maiden back to her side of the village, since he knew her disappearance would spark a violent dispute. When she refused to leave, the Kaumfus were forced to send the Apiems clay bottles, fiber bracelets, and some pork. The gift averted the crisis, and the couple was married. But the Apiems soon grew to resent their affines, who failed to share any more of their meat. As the bride soon learned, the Kaumfus came by this luxury through miraculous means. Not only did Young Man's family know how to hunt, they had korwars. Late at night, summoned by the Head Skull, these ancestral relics did all the gardening. Thus, the Kaumfus could spend their days hunting, enriching their plentiful harvests with plenty of game.

During the day, when their descendants were in the forest, the korwars gathered in the village to amuse themselves. Beating *tifa* drums borrowed from the village's residents, the skulls danced and sang a simple song.

The living sing to the dead.
Kirin kirino.
The dead sing to the living.
Kirino kirin kirino.[15]

Eventually, the racket from the dance ground became more than the Apiems could bear. To find out what their neighbors were up to, they left a boy in the village to spy. When the adults returned, the child reported what he had seen: skeletal drumming, bouncing skulls. When they had pieced together the Kaumfu's secret, the Apiems could not contain their envy. Sneaking into the Kaumfu clan house, they tried to destroy the Head Skull by thrusting a spear through its eye socket. The Apiems could not kill the dead object, but they managed to offend it. The relics hopped off to the cemetery in a huff. From then on the dead Kaumfus refused to work the land.

With the skulls on strike, the Kaumfus had to clear their own land. After a gruesome gardening accident, the Kaumfus were forced to migrate. They moved toward the sea, where they intermarried with the Dasems, another North Biak clan, who gave them a Tidoran title, foreign objects, and some land.[16] This first part of the story ends with the emergence of the current order of production and exchange. Instead of korwar, women and affines have become the startling source of surplus. The working skull has given way to the alien mother: the bride who must come from outside. Instead of the dead shocking the living, brothers shock their sisters with their gifts.

The Kaumfus and the Dasems were not together in the foothills for long before a new pair of "others" discovered them: an old couple who lived on the beach. Old Man "The Food Is Already Prepared" and Old Lady "The Two Who Cannot Die" were the site's original inhabitants.[17] These miraculous beings lived on fish that they caught in the tide pools and cooked in the sun. They did not need to make fires, for at night their simple shelter became a wondrous mansion, complete with running water, appliances, and electric lights.

One day, suspecting that people were living in the interior, the old couple tied a bag of sand onto the back of their pig and sent it into the hills to investigate. A Dasem woman discovered the animal and its strange white burden, which she replaced with some charcoal. She sent it back to its masters, after telling her brothers that someone was living on the shore. Along with their sister's husband, the Dasem brothers followed the trail of pig tracks out of the hills. The brother-in-law stood guard in the forest while the Dasems went to meet the strangers. Led by the old couple toward the sea, the two men suddenly stiffened, shocked at their first sight of a wave. They assumed fighting positions and shouted out curses, convinced that they had come upon a powerful foe. But the old man quickly demonstrated that the sea would not kill them by plunging into the surf.

The old man and woman then made friends with the brothers. The Dasems told the spirits their origin stories; the old couple explained the meaning of their names. It was agreed that the brothers would settle on the beach. But the cordial relationship did not last long. The brothers wanted to smoke, and so they decided to light a fire. When the old couple saw the flames, the terror turned them to stone. Terrified by the transformation, the Dasems fled to the hills. But the two named rocks, plus a third for the pig, marked the Dasems' claim to the region. Having shocked the brothers who shocked them, the spirits became silent landmarks, anchoring a social group to a place. Traces of light soil in the interior and dark soil at the beach serve to corroborate the story. A startling encounter gave rise to objects marking an absence and validating an identity and a tale.

The final segment of the story concerns four korwars that took the form of sacred rocks. These boundary markers were the Dasems' "guardians," objects that defined and defended the clan. When the Dasems decided to convert to Christianity, the missionary ordered them to bring these "idols" to the coast. Near the spot where the clan's ancestors briefly had lived, Pastor Hartweg placed a large Bible on top of one boulder and a ring of small Bibles around the others. Then he knelt down and prayed.

The next morning, the missionary returned to discover that the boulders had vanished, leaving only the Bibles. Hartweg accused the Dasems of hiding the korwars. But the fledgling Christians would not have done this, their descendants assured me; they were far too scared. Hartweg sent the men to check, and, sure enough, the rocks had returned to the forest up a path far too treacherous to tread at night. If the miracle marked the victory of the Gospel over the korwars, it kept their encounter on heathen terrain. By inviting the boulders down to the beach, the missionary set the stage for a reciprocal surprise. Just like the skulls that retired to the cemetery, the magical rocks had gone home. Their route followed the Dasem brothers' path back to the foothills, and like them they left behind their trace. In an outcome that startled both the preacher and his flock, the boulders passed on their powers and headed for the hills.

The myth's conclusion seems to support the missionaries' view of conversion: the Word had vanquished a "horrid idolatry." But the transformation left the uncanny grounds of society intact. By remaining as a monument to outmoded beliefs, the korwar might have founded a new subjectivity, oriented to a choice of "idols" and selves.[18] Their disappearance suggests the persistence of a dynamic that grounds social order in a different sort of trace.[19] What we find in this myth is a genealogy of alien sources of identity: from the anonymous dead to the envious affines to the alien spirits who introduce the brothers to the dangerous sea. Their descent follows an apotropaic logic:[20] the specter of lack evokes the signifer that becomes the specter of lack. By this account, the Bible is not simply the divine Word of God, it is another alien thing.

As novel as it seemed, the Gospel's victory followed an established script. The narrative brings out a principle at work in a range of arenas, where the assumption that startling encounters will become a source of socially significant differences ensures that other orders remain strange. This principle finds its roots in a perspective that takes power as substantive, not abstract (B. Anderson [1972] 1990). As seen by those capable of reading its signs, a constant sum of potency remains at large in the universe, subject to capture and concentration. Divinity is neither omnipresent nor omnipotent. God's kingdom is decidedly "of this world" (compare Durkheim [1893] 1984: 230–31).[21]

A kind of double consciousness persists on Biak, on the one hand memorializing the korwar as a dead tradition, and on the other making its death a source of power. But in stressing the connections between the korwar and the Bible, I do not mean to underplay their differences. In the final section of this chapter, I approach the problem of Biak's conversion by way of mission history. I show how Gossner and Heldring's theories of "rebirth" were put into practice in ways that confounded the relationship between labor, souls, and words.

The Word Comes to Mansinam

In sending Christian Workmen to the Netherlands Indies, Heldring hoped to provide the deserving poor with a new livelihood in the tropics while stemming the advance of Islam and promoting law and order (L. Heldring 1882: 216). Up against a colonial government that treaded lightly in matters of religion, the pastor and his colleagues started small. In 1848, they advertised for candidates, "preferably married, who, on the grounds of their creed and lifestyle, can be sent with confidence, and who, through simple devotion, shall make their light shine for the people, who, in seeing their work, shall come to exalt our Father in heaven" (218). Although many people applied, very few were suitable, and Heldring ended up relying on Gossner for a large proportion of the craftsmen who set out for the Indies in the late 1840s and early 1850s. Of the thirty-six men and nine women sent by Heldring and his associates, one remained in Java; another was dismissed shortly after his appointment; still others did so well in their commercial ventures that they forgot their evangelical goals.

Although Heldring did not mention western New Guinea in his 1847 tract, the territory proved the perfect destination. For the Dutch and German craftsmen dispatched to the "Land of the Papuans," it would have been hard to imagine a more alien land. "The Papuan," one of them argued, "stands on the lowest rung of humanity, and many who have not ruled out all prospect for the civilization and rebirth of other deeply sunken heathens consider this race, at least, as far too bestial for anything vaguely resembling religion to be implanted among them" (Kamma 1977: 1:139). The challenge made the coming victory seem more sweet.

It was not easy for Carl W. Ottow and Johan Gottlob Geissler, the German cabinetmakers designated to establish a post in New Guinea, to get permission to begin work in the isolated region. Claimed in 1828, the western half of the huge island had become a source of discomfort for the Dutch. Nominally, the Netherlands governed New Guinea through the Sultan of Tidore. While Tidore loomed large in the Biak imagination, the island stood in the furthest reaches of the polity, and the Sultan had little impact on day-to-day affairs. During much of the nineteenth century, the colonial government could not guarantee the safety of foreign nationals in coastal areas, let alone draw a profit from the territory. Officials in Ternate, capital of the Residency that encompassed New

Guinea, were far from enthusiastic about the prospect of having witnesses reporting on the government's dismal lack of control.

Ottow and Geissler persisted, however, and some three years after they had arrived in the Indies they were finally on their way to Doreh Bay, a well-known stopping point on the northeastern corner of the Bird's Head Peninsula. A Ternatan merchant who had three trading ships that sailed to Doreh once a year had offered them free passage in return for their agreement to act as his agent in New Guinea. While Ottow, Geissler, and Fritz, their Ternatan servant, were not the first foreigners to disembark at Mansinam Island, at the mouth of the Doreh Bay, they must have made quite a scene. After stepping ashore, the Germans dropped to their knees and prayed for "strength, energy, clarity and wisdom so that everything would begin successfully and God would bestow great pity on the poor heathens here" (Kamma 1981: 1:74). Then they unloaded their supplies. The brothers had brought with them a cow, some chickens, ducks and geese, farming tools, a year's supply of food, a prefabricated house, and several trunks of trading goods, writing materials and books (Kamma 1977: 1:74). They also had brought a letter of introduction from the Sultan of Tidore, written in Malay, the Indies' widely spoken lingua franca, of which some locals knew a few words.

Mansinam's inhabitants were migrants from Numfor, an island close to Biak. The Biaks and the "Meforezen," as they were known to the Dutch, spoke mutually intelligible languages and shared many traits. The Numforese at Mansinam were avid traders. But unlike the Biaks, they relied on slaves to do the gardening instead of integrating captives into their clans. Ottow and Geissler, who described their experiences in voluminous letters to Gossner, were struck by the islanders' indifference to their plight. As the ship pulled away, the Christian Workmen got started. After a quick survey of the island, they concluded that it was unfit for their purposes and that they should move to the mainland, where there was more water and better conditions for farming. To do so, they needed to build a boat, an undertaking that ended in failure. "To fell the tree alone took a half a day, and we worked for three days before the shape became apparent; by then we were very fatigued. Then the wood cracked because the sun was too hot" (Kamma 1981: 1:93). Two attempts later—the last using ironwood, which would have been too heavy to float—Ottow and Geissler finally gave up. "Luckily, that night I saw a new canoe at the Papuan house; fortunately, I was able to buy it for twelve florins" (1:93). In a community where people with status never engaged in manual labor, the missionaries' behavior must have seemed remarkable. Instead of attracting the admiration of the locals, these Christian Workmen became the object of pity and disdain (see Kamma 1977: 1:77).

Following the fiasco with the boat, Geissler developed an infection on his foot that forced him to return to Ternate on the next passing ship. Ottow, who remained behind, took his mentor's advice and attempted to master the local language. In between house building and trips to death feasts, he collected Papuan words. By the end of 1855, Ottow was teaching school, with his cook and a Malay sailor as pupils.[22] If Ottow and Geissler had ever seriously considered making cabinets for the heathens, these early months put that notion to rest. Like the eighteen missionaries who followed them during the nineteenth century (Rauws 1919: 75), the Christian Workmen came to owe their livelihood—and survival—to trade.

From the day they arrived, the local Papuans showed an interest in doing business with the missionaries.[23] Canoes from across the region would stop at the post to exchange birds of paradise, ambergris, wild nutmeg, massoi bark, and other forest products for coins, knives, beads, and cloth. The missionaries soon hit on a lucrative scheme, buying rice from the coastal Papuans at harvest time for imported commodities, and during the lean season reselling the same rice for export goods (Wallace [1869] 1986: 498). The profits they earned from trade paid for the provisions that they periodically received from their Ternatan supplier. But even before they launched this commerce in objects, Ottow and Geissler became involved in the purchase of people. In 1857, the colonial government awarded the missionaries a monthly stipend for coming to the rescue of the crews of shipwrecked vessels, who risked being killed by the coastal Papuans. (It was considered bad luck to shelter the sea spirits' victims.) Able to act on the rumors that circulated in the region, Ottow and Geissler hired paddlers to carry them to distant villages to ransom foreign nationals. Soon the Papuans started saving the missionaries the trouble of seeking them out, by delivering the unfortunates to Mansinam and demanding a reward.

Besides foreign victims, the missionaries also ransomed local men, women, and children. Ottow, Geissler, and the dozen missionaries who followed them in the nineteenth century made a practice of manumitting Papuan slaves. The first slave they received—and baptized—was a young Papuan woman whom they "rented" from a ship's captain to serve as their cook (Kamma 1977: 1:110).[24] Just as the trade in forest products and victims helped the missionaries make ends meet, the trade in slaves lightened the burdens of life in a colonial hinterland where reliable help could not be hired (Adriani et al. 1896). Generally obtained as children, the free-bought slaves became members of the missionaries' households, where they performed menial chores.

But trade had more than a pragmatic function; it helped the missionaries meet their evangelical goals. As Ottow and Geissler saw it, they were not buying people; they were saving lives and souls. The former slaves were more than compensated for their efforts with the blessings of civilization and the joy of faith. The missionaries' wives, dispatched from Ternate, had up to thirty such "foster children" in their care. Soon, a community of "freebought" Christians formed near Ottow and Geissler's homes. The missionaries tried to lure "freeborn" Papuans into their churches and schools with the promise of free tobacco. Trade served as a stick, as well as a carrot: those who violated God's law and worked on Sunday found the Christian Workmen unwilling to do business during the following week. By 1857, Ottow and Geissler were preaching to large gatherings every Sunday, using a mixture of Malay and Mefoorsche words (Kamma 1977: 1:85).[25]

When the Utrecht Mission Society took over the New Guinea mission in 1863, the strategies of the Christian Workmen came under attack. Yet while van Hasselt Sr. and his colleagues received a modest salary from Holland, they soon found themselves conforming to their predecessors' ways (see Adriani et al. 1896).[26] To preach the Gospel, the missionaries needed an audience. The manumission of slaves provided one that was literally captive, while trade caught the free Papuans' eye. By maintaining a commercial center, the missionaries tried to suppress the Papuans' "lust for wandering" off to do business elsewhere or, worse yet, to raid.[27] The allure of the transactions that took place at the mission post helps to make sense of the remarkable security the missionaries enjoyed in this "unpacified" land. In the entire history of the mission, not a single European missionary died by a Papuan hand.[28]

Survival is not success, however, and plenty of missionaries languished in disappointment at the fruitlessness of their work. The most carefully reared foster children disappointed the missionaries by returning to native society and reverting to heathen ways. The freeborn Papuans' apparent imperviousness to God's message was equally discouraging. The missionaries refused to baptize adults who could not demonstrate contrition for their sins by renouncing all heathen customs. Not surprisingly, the only free Papuans whose hearts they managed to touch usually waited until their deathbeds to see the light. But in seeking proof of the state of the Papuans' souls, the missionaries were caught in a trap of their own devising. The very forces that drew the Papuans to Mansinam obstructed the transformation the missionaries hoped to inspire.

The early evangelists provided Biaks and other Papuan visitors with a place to capture the foreign. The booty they obtained through their encounters with the missionaries included not only foreign things, but also foreign words. When Biaks attended services, they acquired more than tobacco; they gathered texts, memorized verbatim, to take home to their kin (Kamma 1977: 1:131). Some snatches of sermons may have been turned into songs; others were repeated word for word (Kamma 1977: 1:131).[29] Imported words seemingly could serve as "proof," the mark of a confrontation in an alien realm.[30] What the missionaries said may have been comic—and in some cases obscene—but it still provided the valid trace of an encounter (Kamma 1977: 1:129).[31] The very strangeness of the evangelists' words was what gave them their potency and appeal.

Given the Papuans' interest in transforming the spoken word into booty, it is not surprising that they took an interest in the missionaries' written texts.[32] Just as the bodies and houses of foreigners possessed a transmissible potency, so, it appears, did their books (Kamma 1981: 1:311, 1939–41: 123). Stored, like a korwar, in the hold of a ship, the Gospel of Luke saved the lives of one group of shipwreck victims (van Hasselt n.d.: 35). When a Biak warrior saw the powerful object, he knew that he could not kill these travelers with impunity and sent word to Mansinam instead. In the 1930s, in the Raja Ampat Islands, among a group of Biak migrants, a missionary discovered an array of foreign volumes being used by the heathens as divinitory texts (Kamma 1939–41: 126).[33] Possessed by the author's spirit, the shaman picked out a letter whose position determined if the patient would survive. This treatment of the Word put a detour in the route to conversion imagined by Heldring, that pathway leading from surprise to admiration, from fear to understanding, from mysterious signifiers to meaningful signs. Instead of internalizing the spirit of the Scriptures, these heathens incorporated the letter as an uncanny medium for summoning absent powers.

One can imagine Mrs. van Hasselt's consternation in 1894 when an old female shaman came to look at the Bible illustrations that had just arrived from Holland. Gazing at a plate depicting Christ, the old woman exclaimed, "You are the Good Lord, you are also my Lord Jesus Christ; even if others don't want you, I worship you and I love you." Kamma reports: "Mrs. van Hasselt asked her, given that she thought so positively and believed in Christ, why hadn't she ever come to church? The one thus attacked defended herself by saying, 'Yes, I know very well that the Great Lord made the heavens and the earth. He is with the Company, not us; we are Papuans.' Mrs. van Hasselt then noted, 'At these words, I could scarcely hold in my laughter, although she betrayed a deeply distressing unbelief' " (Kamma 1977: 2:495).

The old woman's performance highlighted the difficulty faced by the missionaries in their effort to recognize "true" conversion. The only way they could see into the hearts of the heathens was through the medium of words. Inspired by her encounter with what the villagers called "paper korwar" (Kamma 1977: 2:664), the shaman's utterance raised the specter that more convincing "converts" were also merely replicating what they had heard.[34] But at the same time her "unbelief" raised the issue of sincerity, it also revealed something about notions of space. What was so disturbing—and comical—about the shaman's response was her rejection of God's transcendence: God may be great, but he is not here. He is with the company, elsewhere in the world.[35] The missionaries' deity was of a different nature: there was no position in space or consciousness where His presence could not be felt.

At the turn of the century, the Indies government finally responded to the Utrecht Mission Society's pleas and applied a firmer hand in New Guinea (see Smeele 1988; Beekman 1989: 86–87; Locher-Scholten 1994: 107). For close to fifty years, the missionaries had been forced to conform in practice—if not in theory—to "heathen" conventions concerning personhood, justice, labor, and space. The media they put into circulation provided a common ground for two very differing conceptions of the Gospel. From one perspective, the Word was the speech of God, finding resonance in the most deeply sunken of heathen hearts. From another, the Word was an untranslatable mark, a trace that made present the potency of alien lands. It is from the perspective of this mismatch in perspectives that we should consider the mass conversions that accompanied the consolidation of colonial authority. These conversions marked the victory of a God whose power lay in the strangeness of the foreign, who beckoned on the horizon instead of reigning from the heights.

Conclusion

"The preached word does its work," Rauws proclaimed in the conclusion to his guide (1919: 171). "Souls are touched and delivered." But were they? Following the "awakening" at the turn of the century, it was not long before Biak became a net exporter of evangelists. Yet Biak also became famous as the site of a series of messianic uprisings drawing upon and subverting Christian rhetoric. Dating from before the arrival of the missionaries, and continuing to the present day, the Koreri movement, as these uprisings have been dubbed in the literature, brought together Biaks from across the region to greet the ancestor said to have created foreign power (see Kamma 1972). Some call him Manarmakeri, the "Itchy Old Man"; others refer to him as "Tete Manis," "Sweet Grandfather," a term Biaks also use for Jesus Christ. Manarmakeri's arrival would raise the dead and inaugurate an endless age of plenty: *Koreri*, "We Change Our Skin," also described as *kan do mob oser*, "we eat in one place," no longer needing to struggle to survive.

The continuing grip of Koreri on Biak imaginations raises questions regarding the confrontation between Christian words and heathen things with which this chapter began. It has been argued that the transformation that matters in the history of imperial encounters is not "first contact" but the establishment of effective colonial rule (Sahlins 1993: 16; see also Comaroff and Comaroff 1991: 251). The connections between the pacification of coastal New Guinea and the Papuans' Christian awakening were no secret to the missionaries. By the 1860s, some of the "brothers" had already concluded that they would make no progress until the government forced the Papuans to behave—and to believe (see Beekman 1989: 84). Christianity and colonialism's disciplinary regimes were supposed to work together in New Guinea to create a docile Papuan subject. But if the signs in Biak seemed to be pointing in the direction of an accession to "modern" identity, the island's history may not have followed a predictable script. This chapter has drawn on contemporary Biak practices in an effort to make imaginable the logic behind what we know of "Papuan" responses to the mission. In these final paragraphs, I attempt to explain the burning of the korwar as a transformation that made sense in local terms.

In suggesting resemblances between past and present treatments of the Word, I do not mean to imply that there have not been changes in Biak conceptions of Christian writing. While Ottow and Geissler's dependence on trade, instead of production, was a critical factor in mission history, established modes of capture, including the taking of enemy heads, set the stage for the Biaks who "raided" their sermons. Expeditions to the mission post no doubt recalled the tradition of voyaging to Tidore. Besides foreign titles, clothing, and porcelain plates, Biak warriors who made the journey stole magical power by absorbing the Sultan's potency as they crouched before his throne (see Kamma 1982). Like the filling of mission churches on Sunday mornings, the appearance of the Papuan "pirates" at the Sultan's court from one perspective seemed like a gesture of submission. But from another, it was a dangerous act of thievery, carried out for the benefit of distant kin.

What the missionaries and officials hoped to find in the burning of the korwar was an abandoning of the ancestors (see Feuilletau de Bruyn 1920).[36] As they saw it, these arbitrary, inconstant spirits stood behind an unending cycle of violence and revenge. Freed from the bonds of kinship and impulse, the Papuans might finally develop what they so sorely lacked: a fitting awe for God and the State (see Haga 1884: 2:430–43). Yet in descriptions of Biak's awakening, one finds evidence that the ancestors were scarcely left behind. Van Hasselt and his colleagues postponed sending Petrus Kafiar to Biak when his relatives first located him for fear that the islanders would idolize the long-lost captive (Kamma 1977: 2:619). From mission accounts of Kafiar's experience, it appears that they were right (see Kamma 1977: 2:665).[37] In Maundori and other places that Petrus visited, the slave-turned-foreigner was greeted by villagers bearing gifts. The offering of tribute to prophets proclaiming the return of Manarmakeri was a common feature of the uprisings that recurred throughout the nineteenth century. The moment of conversion may well have meant more than a break with the past; it potentially heralded the return of Manarmakeri and the ancestral sources of foreign power.

From a certain perspective, the previous decades appear to have been leading up to this moment. The earliest recorded incidence of Koreri, which took place on Numfor several years before the missionaries' arrival, identified the return of Manarmakeri with a reversal of relations with Tidore. Instead of traveling to Tidore, the followers delivered the Sultan's tribute to the prophet, who claimed to have the power to sink the Tidoran fleet with a single word (Kamma 1972: 106). Over the years, outbreaks occurred on Biak and elsewhere along the shores of Geelvink Bay. Earthquakes and epidemics set off episodes, as did the Mansinam people's failure to rebuild a men's house condemned by the missionaries as "obscene." Coinciding with these crises was the gradual erosion of Tidore's influence in the region, as the Sultan surrendered the last vestiges of his sovereignty to the colonial state. As the century wore on, new elements entered the prophets' repertoire. One prophet preached in an "incomprehensible language"; another performed baptisms; yet another adopted mission rhetoric and complained of the faithlessness of his flock.[38]

The most dramatic outbreaks of the Koreri movement fit a pattern identified by Bruce Knauft before the term *cargo cult* went out of fashion (1978: 186). Most of the movements Knauft reviewed, in a survey of known cases, occurred when Europeans left, not when they arrived. With their inordinate wealth, Europeans posed a problem to Melanesians because these outsiders surpassed them on their own terms. By this logic, foreigners were potential equivalents, whose excessive potency appeared as something that could circulate. This depiction seems to fit the sultan, with his transmissible magic; it also seems apt when one considers the missionaries, who, like it or not, became a node in a regional network of exchange. Whether by virtue of a transformation in the nature of colonial conditions, or the more dramatic ruptures caused by World War II, when relations to these significant others were disrupted, their power suddenly appeared to be at large. But where Knauft viewed the cargo cult as a symptom of distress, the history of Koreri speaks of the resilience of the underlying dynamic. When Koreri failed to materialize, the followers' hopes did not dim; rather they blamed the prophet's self-interest for leading him to misread the signs.[39] In attempting to close the gap between Biak and the Land of the Foreigners, no leader could be "alien" enough.[40] In valorizing the foreign, Biaks set their sights on an impossible object: the source of an utterly unanticipated surprise. Biak society takes shape around an origin that is stubbornly inaccessible.[41] As we learned from the story of the Kaumfus and their korwars, the value of foreignness shifts at the moment its provenance comes to light.

One outcome of Biak's distinctive relation to the foreign is that alternative routes to authority can coexist at a particular moment (see Rutherford 2000, 2003). Another effect of this dynamic is the unfolding of alternative treatments of foreign discourse over time. The Papuans' exposure to writing began before the arrival of Ottow and Geissler. In 1848, on a stop in Doreh Bay, a Dutch lieutenant read out a missive from the Sultan of Tidore to a group of Papuan notables (de Bruyn Kops 1850: 171).[42] Ternatan traders and Dutch colonials persisted in the practice of granting letters of appointment to local leaders, powerful objects that they would present to the captains of passing ships (see Robidé van der Aa 1879: 81, 96). It seems possible to trace a progression from the objectification of foreign documents to the memorization of foreign words to the fragmentation of foreign narratives. This final alternative became apparent in the course of my fieldwork, when I interviewed a prophet who explicated the Scriptures, quoting chapter and verse (see Rutherford 2000). By a reversal born of the logic of Biak prophecy, the Gospel became a translation of the myth of Manarmakeri. A Biak ancestor became the figure who ordered Guttenberg to set up his presses so that the Germans could bring the Bible back where it belonged.

Encompassing a wider repertoire of ways of incorporating Christian discourse, the perspective of contemporary Biaks is clearly different from that of the "indifferent" Papuans portrayed by the missionaries.[43] When we compare contemporary Biak practices with what we know of the past, the burning of the korwar in 1908 appears as a critical point of transition. What was recognized at the surprising moment of conversion was not the hidden soul of the heathens but the hidden significance of the Gospel. What the warriors suddenly saw from the perspective of outsiders was not the sinfulness of their behavior but the unexpected truth of Biak myth. The shaman's statement that God is "with the Company" lost its validity. The collapse of distances could only mean one thing: Manarmakeri, the ancestor, was about to return. This was a different plot than that imagined by Heldring, in which surprise would give way to understanding. True to the logic of Biak sociality, one surprise led to another. The shock of recognition would be repeated, with Biak astonishing the world.

For in fact, I did not need to turn to contemporary Biak to show the error in Director Rauws's assumptions. I could have turned the calendar forward, less than two decades, to 1939 and the most dramatic uprisings the island has ever seen. The Koreri movement in North Biak was led by Biromor, a former convict, who gained invulnerability from a tiny Bible worn like an amulet around his neck. He told his followers that the volume was from Sukarno, the nationalist leader who became Indonesia's first president after the war. After the flight or internment of the Dutch officials and missionaries, Biromor ascended to power on the strength of a rumor that the Dutch had torn the opening pages from the Scriptures—the ones that proved that God was really Manarmakeri and Biak was really Israel, His chosen land. Biromor, like leaders in other parts of the island, required his followers to turn over their Bibles. The bonfire this time included the possessions of local teachers, who, like it or not, were forced to surrender their texts. If my informants were correct, the burning of the Bibles by this warrior was not intended to destroy the source of their potency. The destruction of the texts, like the annihilation of pigs and gardens, was a peculiar act of faith. An impossible confrontation with the origin of difference, Koreri would bring new and better books.

Biromor did not succeed in "opening Koreri." But his failure has not prevented contemporary Biaks from finding power—and their forebears—in the Word.

......

Notes

1 At the invitation of the people in Maundori, van Hasselt also took the two large statues that guarded Meosbepondi, the island where Biaks deposited the bones of the dead. Depicting an eagle and a snake, said by Kamma to be the signs of the masculine and the feminine, these ended up in a museum in Holland and later at the Paris Exhibition, where, ironically, they were destroyed in the fire that gutted the Indies exhibition. See Kamma 1977: 2:621–62.

2 Schrauwers 2000 offers an alternative version of this argument, which takes into account the impact of Dutch religious and political dynamics on missionary practice in Sulawesi.

3 As the Pietist count von Zinzendorf put it, "Faith was not in thoughts or in the head, but in the heart, a light illuminated in the heart" (Armstrong 1993: 317). Weber ([1930] 1992: 137) found that von Zinzendorf's German Pietism offered less of a support for the development of the "spirit of capitalism" than Calvinism. "But compared to Calvinism," he wrote, "the rationalization of life was necessarily less intense because the pressure of occupation with a state of grace which had continually to be proved, and which was concerned for the future in eternity, was diverted to the present emotional state."

4 See L. Heldring 1882: 128. "The potato is today's Tower of Babel," Heldring pronounced, finding the hand of God in the massive displacement of populations caused by the famine. (L. Heldring was O. G. Heldring's biographer.)

5 He had just broken with the Berlijn Missionsgesellschaft over that organization's restrictive selection policies.

6 Gossner provided a convincing example for his charges: when facing a tough decision, he would pray and "throw the dice." Drawing lots to determine the will of God was advocated by von Zinzendorf as well. See Weber [1930] 1992: 135.

7 Heldring's descriptions of his own open-air sermons for Dutch audiences make it clear that he imagined awakening in universal terms. "In connection with the local surroundings, I sketch in broad strokes the coming of Chris-

tianity, such as it was once brought here by the first evangelists, and through which heathendom, to which so many reminders from antiquity in the immediate neighborhood testify, was driven from the region" (L. Heldring 1882: 231). Speakers also described the conversion of contemporary heathens: "Stories from the rich terrain of evangelism seem to me to be most suited to festivals like these, where such a number of strangers, some entirely foreign to the mission, are gathered. There, among the thousands, only an impression, an unforgettable word, a holy thought, a divine seed needs to be strewn that possibly, through the grace of the Highest, will grow to fruition" (231).

Heldring's accounts of ancient history enabled the audience to relive their ancestors' own Christian awakening when they heard evangelical tales from afar. Recalling God's power and love, the audience hung on the words of the speakers, touched by a "great word," "rebirth" (L. Heldring 1882: 232). This word took the faithful back to the future, as it were; they saw contemporary awakenings from the perspective of the congregation to come, when all would be joined in "one heart and one spirit"; when one would no longer need to ask, "Who is still a stranger here?" (233). The universal congregation would include not only the Dutch audience, but also the souls described in the testimonials, those descriptions of heathen hearts touched in distant lands.

8 This undermining of inherited forms of status has also been noted in Southeast Asian societies. See Siegel 1979, Wolters 1982; Errington 1989, 1990; and Kenji and Siegel 1990.

9 In 1893, in his catalogue of objects collected from northern New Guinea, de Clerq and Schmeltz (1893: 186) explain that the people of "Wiak" bury the bodies of the dead but decorate the graves of brave men with a little casket, in which the skull of the deceased is placed. Evidence suggests that the carving of the korwar was a moment in a protracted series of mortuary rituals, including the "second burial" for which Southeast Asia has long been known. See Hertz 1960.

10 Van Baaren (1968: 52) cites Feuilletau de Bruyn's report on the *nin* and the *rur*: "According to this report the inhabitants of Biak believe in two souls, the *nin* and the *rur*; the first is brought into relation with the shadow, the second is the principle of life, mind, consciousness and personality."

11 See van Baaren 1968: 27: "Although the Papuans have a great respect for their korwar, they can get very angry with them if the prophecy has not turned out according to the desire of the person concerned, and in such a case they may throw them against the wall or against a post so that an arm or a leg or the point of its usually immense nose breaks off. Such a korwar that is no use anymore is sometimes offered us for sale, as it no longer has any power; otherwise they remain firmly attached to this idolatrous worship, and go in fear of all kinds of mishap should it be taken from them by a foreigner."

12 According to Rauws (1919: 37), the Papuans remained in the age of ani-

mism, which he defined not as a religion but as a "worldview to which religious notions are connected. The heathens are in general 'religious in every respect;' likewise the Papuans, although among them few 'religious natures' are found. If one comes into contact with them one in fact remarks that the indications of religiosity do not have a certain connection with God or gods. Religion, worship of God, means for us, connection to God. For them, religion is much more a feeling of dependence on all sorts of powers, spirits and souls who are often pernicious. For this reason, the feeling of dependence usually expresses itself in the form of fear. Fear governs their lives, and they seek ways and means to escape the feared powers. Above all, people fear the spirits of the dead; to these they ask about the uncertain future; to these they make offerings to propitiate them and to preserve for themselves a long life. To understand this worship of spirits, one must know the soil out of which this plant grows. That soil is animism."

13 Prompted by rumors of this new and valuable thing, in 1916, one warrior took three perilous journeys to get the Scriptures for his North Biak village. First he paddled to the mainland in an enormous canoe to ask the missionaries for the Gospel. Then he paddled to Biak's east coast, to wait for an evangelist to arrive on a ship. His first attempt failed when colonial soldiers, spotting the famous troublemaker, beat him up and threw him in jail. This much-told saga repeats itself in various versions along the north coast. In Sansundi, I was told that four renowned killers joined forces to "buy" the Bible and bring it home.

14 See Rutherford 2003 for songs that compare the Gospel to a delicious smoked fish.

15 The Biak text goes: "Ikenem iwor imaroke. / Kirin kirino. / Imaro iwor be ikenemoke. / Kirino kirin kirino." My informants could not translate *kirino*, although the mission dictionary defines *kir* as "through and through." See van Hasselt and van Hasselt 1947: 122.

16 Instead of the skulls, my informant noted, it was this foreign name that protected the Kaumfus from becoming extinct.

17 Biaks call the spirits that haunt special sites, *tuan tanah*, the "lords of the land."

18 It is worth comparing the behavior of Biak's boulders to that of Surakarta's Court. In 1745, after a defeat by the Dutch colonial army, instead of heading for Java's hills—and magically disappearing—the sultan participated in a grand procession / retreat that transferred him to "a new department in the changing political cosmos of eighteenth-century Java." Pemberton takes this paradoxical procession / retreat as a trope for the "seminal contradiction" at the origin of the subject of "Java." See Pemberton 1994: 35. On the monuments of the "vanishing" as a symptom of the modernity, see also Ivy 1995: 141–91.

19 A way of approaching this logic is suggested in Sangren 1993. Steven Sangren draws on T. Turner 1977 in describing how the source of the worshippers' communities' self-productive power is represented through the rhet-

oric of the pilgrimage in an alienated, fetishized form. The pilgrimage takes the adherents of local temples to the "home" temple of the deity, Ma Tsu, located in an unfamiliar city, beyond the range of their day-to-day travels. Their appearance in the parade signifies not only their quest for renewed spiritual power, but also their gratitude for the miracles Ma Tsu has already performed. The ideological alienation that Sangren describes is repeated in each phase of this myth: the product takes the place of the producer. But what proves more significant for the argument put forward in this chapter is the form of the transformations that link the different episodes into an overarching plot. In each episode, a different entity represents the power to produce the distinctions that define Biak society; relations to the dead, affines, ancestral territory, and dangerous strangers all play an important role in the constitution of social identity in Biak. The power not only to institute a set of relations but also to transform them historically is given substance in a somewhat different way. On this level, the fetish is not a particular entity, but the quality that defines particular entities as foreign.

For Sangren (1993: 571), the spatial and historical murkiness that exists at the highest level of cult organization is in a certain sense fortuitous; it has to do with the worshippers' unfamiliarity with particular places and times. What Sangren suggests, but does not explicate, is the way in which the quality of unfamiliarity is equally as fetishized as the deity figures themselves. In Biak rhetoric, figures of power must be alien in an explicit sense; they must come as a surprise within a local social world. Not only does this tendency underlie the social production of peripherality; it ensures the conflation of Sangren's first two definitions of transcendence: the deity as an alienated representation of socially productive power is never allowed to dislodge itself from space. The encounter with a broader world is never normalized, even as travel becomes easier. The substance of the fetish, the target of the metaphor, stubbornly remains a shock.

20 *Apotropaic* is the word that Freud used to describe the act of displaying one's genitals—female or male—to drive off an enemy. Projecting one's terror onto a rival, what one doubly evokes in either case is the threat of castration. The act expresses both the presence of the penis and its potential absence. See Freud [1922] 1963: 203.

21 Durkheim wrote, "It is only with Christianity that God finally goes beyond space; His Kingdom is no longer of this world. The dissociation of nature and the divine becomes so complete that it even degenerates into hostility. At the same time, the notion of divinity becomes more general and abstract, but it is formed not of sensations, as it was in the beginning, but from ideas" ([1883] 1984: 230–31).

22 Attendance was not high, as a rumor soon was circulating in Doreh that the missionaries had plans to turn the locals into Christians, "just like the people in the Company." See Kamma 1981: 1:109. Others are said to have suspected the Germans of plotting to sell their children as slaves.

23 "The Papuans are very lazy and curious," wrote Geissler. "Our house is

almost always full and many bring something along to sell" (Kamma 1977: 1:74).

24 Selected in part because she spoke some Malay—and thus could serve the missionaries as an interpreter—ironically enough, she was a Muslim, having converted during the time she spent with a Ternatan trader.

25 Left alone in Doreh, Ottow had "immersed himself in the local language, but wrote that he had to use many Malay words since in Numforese there were no words for spiritual matters." When he asked people what a word meant, they always responded, "I don't know." "And he wrote that he had to steal, as it were, words" (Kamma 1977: 1:85). Ottow, like his successors, complained about the "materialism" of the Papuans, whose language, as he saw it, lacked words for spiritual things.

26 By the end of the century, 80 of the 135 baptized Papuans at the five New Guinea posts were free-bought slaves. A report commissioned by the Utrecht Mission Society board concluded that the free buying of slaves and trade with the local Papuans were crucial to any success the missionaries had enjoyed. See Adriani et al. 1896.

27 Ottow and Geissler read the increase in intertribal violence that occurred during their first decades in the field as Satan's reaction to the Gospel's arrival. "The more than normal restlessness of the population," the Utrecht Mission Society's journal reported, "appears to indicate that the power of darkness comes into turmoil with the approach of the news of the kingdom of light" (Kamma 1977: 1:159). The missionaries' purchase of slaves, of course, provided both means and an incentive for raiding to warriors who traded captives for guns.

28 Quite remarkably, in 1859, Ottow and Geissler managed to prevent the Mansinamers from rebuilding their *rumsram*, the "heathen temple" where they had initiated youths. Even an outbreak of smallpox—to the Mansinamers a clear sign of the ancestors' displeasure—did not lead local villagers to vent their anger on the Germans.

29 The Biak song genre, *wor*, has long featured a structure that repeats the startling moment of an encounter (see Rutherford 1996, 2003).

30 The authority gained from this "proof" could be cut loose from the adventurer who obtained it. A visitor from Numfor once asked a missionary if he could have the monopoly on a story; he planned to take it to a distant village to exchange for rice (Kamma 1977: 1:130).

31 This focus on the materiality of mission discourse may well account for the failure of local people to correct the Europeans when they made mistakes in "Mefoorsche"—instead, they adopted the incorrect usages themselves. See Kamma 1977: 2:434.

32 The missionaries were eager to make Christian materials accessible to newly literate Papuan students as a way of extending the reach of their tidings. Less than a year after the missionaries' arrival, Ottow had written to Holland for a handpress, so that he could produce "Papuan language" books. See Kamma 1977: 1:55. Over the years, the missionaries produced a variety of edi-

tions: from a primer titled *Goeroe ma Moerid* (*Teacher and Pupil*) to a translation of the Ten Commandments to a geography text consisting of an imaginary tour of the Indies archipelago by steamship and train.

33 Kamma learned about the cosmology of the Biak migrants who inhabited Besewer when shamans who had converted to Christianity turned over their "mon books," divinitory texts featuring drawings of the "demons" who inhabited the *doenia wam*, "world of the winds." While the Besewers had some conception of a highest power in the figure of Manseren Nanggi, "the Lord of the Heavens," and some sense of a moral struggle between the "good" kings of the eastern and northern winds, and the "bad" kings of the western and southern, for the most part, they concerned themselves with the ambivalent, heterogenous host of spirits in their immediate vicinity, who manifested themselves in the shape of dragons, octopuses, mosquitos, flies, women, and men. To mediate between the world of the living and the world of the spirits, the shamans had familiars, also known as *mon*, who were usually the ghosts of recently deceased people, including foreign shipwreck victims and local kin. Sometimes the shaman summoned the mon; other times the spirit simply possessed him. See Kamma 1939–41: 206–13, esp. 208; 247–58. Kamma describes how shamans in Besewer sometimes used their "mon books" for curative purposes. They would rub the image of the suspected culprit on a sick child's head, in hopes of luring the demon out.

34 The women who "reprimanded her in the classic manner" shared the same vulnerability to infelicity that constitutes and threatens every performative (see Austin 1976; Derrida 1982). For an act of worship to be recognized as such, it must be subject to repetition in a context that drains it of its expected intent.

35 See also Kamma (1977: 2:259–60) for a kindred statement. A man from Numfor explained his point of view to a missionary: "You see, this is what I think: the Lord in Heaven loves the Dutch very much; they know everything and have everything. He loves us Meforezen a little; we have a pastor and a few goods, not much. But He doesn't love the Arfakkers or the Wandammers at all, because they have nothing, no pastor and no goods."

36 This Dutch lieutenant, who conducted a punitive campaign on the island after the killing of an Ambonese teacher, referred to the Biaks as both overly individualistic and enslaved to their clans.

37 Kamma refers to the stories that circulated on Biak at the time of the awakening. "No one will ever ascertain what the contents of the propaganda was, which went before the request for a teacher and the burning of the sacred objects. One thing one can be certain of: it would have had little to do with the Gospel, lots with Koreri expectations, now translated into Christian terminology for the evangelists and teachers, as far as people were in a position to do this."

38 "Oh Sir, people are so bad; they do not want to go to church or school. They are very bad, very bad, they do not listen to me," he told van Hasselt Sr. after his followers lost the faith. See Kamma 1972: 126.

39 Something like the dilemma faced by Koreri leaders is described in Susan Stewart's 1995 account of the paradox of "willed possession." See also Bataille 1985, and [1967] 1991: 63–77 on the distinction between lordship and sovereignty.

40 See Kamma 1977: 2:687. When van Hasselt visited the islands, people told him that they had long known about the Gospel, but that they had to hear a story from several different sources before they believed it. An interesting dynamic seems to have applied in the evaluation of words as booty—there seems to have been a tension between audiences, who demanded a perfect repetition of a story, and orators, whom rivals stood ready to accuse of pulling the wool over their eyes. In my interviews with Biaks who recalled the Koreri movement of 1938, the most respected leader seemed to be Angganeta, a female medium who spoke in the voices of foreigners and the dead, as opposed to the male generals who took up her cause.

41 I have argued elsewhere (2003) that the resilience of this logic reflects the tenacity of fetishistic desire. William Pietz (1985: 8) has depicted how European thinkers viewed the fetish, with its "irreducible materiality," as reflecting the irrationality of societies founded on the "chaotic principle of contingency." For Hegel, the classic fetishist is "the African," who arbitrarily chooses as his fetish "the first thing that comes in his way" ([1822] 1956: 94). Ruled by "fancy," instead of reason, when the fetish stops working, the Africans "bind and beat or destroy the Fetich and so get rid of it, making another immediately, and thus holding it in their power" (94). Thus Africa remains stalled on the threshold of history, since its inhabitants are unable to maintain a stable relationship to the sign. Derrida has described how Hegel's depiction of Africa as "lacking the category of Universality" underwrites his wider project (1986: 207–11). At once miming and defining the progress of "Spirit," Africa stands as the substitute that turns the "rational" into the "real." But there may be another way of redeploying Hegel's depiction of the fetish. Just as there is nothing "natural" in Biak's notion of the foreign, there can be no unmediated relation to "contingency." In Biak, one finds a particularly resilient "Universal"—an ideology that elevates an "unconscious" sort of "consciousness"—not of the sign, but of shock.

42 It is worth noting that the Biak term for the Bible is not a loan word from Malay or Dutch, but a borrowing from Tidore: *refo* from *lefo*, which means "written script." See van Hasselt and van Hasselt 1947: 190.

43 "Let the Dutchmen, the whites keep their *adat* [religion] to themselves," a typical Papuan is recorded saying. "We are Papuans, and we'll keep our own adat as well" (Kamma 1977: 1:303). One could multiply the examples of how contemporary Biaks have wholeheartedly embraced Dutch adat—not only in religious matters, but also in the family, where, like the wives of the missionaries, mothers take credit for making "humans" out of their daughters and sons. But a distinctly local perspective lurks behind a rhetoric that makes the Biaks seem more Dutch than the Dutch. It is "foreigners," for instance, and not simply well-behaved Christians, whom Biak women ex-

plicitly seek to produce. In an ironic rereading of the history of the mission, Biaks today often comment that the best speakers of "formal Biak" were the missionaries who served on the island. When today's Biak pastors give sermons in "high Biak language," they present their speech as an imitation of the Dutch.

···Nine···

Scripture Study as Normal Science

Seventh-Day Adventist Practice on the East Coast of Madagascar

Eva Keller

This chapter attempts to capture the subjective value that ordinary members of the Seventh-Day Adventist church in Madagascar attach to their religious commitment. The analysis focuses on the question of what kind of experience Adventist religious practice is and what church members in Madagascar consider to be the nature of the religion they have embraced. It follows from this focus on the subjective value of Adventism that I am interested in the nature of people's long-term commitment rather than the reasons that might have led to conversion.

This perspective has been largely ignored in the literature (but see J. Robbins 2004). Social scientific work on Christianity in general has concentrated on the sociology of religion, and in particular the sociology of conversion (see Cannell in this volume). Studies of New Churches[1]—such as Pentecostal churches, Jehovah's Witnesses, or the Seventh-Day Adventist Church—have not been an exception.

As a consequence of the mushrooming of New Churches in many parts of the world, scholarly attention has become increasingly focused upon them. What have we learnt from these studies? In the great majority of cases, the focus lies on establishing the structural conditions that foster conversion to New Churches, and on defining the social profile of those who might be particularly likely to convert. The answers offered in the literature to the questions of what kinds of people convert and of why they do so, are strikingly uniform and may be summarized as follows.

In characterizing the sociological profile of converts, most theorists focus on their socioeconomic position and write of people who have been uprooted, dislocated or otherwise disoriented as a result of the impact of globalization and modernity upon their lives. Such disoriented people, it is argued, feel economically and socially marginalized and are therefore particularly prone to listen to those who promise them a new future. The promises made to prospective new converts may be of a rather blunt economic nature; this is so especially with New Churches advocating the Prosperity or Faith Gospel, which states that true believers will be wealthy and healthy and that the rich are blessed by God (Gifford 1998; Maxwell 1998; and see Coleman in this volume). But membership of New Churches is not always motivated by the hope of material advancement. For many converts, their core attraction is the fact that they offer orientation at a time of rapid social change, and that they provide a new anchor of identity in situations when traditional securities have become jeopardized. This, in a nutshell, is what we know about the attraction of New Churches for millions of people in the Third World. As we will see, however, this hardly seems sufficient to understand what motivates Malagasy Seventh-Day Adventists in their commitment to the church.

What is extremely striking in almost all of the literature on New Churches is the way the people concerned seem distant, and in many cases, their complete absence from the analysis. With a handful of exceptions—in particular Birgit Meyer's 1999 study of Pentecostalism among the Ewe of Ghana and several publications by Joel Robbins (2001b, 2001c, 2004) on a community of Baptists in Papua New Guinea—these are top-down studies describing the structural conditions of the growth of New Churches and the interrelationship between the global and the local. The members of the New Churches themselves—who, after all, are those, whose motivation to be in such churches we want to understand—remain in the shadow. Borrowing from Sherry Ortner (who in this context refers to studies on resistance by the marginalized more generally), the literature on New Churches can be described as "ethnographically thin . . . thin on the subjectivity—the intentions, desires, fears, projects—of the actors engaged in these dramas" (1995: 190; see also Bruce 2000). Few of those who study New Churches seem to have approached the people concerned and, with the aforementioned exceptions, those who have done so, including anthropologists, have tended to focus on leaders and their public rhetoric rather than ordinary members of such churches.[2]

This chapter attempts to counterbalance the existing literature in a number of ways. It does not focus on the moment of conversion but examines the time thereafter.[3] Given this focus, I will not analyze the structural conditions inducing particular sections of Malagasy society to convert to Adventism; my interest lies with the nature of people's long-term commitment to the Seventh-Day Adventist church. Finally, I discuss not leaders' programs and tactics to recruit followers but the everyday religious experience of ordinary church members. What I want to advocate, in short, is the importance of "approaching people" and of making their subjective religious experience beyond initial conversion one of our primary concerns. I will do so in this chapter by looking closely at Adventist religious practice in the context of church services, but also outside of these. Daily religious practice is then linked up to an analysis of what the members of the church consider to be the core of their religion and what they consider themselves to be doing when practicing Adventism. Finally, I will suggest that their subjective experience as Adventists is akin to what Thomas Kuhn has called "normal scientific" activity.

The argument is based on nineteen months of fieldwork between 1998 and 2000 among Seventh-Day Adventists in Maroantsetra, a small town on the northeast coast of Madagascar, and Sahameloka, a village a five-hour canoe journey upriver from the town.[4] Before I present my ethnography, let me give some background information on Seventh-Day Adventism in Madagascar and beyond.

From America to Sahameloka

The Seventh-Day Adventist church grew out of an apocalyptic-millenarian movement that developed in the United States around William Miller in the 1840s,[5] one of many movements of religious revival at the time (Vance 1999: 1). The core of Miller's prophecies was the expected Second Coming of Christ in October of 1844.[6] As the date passed uneventfully, resulting in what has become known among Adventists as "The Great Disappointment," many of Miller's followers lost hope and the rest of the movement split into numerous directions and factions. One of these, however, resurrected around a young woman, seventeen-year-old Ellen G. White (1827–1915), whose spiritual leadership of what later became the Seventh-Day Adventist Church[7] was based on the dramatic visions she had been experiencing since the Great Disappointment. She became recognized as the contemporary medium of the Holy Spirit and thus as a true prophetess.[8]

From its cradle in the United States, Seventh-Day Adventism soon spread all over the globe, and by 1903 it had reached every continent of the world (Pfeiffer 1985: 18). By now, the vast majority of its 13 million worldwide members are to be found outside the United States, with one-third in Africa alone.[9]

The first Seventh-Day Adventist missionary couple set foot in Madagascar in 1926 and immediately set up a press in the capital and started publishing. The first Adventist mission school was opened in the capital in 1934. Within a year, a hundred pupils were taught there, and their number was to rise to some seven hundred within a decade. In the course of the twentieth century, the Adventist Church continued to grow and to expand to many different parts of Madagascar, and by 2003, over 70,000 Malagasy had been baptized as Seventh-Day Adventists. Although this seems a large number, it represents only 0.5 percent of the total population of the country.[10] The church is unevenly distributed across the island with the highest percentages of converts in already strongly Christianized regions. One of these regions is the district of Maroantsetra, where roughly half of the population is at least officially members of either the Protestant or the Catholic Church.

Archival sources[11] document Seventh-Day Adventist presence in the district of Maroantsetra already in the late 1930s, but local memory goes back only to the 1960s when, according to the oldest members of the church, the first Adventist pastor arrived and began the task of building a congregation. At present, approximately 1 percent of the district's population has been baptized as Seventh-Day Adventists. In some villages, the number of church members is much higher. In Sahameloka, where I conducted fieldwork and where Adventism arrived only a decade ago, almost 10 percent of the adult population is Adventists. The reasons for this are far from clear and too complex to be discussed in the space of this chapter. However, Sahameloka's Adventists are in no way exceptional villagers, and they do not belong to one particular socioeconomic section of the village's population. The reason for the concentration of church members in certain villages of the district is likely to be the result of chain conversion within particular kin groups, which results from the complex and difficult relationship between Adventist and non-Adventist kin (see Keller 2005).

Studying and Learning

What struck me most during fieldwork among the Seventh-Day Adventists in Maroantsetra town and the village of Sahameloka was the enthusiasm with which men and women, boys and girls, actively engaged in Bible study and the effort they made to improve their biblical knowledge. This happened in two different contexts.

On the one hand, there was a very strong focus on Bible study and discussion of biblical text as part of the institutionalized setting of Seventh-Day Adventist church services. On the other hand, the members of the church also studied the Bible at home throughout the week. I will first discuss this more informal context of Bible study and then move on to its more institutionalized forms.

STUDYING AT HOME

The basis of Seventh-Day Adventist Bible study, whether at home or in church, is the *Bible Study Guide*. This is a three-monthly booklet translated from the original English version, which is produced in the United States, into hundreds of languages, including Malagasy. For every day, there is a specific lesson dealing with topics such as "Testing the Prophetic Gift," "Science and the Bible," "The Cosmic Conflict Extended to Earth" or "What about the Versions [of the Bible]?"[12] These daily lessons—which include references to the books of both the Old and the New Testament—are meant to be read and discussed by all Seventh-Day Adventists worldwide.[13] In each of my field sites I lived with a Seventh-Day Adventist family; this gave me the opportunity to observe the reality of daily Bible study in two unrelated households. Apart from the fact that both families are members of the Adventist Church, they have little else in common.

Papan' i Beby (Beby's dad) of my host family in Maroantsetra town works for the local Service du Génie Rural (which is associated with the Ministry of Agriculture) and goes to work in his office almost every day (except for Saturdays, Seventh-Day Adventists' holy day, during which they are not allowed to do any work or to handle money). Maman' i Beby (Beby's mom), his wife, is responsible for buying food at the market, cooking, and other household-related activities. Their two children—Beby, a fifteen-year-old girl, and Kiki, a boy of eighteen—go to school. The family joined the Adventist church soon after Kiki was born. The most shining character in the family, it seems to me, is Papan' i Beby. He is extraordinarily knowledgeable, although, coming from a poor background, he did not receive higher education. Yet he has always loved to read and has learned a great deal about world history, geography, scientific inventions, and more by self-study. I was amazed, for example, to hear him explain the meaning of the expression *pachyderm*, or the fact that it was the Roman Emperor Vespasian who first introduced public toilets and that therefore male public toilets are called *vespasienne* in France. Neither is he at a loss to list the Seven Wonders of the World or to explain to his children what a *mausolée* is and why it is called such (did *you* know that it was a king called Mausolos who first had himself built a tomb in the style of what came to be known as a mausoleum?). Papan' i Beby also speaks French fluently, and moreover, apart from the pastor, he is the greatest expert on the Bible and Adventist doctrine of all the members in the entire district.

Maman' and Papan' i Claude of my host family in Sahameloka are rice farmers like everyone else in this remote village, which can only be reached on foot or by canoe and is surrounded by the rainforest. As do the other villagers, they spend almost all their time caring for their crops. Of their six children, four are still alive; two died at a young age, probably from malaria. Claude, their eldest child, is twenty and is an indispensable help for his parents. Both Maman' and Papan' i Claude went to a local primary school for a few years, but neither of them is fluent in reading or writing. In fact, Papan' i Claude is practically illiterate, while Maman' i Claude can manage to read a fairly long text, though slowly and not without stumbling over a word or expression here and there. The family joined the Adventist Church nine years ago. But although they were the very first Adventists in Sahameloka, they do not play a leading role in the local church because of their lack of literacy and, consequently, biblical expertise, unlike Maman' and especially Papan' i Beby, who are among the leading members of the church in Maroantsetra town.

Because Papan' i Beby is by far the most knowledgeable of his family, he would normally guide us through the daily Bible study session lasting between fifteen and forty-five minutes. Almost every evening after dinner we all sat together on the eating mat in order to study the day's lesson provided in the *Bible Study Guide*. After an initial prayer spoken by Maman' i Beby and sometimes a song, Papan' i Beby began to read and explain the text of the day. However, he did not act as teacher to the others, but considered it his job to encourage everyone's participation. The emphasis during the family's Bible study sessions at home always lay on discussion and comprehension of what was being read, rather than instruction. It would be an exaggeration to claim that all members of the family were equally keen participants every day, but it is no exaggeration to say that most days there was a spirit of learning in the room, with all of us asking questions and offering our own thoughts and views on the topic at issue.

In Sahameloka, Claude was the most literate and educated of the family, and so the job of Bible study leader was usually his. His mother also very often played an active role in shaping the nature of the family's discussions, while the lack of his literacy made Papan' i Claude shy and predominantly silent in these situations. It was usually Claude who read the actual text from the *Bible Study Guide* and who offered most explanations and often clarifications for the others. His mother, and rarely his father, too, made comments and suggestions as to how the text could be understood. The family's enthusiasm for Bible study, depending on a number of aspects, came and went. But when they went through a good phase, which could last for several weeks at a time, they always studied the day's lesson very properly and not at all hastily, even after a long, tiring day out in the rice fields.

In both families, Bible study was a prominent feature of daily life, and I was often impressed by the eagerness with which they went about it and the genuine engagement with, and discussion of, the presented text. However, what to me was even more remarkable was to see people engaging in Bible study on the spur of the moment, that is outside the somewhat routinized context of studying the daily lesson. I often observed such spontaneous learning efforts in the families I lived with, as well as with many other Adventists in Sahameloka and Maroantsetra.

Claude, for example, could often be seen sitting on his bed or on the veranda completely absorbed in Bible study, sometimes taking notes on a loose sheet of paper. His mother found time to read the Bible while sitting in the kitchen waiting for the rice to cook. Kiki of the family in town was an equally eager student. Often I found him lying on a mat on the veranda reading the Bible opened up in front of him and—equipped with a ruler and a number of colored pencils I had brought him from Europe—underlining those passages he considered particularly important. At other times, he would revise the sermon of the previous Sabbath, during which he had taken quick notes.

In fact, the local Adventists use the Bible very much like people in Europe would use a schoolbook, writing references and notes in it, circling, or otherwise marking specific passages. The book itself is not treated particularly respectfully. The Bible is not a fetish that has intrinsic power; it is a collection of wise and truthful words that need to be read, analyzed, and understood. On one occasion, Papan' i Beby, who is such a devout church member, glued into his Bible a newspaper clip I had brought him from Europe which concerned the Creation versus Evolution debate in America.

In the course of my stay in Maroantsetra and Sahameloka, I witnessed countless examples of church members engaging in Bible study on the spur of the moment. When strolling around town or in the village intending to stop for a visit at one of my Adventist friends' house, it was not unusual to find one of them studying the Bible alone or together with another member of the church. On one such occasion I encountered Papan' i Fredel and his nephew Ranary sitting on a bench outside Papan' i Fredel's house. Both men had bent their heads over their Bibles and hardly noticed my arrival. It turned out that they were involved in a discussion of a Bible passage which Papan' i Fredel had asked his nephew, who was well versed in biblical matters, to clarify to him. The person who impressed me most, however, was Papan' i Claude of the family I lived with in the village.

As I already mentioned, Papan' i Claude is practically illiterate. Writing especially is extremely difficult for him, and he struggles to sign his name. His ability to read is a little better, but to read more than a few words requires his full concentration and tremendous effort. Notwithstanding these difficulties, sometimes on a rainy afternoon or at another free moment, he picked up the Bible and tried to read from it. I do not know which passages he chose on such occasions, because he was very shy about being overheard or seen when studying privately. But whatever he read, he was very much involved in what he was doing, and could go on for half an hour or more. He sat there, by himself, struggling with the particular passage he had chosen, mouthing every word with his lips, muttering to himself. Although he probably managed to read only a couple of Bible verses at a time, his effort was enormous.

Papan' i Claude cannot use the Bible or the *Study Guide* in the same sophisticated manner as Papan' i Beby, who can give lengthy explanations and interpretations of almost any Bible passage one asks him about. But although there is a vast gap between the levels of literacy of the two men, their education more generally, and their actual degrees of biblical expertise, they are alike in their eagerness for Bible study and in their effort to learn.

These examples might have given the impression that Adventist Bible study is predominantly an activity the male members of the church engage in. However, although certain offices (pastor, elder) and duties are only open to men, and although the Seventh-Day Adventist doctrine is patriarchal, Adventist practice in Maroantsetra and Sahameloka, at home and in church, was characterized by comparatively remarkable gender egalitarianism, as is life in Madagascar generally (see Bloch 1987). This is why I do not make a separate issue of gender relations in this chapter.

STUDYING IN CHURCH

Several times a week, the Seventh-Day Adventists in Maroantsetra and Sahameloka meet in church for a service. Adventist church services follow a ritualized procedure, specifying when to pray, when to sing, when to say what sort of thing, when to stand up and when to kneel. But during any service, there is also space to discuss things, or to put forward questions or one's opinion on a particular matter for anyone, young and old, women and men, who wishes to do so. Let me give an example.

Hery, a boy of eighteen, had been studying the Book of Genesis at home. But reading "In the beginning God created the heaven and the earth. And the earth was without form, and void; and darkness was upon the face of the deep" (Genesis 1:1–2) had left him muddled about the origin of evil, of which he took the word *darkness* to be a metaphor. Had God also created darkness and evil? If yes, why? If no, where did darkness come from? Having failed to find a satisfactory answer by himself, he presented the assembled congregation with these questions. It was then discussed what exactly was meant by darkness—was it to be understood metaphorically or did it refer to darkness as opposed to light?—and whether the darkness one reads of in Genesis referred to the earth or the entire universe.

Such questions can be posed during any Adventist church service and often lead to lengthy discussions of an issue. On Sabbath, however, there are particular times especially designated for learning, studying, and discussion. One of two central parts of every Sabbath morning is what Adventists call Sabbath school.

The main purpose of Sabbath school is to discuss in small groups of about ten participants the past week's lessons of the *Bible Study Guide* (these groups are gender-mixed in Maroantsetra and Sahameloka). The seven lessons of a week are organized around a specific topic, such as "The Uniqueness of the Gift of Prophecy" or "The Languages and

Translation of the Bible," thus forming a chapter. Every weekly chapter at the end contains a number of questions relevant to the overall topic. Members of the church jointly explore these during Sabbath school, exchanging their interpretations of the text, discussing their respective points of view, citing biblical verses as evidence for their opinion and weaving their own experiences into their expositions. In every discussion group, one participant, in most cases a man, acts as chairperson and encourages everyone to participate. The purpose of Sabbath school is to exchange ideas, opinions, and interpretations of what everyone has read over the week at home, and to possibly develop in group discussion a common understanding of the past week's chapter. The members of the church are encouraged to reflect and ponder and to form their own opinion on a given matter. Many people have both Bible and *Study Guide* at hand, and some take notes of particularly important points or of biblical references on a flimsy piece of paper or in a school exercise book, or they may underline a paragraph in their Bible that they consider to be especially significant. Adventist Bible study is not a matter of the truth being taught by some to others; and this includes the pastor, whose office per se does not authorize his interpretations of biblical text. Rather, it is a matter of everyone discovering the truth contained in the Bible for themselves by way of study, reflection, and discussion. The goal of such discussions is not to establish one correct answer (very much in contrast to what Simpson describes as "right-answerism" [2003: 87] among Seventh-Day Adventist students in Zambia); the main purpose of Sabbath school, as of Bible study at home, is to enable the discussion to take place. It is because of the absence of top-down instruction and the focus on discussion that I call Adventist Bible study Socratic (see Keller 2005).

To me, with my limited experience of Protestant church services in Switzerland, during which the congregation does nothing but listen and perhaps sing a song or two, the atmosphere of Adventist services was more reminiscent of school than of church. This was so also during Sabbath afternoons, although, in contrast to the mornings with their focus on serious Bible study, the afternoon part of the Sabbath service was often a rather playful event. Children, teenagers, and adults performed songs and other kinds of entertainment they had practiced at home. Twice I witnessed the performance of an Adventist-inspired sketch that involved several members of the church acting their part dressed up in appropriate costumes and everyday scenes at the market or at a doctor's being reproduced in church.

At the same time as being light and often fun, Sabbath afternoons remained distinctly knowledge oriented. On one occasion in Sahameloka, for example, a young woman came forward to read two different Bible texts she had chosen and practiced at home. She read very slowly and a couple of times got stuck with a particular passage, which she had to spell out, but the audience appreciated her effort and applauded. One of the most popular Sabbath afternoon happenings were quizzes, which were designed and presented by whoever had the appetite to do so, and which were aimed at the same time at entertainment and knowledge acquisition. Such quizzes would test the Bible expertise of the members of the church, who were asked, for example, to find a passage in the Bible that speaks of the Last Supper or to state the name of Moses's wife and the exact "chapter and verse" which contains this information.

Sabbath afternoons did, for the most part, not involve the Socratic type of discussion typical of Sabbath school. It was geared toward acquiring factual knowledge contained in the Bible and toward its display in public. However, it would be mistaken to treat these two aspects as disconnected, because the knowledge memorized during such events as quizzes—for instance, knowledge of what exactly happened during the Last Supper—helps the members of the church to think about the questions addressed during Sabbath school.

"True Things Have Proof"

The local church members are not only very committed to Bible study; they also define what it means to be an Adventist as intimately linked to knowledge and comprehension of the Bible. This was captured in the phrase "Adventists are people who know the Bible" (*ôlo mahay baiboly ny advantista*), which was regularly and emphatically voiced. To be an Adventist is to study the Bible and to be knowledgeable of its content. But biblical knowledge is not understood to be isolated. On the contrary, it is closely connected to other sources of knowledge, in particular scientific findings. Naturally, from the Adventist point of view, the Bible is the ultimate source of truth, and hence science will always remain infinitely inferior to it, but it nevertheless can help to confirm biblical truth.[14] Seventh-Day Adventists categorically reject the theory of evolution, because it contradicts the Book of Genesis and in their view belittles God's creation. But this does not imply the rejection of science per se, but merely, in their eyes, the rejection of a particular scientific theory that happens to be wrong.

Church members in Maroantsetra and Sahameloka found scientific confirmation of biblical truth in such fields as geology or astronomy, which was presented to them mainly by the pastor during church services. Once, for example, the pastor had attended a training course in the Adventist center in Antananarivo, the capital city of Madagascar, from where he brought back a notebook full of astronomical findings. It is important to note that this was not information provided by Adventist scholars, but by astronomers who had nothing to do with the church. But because the Adventists are constantly on the lookout for new proof of what they are already convinced of, they are extremely eager to absorb, and integrate into their stock of knowledge, any piece of new information that comes their way and which they interpret as confirming biblical truth. When talking to the assembled congregation about what he had learned, the pastor had things to tell about the development of the sun and how, one day, it would become so hot that life on earth would become impossible. This, he suggested, was proof of the biblical prophecy of the destruction of this earth by a "lake of fire" (Revelation 20:9–15); many of those who listened to him took note of this new piece of information. The pastor also spoke of a black hole that astronomers had discovered in the constellation of Orion. Weeks later, one young man explained to me with shining eyes that it would be through this hole that Christ would descend to earth at the time of his Second Coming, which Seventh-Day Adventists believe lies in the not too distant future.

Thus although not everyone has direct access to scientific data—in particular not the rural members of the church, who hardly ever venture further than Maroantsetra—such information travels a long way through Adventist communication channels and is appropriated by the members of the church as new food for thought and discussion. The dissemination of new information, of new confirmation of the truthfulness of Seventh-Day Adventism, is particularly easy during district meetings of the church, which happen every three months. At such meetings, several hundred people from every Adventist congregation in the district gather in town, from where they take back such news as the existence of a black hole in the sky.

It emerges, then, that the Malagasy Adventists do not see themselves as defending religion against science. Indeed, for them, there is no such distinction, because scientific news—such as the development of the solar system—is also religious and vice versa. Rather, what outsiders call

Seventh-Day Adventist religion, insiders consider to be primarily a matter of true knowledge.

The local church members are keen to absorb scientific information, to discuss Adventist theory, and to thus be involved in a debate over such issues as the origin of humankind and its future. The truthfulness of the Bible is not only confirmed by specific information provided during church services, or in Adventist publications, but the local Adventists seek to discover such proof daily all around them. Almost anything that happens can be interpreted as a manifestation of what is written in the Bible. One of the tenets of Adventist theory is that human history is the outcome of the "great controversy" between God and Satan. The devastating cyclone that struck Sahameloka in April 2000 exemplified this. The Adventist church was razed to the ground, while the Catholic one was hardly damaged at all and the Protestant only needed its roof repaired. Satan had chosen his targets carefully: he had chosen the Adventists who, in his and their own eyes, are the only true Christians and as such his main adversaries. At the same time, church members noticed and commented that none of their own houses, in contrast to many others in the village, had been completely destroyed. As the cyclone howled above our heads and made the corrugated-iron roof of our house shake and lift, the whole family fell on their knees, praying to God for protection. The house withstood the storm undamaged, like only a few others in the village—a clear sign that God had heard them. Two days after the cyclone, the water had receded enough to make it possible for people to go and inspect the damage done to their fields and their land in the forest. The family had been badly hit. Much of their rice harvest had been destroyed, and hardly a clove tree still stood upright. Satan had targeted them because they were Seventh-Day Adventists. In short: everything, good and bad, is a manifestation of biblical truth. As for other Christians who believe in the closeness of Christ's Second Coming, however, the Book of Revelation is of particular importance for Seventh-Day Adventists. Thus the local Adventists are particularly attentive to possible signs of Christ's impending advent, which, it is believed, will be foreshadowed by an unusual concentration of misfortune of all kinds. Thus many ordinary problems such as bad relations between neighbors or even bad weather conditions are interpreted as further evidence of the truthfulness of Adventist teachings.

"True things have proof" (*misy porofo ny zavatra marina*), members of the church would sometimes state. It is important to note, however, that although local church members are continuously looking for new evidence of biblical truth, they do not for a moment doubt that the Bible is God's word and as such beyond question. To find new proof of what the Bible says is not to establish the Bible's truthfulness, but merely to add a new piece of knowledge confirming it.

Are They Normal Scientists?

The Seventh-Day Adventists in Maroantsetra and Sahameloka struck me as what I will call "scientifically minded" for the reasons I have discussed. First, in their daily approach to Bible study, the emphasis lies on investigation and comprehension, rather than mere absorption, of what is being proposed. Second, to be an Adventist is understood to be based on expert knowledge. Third, local church members consider it imperative to match empirical evidence with theory and to thus collect more and more proof of Adventist doctrine.

However, there is clearly a limit to what sincere Seventh-Day Adventists can possibly accept as true. In spite of their focus on individual reflection, there are certain fundamental aspects of Adventist doctrine concerning which there is no scope for disagreement. One of these, for example, is the rejection of the theory of evolution. Thus whatever proof of it may come their way, Seventh-Day Adventists cannot accept evolution, because to do so would be to reject the story of Creation as told in Genesis, and this in turn would imply to give up Adventism, which is based on a literal reading of the Bible. Therefore, are they really "scientifically minded"?

If one assumes a positivist understanding of science, that is, science as the pursuit of objective knowledge guided by the discovery of facts, the Malagasy Adventists are scientifically minded. However, they are looking at facts within a closed framework of thought determined by Adventist teachings, and they are at pains to squeeze new facts into that framework. Hence the destruction of the Adventist church in Sahameloka during the cyclone was interpreted as a sign of Satan's anger, while the fact that church members' private houses withstood the storm was clear evidence of God's protection. Therefore, scholars with a view of science as unrestricted in its openness toward the interpretation of new facts would not agree that the Malagasy Adventists are true scientists although they are scientifically minded. However, if one assumes, with Thomas Kuhn, that normal scientific inquiry, too, is guided by a particular framework of thought, then one might propose an analogy between the religious practice the local Adventists engage in and what Thomas Kuhn has called "Normal Science" ([1962] 1996).

Kuhn's principal claim is that normal scientists—that is, most scientists at most times—are not involved in open discovery, indiscriminately accepting any evidence available to them and ready to change their theory accordingly, although they claim and are convinced that they are. Instead they work and think within an accepted paradigm that determines and restricts their vision and their perception of reality. Thus normal scientific activity is not based on continual skepticism, as generally assumed, Kuhn argues, but on a search for information that confirms the paradigm. Starting from his observations regarding normal science, Kuhn develops a theory of "the structure of scientific revolutions." These are caused by "paradigm shifts" and, unlike normal science, do lead to genuine scientific progress. However, here I am mainly concerned with Kuhn's analysis of normal science. Let us look at his provocative argument in more detail. He defines paradigms as "universally recognized scientific achievements that for a time provide model problems and solutions to a community of practitioners" ([1962] 1996: x). Normal science Kuhn characterizes as "research firmly based upon . . . achievements that some particular scientific community acknowledges for a time as supplying the foundation for its further practice" (10). "No part of the aim of normal science is to call forth new sorts of phenomena," he writes; "indeed those that will not fit the box are often not seen at all. Nor do scientists normally aim to invent new theories, and they are often intolerant of those invented by others. Instead, normal-scientific research is directed to the articulation of those phenomena and theories that the paradigm already supplies" (24). "Novelty . . . is not a desideratum," he adds (169).

I want to suggest an analogy between this normal scientific activity as interpreted by Kuhn and Seventh-Day Adventist religious practice. I have described the local Adventists as scientifically minded because the nature of their religious commitment is based on study, evidence, and expert knowledge. At the same time though, their search for knowledge is clearly limited by the fact that they think, and interpret, evidence within a particular paradigm, namely the literal truth of the Bible. And as with Kuhn's normal scientists, what does not fit the box tends not to be seen.

In the course of his discussion, Kuhn likens the activities of normal scientists to the process of solving a puzzle, either a jigsaw or a crossword puzzle ([1962] 1996: 35–42); I especially like the image of the jigsaw. Kuhn uses this metaphor to point out that the purpose and the thrill of doing a jigsaw is not to produce a novel outcome, but the discovery of how to get to the predetermined solution. Like Kuhn's normal scientists, the Adventists might be compared to people doing a jigsaw. They are first and foremost interested in the process of searching for and finding fitting pieces and of making the picture grow, rather than in creating their own picture. The local Adventists are not concerned with investigating whether or not the Bible is true, they know that it is. They are motivated by a desire to discover the detailed facts of biblical truth and to fully understand them, rather like someone who makes an X-ray of a body in order to see what is inside and understand how it all works and how every organ relates to the body as a whole. They are motivated by a desire to discover where exactly every piece of the jigsaw belongs and what it contributes toward the overall outcome; this is the fascinating inquiry that Bible study is.

The analogy I propose here has important limits, though. Normal science, according to Kuhn, has a built-in mechanism which eventually causes an existing paradigm to be abandoned and a new one adopted. This is a mechanism which is triggered by exceptional individuals who realize that certain evidence does not match the theory and which, in short, leads, from time to time, to scientific revolutions. Is such a revolution also conceivable within Adventism? First of all, Adventism does not recognize a built-in mechanism, as Kuhn describes is the case with science, which will eventually and inevitably lead to constant reformulation of what is considered to be true. Because the whole point about biblical truth is that it is eternal. However, it is conceivable—here we move away from Maroantsetra and Sahameloka to places where Adventist doctrine is established—that Adventist scholars come to interpret differently what is written in the Bible. For example, it is theoretically possible that the theory of evolution comes to be accepted by Seventh-Day Adventists if, as a result of thorough study, proof of it were to be found within the Bible. Such a change of paradigm (acceptance of evolution) within the ultimate paradigm (literal truth of the Bible) might be caused, for instance, by the realization that the Book of Genesis has been mistranslated, and that indeed God tells us in the Bible that He will cause evolution to happen bringing about ever new creatures to exist on this earth. Such a radical reformulation of Adventist theory would, however, not be a total paradigm change, as it does not challenge the trust in the Bible as God's word. I must emphasize that all of this is my own speculation about possible paradigm shifts within Adventism; I have no information actually suggesting such a shift to be in the process of occurring. Be that as it may, what is easily conceivable is a paradigm shift in the biography of individuals, and here we move back to the level of Maroantsetra and Sahameloka. If individual church members should come to the conclusion that Adventist theory is not borne out by the evidence they encounter, they would then be justified to leave the church. Indeed, this has happened many times in the past in the district, though it is extremely difficult, not to say impossible, to establish why certain members of the church withdraw from it and whether or not this has anything to do with their view of what is true. However, there is at least one paradigm shift that all the members of the local Adventist church have already undergone during their lives: conversion to Seventh-Day Adventism.

The Beauty of the Picture

I have used Kuhn's metaphor of the activity of doing a jigsaw puzzle to underline the excitement the Adventists in Sahameloka and Maroantsetra derive from the very process of studying the Bible. However, although that process is key to understanding the nature of their commitment to the church, they also take joy in seeing the picture develop and grow. Not only the process of doing the jigsaw is exciting, but also the anticipated satisfaction of seeing the entire picture in its full size and in all its colors and shapes. People get a taste of that satisfaction every time they find a new piece that fits, every time they feel they understand more of what they read about in the Bible and the *Study Guide*. A bag full of muddled jigsaw pieces, to borrow Kuhn's metaphor once again, contains the entire picture, yet we cannot see it without making the effort of turning over every piece and putting it in its right place. The whole picture the Seventh-Day Adventists want to see is, quite simply, the truth: the truth about the world and life beyond, and about human nature. The truth is there available in the Bible, yet we cannot see it unless we study what the Bible says. Hence to study the Bible is to make the picture appear; it is the road leading to the completion of the jigsaw. Neither Kuhn's normal scientists nor the Adventists in Maroantsetra and Sahameloka question their basic epistemology, yet they want to discover and understand the internal logic of truth.

To discover the truth is, however, made extremely difficult by the fact that Satan—who, on the Adventist stage, is a key player—channels all his power into hiding the truth from people. Thus the Bible student's job is to rescue the truth from beneath a cover that has been intentionally laid upon it. In this sense, to study the Bible is to recover or uncover rather than to discover true knowledge (see Parry 1985). However, the road that leads to the truth being fully recovered—uncovered from Satan's lies—is a process of normal-scientific discovery. It is a process of discovering, understanding, all the bits and pieces the truth is made up of.

As a result of discovering the truth hitherto buried, the Adventists gain a particular kind of power. They gain no power in a narrow socioeconomic or political sense. Indeed, people are perfectly aware that church membership will not give them access to any material riches or advantages such as free medical care or schooling or a better position in society. In fact, if anything, conversion to Adventism entails considerable social problems—a topic I have no space to discuss in this chapter (but see Keller 2005). Bible study gives them the subjective feeling of being powerful in the sense of intellectually being in control, of intellectually being on top of things.

Elsewhere (Keller 2004, 2005) I have discussed in detail how the Adventists' notion of being in possession of true knowledge is linked to an image of clarity. Let me briefly recapitulate the argument. Going back to the metaphor of the jigsaw puzzle, when the Adventists anticipate to see the entire picture in all its colors, they anticipate to see complete clarity. The clarity they envision not only includes the truth about our life here on earth but extends to what in Christian vocabulary is normally referred to as the afterlife or another, transcendental world. As I mentioned earlier, the Adventists believe that Christ will come back to this earth in the not too distant future, though nobody can know when exactly this will happen. He will come back in order to take all true believers (which includes both living people and dead Christians who will be resurrected) with Him to heaven, where they will live for one thousand years. At the end of the millennium, Satan and all evil will be annihilated forever, and all true Christians who have ever lived will enjoy eternal life in paradise. Not only will they be blessed with an eternal existence; they will live together with God Himself. God will live among them and He will be of flesh and blood and people will be able to speak to Him, even to touch Him. In paradise, absolutely everything, even God, will be accessible to the human senses. There won't be anything mysterious any longer, nothing that escapes human capabilities, nothing that humans do not or cannot understand. There won't be anything "transcendental" or "supernatural," but everything will be perfectly clear. And herein lies the beauty of the picture the Adventists are in the process of making appear. The anticipated clarity—which is foreshadowed by *knowledge* of the truth, but which will manifest itself completely only in paradise—thus dissolves the distinction between this and another worldly existence.

Conclusion

There is no doubt that the anticipation of seeing the picture in all its beauty, with nothing hidden anymore to the human eye and nothing beyond the capabilities of the human intellect provides great satisfaction to the local members of the Adventist church. The promise of bliss, which is highlighted in many studies on millenarian movements (Worsley [1957] 1970: 22; T. Robbins and Palmer 1997: 9; Bozeman 1997: 140), completely fades in comparison. This part of my argument discussing the satisfaction of the worldview offered by the new religion, Seventh-Day Adventism in this case, has obvious affinities with the intellectualist approach to conversion, which holds that people convert to Christianity because they see it to offer satisfactory answers to existential questions of meaning. The intellectualist approach to conversion is usually juxtaposed in the literature to the utilitarian approach explaining conversion primarily in terms of worldly advantages; I discussed the shortcomings of this latter line of argument in the introduction to this chapter. However, in contrast to the intellectualist approach, I want to emphasize that the *prime* attraction of Adventism for people in Maroantsetra and Sahameloka is not the answers it offers to basic questions of life, but the very *activity* of Bible study and scientific inquiry that lies at the heart of local people's commitment to the Adventist church. Thus despite the prominence of the word *intellectual* throughout this chapter, my argument is that Bible study and research about the world is not simply a means to an end, either in an utilitarian or in an intellectualist sense. The core of local people's commitment to the church is the excitement of the intellectual process itself.

It has sometimes been argued—in particular with regard to Pentecostalism, with its emphasis on emotional and sensual experience (Martin 1990: 231; Corten 1999: 25–67; Meyer 1999: 117–18)—that illiterate or semiliterate people feel estranged by forms of Christianity that emphasize biblical text. Among the Seventh-Day Adventists in Madagascar, many of whom are poorly educated and can barely read and write, it is quite the opposite. There I found people who despite their lack of literacy and education are enthusiastically engaging in studying and learning, rather like scientists in search of truth about the world.

Many observers of New Churches in Africa and elsewhere have noted the tremendous significance of Bible study as part of religious practice (MAC 1993: 35; Levine 1995: 162; Gifford 1998: 78, 169; Meyer 1999: 135–36). Several of them have mentioned a focus on discursive Bible study among such varied groups as North American Baptists (Ault 1987: 15–16), Seventh-Day Adventists in Fiji (Miyazaki 2000: 34–35), and Jesus Saves Christians in Madagascar (Walsh 2002: 376). However, these observations are made in passing and their significance is not further elaborated. Nevertheless, they encourage me to think that it might not only be the Adventists in Maroantsetra and Sahameloka whose religious commitment is motivated very largely by enthusiasm for a Socratic type of Bible study, but that this may be true for other adherents of New Churches, and elsewhere, too.

Toward the end of his analysis, Kuhn suggests that the adoption of a new paradigm—which is what leads to scientific progress—is based not primarily on acquaintance with new scientific proof, but on *faith* in the new paradigm, on faith that it will keep what it promises. Therefore, the adoption of a new paradigm is a matter of conversion. The individual scientist who adopts a new paradigm is not convinced to do so by factual knowledge but is persuaded to believe in the new paradigm (Kuhn [1962] 1996: 151–59). In presenting this analysis and using words like *conversion*, *faith*, and *persuasion*, Kuhn certainly alludes to his view that science is in fact much more similar to religion than most scientists would be keen to stress, although he does not explicitly say so. My research with Malagasy Seventh-Day Adventists illustrates the other side of the coin: that sometimes at least, religion is much more similar to science—that is, the activity of science as it is practiced daily, if we believe Kuhn—than is normally believed.

......

Notes

This essay is based on research that was supported by several institutions and people. I wish to express my gratitude to the Janggen-Pöhn Stiftung in St. Gallen in Switzerland, which provided substantial financial aid. I wish to thank my father Alfred Keller for his moral and financial support, and thanks to my friend Christian Suter, who lent me money when I needed it. In

Britain, my research was generously supported by the Overseas Research Student Award Scheme and the Department of Social Anthropology at the LSE (Alfred Gell Memorial Studentship, 2000). I also received financial support from the Central Research Fund of the University of London and the Royal Anthropological Institute (Sutasoma Award, 2001). I feel deeply indebted to my supervisors Maurice Bloch and Rita Astuti for their continual support and intellectual inspiration over many years. I also thank Fenella Cannell for constructive comments throughout the process of writing this essay. Finally, I thank two anonymous reviewers for Duke University Press for their comments on an earlier draft.

1 Following Gifford 1994, I use the term *New Churches* to refer to outstandingly popular forms of contemporary Christianity in the Third World. New Churches are not necessarily new in the sense of not having existed before; Seventh-Day Adventism, for example, has been present in many African countries since the beginning of the twentieth century. What appears to be new about them is their tremendous popularity among various sections of society, so that they have become a serious challenge and threat to the mainline Catholic and Protestant denominations (MAC 1993). Although Seventh-Day Adventism is often subsumed under the heading "fundamentalism," I avoid the term *fundamentalist* because it has given rise to much dispute about its appropriateness (see Caplan 1987c: 4–5; Marty 1992: 5; Marty and Appleby 1993: 2, 1995: 5–6; Bruce 2000: 10).

2 This is true, for example, of Susan Harding's excellent work on North American Baptists (1987, 1991, 1992, 1994, 2000), of Stoll's study of neo-Pentecostalism in Guatemala (1994), and of the work of Paul Gifford (1998) and David Maxwell (2001) on Pentecostalism in Africa.

3 The one-sided concern with initial conversion is evident, for example, in the contributions in Caplan 1987b; J. Barker 1990; and Hefner 1993, although several authors, including Hefner in his contribution to *Conversion to Christianity* (1993a: 117, 120–21), have mentioned in passing the necessity to differentiate between unfolding levels of the conversion process and religious involvement (Heirich 1977: 654; Snow and Machalek 1983: 261–64, E. Barker 1984: 8; Meyer 1998: 320). But see Robbins 2004 for a thorough discussion of this point.

4 In 1998, Maroantsetra had a population of 20,000 people, while Sahameloka counted roughly 1,000 inhabitants (statistics provided by the local Ministry of Population).

5 For details on William Miller's life and prophecies, see Knight 1993 (in particular chapters 2 and 3) and Vance 1999: 14–22.

6 This was based on complicated calculations based on the Book of Daniel and the Book of Revelation (for details, see Hoekema 1963: 90–94; Nyaundi 1997: 15–19; Vance 1999: 18–27).

7 The name Seventh-Day Adventist refers to the church's stress on the importance of keeping the Holy Sabbath on the seventh day of Creation, considered to be Saturday, and to the certainty of Christ's second advent.

8 On Ellen G. White, see Hoekema 1963: 96–98; Knight 1993: 300–303; Vance 1999: 22–25, 42–44. Several publications have been devoted to her life and work, including Numbers 1976 on her work as a health reformer.

9 Seventh-Day Adventist Yearbook 2003, available online at http://www.Adventist.org.

10 This number reflects the sub-Saharan African average. Most sub-Saharan African countries count between 0.5 and 1 percent Seventh-Day Adventists of the overall population. An exceptionally high concentration of Adventists exists in Rwanda (4.7 percent). This, however, does not seem to be related to the genocide of 1994.

11 Centre des archives d'outre-mer (CAOM), Aix-en-Provence, Sous-série Affaires Politiques, MAD ggm 6(4)D51; 6(4)D58; 6(4)D48. See also Tronchon 1986: 353–54.

12 These and other examples to follow are taken from the adult Sabbath school *Bible Study Guide* of January–March 1999.

13 The intention behind these international publications is clearly to create a kind of imagined community among church members worldwide. Although the idea got through to the local congregations, the international connection is not a very pronounced sentiment, particularly not in the village, where not everyone is even aware that there are other Adventists across the sea.

14 It has long been recognized that Christian and other fundamentalists are not opposed to science, but rather attempt to validate religious truth on scientific grounds (see Caplan 1987c: 11–12; Marty and Appleby 1992: 31–33; Mendelsohn 1993; Moore 1993; Tibi 1993). However, existing research on the incorporation of science into fundamentalist religions (through the use of high-tech media, for instance) has focused entirely on the level of leadership and public rhetoric.

···Ten···

Appropriated and Monolithic Christianity in Melanesia

Harvey Whitehouse

In her introduction to this volume, Fenella Cannell points out that anthropological interest in the study of Christianity was remarkably slow to develop. Voluminous literatures on Islam, Hinduism, and Buddhism were established much earlier. Meanwhile, in heavily missionized European colonies, traditional cosmology and ritual were often distinguished somewhat crudely from Christian beliefs and practices, and the latter largely ignored. Among the causes of this neglect was the assumption, not always explicit, that Christianity was an inauthentic accretion to the cultures of Africa, Oceania, Asia, and so on—a colonial importation that obscured the real objects of ethnographic interest. This way of thinking was integral to salvage anthropology, which aimed to gather as much information as possible about cultures thought to be dying out or undergoing radical transformation. More recently, however, anthropologists have been arguing that processes of colonization, missionization, and globalization do not involve simply the imposition of Western culture onto local traditions but, rather, highly variable processes of local reinterpretation and contestation. While appearing to be a context-independent monolith, Christianity is in fact a vast array of fragments, uniquely shaped by local discourse and politics.

In this chapter, I argue that there are drawbacks, but also advantages, associated with both the above viewpoints. From a twenty-first-century viewpoint, the drawbacks of salvage anthropology seem quite obvious. In former European colonies, as anywhere else, religious beliefs and practices are adaptations to changing circumstances, such that what appears to be "traditional" often turns out to be recently inspired, and what seems to be "imported" (e.g., Christian) often turns out to have ancient local roots. The problem, however, with currently more fashionable, antimonolithic views of Christianity is that they can obscure the fact that missionization really did impose some radically new sociocultural models on colonized peoples, and did so in ways that are broadly comparable cross-culturally. Thus, a strength of salvage anthropology was that it recognized something of the monolithic character of Christianity and a weakness was that it then ignored the subject more or less entirely. Recent research has done much to rectify this neglect, but it has sometimes gone too far in stressing the local appropriation and creative manipulation of missionary teaching and practice, as if the general monolithic features of Christianity simply do not exist.

Appropriated Christianity

A highly instructive example of the antimonolithic view of Christianity is provided in the recent publications of John Barker (1987, 1990, 1993). According to Barker, anthropologists working in Melanesia have systematically overlooked the subject of Christianity on the assumption that it is a Western-imposed system that obstructs access to bona fide indigenous culture. Many detailed studies of Melanesian religion (Barth 1975; Gell 1975; Schieffelin 1976; Tuzin 1980; Herdt 1981; Juillerat 1992, 1996) have dealt with societies that had comparatively little experience of Christianity. Meanwhile, research in heavily Christianized areas has tended to focus heavily on traditional religious concerns, revealing little or nothing about local church organizations and prevalent Christian attitudes, beliefs, and practices. Barker (1992: 147) singles out the highly respected work of Nancy Munn (1986) on Massim Island and Roy Wagner (1986) on New Ireland to illustrate the point. The marginalization of Christianity in ethnographic writing on Melanesia is long-standing. That famous pioneer of salvage anthropology, Bronislaw Malinowski, wrote many substantial volumes about the Trobriand Islanders of Papua New Guinea in which he scarcely mentioned Christianity, even though the Methodist Church was firmly established on these islands in the late nineteenth century. Malinowski's rare allusions to Christianity were mostly negative, suggesting that missionaries were engaged in the destruction or corruption of indigenous culture and social organization. What Malinowski never seriously considered was that, like it or not, Trobrianders were making Christianity part of their culture.[1]

In a lucid critique of anthropological writing on Melanesian religion, Barker (1992) suggests that the opposition between traditional Melanesian culture and Western Christianity assumes three main guises: first, as an opposition between indigene and missionary; second, as an opposition between Melanesian and Christian religious systems; third, as an opposition between traditional subsistence society and Western colonial capitalism. Barker challenges each of these oppositions in turn, and his argument is worth examining in detail.

With regard to the opposition between indigene and missionary, Barker points out that, for the most part, Christianity was spread throughout Papua New Guinea by Polynesian and Melanesian converts, rather than by Europeans. Even generalizations about European missionaries are problematic due to their diverse national and denominational backgrounds. Moreover, Barker counsels against attempting to derive missionary attitudes and practices from centrally codified church policies, not only because of the heterogeneity of missionaries in the field, but because a wide range of lay Christians contributed to the shaping of local religious thinking and behavior (including European planters, traders, government officers, and missionary wives, as well as indigenous big men, mediums, prophets, and other interpreters of church teachings). Finally, Barker points out that most Melanesian missions (with the notable exception of Roman Catholic orders) rapidly developed into nationally based churches. In short, the simplistic opposition between indigene and missionary breaks down in the face of a far more complex reality. Barker maintains that Melanesian Christianity cannot be envisaged as a monolithic Western import, since it has in fact been forged in different ways and at different times by a great diversity of agents of religious change.

Barker's critique of the opposition between "traditional" Melanesian religion and Christianity follows in a similar vein. Melanesian religion, he argues, is a complex and fundamentally indissoluble mixture of heterogeneous elements, some of which appear to be "traditional," others Christian, and others syncretic or recently invented. But even those elements of Christianity that appear to be most distinctively Western may in fact have ancient local roots. As Barker notes, some Fundamentalist Christian sects in Papua New Guinea proscribe certain forms of behavior, such as smoking, drinking, and chewing betel nut; they are also very strict about the observance of the Sabbath as a day of rest. Although these are undeniably aspects of church teaching, they may also be locally understood as expressions of more ancient taboos. On the island of Malaita, for instance, the rules of Fundamentalist Christianity merge with local traditions of abstinence and enforced idleness in connection with ritual cycles (Barker 1992: 160). In such cases, what people describe as modern and Christian is impossible to disentangle from what is traditional and local.

Conversely, those forms of religion that appear thoroughly traditional may well engender Christian ideas and attitudes (Barker 1992: 160–61). This was brought home to me forcibly by the experience of carrying out fieldwork among the Baining of East New Britain. The Baining are renowned for their spectacular fire dances, in which men dance all night, wearing huge masks, to the accompaniment of drumming and choral music (Whitehouse 1995: 20–22). This is a very dangerous and exhilarating ritual. Some of the participants carry pythons up to fourteen feet long, and many of the dancers rush into the fire, sustaining terrible burns. Fire dances were described to me as an ancient local custom, and when I first attended such an event, early in my fieldwork, I saw little that reminded me of Western or specifically Christian culture. Nevertheless, I soon learned that, although the red markings on the dancers' masks would in the past have been painted with blood, painfully extracted from the tongue, they were nowadays produced using paint because, in local Christian teaching, self-mutilation is proscribed. Moreover, buried in the complex designs painted on the masks, crucifixes could often be deciphered. Fire dances are now most commonly staged to celebrate the completion of church projects or the arrival of a new missionary. It did not take me long to discover that the dance I first witnessed had been learned, quite recently, from a neighboring group, also classified locally as Baining, but speaking a different language. There is no doubt that my informants regarded the fire dance as traditional rather than modern or imported. Nevertheless, it was clearly an adaptation to quite recent circumstances. It resulted from contemporary ties with neighbors and was steeped in Christian thinking.

The conclusion Barker reaches is that the opposition between Christianity and traditional religion is at best a distortion, and at worst an expression of essentializing, ethnocentric prejudices dividing Them and Us (1992: 153). In critiquing, rather more gently, the opposition between

Western colonial capitalism and traditional subsistence activity, Barker makes a fundamentally similar point. Acknowledging that Christianity is, in diverse ways, an instrument of Western capitalism, does not require a monolithic view of the religion. Barker envisages Melanesia as a region of "religious pluralism" in which heterogeneous Christian and pagan ideas and attitudes mingle in a way that, despite the diversity of this repertoire, is nevertheless compliant with economic exploitation and political domination by the West. More specifically, Barker argues that Melanesian religion is a multilayered phenomenon, operating in distinctive registers at the local / rural, regional / urban, and international / global economic levels.

The many local varieties of Christianity now distributed across Papua New Guinea, as well as the layering of domains of Christian discourse, are undoubtedly outcomes of what Barker calls "indigenous peoples' total religious dialogue with the forces affecting their world" (1992: 152). Consequently, Western and indigenous elements of contemporary Melanesian culture are indeed often difficult to disentangle. In the next section, however, I show that there remain some important differences between indigenous and Christian sociocultural models, which Barker overlooks. A clue to why he does so is to be found in his caricature of salvage anthropology as an enterprise that not only distinguished Christianity and tradition but saw them as intrinsically incompatible and irreconcilable. According to Barker, "If one thinks of religious change as a contest between two incompatible religions and cultures then there can be but three possible outcomes of missionization: displacement of Melanesian religion by Christianity, temporary accommodation between the two sides, or rejection of Christianity by indigenous peoples" (1992: 148). What Barker fails to appreciate, however, is that the postulation of differences between traditional Melanesian religions and Christianity does not necessarily imply that the two systems are incompatible. Moreover, their mutual accommodation can be permanent or long-term, as well as temporary, in principle preserving distinctive features of both.

Monolithic Christianity

In order to envisage Christianity as a kind of monolithic entity, we do not have to demonstrate the cultural homogeneity of its agents of transmission or to deny the existence of highly variable patterns of local appropriation or reinterpretation of missionary teaching and practice. We do have to show that, despite this diversity, some historic features of missionary Christianity are systematically different from those of precontact Melanesian religion. If this can be established, then it is legitimate to distinguish contemporary sociocultural forms in Melanesia inspired by traditional and Christian models respectively.

There are at least six parameters of variation in relation to which missionary Christianity stands in rather striking contrast to precontact Melanesian cults. These parameters concern the distribution of authoritative religious knowledge, modalities of revelation, frequency of transmission, patterns of remembering, types of communal identity, and the scale and structure of religious communities. The polarization of indigenous and Christian religious forms in relation to these parameters is not accidental. I will presently suggest a cognitive explanation for the divergence.

The first consideration is the distribution of explicit authoritative religious knowledge. The aim of missionary Christianity is to spread the Word, to draw everybody's attention to the content of the Gospels and other orthodox sources of Christian teaching, and to exclude nobody. By contrast, a characteristic feature of many precontact Melanesian cults was the restriction of religious knowledge to particular categories of people (e.g., initiated men, ritual experts, etc.). Barth (1990: 641–42) has characterized the Melanesian model of religious transmission as a set of transactions upward (directed toward extranatural agencies) rather than downward (directed toward lay audiences or pupils). But we do not really need elaborate tropes to make the point. The fact is that nowhere in Melanesia has evidence been found of precontact religious systems of a systematically evangelical type. Indigenous religions were not founded on a teacher-pupil model of religious transmission in which access to revelations and dogma was theoretically unrestricted and their dissemination construed as a moral imperative. Conversely, nowhere in the history of missionization do we find evidence of the systematic withholding of Christ's teachings or the designation of categories of people deemed ineligible to learn the cardinal principles of Christianity.

A second parameter of variation relates to processes of revelation. Christianity attempts to win people's hearts and minds primarily through the rhetoric of sermons and moral discourse. People have to be talked into following Christ by entering into a dialogue with other Christians and, by extension, with God. Rhetoric, dialogue, and narrative are the fundamental tools of revelation and conversion in missionary Christianity. By contrast, the revelatory power of precontact Melanesian religions relied heavily on people's abilities to draw salient inferences from ritual actions and paraphernalia, rather than on the verbal transmission of logically connected dogma and exegesis. In all forms of Christianity, knowledge of ritual (e.g., how to participate correctly in a Sunday service) is largely implicit, based on procedural learning through repetition, whereas knowledge of exegesis (e.g., what it means to receive the Eucharistic Host) is for the most part explicitly codified and transmitted. In the precontact religions of Melanesia it tended to be the other way around. Participants in major rituals had explicit knowledge of what went on at these events but did not transmit their exegetical understandings as a set of connected teachings codified in language. This issue has been widely and frequently revisited in the anthropological literature (see Gell 1975, 1980; Barth 1987; Tuzin 1992). Revelations, in traditional Melanesian religions, tended to be formed very gradually, through experience of major rituals over the course of a lifetime rather than transmitted full-blown in an explicitly formulated and connected worldview, for instance codified in religious sermons (see Juillerat 1980: 732–33).[2]

A third point of contrast concerns the frequency of religious transmission. Missionary Christianity offers highly routinized regimes of congregational worship, involving the regular (e.g., weekly) repetition of liturgical rituals and textually oriented orations. Nothing like this was to be found in precontact Melanesia, at least not in the form of collective ritual performances. Before European settlement and colonization, communal religious activity tended to be focused on periodic ceremonial of varying frequency, ranging from annual fertility rites in parts of the West Sepik (Gell 1975) to the twenty-five-year *Hevehe* ritual cycle of the Papuan Gulf (F. E. Williams 1940). Many such activities were linked to natural developmental processes, such as ten- to fifteen-year initiation cycles organized around the physical maturation of boys (Barth 1975) or somewhat more variable cycles influenced by fluctuations in both human and pig populations (Rappaport 1968). At any rate, the major communal religious occasions of precontact Melanesia were markedly less frequent that those of Christianity.[3]

The fourth consideration is how religious knowledge is remembered. Christian teachings are part of the worshipper's general or encyclopedic knowledge. When we recall something about the Decalogue or the Sermon on the Mount, we are drawing on knowledge we generally do not remember acquiring. Psychologists refer to these sorts of memories as "semantic" (following Tulving 1972). Similarly, procedural memory for

Christian rituals, although it may be unavailable for verbal report (unlike knowledge in semantic memory), is not anchored to specific episodes in the worshipper's experience. Thus, I may know the general sequence of actions in the Catholic Mass, as incorporated habits and a set of schemas (scripts or rules for how to behave), but I do not necessarily recall the moment when I first learned all this. By contrast, the rare and climactic ceremonies or precontact Melanesia were to some extent remembered as distinctive episodes in people's lives. This involved the use of "episodic" and "autobiographical" memory (again, see Tulving 1972). Of course, some of the elements from which these ceremonies were constructed may have been derived from more familiar, even everyday schemas, but much of what people in Papua New Guinea know about their precontact rituals is generated through private rumination on the meanings of quite extraordinary ritual experiences, encoded as vivid and haunting episodic memories.

A fifth parameter of variation concerns patterns of communal identity evoked by religious activity. Christians do not see themselves as members of an exclusive group of adherents, who know each other personally. One's identity as a Christian is premised on the presumed commonality of forms of worship and belief within a vast population of anonymous others. By contrast, precontact Melanesian religions encompassed face-to-face communities of ritual participants—actual groups of flesh-and-blood people rather than an abstract, faceless fellowship.

Finally, the scale and structure of Christian and traditional religious communities may be contrasted. All forms of missionary Christianity are, by definition, expansionary and inclusive. Christian churches are also centralized and hierarchical. The preservation of denominational identity rests on the maintenance of at least some kind of definitive orthodoxy of belief or practice, and this, in turn, justifies the supervisory prominence of a religious center. The scale on which Christian churches operate tends to require the central formulation of policy that is most effectively imposed via an ecclesiastical hierarchy with jurisdiction, for instance, over a graded series of national, provincial, district, and local units. None of the religions of precontact Melanesia operated on such a scale or operationalized this kind of centralized and hierarchical structure. Although indigenous Melanesian religions sometimes involved quite extensive regional cooperation, facilitated by trading networks and ties of kinship and alliance (see Biersack 1996), they did not give rise to centrally monitored orthodoxies and ranked priesthoods. Religious communities exercised considerable autonomy over matters of ritual and cosmology and, in practice, the members of local cults saw themselves as fundamentally distinct from, and often pitted against, their neighbors. This point is nicely illustrated by Barth, who tries to imagine what the religious fragmentation and heterogeneity of inner New Guinea would be like if transposed onto Christian England: "If one were to imagine a Christian from one English village who entered the church of a community some miles away and found an image of the devil on the crucifix, and the altar wine being used for baptism, this seems the closest analogy I can construct. But by no means do all the contrasts have this stark character of inversion. In other cases, sacred symbols explicitly elaborated by some Mountain Ok communities are left entirely tacit or unelaborated by others" (1987: 5).

We therefore have at least six points of fundamental contrast between indigenous (Melanesian) and Christian (Western) religious systems. These contrasts can be explained, to a considerable extent, in cognitive terms. Procedural, schema-based, and semantic knowledge for Christian ritual and dogma is clearly an outcome of highly routinized worship. The repetitive nature of Christian practices cannot sustain episodic memories for most of those activities (discursive and embodied) that identify people as Christians. An indispensable part of what it means to be an Anglican or a Catholic, for instance, is to know what Anglicans and Catholics distinctively do and believe (e.g., the rituals they perform and the dogmas they espouse). But this knowledge is not intrinsically connected to distinctive transmissive episodes and, thereby, to concrete agents of transmission or coparticipants in ritual. The Anglican liturgy is not a particular action that I performed in concert with John and Mary but a general type of action that anybody could in principle engage in. As a set of schemas for how to behave in church, it stipulates a general sequence of worshipful behavior in which agents, actions, and patients are abstracted. It is partly for this reason that Christians form an anonymous community, conceptualized *in abstracto*. But transmissive frequency is also required for the stable and widespread reproduction of a complex, logically motivated body of doctrine. The intricate rhetorical arguments and narrative structures of Christianity, if only rarely transmitted, would have a greatly diminished impact on religious sensibilities during intervening periods (see Whitehouse 1992). Thus, the techniques of revelation elaborated in Christianity are intimately linked to a regime of procedural and schema-based learning, subject to continual review and consolidation through regular repetition.

Conversely, many of the major rituals of precontact Melanesia were resistant to formulation in procedural and semantic memory. The tendency was to recall climactic ceremonies, often planned and prepared months or years in advance, as distinctive and life-changing episodes. Declarative, exegetical knowledge, codified as abstract generalizable religious principles, was comparatively hard for all but the most experienced religious adherents to achieve. Instead, rituals were consciously recalled as a series of particular events in which concrete, flesh-and-blood actors were specified. It is this, above all, that undergirds the cohesiveness of religious groupings in traditional Melanesian society and militates against expansionary, evangelical regimes. The ritual community is not an abstract, potentially inclusive category but a concrete, exclusive group whose members figure centrally in one's memories of previous ceremonial activities.

Christianity and Contemporary Melanesian Religion

In a series of publications (Whitehouse 1995, 1996a, 1996b, 1996c, 1996d, 1998, 2000, 2004), I have suggested that many traditional Melanesian religions used an "imagistic mode of religiosity," whereas missionary Christianity has tended to exhibit features of a "doctrinal mode of religiosity." The point of this distinction between modes of religiosity has been to characterize and explain, in as much detail as possible, the contrasting cognitive, transmissive, and political characteristics of various religious traditions in Melanesia, as I have summarized briefly. What seems to emerge is that contemporary Melanesian religions may incorporate both modes of religiosity, inspired by indigenous and Christian models respectively. When this happens, however, the two modes do not simply collapse into each other, as if in the sort of melting pot envisaged by Barker, but retain their distinctiveness and, at the same time, impact on each other in specifiable ways.

In *Inside the Cult* (1995), I showed, through a detailed study of Christian-syncretic religion, that doctrinal and imagistic practices corresponded to distinct domains of operation—on the one hand, a mainstream movement with an elaborate churchly apparatus and, on the other, a tradition of localized splintering modeled on traditional cycles of initiation. More recently, in *Arguments and Icons* (2000), I generalized my model to a wider range of Melanesian case studies, suggesting that indigenous and Christian models are distinguishable throughout Papua New Guinea. In attempting to explain why this is the case, I have had to examine the historical conditions that gave rise to missionary Christianity, dating back at least as far as the European Reformation (Whitehouse 2000, chapter 7).

The central project of early Protestantism, and in many ways also of the Catholic Reformation, was to produce and uphold a purely doctrinal mode of religiosity.[4] Although this project was largely unsuccessful, even from the very start, it accounts in large part for the rapidity with which Protestantism spread in the sixteenth and seventeenth centuries, and this experience provided the template for subsequent varieties of missionary Christianity. Thus, the intellectual imperialism of sixteenth-century reformers in Europe was the indirect inspiration to nineteenth- and twentieth-century missionaries in Papua New Guinea, whether they were ethnically European, Polynesian, or Melanesian. Although the extraordinary variety of people who acted as agents of Christianization in Melanesia exhibited very different degrees and types of tolerance toward indigenous cultures, their primary concern was with the dissemination of a set of doctrinal practices. Since these were entirely alien to the peoples of Papua New Guinea, their country became the site of an exceptional confrontation between contrasting modes of religiosity that is still going on and shows little sign of abating.

Formulating the issues in this way has enabled me to develop a series of subsidiary arguments about the development of new forms of political identity in Melanesia (Whitehouse 1994). At the same time, however, it has brought me onto a collision course with scholars like Barker who regard traditional Melanesian and Christian religious forms as indistinguishably enmeshed. As Barker puts it (1999: 98): "Whitehouse reiterates repeatedly the fundamental contrast between Christian doctrinal and Melanesian imagistic modes of religiosity. . . . What he entirely overlooks, however, is that . . . local peoples appropriated, reinterpreted, and rejected mission Christianity, giving rise to a multitude of syncretic forms. . . . As White [1991: 179] cogently argues, Christian ideology has not been simply passively recorded on Pacific minds like a tape-recorder left running in the background of a Western conversation."

I have answered Barker's criticisms elsewhere (Whitehouse 1999), but what requires clarification in the present context is that a notion of thoroughly "appropriated" Melanesian Christianity is in no way inconsistent with the arguments I am advancing, nor do I subscribe to the cognitively absurd claim that the minds of Melanesians resemble tape recorders. Barker is right to criticize salvage anthropology for ignoring Christianity in Melanesia, but he is probably not justified in suggesting that Christianity completely lacks monolithic features that mark it off from indigenous religious forms. In appropriating, reinterpreting, or rejecting missionary Christianity, Melanesians have been grappling with profoundly alien models of codification, transmission, and political association. The fact that they have often applied these models in highly innovative ways does not mean that the models themselves are no longer distinguishable from those of traditional Melanesian societies.

Conclusion

Although Barker has, as he puts it, repeatedly "bemoaned the state of anthropological research on Melanesian Christianity" (1999: 98), he rightly acknowledges that this subject is belatedly attracting considerable interest.[5] More widely, too, in social and cultural anthropology, the study of Christianity is clearly taking off and rapidly maturing, as the contributions to this volume amply demonstrate.

Perhaps the most important feature of this work has so far been to reveal the extraordinary plasticity of local Christianities, viewed within microhistorical processes of accommodation, contestation, and discursive innovation. Part of the reason recent research has followed such a course is that postmodern sensibilities direct our attention to the creativity and distinctiveness of anthropological subjects. In this way, heterogeneity paradoxically becomes an argument for the generic oneness of humanity, in which the division between Us and Them is dissolved. While the ethnographic achievements of this trajectory are undeniable, comparative and generalizing projects will be inhibited. Christianity, wherever it flourishes, is locally appropriated, but that does not mean it lacks monolithic characteristics, equally worthy of examination. The anthropological study of Christianity will ideally encompass both dimensions, curbing the extravagant dogmatism of both scientific theory building and unconstrained relativism.[6]

Notes

1 Barker (1992: 149–52) provides a detailed discussion of anthropologists' neglect of Christianity on the Trobriand Islands, which covers Malinowski's work.

2 In drawing this contrast, I do not mean to suggest that bodies of Christian knowledge can be transmitted instantaneously—or that, having been transmitted, such knowledge remains somehow fixed in the worshipper's mind and is thus incapable of being developed or enriched through ongoing experience and rumination. Obviously, neither is the case, and we have plenty of evidence in this volume alone (if evidence were needed) that the religiosity of Christian individuals can be both fluid and dynamic. The crucial point is that much of the distributed knowledge that one may identify as distinctively Christian (or distinctive to a particular church or sect) is relatively fixed and publicly standardized—and it is largely to this kind of knowledge that Christians appeal in their attempts to trigger religious conversions. By contrast the rituals of many precontact Melanesian cults generated no such bodies of distributed, stereotyped religious knowledge and the process of being inducted into religious secrets more or less exclusively depended upon personal inspiration or revelation rather than on verbal persuasion. For a more detailed discussion of these issues, see Whitehouse 2004; Whitehouse and Laidlaw 2004; and Whitehouse and Martin 2004.

3 Of course, one could also identify some aspects of Melanesian religiosity that are subject to frequent—perhaps even daily—transmission, as Gilbert Lewis (2004) has pointed out. And some important aspects of Christian religious experience may be very rare or even once-in-a-lifetime events (conversion experiences furnish obvious examples), as Ilkka Pyysiäinen (2004) has observed (see also McCauley and Lawson 2002). My principal concern, however, is with the processes by which conceptually complex and highly motivating religious concepts are reproduced, and these are generated and transmitted through fundamentally contrasting strategies in missionary Christianity and in precontact Melanesian religions respectively.

4 This argument has been the subject of much recent discussion among anthropologists and historians (see in particular Howe 2004; Clark 2004; Vial 2004).

5 Much recent work has been characterized by a high degree of sophistication ethnographically (see Keesing and Tonkinson 1982; Robin 1982; Burt 1983; Smith 1980; Jolly and Macintyre 1989).

6 These issues have been explored at length in recent debates among anthropologists and historians, focused on the theoretical arguments outlined in this chapter, thanks to a British Academy Networks Grant on modes of religiosity that supported a series of conferences in Cambridge, Vermont, and Atlanta (Whitehouse and Laidlaw 2004; Whitehouse and Martin 2004; and Whitehouse and McCauley 2005).

···Epilogue···

Anxious Transcendence

Webb Keane

With this volume the return of the repressed takes a significant step forward. As Fenella Cannell astutely observes in her introduction, Christianity has not only been avoided by the mainstream of the anthropological tradition, it also lurks as the suppressed core of much of what goes under the name Western Culture. Indeed, this suppression may have been necessary for the emerging self-understanding of modernist art and science. According to this self-understanding, which since Weber has percolated into common sense, the defining practices of modernity such as scientific procedure, bureaucratic rationality, nationalist politics, free markets, and the liberation of art for art's sake, both depended on and contributed to processes of secularization. Even if the world is not yet—or ever will be (see Casanova 1994)—fully disenchanted, by this account at least it has been heading that way, led by those positioned in the vanguard of modernity. And from the nineteenth century onward, the social sciences were foremost in this vanguard, having named the condition and offered a diagnosis. In the process, they had to forget the sources of their core questions and concepts in a world for which Christianity was both pervasive background and specific instigation for research and theorization. The religious preoccupations of Durkheim, Freud, and Weber are self-evident; but one might recall as well the theological roots of Hegel and the young Marx.[1] In the twentieth century, these repressed origins continue to haunt social and cultural studies, and their kin in critical and humanistic theory. This haunting is evident in their core concerns with and ways of conceptualizing the self, objectification, agency, authority, power, and materialism. Consider, for example, the practice of anthropology as critique. Critique, moral or political, presupposes some normative ground. Much contemporary academic critique, however, does not give any explicit account or even acknowledgment of its own normative foundations (see A. Anderson 1992). I propose that this may be, at least to some extent, because its driving concerns and basic assumptions about human identity, rights, liberation, individuals, and society cannot fully know the extent to which their own foundations lie in the apparently alien and even obsolescent Judeo-Christian world.

A number of anthropologists have, of course, begun to confront the persistence of Christianity in the contemporary world, with attention to the politics of resistance (Comaroff 1985) and identity (van der Veer and Lehmann 1999; Viswanathan 1998), missions colonial (Beidelman 1982; Comaroff and Comaroff 1997) and postcolonial (J. Barker 1990), disciplinary regimes (Asad 1993), and rationalization (Hefner 1993). Such approaches share a tendency to subordinate Christianity as a religion of transcendence to its institutional forms or its service to the this-worldly problems with which the secular scholar, naturally, feels more at home.

Here I would like to sketch out a problematic that has been less prominent in the literature but is abundantly in evidence in the contributions to the present volume. Moreover, I contend that it informs some of the most pressing concerns of social and cultural studies. In its broadest and most abstract formulation, this problematic concerns the relations of subject and object. As I have argued elsewhere (Keane 1996, 1997b), the constitution of the human subject in contrast to objects is a persistent and disturbing problem for modernity, at least insofar as modernity is something that living people attempt self-consciously to inhabit. It worries both high theory and everyday practices. That the relations of subject and objects are a source of not just conceptual puzzles but also anxiety is suggested by the appropriation of the word *fetishism* by Marx and Freud from the study of religion (Pietz 1985). Uses of the word *fetishism* point to the folly of others and evoke a paradoxical combination of responses to that folly, ranging from contempt to fear lest that folly be contagious and even inescapably desirable. I propose that this anxious tension between contempt, temptation, and fear is a function of fundamental problems in the ways in which the subject has been conceptualized and lived in Western modernity. It arises from the conflict between the desire for transcendence and abstraction on the one hand, and the persistence of material embodiment and social embeddedness on the other. Transcendence, I suggest, haunts modernity in three unrealizable desires: for a self freed of its body, for meanings freed of semiotic mediation, and for agency freed of the press of other people.

These problems, moreover, have an important relationship to Christianity. I do not intend to place Christianity, or Judeo-Christianity, or even religion, uniquely at their origin; surely a full historical account would discover a hugely complex set of relations among ideology, political economy, technological developments, and so forth. (Nor do I simply mean that Judeo-Christianity continues to lurk fully formed beneath the surface of social science at the end of the twentieth century.) What I do want to suggest, however, is that Christianity has a special place in the articulation of these problems. It should therefore provide us with privileged insight into how these problems have been conceived and, perhaps more significantly, become part of people's everyday lives. In conceptual terms, Christianity has given rise to key discourses of iconoclasm, spirituality, conscience, agency, worldliness, and transcendence that persist even where their religious supports have fallen away. Where Christianity does persist, the pervasive presence of its discourses in churches, schools, pamphlets, the press, everyday expressions, political speeches, and so forth have long been available to all sorts and manners of people in ways that more esoteric discourses of philosophy, political thought, and science have not. Moreover, because Christianity in whatever form it takes is embedded in ordinary practices, it creates recurrent practical means by which these concepts can be lived in concrete terms (Asad 1993), even when the result contradicts official ideology (see Toren's contribution to this volume).[2] And through missionization, Christianity has become one of the most vigorous and deeply accepted forms by which the West has entered into nonelite discourses and daily practices across the globe.

Words, Things, and the Invisible

In the essays in this volume, the problem of the human subject emerges as an empirical problem especially in questions involving words and things. This should not be surprising. By virtue of their peculiar properties, both language and material objects help make it possible for living people to be aware of and interact with beings and powers that are otherwise not perceptible to the human senses. They are also crucial media for the self-objectification by which, I argue, human subjects know themselves and make themselves recognizable to others (see Keane 1997a).

Material things play such varied and ubiquitous roles in religious practices that they are easy to overlook. As icons they serve pedagogy and memory; as relics they draw otherworldly powers near to hand; as offerings and sacrifices they travel from the near to distant worlds. They are able to do so by virtue of their objective character, which articulates causal with logical or semiotic properties. For example, the relic, as something that connects the living with the distant and the dead, depends for its plausibility on the material property of brute persistence over time. Moreover, physical durability permits objects to circulate across contexts. Thus, for instance, the donor of offerings can reasonably hope that eventually they will arrive at a distant recipient. But objects are also vulnerable to destruction, and this serves their religious functions as well. This property is at the heart of sacrifice in two respects, both as a real loss—a cost—on the part of the owner (Bataille 1988), and in crossing from the domain of the visible to the invisible.

These examples have in common the fact that the very materiality of objects is inseparable from their capacity to signify. This is not simply a matter of conventional symbolism (as the lamb signifies Christ) or iconic resemblance (red signifies blood), matters of contestable social agreement, whose appeal is often limited to explicit pedagogy or intellectualist speculation. Rather, the realism and intuitive power of objects often derives from indexicality, their apparent connection to the things they signify by virtue of a real relation of causality or conjunction. That is, they point to the presence of something (if not here, at least at some time and place).[3] Under manipulation, they transform the spatial and or temporal dimensions of identity and experience—for instance, bringing the distant closer or the past into the present. As Rutherford puts it in this volume, by responding to the "seductive materiality of the Bible," the Biak were able to tap into the power of spatial distance, taking it as "another alien thing" that had traveled from afar. But objects are also mute. Their possible interpretations are underdetermined. As they travel across space and time, they elude hermeneutic control. The latter is one reason objects may be seen as problematic for true doctrine. Indeed, this is how John Calvin chose to illustrate humans' inescapable propensity for idolatry: in a certain religious festival, men took on the parts of those who had martyred St. Stephen. But mistaking them for Stephen's companions, the populace gave candles to them as well as to the saint (Eire

1986: 317–18). That is, the inability of objects fully to determine their interpretation leads people into false beliefs.

Material objects can become a problem for any religion, depending on the kinds of claims it makes about transcendence. This is evident, for example, in the antimaterialism of some versions of Buddhism. Western hostility to icons is manifest in the second commandment, later Jewish teachings, and the early church. But the nature of this problem will vary, with varying implications. According to Carlos Eire (1986), the Reformation popularized an understanding of God's transcendence so radical that, given the chasm between the divine and this world, the latter was left to follow the purely mechanical laws of Copernican science. As this worldview came to dominate the West, material objects came increasingly to pose a problem, to the extent that claims of transcendence become involved with modernity's own conflicted relationship to materiality.[4] This is evident in the apparent conflict between the spiritual purity and materialistic acquisitiveness of the evangelicals described in Coleman's contribution to this volume.

If the fundamental material properties of things undergird their causal and logical role in religious practice, so too the structure and phenomenology of language give it special importance in bridging the ontological gap between visible and invisible worlds, however these may be locally construed. For this reason, words are likely to have a special place in the practices of *any* religion that attempts to deal with invisible or immaterial aspects of the world (Keane 1997c). This is due in part to the double character of language as type and token, virtual system and concrete instance. In any instance of use, language is embedded in its context by a variety of means, including the pronouns that refer to actual participants, temporal and spatial deixis, and so forth. But words can always be extracted from one context and inserted into another. This is, after all, what makes it possible to read something that was written in another time and place, or to quote another's speech.[5] In addition to making words portable across occasions and, perhaps, ontological divides, as we find in the case of ancient scriptures, the textual character of language gives rise to an enormous range of other possibilities. For example, prayers and chants that are stripped of contextualization cues can make the moment in which they are used seem to stand beyond a particular time and place. Conversely, words spoken in trance, spirit possession, or glossolalia can bring into the immediate context voices attributed not to the bodily speaker but to normally distant beings like spirits, gods, or the dead. In either case, words are detachable from the identities of bodily present people and capable of invoking or producing other participants, times, and places.

There is a second respect in which language has powerful implications for the religious construction of subjects and subjectivities. This is the relationship between the experience of words as internal and external. On the one hand, to the extent that people experience inner thought as a kind of speaking, language mediates the intimacy of individual self-consciousness.[6] On the other hand, language is inescapably public, something that is always learned from other people and is encountered outside oneself in the concrete forms of sound or inscription. Even interior speech seems to echo the material forms of a given linguistic structure. As Bakhtin insisted (1981), one's own words are always already someone else's, something of which different constructions of the subject are more or less accepting. Overall, how a given religious tradition thinks about and handles words and things has important implications for how it thinks about the character, distinctiveness, and boundaries not just of the otherworld, but of the human subject.

According to their respective properties, words and (other) material things thus contribute to the objectification of the identities of subjects. Both words and things have properties that implicate them in the general condition of human sociability: to the extent that words and things circulate among people, the very conditions for people's objectification, self-knowledge, and identity necessarily involve other people. For many modern varieties of Christianity, this embeddedness often poses problems. These problems in turn resonate with certain foundational concerns of social and cultural theory, such as the relation of individual and society, autonomy, agency, and authenticity. It is, after all, the conjunction of Protestantism with scientific and political modernities—however we understand the precise historical development—that underlies the peculiar coexistence of a mechanistic worldview, a capitalist economic system, and the view that material goods are corrupting. Faced with this tension, social thought has long acted as if people, words, and even things could be only totally reduced to or completely abstracted from materiality. If the rethinking of Christianity in the contemporary world has any implications beyond the study of religion, it may be in challenging these dual reductivisms and offering a more realistic alternative.

Human Value and Its Transaction

In the two sections that follow, I want to trace out one way in which the materiality, semiotics, and sociality of human subjects might be rearticulated, with brief reference to examples from my own fieldwork on the eastern Indonesian island of Sumba (see Keane 1997a), whose ancestral ritualists have been undergoing conversion, largely to Dutch Calvinism, since early in this century.[7] I start with the problem of marriage exchange, given Christian views of the self and modern models of economic value. I then turn to the practical construction of sincere speech.

As Marcel Mauss ([1925] 1990) pointed out, ceremonial exchange, especially that which forges marriage alliances, seems to conflate people and things. For the West, whether conservative missionaries or progressive feminists, the apparent "traffic in women" (Rubin 1975) has often been a scandal, since it seems to dehumanize the subject. To assume that the articulation of people and objects in exchange is dehumanizing presupposes both that exchange treats people and things as equivalent values, on the model of commodity exchange, and that the value of the human is defined in its distinctiveness from, and superiority to, the material world. The former assumption shows its origins in capitalism, the latter, or so I am suggesting, in the assumptions of religious transcendence.[8]

Since Mauss, an enormous literature on marriage exchange has revealed the complexity of the matter. For one thing, people who engage in marriage exchanges usually take them to exemplify rather than threaten the distinctiveness of human self-worth. Thus, one elderly Sumbanese woman friend of mine was shocked to hear that Americans do not carry out marriage exchanges—for her, this meant we thought of ourselves as no better than animals in all their promiscuity. Marriage exchanges, at the very least, are a vigorous working through of the implications that people are, or should be, embedded in social relations with others, both living and dead, and that these relations are inseparable from their material entailments.

This sense of embeddedness and the work needed to sustain it is often expressed with reference to ancestral mandates and spiritual sanctions. This poses a host of problems for Christians. Those who celebrate modernity and economic rationality must have some account of the respective values of exchange and its alternatives. This is where Christian discourses of interiority and materialism often come into play, discourses that help give expression to shifting distinctions between subject and object. Talk about materialism seems to incite people to a certain dematerialization in their understandings of the world. This is evident, for instance, in the effort to treat material goods as merely symbolic. For example, Indonesian Christians must often face the question: What is the value that is transacted in marriage exchange? Few are willing to reject exchange out of hand, yet they also cannot accept the world of ancestor spirits and rituals at its foundations. One solution, which I often heard, is to explain marriage exchange in terms of immaterial human values. Consider this newspaper essay by a Catholic high school student from the island of Flores:

> Bridewealth in the form of traditional valuables like ivory, gold, buffalo, is at base only a symbol in order to raise a woman's value and dignity. Demands for bridewealth show that a woman must be honored, valued. . . . Bridewealth is only a symbol of the woman's self-respect. . . . It is proper that bridewealth be retained, on the basis of its essence as a symbol of woman's own value and dignity—and not tend towards business or "trade" in daughters. On the part of women themselves, the most important problem is as far as possible that she be able to guard her self-respect so that the demand for bridewealth which is to be discussed by her family doesn't put her to shame. One should value oneself by way of one's patterns of thinking, attitude, and praiseworthy behavior, before one is valued by others, especially the groom, by way of the bridewealth that will be discussed. (Witin 1997)

Like many anthropological analyses of exchange, the author assumes a clear opposition between material and social values. She dematerializes exchange to treat material objects as being merely signs of an immaterial value. This dematerialization accords well with the world of commodities, in which the subject is supposed to be clearly separated from its objects, and in which value can be fully abstracted from concrete practices and material forms. Yet in seeking to account for the value those objects hold for the subject, one is left with little but the desires of a willful subject as its source.

Put in other words, the writer is describing how the modern subject must be the source of its own value. It is hard to confine material objects to conventionalized symbolism and to constrain their motion to prescribed pathways. In exchange, the person manipulates the tokens of value in deference to the displaced agents of ancestral mandate. But when Christians deny that the materiality of objects is meaningful, they transform them into signs of invisible and abstract values such as social solidarity, tradition, or self-worth. Behind these signs stand abstract agentive subjects. But where do they stand?

Words Spoken from the Heart

The modern subject, as I have been describing it, seeks to act as the source of its own authority. In the most austerely Protestant versions, at least, this source cannot be the physical body or social standing. It derives, rather, from a sincere relationship to its own interiority.[9] To make sense of this, I ask what we mean when we speak of "sincerity"; the answer brings us back to the materiality of semiotic practices.

First, *sincerity* is a metadiscursive term. It characterizes a relationship between words and interior states. To be sincere is to utter words that can be taken to be isomorphic with beliefs or intentions.[10] As a metadiscursive term, then, *sincerity* is a component of linguistic ideology. It posits a relationship between speech and its imputed sources in the speaker's self: sincere speech makes that interior state transparent. It adds and subtracts nothing in words that was not already there in thought. The concept of sincerity thus seems to assume a clear distinction between words and thought, as parallel discourses (interior and exterior) such that they either could or could not match up. It seems as well to propose a hierarchical relation between these two, since the thought seems to come first, and to determine and impose a limit on the words. Moreover, as linguistic ideology, the concept of sincerity also seeks the authority of words in that relationship of matching. To take words as insincere is to cast at least some doubt on them. If I characterize your praise or promise as insincere, I am suggesting that I take the thought to hold primacy over the word, discrediting the latter. Moreover, sincerity seeks to locate the authority for words in the speaker as a self, as the responsible party.

Insofar as the concept of sincerity assumes that words could reflect inner states, it involves us in the linguistic questions about intentionality. Insincerity typically involves an intentional divergence between expression and thought: that, for example, is the difference between a lie and an error. What about the reverse: can one be unintentionally sincere? I suppose it might be possible to think of examples of unintentional sincerity, but the heart of the concept lies elsewhere. As I understand it, sincerity is a matter not just of imputed isomorphism between expression and interior state, but also a product of one's desire to make one's expressions isomorphic in this way.[11] That is, sincerity says something not just about speech or about speech and thought, but also something about the character of the speaker. That is why one also hears of people, and not just particular acts of speaking, being described as sincere.

Thus, the concept of sincerity seems to link ideas about language to moral questions. I think we should take the concept of sincerity to be inseparable from some kind of judgment—it's hard to make sense of a neutral concept of sincerity. And the speaker's efforts at producing sincere expressions would likewise seem to be a function of that judgment. The concept of sincerity weds metadiscourse with the sphere of moral evaluation. It is a guide to the linkage between linguistic ideology and other cultural values. This leads me to the third aspect of the concept of sincerity: it is interactive. For in being sincere, I am not only producing words that are transparent to my interior states but am producing them for you; I am making myself—as a private and inner self—available for you in the form of public, external expressions. Thus sincerity is a certain kind of public accountability to others for one's words with reference to one's self.[12] But there remains a hierarchy in which the self is the ultimate foundation, since it is an accountability that presupposes a self that knows itself. For, in order to be sincere, for words to match thoughts, those thoughts must be no more ambiguous or opaque than the words that express them. Moreover, both thoughts and words must be fully under the control of the speaking self: it doesn't seem to make sense, for example, to speak of the sincerity of dialogues as such, apart for the respective sincerity of each participant separately.

So I propose that the concept of sincerity, as an ethnographic problem, be posed as a question with two parts to it: (a) As an element of a metadiscursive vocabulary, what linguistic ideology does "sincerity" presuppose? What does it assume about the normal relations between speakers and speech? (b) As an element of a cultural value system, what is the moral load of the concept of sincerity? What does it assume about the value and authority of the relations between speakers, their speech, and other people? What does it say about the self and its relations to others?

I treat these as separate questions in part because I take it to be at least possible that historically one could change and not the other; that, for instance, members of a given society might maintain a certain view of language and its speakers, but alter how they evaluate them. I propose that this is precisely the sort of thing that might happen in a case of religious conversion, to the extent that the relatively tacit pragmatic assumptions underlying interaction are less susceptible to intentional, self-conscious, ideologically motivated change than are explicit evaluations.

Now as I've been suggesting, the semantic and moral load carried by the concept of sincerity for contemporary speakers of English bears strong traces of a religious genealogy in which Protestantism plays an important role. Or at least the implicit individualism, the distrust of language, and the authority granted to interior states find especially strong and influential expression in those strands of popular thought associated with the Protestant Reformation and its effects on Euro-American cultural and political formations. Moreover, it is as formulated by Protestant churches that the concept of sincerity often has its most direct impact on non-Western ways of thinking about language, selves, and interaction.

One of the critical problems that Protestants have had to contend with is the power of local discourse pragmatics and their underlying assumptions. For example, Sumbanese Protestants are deeply concerned about the problem of authentic speech in prayer (Keane 1997b). They are highly critical of both ancestral ritual, which makes use of formulaic couplets supposed to have been handed down unchanged from the ancestors, and Catholic ceremonies, in which people rely on printed prayer books. In contrast, Protestant prayers should come from the heart, be spontaneous and truly felt—they should, that is, be sincere. But the problem is, these words remain in the form of human language. And so, to the extent that words always bear with them some trace of their origins elsewhere, beyond the speaker in society (or wherever one imagines particular languages to come from), they pose a problem for the ideal that one should claim one's own words. It turns out to be difficult even for purportedly spontaneous speech to abolish all traces of its externality to the speaker.

Among other things, the act of conversion gives substance to the idea that upon entering modernity (*massa moderen*) one becomes free. This freedom is expressed in releasing oneself from the ritual obligations imposed by ancestral mandates and joining a voluntary organization in response to consultation with one's own conscience. This confirmation requires a public performance. Typical of such performances is one I recorded in August 1993. A minor local official with a wife and several children set out to regularize his union with a church marriage. First, however, he had to confirm his faith. This involved standing before the congregation while the minister delivered a sermon. The voice of the church, articulated by a single speaker, delivered itself to a split addressee: a single individual and a congregation. Here the minister addresses the audience by naming the authority on whose part he speaks:

> We are called and—at this moment we are called to implement the announcement of the Parish Council in successively implementing various kinds of activities, and the first opportunity we are called to implement the carrying out of the declaration of the confession of faith by the brother whose name has already been mentioned in the announcement and we all are invited to follow him. And before that, we are invited to listen to the reading of the declaration, which is connected with the aforementioned activity. Beloved brethren, congregation of God, at today's hour of religious service there is a brother of ours who desires to acknowledge and declare his belief before God and before his congregation here. He has requested and been received in an ecclesiastical manner to become a member with full responsibility in the congregation of God. He has been cultivated and educated to take a change of faith and promised this to his parents when he was baptized while still small.

So the action to take place here makes explicit reference to a parabureaucracy with all the appropriate forms of proper procedure including the preliminary announcement of the upcoming event and the retrospective reference to those announcements assuring the listener that what now occurs follows the rules and is not unexpected. In pragmatic terms, the minister's authority is immanent in rational procedures, the pedagogy referred to with the words like *cultivated* and *educated* and the formal Indonesian language he wields.

The minister continues:

> The regulations for the confession of faith are bestowed by our Lord Jesus Christ, who always accompanies his community and helps us hold fast to the promise bestowed by God from generation to generation. In order that our brother's confession of faith be evident before God and before the congregation, I invite [him] to stand before God and declare his faith to answer the questions that I am about to submit. I will read the questions in their entirety and then I will give an opportunity to answer them. The first: Do you believe in the teaching of this Bible and the twelve articles of the confession of apostolic faith as teaching that is true and perfect for the purpose of your salvation? . . . Do you believe, acknowledge, and promise? [Answer]: I believe, acknowledge, and promise. [Minister]: Therefore you have become a member with full responsibility in the holy congregation of God.

The minister then turns the groom to face the congregation and tells them to receive him as a friend and sing a hymn.

The congregation here serves as a single collective witness. To the extent that the sermon is addressed to the groom, this witness overhears the summoning of an individual conscience. I would suggest that the church ceremony enacts a scene in which each individual member's conscience itself is subject to the overhearing of others.[13] Each is kept true to his or her own conscience by this repetitious recalling of the moment of his or her own summoning by the church.

The sermon is supposed to address the listener's conscience. This doctrinal stress on interiority works in tension with the highly formalistic procedure that enacts not belief per se—there is no testimony, no cries of anguish or exultation here—but rather the discourse of belief. The church summons the groom here to give an accounting of himself. He must reply in the language of belief. What interests me about this scene is precisely its schematic nature, its theatricality, its lack of psychology. Nothing requires us to assume any belief on the part of the groom. What is important here is rather that he understand that he must stand ready to give an account of himself in the language of belief—he must at least be able to say "I believe" if summoned to do so by the church.

The congregation is also constituted as those before whom this profession is witnessed: they form the public who provide the warrants for such acts of self-accounting, who are owed such an accounting of an invisible interior state of belief, or at least of the responsibility of the groom's future outward acts toward this declaration of interiority. And they are given the right and responsibility in the future to call him into account if he should stray. His sense of responsibility is not his alone; it is mirrored in that of the community.

In this respect, the church ceremony remains within the parameters of certain interactive norms of Sumbanese society that limit the acceptable expressions available to the sincere conscience. Assumptions embedded in the pragmatics of performance in Sumba still require public recognition of the self in formalized interactions. The church service, for all its appeal to, on the one hand, bureaucratic rationality and, on the other, the language of interiority and belief, responds to persistent Sumbanese intuitions about how to act in the world. Even sincere speech, if it is to have any authority for Sumbanese, must take the form of a public performance and demand a public affirmation.

Public performance is, of course, a highly marked kind of event and involves specific sorts of speech genres. For Sumbanese Protestants, the demand for the performance of sincerity is most evident at weddings and funerals. It is as if one should enact one's moral subjecthood at moments when one's embeddedness in the world of other people is most apparent. Obviously we are not justified in concluding from events like this that no other expectations of or concepts of sincerity exist in Sumbanese society. It is possible, for example, that husbands and wives might demand sincerity of one another in the home, although my own experience in a Sumbanese household suggests not.

What, then, can we conclude from this? First, in reflecting on these public objectifications of the self and the demand for recognition, we should ask not just who has sincerity but when it should appear, when it should count. Second, we are witnessing a clash between language ideology and religious doctrine, between the presuppositions of speech pragmatics and explicit, public concepts. If we want to talk about different kinds of selves, we cannot ignore the possibility that such clashes between the tacit and the explicit, among different speech genres, and among presupposable selves, are, in fact, commonplace.

Anxious Transcendence

The examples of material exchange and sincere speech I have just offered have two things in common. One is that they both concern clashes in assumptions about the human subject that emerge in changes in its material mediations and objectifications. The second is that these clashes align Christianity with modernity in opposition to paganism and the past. In this alignment, Christianity and modernity both seek to abstract the subject from its material entanglements in the name of freedom and authenticity. It is in this, I think, that we can see one suppressed link between modernist rationality and theology (however much the explicit claims of the latter have fallen away): the value of freedom and abstraction lies, at least in part, in their offer of transcendence. Gifts symbolic of intentions, words true to the heart, and, perhaps above all, money are transcendence's quotidian forms.

But, at the same time, I have argued that even in its most abstract and transcendent, the human subject cannot free itself from objectification. It retains a body, it continues to work on, transact, and possess objects. And it cannot even be sincere without the publicly known material forms of speech (even the limit cases of Quaker silence, Hindu mantra, and Pentecostal glossolalia do not entirely escape this condition). As I have argued elsewhere, agents continually constitute themselves through semiotic practices that contain an irreducibly material dimension. Which also means that they cannot free themselves from the practices by which they are embedded in the world of other people. It is this irresolvable tension between abstraction and the inescapability of material and social mediations that I call the modern subject's anxious transcendence. And Christianity is an especially rich ethnographic domain for exploring the genealogies and futures of this troubled subject.

......

Notes

1 The invocation of Durkheim, Freud, and Marx obviously raises questions about the role of Judaism in this story. For my purposes here, it suffices to say that their intellectual careers unfolded in an institutional and discursive world dominated by Christianity. Different points I raise in this chapter apply at different levels of generality, which I will try to keep clear by referring, respectively, to Judeo-Christian, Christian, Protestant, or Calvinist contexts.

2 Charles Taylor (1989: 184) claims that Protestantism has a special historical role in this practical percolation, since it demands the commitment of each individual, not just members of the elite.

3 Simply by virtue of being material objects, things are subject to scarcity. Thus their very presence in any given instance indicates at least the fact that they have been obtained and retained, matters that are not always insignificant, as shown by the aura of things that are rare, expensive, fragile, or much in demand. For some of the social-structural implications of the retention of objects, see Weiner 1992. For an insightful discussion of the sheer materiality of relics in a non-Christian context, see Sharf 1999.

4 Modernity is, of course, a highly contested word. In using it here, I take it above all to be a term of self-description: modernity is what people who think they are or are not modern think it is. In this essay, I follow Marshall Berman (1982) in emphasizing the special place of agency and self-creation in the self-conception of modernity, and Charles Taylor (1989) in defining the modern subject with respect to its sense of inwardness and freedom.

5 The philosophical implications of this are most famously developed in Derrida 1976. For recent theoretical developments building on empirical research on the "textual" dimensions of both written and spoken language, see Silverstein and Urban 1996.

6 Psychologists are divided on the role of language in thought. But the intuitive perception of thought as language is widespread. For instance, in Sumba, in eastern Indonesia, the normal way of representing one's own inner thoughts is in reported speech: "As my heart said" (*wina na atigu*).

7 Portions of these two sections appear in somewhat different form in Keane 2002.

8 On the role of material things in constituting human subjects, see especially Daniel Miller's appropriation of Hegelian dialectic in an effort to remove the stigma attached to the concept of "objectification" (Miller 1987).

9 I am oversimplifying history, of course. Appadurai (1990: 93) claims that the New Testament is the first appearance in the West of a distinction between act and actor. Taylor (1989) defines the modern subject (going back to Descartes in this respect) in terms of inwardness and freedom. Lionel Trilling (1972) argues that sincerity develops as a specific historical formation in early modern Europe. Talal Asad (1996) sees the Enlightenment as the moment in which internality was developed as a site free of political coercion.

10 I think we would say that nondiscursive actions are sincere only insofar as they can be translated into discourse or at least be treated as some sort of signification. To call a smile or a gift insincere is to say that we find a mismatch between the smile a person has and the invisible feelings we conventionally expect to produce a smile or gift. In doing so, I warrant that we treat them as signs.

11 The philosophical importance of being able to stand back from, evaluate, and reform one's desires was expressed by Locke, something Taylor (1989: 170) takes as a crucial moment in the development of the modern self. Note that this capacity for "second order desires" (Dennett 1976) is a condition of possibility for religious conversion, at least in its most demanding Protestant forms.

12 Taylor defines the "inwardness" characteristic of the modern self in terms of what we hold back from others. Thus part of the morality of sincerity would lie in not holding back that which one defines oneself in terms of being capable of holding back. For a contrasting morality, concerning the expression of publicly shared sentiments, see Appadurai 1990.

13 Here are two significant points of contrast from the role of confession as portrayed by Rafael (1988). One concerns the role of the Protestant congregation over that of the Catholic Church hierarchy. The other concerns the self-reproducing nature of these practices. At least some of Rafael's claims seem to be peculiar to the initial period of early missionization and linguistic confusion, whereas my concern here is with the subsequent fate of norms of sincerity as ways of living.

References

à Campo, J. 1985. Een maritiem BB: De rol van de Koniklijke Paketvaart Maatschappij in de integratie van de koloniale staat. In *Imperialisme in de Marge: De afronding van Nederlands-Indië*, ed. J. van Goor; 123–78. Utrecht: HES.

Abella, Domingo B. 1954. *Bikol annals: A collection of vignettes of Philippine history*. Vol. 1. Manila: Privately published.

Abercrombie, T. 1998. *Pathways of memory and power, ethnography, and history among an Andean people*. Madison: University of Wisconsin Press.

Abraham, Nicolas, and Maria Torok. [1972] 1994. Mourning or melancholia: Introjection versus incorporation. In *The shell and the kernel: Renewals of psychoanalysis*, ed. and trans. Nicholas T. Rand, 1:125–38. Chicago: University of Chicago Press.

Ackerman, S. E. 1981. The language of religious innovation: Spirit possession and exorcism in a Malaysian Catholic Pentecostal movement. *Journal of Anthropological Research* 37:90–100.

Adriani, M. A., W. B. Bergsma, E. H. Van Leeuwen, and A. Voorhoeve. 1896. Response to question posed by Mr. W. B. Bergsma and Ds. A. Voorhoeve in Algemeene Vergadering of 1895. Library copy Irian B5b / 290. Archives of the Hendrik Kraemer Institute, Oegstgeest, the Netherlands.

Albo, X. 1991. La experiencia religiosa aymara. In *El rostro indio de Dios*, ed. M Marzal. Lima: Pontificia Universidad Católica del Perú.

Allen, N. J. 1985. The category of the person: A reading of Mauss's last essay. In *The category of the person: Anthropology, philosophy, history*, ed. Michael Carrithers, Steven Collins, and Steven Lukes. Cambridge: Cambridge University Press.

Alvarez, Ricardo. 1960. *Los Piros*. Lima: Litografía Universo.

———. 1984. *Tsla: Estudio etno-histórico del Urubamba y Alto-Ucayali*. Salamanca: Editorial San Estebán.

Amich, José. 1975. *Historia de las misiones del Convento de Santa Rosa de Ocopa*. Lima: Editorial Milla Bastres.

Andaya, Leonard Y. 1993. *The world of Maluku: Indonesia in the early modern period*. Honolulu: University of Hawai'i Press.

Anderson, Amanda. 1992. Cryptonormativism and double gestures: The politics of post-structuralism. *Cultural Critique* 21:63–95.

Anderson, Benedict. [1972] 1990. The idea of power in Javanese culture. In *Language and power: Exploring political cultures in Indonesia*, 17–77. Ithaca, N.Y.: Cornell University Press.

Appadurai, Arjun. 1990. Topographies of the self: Praise and emotion in Hindu

India. In *Language and the Politics of Emotion*, ed. Catherine A. Lutz and Lila Abu-Lughod. Cambridge: Cambridge University Press.

Appadurai, A., and Breckenridge, C. 1976. The south Indian temple: Authority, honour and redistribution. *Contributions to Indian Sociology*, n.s., 10:187–209.

Aragon, Lorraine. 2000. *Fields of the Lord: Animism, Christian minorities and state development in Indonesia*. Honolulu: University of Hawai'i Press.

Archdiocese of Madurai. 1983. *Archdiocese of Madurai: Origins development*. Madurai: Nobili Pastoral Centre.

Ariès, Philippe. 1981. *The hour of our death*. Harmondsworth: Penguin Books.

Armstrong, Karen. 1993. *A history of God: The 4,000 year quest of Judaism, Christianity and Islam*. New York: Ballantine Books.

Arriaga, P. J. de. [1621] 1920. *La extirpación de idolatria en el Peru*. Colección de libros y documentos referentes a la historia del Perú, 1st ser., 1.1. Lima: Imprenta y Libreria Sanmarti.

Asad, Talal. 1993. *Genealogies of religion: Discipline and reasons of power in Christianity and Islam*. Baltimore: Johns Hopkins University Press.

——. 1996. Comments on conversion. In *Conversion to modernities: The globalization of Christianity*, ed. Peter van der Veer, 263–73. New York: Routledge.

Ault, James. 1987. Family and fundamentalism: The Shawmut Baptist Church. In *Disciplines of faith: Studies in religion, politics and patriarchy*, ed. Jim Obelkevich, Lyndal Roper, and Raphael Samuel. London: Routledge and Kegan Paul.

Austin, J. L. 1976. *How to do things with words*. London: Oxford University Press.

Austin-Broos, D. 1997. *Jamaica genesis: Religion and the politics of moral orders*. Chicago: Chicago University Press.

Bakhtin, M. M. 1981. *The dialogic imagination: Four essays*, ed. Michael Holquist, trans. Caryl Emerson and Michael Holquist. Austin: University of Texas Press.

Barker, Eileen. 1984. *The making of a Moonie: Choice or brainwashing?* Oxford: Basil Blackwell.

Barker, J. 1987. Optimistic pragmatists: Anglican missionaries among the Maisin of Collingwood Bay, Northeastern Papua, 1898–1920. *Journal of Pacific History* 22:66–81.

——. 1992. Christianity in western Melanesian Ethnography. In *History and Tradition in Melanesian Anthropology*, ed. J. Carrier, 144–73. Berkeley: University of California Press.

——. 1993. "We are Ekelesia": Conversion in Uaku, Papua New Guinea. In *Conversion to Christianity: Historical and anthropological perspectives on a great transformation*, ed. R. W. Hefner. Berkeley: University of California Press.

——. 1999. Comment. *Journal of the Royal Anthropological Institute*, n.s., 5:97–99.

Barker, J., ed. 1990: *Christianity in Oceania: Ethnographic perspectives*. ASAO monograph no. 12. Lanham, Md.: University Press of America.

Barnes, M. 1992. Catechisms and confesionarios: Distorting mirrors of Andean societies. In *Andean cosmologies through time*, ed. R. Dover, K. Seibold, and J. McDowell. Bloomington: Indiana University Press.

Barnhart, B. 1990. Prosperity Gospel: A new folk theology. In *Religious television: Controversies and conclusions*, ed. R. Abelman and S. Hoover, 159–64. Norwood, N.J.: Ablex.

Barron, B. 1987. *The health and wealth gospel*. Illinois: Inter Varsity.

Barth, F. 1975. *Ritual and knowledge among the Baktaman of New Guinea*. New Haven: Yale University Press.

——. 1987. *Cosmologies in the making: A generative approach to cultural variation in inner New Guinea*. Cambridge: University Press.

——. 1990. The guru and the conjurer: Transactions in knowledge and the shaping of culture in Southeast Asia and Melanesia. *Man*, n.s., 25:640–53.

Bataille, Georges. 1985a. The notion of expenditure. In *Visions of excess: Selected writings, 1927–1939*, ed. Allan Stoekl, 116–29. Theory and History of Literature 14. Minneapolis: University of Minnesota Press.

——. [1967] 1988. *The accursed share: An essay on general economy*. Vol. 1, *Consumption*, trans. Robert Hurley. New York: Zone Books.

Bauman, R. [1974] 1989. Speaking in the light: The role of the Quaker minister. In *Explorations in the ethnography of speaking*, ed. R. Bauman and J. Sherzer, 144–60. Cambridge: Cambridge University Press.

Bauman, R., and C. L. Briggs. 1990. Poetics and performance as critical perspectives on language and social life. *Annual Review of Anthropology* 19:59–88.

Bayly, S. B. 1989. *Saints, goddesses and kings: Muslims and Christians in south Indian society, 1700–1900*. Cambridge: Cambridge University Press.

Beck, B. E. F. 1981. The goddess and the demon: A local south Indian festival and its wider context. *Puruṣārtha* 5:83–136.

Beekman, Elke. 1989. *Driekleur en Kruisbanier, De Utrechtsche Zendingsvereeniging op Nederlands Nieuw-Guinea, 1859–1919*. PhD diss., Erasmus University, Rotterdam, the Netherlands.

Beidelman, Thomas O. 1982. *Colonial evangelism: A socio-historical study of an East African mission at the grassroots*. Bloomington: Indiana University Press.

Berg, H. van den. 1990. *La tierra no da así no más: Los ritos agrícolas en la religión de los aymara-cristianos*. La Paz: Hisbol.

Berman, Marshall. 1982. *All that is solid melts in air: The experience of modernity*. New York: Penguin.

Besse, L. 1914. *La Mission du Madure: Historique de ses Pangous*. Tiruchinapoly: Imprimerie de la Mission Catholic.

Biak Numfor dalam Angka. 1991–92. Biak: Kantor Statistik dan Bappeda Tk. II.

Biersack, A., ed. 1996. *Papuan borderlands: Huli, Duna, and Ipili perspectives on the New Guinea highlands*. Ann Arbor: University of Michigan Press.

Bloch, M. 1971. *Placing the dead: Tombs, ancestral houses and kinship organization among the Merina of Madagascar*. London: Seminar.

——. 1986. *From blessing to violence: History and ideology in the circumcision ritual of the Merina of Madagascar*. Cambridge: Cambridge University Press.

——. 1987. Descent and sources of contradiction in representations of women and kinship. In *Gender and kinship: Essays towards a unified analysis*, ed. J. F. Collier and S. J. Yanagisako. Stanford, Calif.: Stanford University Press.

——. 1994. The slaves, the king and Mary in the slums of Antananarivo. In *Shamanism, history and the state*, ed. N. Thomas and C. Humphrey. Ann Arbor: University of Michigan Press.

——. 2002. Are religious beliefs counterintuitive? In *Radical interpretation in religion*, ed. N. Frankenberry, 129–46. Cambridge: Cambridge University Press.

Bloch, M., and S. Guggenheim. 1981. Compadrazgo, baptism and the symbolism of a second birth. *Man*, n.s., 16:376–86.

Bloch, M., and J. Parry, eds. 1982. *Death and the regeneration of life*. Cambridge: Cambridge University Press.

——, eds. 1989. *Money and the morality of exchange*. Cambridge: Cambridge University Press.

Boddy, J. 1994. Spirit possession revisited: Beyond instrumentality. *Annual Review of Anthropology* 23:407–34.

Bodley, John H. 1970. Campa socio-economic adaptation. PhD diss., University of Michigan.

Bouysse-Cassagne, T., and O. Harris. 1988. Pacha: En torno al pensamiento aymara. In *Raíces de América: El mundo aymara*, ed. X Albo, 217–82. Madrid: Alianza / UNESCO.

——. 1997. De Empedocles a Tunupa: Evangelización, hagiografia y mitos. In *Saberes y memorias en los Andes*, ed. T. Bouysse-Cassagne. Paris and Lima: Centre de Recherche et Documentation sur l'Amérique Latine / Institut Français des Études Andines.

Bowie, Fiona. 2000. *The anthropology of religion: An introduction*. Oxford: Blackwell.

Boyer, Pascal. 2001. *Religion explained: The human instincts that fashion gods, spirits and ancestors*. London: William Heinemann.

Bozeman, John M. 1997. Technological millenarianism in the United States. In *Millennium, messiahs, and mayhem: Contemporary apocalyptic movements*, ed. Thomas Robbins and Susan Palmer. London: Routledge.

Bradford, N. J. 1983. Transgression and the cult of Yellamma: Heat, sex and sickness in a South Indian ritual. *Journal of Anthropological Research* 39:307–22.

Brandon, A. 1987. *Health and wealth: Does God always promise prosperity?* Eastbourne: Kingsway.

Brandon, S. 1964. *History, time and deity*. Manchester: Manchester University Press.

Brockington, J. 1992. *Hinduism and Christianity*. London: Macmillan.

Brooke, John L. 1996. *The refiner's fire: The making of Mormon cosmology, 1644–1844*. Cambridge: Cambridge University Press.

Brotherston, G. 1992. *Book of the fourth world: Reading the Native Americas through their literature*. Cambridge: Cambridge University Press.

Brown, Michael F., and Eduardo Fernandez. 1991. *War of shadows: The struggle for utopia in the Peruvian Amazon*. Berkeley: University of California Press.

Brown, Peter. 1981. *The cult of the saints: Its rise and function in Latin Christianity*. London: S. C. M. Press.

——. 1988. *The body and society: Men, women and sexual renunciation in early Christianity*. New York: Columbia University Press.
Bruce, Steve. 1996. *Religion in the modern world: From cathedrals to cults*. Oxford: Oxford University Press.
——. 2000. *Fundamentalism*. Cambridge: Polity.
Burke, K. [1950] 1969. *A rhetoric of motives*. Berkeley: University of California Press.
Burt, Ben. 1983. The remnant church: A Christian sect of the Solomon Islands. *Oceania* 53:334–46.
Busby, C. 1997. Of marriage and marriageability: Gender and Dravidian kinship. *Journal of the Royal Anthropological Institute* 3:21–42.
——. 2000. *The performance of gender: An anthropology of everyday life in a South Indian fishing village*. LSE Monographs on Social Anthropology 71. London: Athlone / Continuum.
Cameron, Averil. 1991. *Christianity and the rhetoric of empire: The development of Christian rhetoric*. Berkeley: University of California Press.
Campbell, John. 1964. *Honour, family and patronage: A study of institutions and moral values in a Greek mountain community*. Oxford: Clarendon.
Cannell, Fenella. 1991. Catholicism, spirit mediums and the ideal of beauty in a Bicolano community, Philippines. PhD thesis, University of London.
——. 1995. The imitation of Christ in Bicol, Philippines. *Journal of the Royal Anthropological Institute*, n.s., 1 (2):377–94.
——. 1999. *Power and intimacy in the Christian Philippines*. Cambridge: Cambridge University Press.
——. 2005a. Immaterial culture: "Idolatry" in the lowland Philippines. In *Spirited politics: Religion and politics in Southeast Asia*, ed. Kenneth George and Andrew C. Wilford. Ithaca, N.Y.: Cornell Southeast Asia Program Publications.
——. 2005b. The Christianity of anthropology. *Journal of the Royal Anthropological Institute*, n.s., 11 (2): 335–56.
Caplan, Lionel. 1983. Popular Christianity in urban south India. *Religion and Society* 30:28–44.
——. 1985. The popular culture of evil in urban South India. In *The anthropology of evil*, ed. D. Parkin. Oxford: Basil Blackwell.
——. 1987a. *Class and culture in urban India: Fundamentalism in a Christian community*. Oxford: Clarendon.
——, ed. 1987b. *Studies in religious fundamentalism*. Basingstoke: Macmillan.
——. 1987c. Introduction. In *Studies in religious fundamentalism*, ed. L. Caplan. Basingstoke: Macmillan.
——. 1989. *Religion and power: Essays on the Christian community in Madras*. Madras: Christian Literature Society.
——. 1991. Christian fundamentalism as counter-culture. In *Religion in India*, ed. T. N. Madan. Delhi: Oxford University Press.
Carrier, J. 1995. *Gifts and commodities: Exchange and Western capitalism since 1700*. London: Routledge.

Carrithers, Michael, Steven Collins, and Steven Lukes, eds. 1985. *The category of the person: Anthropology, philosophy, history*. Cambridge: Cambridge University Press.

Casanova, José. 1994. *Public religions in the modern world*. Chicago: University of Chicago Press.

Catedra, Maria. 1992. *This world, the other worlds: Sickness, suicide and death among the Vaquieros de Alzada of Spain*. Princeton, N.J.: Princeton University Press.

Cawelti, J. 1965. *Apostles of the self-made man*. Chicago: Chicago University Press.

Cervantes, F. 1994. *The devil in the New World: The impact of diabolism in New Spain*. New Haven, Conn.: Yale University Press.

Chandler, J. S. 1909. *History of the Jesuit mission in Madura South India in the seventeenth and eighteenth centuries*. Madras: M. E. Publishing House.

Christian, William A., Jr. 1972. *Person and God in a Spanish valley*. New York: Seminar.

——. 1981. *Local religion in sixteenth-century Spain*. Princeton, N.J.: Princeton University Press.

——. 1989. *Person and God in a Spanish valley*. Rev. ed. Princeton, N.J.: Princeton University Press.

——. 1992. *Moving crucifixes in modern Spain*. Princeton, N.J.: Princeton University Press.

Clark, Anne. 2004. Testing the two modes theory: Christian practice in the later Middle Ages. In *Theorizing religions past: Historical and archaeological perspectives*, ed. Harvey Whitehouse and Luther H. Martin. Walnut Creek, Calif.: AltaMira.

Coleman, Simon. 1989. *Controversy and the social order: Responses to a religious group in Sweden*. PhD thesis, University of Cambridge.

——. 1993. Conservative Protestantism and the world order: The Faith movement in the United States and Sweden. *Sociology of Religion* 54:353–73.

——. 1995. America loves Sweden: Prosperity theology and the cultures of capitalism. In *Religion and the transformation of capitalism: Comparative approaches*, ed. R. Roberts, 161–79. London: Routledge.

——. 1996. Words as things: Language, aesthetics and the objectification of Protestant evangelicalism. *Journal of Material Culture* 1:107–28.

——. 2000. *The globalization of charismatic Christianity*. Cambridge: Cambridge University Press.

——. 2004. The charismatic gift. *Journal of the Royal Anthropological Institute*.

Comaroff, Jean. 1985. *Body of power, spirit of resistance: The culture and history of a South African people*. Chicago: University of Chicago Press.

Comaroff, Jean, and John Comaroff. 1991. *Of revelation and revolution: Christianity, colonialism and consciousness in South Africa*. Vol. 1. Chicago: University of Chicago Press.

Comaroff, John L., and Jean Comaroff. 1997. *Of revelation and revolution*. Vol. 2, *The dialectics of modernity on a South African frontier*. Chicago: University of Chicago Press.

Correia-Afonso, John. 1997. *The Jesuits in India, 1542–1773: A short history*. Anand, Gujarat, India: Gujarat Sahitya Prakash.

Corten, André. 1999: *Pentecostalism in Brazil: Emotion of the poor and theological romanticism*. Basingstoke: Macmillan.

Crocker, Christopher J. 1985. *Vital souls: Bororo cosmology, natural symbolism and shamanism*. Tucson: University of Arizona Press.

Cronin, Vincent. 1959. *A pearl to India: The life of Roberto de Nobili*. London: Rupert Hart-Davis.

Csordas, T. 1995. Oxymorons and short-circuits in the re-enchantment of the world: The case of the Catholic charismatic renewal. *Etnofoor* 8:5–26.

Daniel, E. V. 1984. *Fluid signs: Being a person the Tamil way*. Berkeley: University of California Press.

Darrieutort, Fr. 1876. Diableries. *Scholasticat de Vals*, 1876–1880, 1–6. Shembaganur: Jesuit Madurai Mission Archives.

de Bruyn, Jan Victor. 1948. Jaarverslagen. 1947 en. 1948 van Onderafdeling Biak. Nummer Toegang. 10–25, Stuk. 188. Nienhuis Collectie van de Department van Bevolkingszaken Hollandia Rapportenarchief. The Hague: Algemeene Rijksarchief.

de Bruyn Kops. 1850. Bijdrage tot de kennis der Noord- en Oostkusten van Nieuw Guinea. *Natuurkundig Tijdschrift voor Nederlandsch Indië* 1:163–235.

de Clerq, F. S. A., and J. D. E. Schmeltz. 1893. Ethnographische beschriving van de West—en Noordkust van Nederlandsche Nieuw-Guinea. Leiden: Trap.

Delaney, C. 1991. *The seed and the soil: Gender and cosmology in a Turkish village*. Princeton, N.J.: Princeton University Press.

Deliège, Robert. 1997. *The world of the "Untouchables": Paraiyars of Tamil Nadu*. Trans. David Phillips. Delhi: Oxford University Press.

Dennett, Daniel. 1976. Conditions of personhood. In *The identities of persons*, ed. Amelie Oksenberg Rorty, 175–96. Berkeley: University of California Press.

Derrida, Jacques. 1976. *Of grammatology*. Gayatri Chakravorty Spivak. Baltimore: Johns Hopkins University Press.

——. 1981. Plato's pharmacy. In *Dissemination*, trans. Barbara Johnson, 61–172. London: Athlone.

——. 1982. Signature, event, context. In *Margins of philosophy*, trans. Samuel Weber, 307–30. Chicago: University of Chicago Press.

——. 1986. *Glas*. Trans. John P. Leavy Jr. and Richard Rand. Lincoln: University of Nebraska Press.

——. 1995. *The gift of death*. Trans. David Wills. Chicago: University of Chicago Press.

Descola, Phillippe. 1992. Societies of nature and nature of society. In *Conceptualizing society*, ed. Adam Kuper, 107–26. London: Routledge.

——. 1996. *The spears of twilight: Life and death in the Amazon jungle*. London: HarperCollins.

Dijk, R. van. 2000. Ngoma and born-again fundamentalism. In *The quest for fruition through Ngoma*, ed. R. van Dijk, R. Reis, and M. Spiererburg, 133–54. London: James Currey.

Dillon, M., and T. Abercrombie. 1988. The destroying Christ: An Aymara myth of conquest. In *Rethinking history and myth*, ed. J. Hill, 50–77. Urbana: University of Illinois.

Dumont, Louis. 1980. *Homo heirarchicus: The caste system and its implications*. Rev. ed. Chicago: University of Chicago Press.

——. 1982. A modified view of our origins: The Christian beginnings of modern individualism. *Religion* 12:1–27.

——. 1985. A modified view of our origins: The Christian beginnings of modern individualism. In *The category of the person: Anthropology, philosophy, history*, ed. Michael Carrithers, Steven Collins, and Steven Lukes. Cambridge: Cambridge University Press.

Durkheim, E. 1969. Individualism and the intellectuals. In *Durkheim on religion*, ed. W. Pickering. New York: Scholars.

——. [1893] 1984. *The division of labour in society*. Intro. Lewis Coser, trans. W. D. Halls. London: Macmillan.

——. [1893] 1997. *The division of labour in society*. Trans. W. D. Halls. New York: Free Press.

Duviols, P. 1971. *La lutte contre les réligions autochthones dans le Pérou colonial*. Lima: Institut Français d'Études Andines.

Eck, D. 1980. *Darsan: Seeing the divine image in India*. Chattersborg, Pa.: Anima Publications.

Ehrman, Bart D. 2000. *The New Testament: A historical introduction to the early Christian writings*. 2d ed. New York: Oxford University Press.

Eire, Carlos. 1986. *War against the idols: The reformation of worship from Erasmus to Calvin*. Cambridge: Cambridge University Press.

Ekman, U. 1985. *Tro som övervinner världen*. Uppsala: Livets Ords Förlag.

——. 1989. *Financial freedom*. Uppsala: Word of Life Publications.

Eliade, M. [1954] 1989. *The myth of the eternal return: Cosmos and history*. London: Arkana.

Engelke, M. 2002. The problem of belief: Evans Pritchard and Victor Turner on "the inner life." *Anthropology Today* 18(6): 3–8.

——. 2004. Discontinuity and the discourse of conversion. *Journal of Religion in Africa* 33(1–2): 82–109.

Englund, Harri, ed. 2002. *Democracy of chameleons: Politics and culture in the New Mozambique*. Uppsala: Nordic African Institute.

Errington, Shelly. 1989. *Meaning and power in a Southeast Asian realm*. Princeton, N.J.: Princeton University Press.

——. 1990. Recasting sex, gender, and power: A theoretical and regional overview. In *Power and difference: Gender in island Southeast Asia*, ed. Jane Monnig Atkinson and Shelly Errington, 1–58. Stanford, Calif.: Stanford University Press.

Evans-Pritchard, E. E. 1960. Religion and the anthropologists. The Aquinas Lecture in *Blackfriars*, April 1960. Reprinted in *Essays in social anthropology*, 29–46. London: Faber, 1962.

Fasenille, Fr. 1896. Diableries, extract d'une lettre du P. Fasenille. *Lettres de Vals*, 1896–1880, 13–14. Shembagamur: Jesuit Madurai Mission Archives.
Fernandes, Walter, 1991. Jesuit contribution to social change in India: Sixteenth to twentieth centuries. *Vidyajyoti Journal of Theological Reflection* 55:309–26, 369–84.
Fernandez, Doreen G. 1996. *Palabas: Essays on Philippine theater history*. Quezon City: Ateneo de Manila University Press.
Fernandez, James W. 1982. *Bwiti: An ethnography of the religious imagination of Africa*. Princeton, N.J.: Princeton University Press.
Feuilletau de Bruyn, W. K. H. 1920. *Schouten en Padaido-eilanden*. Vol. 21 of *Mededeelingen Encyclopaedisch Bureau*. Batavia: Javaasche Boekhandel.
Forstorp, P.-A. 1992. *Att Leva och Läsa Bibeln: Textrpraktiker i Två Kristna Församlingar*. Linköping: Linköping University Press.
Forsyth, N. 1987. *The old enemy: Satan and the combat myth*. Princeton, N.J.: Princeton University Press.
Fortes, Meyer. 1965. Some reflections on ancestor worship. In *African systems of thought*, ed. M. Fortes and G. Dieterlin. London: Oxford University Press.
——. 1970. Pietas and ancestor worship. In *Time and social structure*. London, Athlone.
Foucault, Michel. 1976. *A history of sexuality*. Harmondsworth: Penguin Books.
Frankl, R. 1987. *Televangelism: The marketing of popular religion*. Carbondale: Southern Illinois University Press.
Freud, Sigmund. [1922] 1963. Medusa's head. In *Sexuality and the psychology of love*, ed. Philip Rieff, 202–3. New York: Macmillan.
Friedl, Ernestine. 1962. *Vasilika: A village in modern Greece*. New York: Holt, Rinehart and Winston.
Fuller, C. 1976. Kerala Christians and the caste system. *Man* 2:53–70.
——. 1992. *The camphor flame: Popular Hinduism in India*. Delhi: Viking.
Geissler, Johan Gottlob. 1857. Letter of January 29 (UZV K41 D3). Oegstgeest, Neth.: Archives of the Hendrik Kramer Institute.
Gell, Alfred. 1975. *Metamorphosis of the Cassowaries: Umeda society, language, and ritual*. London: Athlone.
——. 1980. Correspondence. *Man*, n.s., 15:735–37.
——. 1988. Technology and magic. *Anthropology Today* 4(2): 6–9.
Gellner, D. N. 1994. Priests, healers, mediums and witches: The context of possession in the Kathmandu valley, Nepal. *Man*, n.s., 29:27–48.
Gifford, Paul. 1994. Some recent developments in African Christianity. *African Affairs* 9:513–34.
——. 1998: *African Christianities: Its public role*. London: Hurst.
Gill, L. 1993. Religious mobility and the many words of God in La Paz, Bolivia. In *Rethinking Protestantism in Latin America*, ed. V. Garrard-Burnett and D. Stoll. Philadelphia: Temple University Press.
Gilligan, C. 1982. *In a different voice*. Cambridge, Mass.: Harvard University Press.

Ginsburg, Faye. 1989. *Contested lives: The abortion debate in an American community*. Berkeley: University of California Press.
Gisbert, T. 1980. *Iconografia y mitos indigenas en el arte*. La Paz: Gisbert y Cia.
Gluckman, Max. 1937. Mortuary customs and the belief in survival after death among the South-eastern Bantu. *Bantu Studies* 11(2): 117–36.
Good, Anthony. 1983. A symbolic type and its transformation: The case of South Indian Ponkal. *Contributions to Indian Sociology*, n.s., 17:223–44.
——. 1985. The annual goddess festival in a south Indian village. *South Asian Social Science* 2:119–67.

Goody, Jack. 1986. *The logic of writing, and the organization of society*. Cambridge: Cambridge University Press.
——, ed. 1987. *The interface between the written and the oral*. Cambridge: Cambridge University Press.
Gouda, Frances. 1995. *Poverty and political culture: The rhetoric of social welfare in the Netherlands and France, 1815–1854*. Lanham, Md.: Rowman & Littlefield, 1995.
Gow, Peter. 1989. The perverse child: Desire in a native Amazonian subsistence economy. *Man*, n.s., 24:299–314.
——. 1990. Could Sangama read? The origin of writing among the Piro of eastern Peru. *History and Anthropology* 5:87–103.
——. 1991. *Of mixed blood: Kinship and history in Peruvian Amazonia*. Oxford Studies in Social and Cultural Anthropology. Oxford: Oxford University Press.
——. 1997. O Parentesco como Conciência Humana: O Caso dos Piro. *MANA* 3 (2): 39–65.
——. 2000. Helpless: The affective preconditions of Piro social life. In *The anthropology of love and hate: The aesthetics of conviviality in native Amazonia*, ed. Joanna Overing and Alan Passes, 46–63. London: Routledge.
——. 2001. *An Amazonian myth and its history*. Oxford: Oxford University Press.
Green, M. 2003. *Priests, witches and power: Popular Christianity after mission in southern Tanzania*. Cambridge: Cambridge University Press.
Gregory, C. 1982. *Gifts and commodities*. London: Academic.
Haga, A. 1884. *Nederlandsch Nieuw-Guinea en de Papoesche eilanden: Historische bijdrage*. 2 vols. Batavia: Bruining's-Gravenhage.
Harding, Susan. 1981. Family reform movements: Recent feminism and its opposition. *Feminist Studies* 7:57–75.
——. 1984. Reconstructing order through action: Jim Crow and the southern civil rights movement. In *Statemaking and social movements: Essays in history and theory*, ed. Charles Bright and Susan Harding. Ann Arbor: University of Michigan Press.
——. 1987. Convicted by the holy spirit: The rhetoric of fundamentalist Baptist conversion. *American Ethnologist* 14:167–82.
——. 1991. Representing fundamentalism: The problem of the repugnant cultural other. *Social Research* 58:373–93.
——. 1992. The gospel of giving: The narrative construction of a sacrificial

economy. In *Vocabularies of public life: Empirical essays in symbolic structure*, ed. R. Wuthnow. London: Routledge.
——. 1994. Imagining the last days: The politics of apocalyptic language. In *Accounting for fundamentalisms*, vol. 4 of *The fundamentalism project*, ed. M. E. Marty and R. S. Appleby. Chicago: University of Chicago Press.
——. 2000. *The book of Jerry Falwell: Fundamentalist language and politics*. Princeton, N.J.: Princeton University Press.
Harris, Olivia. 1982. The dead and the devils among the Bolivian Laymi. In *Death and the regeneration of life*, ed. Maurice Bloch and Jonathan Parry. Cambridge: Cambridge University Press.
——. 1985. From asymmetry to triangle. In *Anthropological history of Andean polities*, ed. J. V. Murra, N. Wachtel, and J. Revel. Cambridge: Cambridge University Press.
——. 1989. The earth and the state: The Sources and meanings of money in Northern Potosí. In *Money and the morality of exchange*, ed. M. Bloch and J. Parry, 232–68. Cambridge:Cambridge University Press.
——. 1995. Knowing the past: Plural identities and the antinomies of loss in highland Bolivia. In *Counterworks: Managing divers knowledges*, ed. R. Fardon London: Routledge.
——. 2000. *To make the earth bear fruit: Ethnographic essays on fertility, work and gender in highland Bolivia*. London: Institute of Latin American Studies.
Harvey, P. 1991. Drunken speech and the construction of meaning: Bilingual competence in the southern Peruvian Andes. *Language in Society* 20:1–36.
Hefner, Robert W., ed. 1993. *Conversion to Christianity: Historical and anthropological perspectives on a great transformation*. Berkeley: University of California Press.
——. 1993a. Of faith and commitment: Christian conversion in Muslim Java. In *Conversion to Christianity*, ed. R. Hefner. Berkeley: University of California Press.
Hegel, G. W. F. [1822] 1956. *The philosophy of history*, trans. J. Sibree. New York: Dover.
——. [1807] 1975. The spirit of Christianity and its fate. In *Early theological writings*, trans T. M. Knox, 182–301. Philadelphia: University of Pennsylvania Press.
Heirich, Max. 1977. Change of heart: A test of some widely held theories about religious conversion. *American Journal of Sociology* 83:653–680.
Heldring, L. 1882. *O. G. Heldring: Leven en Arbeid*. Leiden: E. J. Brill.
Heldring, O. G. 1847. De Christen-Werkman den Zendeling Toegevoegd als Mede arbeider. Uitreksel uit het *Tijdschrift de Vereeniging Christelijke Stemmen*. Amsterdam: H. Höveker.
Hellberg, C.-H. 1987. *Gud och Pengar. Om Framgångsteologi I USA och I Sverige*. Stockholm: Verbum.
Helms, Mary W. 1988. *Ulysses' sail: An ethnographic odyssey of power, knowledge, and geographical distance*. Princeton, N.J.: Princeton University Press.
——. 1993. *Craft and the kingly ideal: Art, trade and power*. Austin: University of Texas Press.

Herdt, G. H. 1981. *Guardians of the flutes: Idioms of masculinity*. New York: Columbia University Press.

Hernandez, Tranquilino, trans. [1866] 1984. *Casaysayan can mahal na Pasion ni Jesucristo Cagurangnanta: Na sucat ipagladd nin puso nin siisay man na mabasa. ("Pasion Bicol.")* Manila: University of Santo Tomas.

Herrin, J. 1987. *The formation of Christendom*. London: Fontana.

Hertz, Robert. 1960. *Death and the right hand*. Trans. Rodney Needham. London: Cohen and West.

Hocart, A. M. [1912] 1929. *Lau Islands, Fiji*. Bernice P. Bishop Museum Bulletin, no. 62. Honolulu: Bernice P. Bishop Museum.

Hoekema, Anthony A. 1963: *The four major cults: Christian Science, Jehovah's Witnesses, Mormonism, Seventh-Day Adventism*. Grand Rapids, Mich.: William B. Eerdmans.

Höfer, András. 1974. A note on possession in South Asia. In *The anthropology of Nepal*, ed. Christoph von Furer-Haimendorf, 159–67. Warminster: Aris and Phillips.

Hollinger, D. 1991. Enjoying God forever: An historical / sociological profile of the health and wealth gospel in the USA. In *Religion and power, decline and growth: Sociological analyses of religion in Britain, Poland and the Americas*, ed. P. Gee and J. Fulton, 53–66. London: British Sociological Association.

Hooper, S. 1982. *A study of valuables in the chiefdom of Lau, Fiji*. PhD thesis, University of Cambridge.

Houtart, F., et al. n.d. *A socio-religious analysis of East-Ramnad District*. Unpublished report prepared for the Madurai Archdiocese.

Howard-Malverde, R. 1990. *The speaking of history: Willapaakushayki or Quechua ways of telling the past*. London: Institute of Latin American Studies, research paper no. 21.

Howe, L. 2004. The doctrinal mode of religiosity: Some ethnographic and theoretical problems. In *Ritual and memory: Towards a new comparative anthropology of religion*, ed. Harvey Whitehouse and James A. Laidlaw, 135–54. Walnut Creek, Calif.: AltaMira.

Hugh-Jones, Stephen. 1994. Shamans, prophets, priests, and pastors. In *Shamanism, history and the state*, ed. Caroline Humphrey and Nicholas Thomas, 32–75. Ann Arbor: University of Michigan Press.

Humphrey, Caroline, and Nicholas Thomas, eds. 1994. *Shamanism, history and the state*. Cambridge: Cambridge University Press.

Hunter, J. D. 1983. *American evangelicalism: Conservative religion and the quandary of modernity*. New Brunswick, N.J.: Rutgers University Press.

Ileto, Reynaldo. 1979. *Pasion and revolution: Popular movements in the Philippines, 1840–1910*. Quezon City: Ateneo de Manila University Press.

Irurozqui Victoriano, M. 1994. La pugna por el indio. La iglesia y los liberales en Bolivia, 1899–1920. In *La venida del reino. Religión, evangelización y cultura en america latina*, ed. G. Ramos, 377–402. Cusco: Centro Bartolomé de las Casas.

Ivy, Marilyn. 1995. *Discourses of the vanishing: Modernity, phantasm, Japan*. Chicago: University of Chicago Press.

Jagor, Feodor. [1875] 1965. *Travels in the Philippines (Reisen in der Philippinnen)*. Manila: Filipiniana Book Guild.

James, W., and D. Johnson, eds. 1988. *Vernacular Christianity: Essays in the social anthropology of religion*. JASO occasional papers, no. 7. Oxford: JASO.

Jarvis, Simon. 2000. "Old idolatry": Rethinking ideology and materialism. In *Between the psyche and the polis*, ed. Michael Rossington and Anne Whitehead, 21–37. Aldershot: Ashgate.

Javellena, Rene, SJ. 1983. Pasyon genealogy and annotated bibliography. *Philippine Studies* 31:451–67.

——. 1984. The sources of Aquino de Belen's Pasyon. *Philippine Studies* 32:305–21.

——. 1988. *Casaysayan nang Pasiong mahal ni Jesucristong Panginoon natin na sucat ipaglaab nang puso nang sinomang babasa (with an introduction, annotations and translation of the 1882 edition)*. Quezon City: Ateneo de Manila University Press.

——. 1990. Gaspar Aquino de Belen's poetic universe: A key to his metaphorical theology. *Philippine Studies* 38:28–44.

The Jesuit in India: Addressed to all who are interested in the foreign missions. 1852. London: Burns and Lambert.

Jolly, M., and Macintyre, M., eds. 1989. *Family and gender in the Pacific: Domestic contradictions and the colonial impact*. Cambridge: Cambridge University Press.

Journet, Nicolas. 1995. *La paix des jardins: Structures sociales des indiens curripaco du haut Rio Negro (Colombie)*. Institut d'Ethnologie, Musée de l'Homme: Paris.

Juillerat, B. 1980. Order or disorder in Melanesian religion? *Man*, n.s., 15:732–34.

——, ed. 1992. *Shooting the sun: Ritual and meaning in West Sepik*. Washington: Smithsonian Institution Press.

——. 1996. *The children of the blood: Society, reproduction, and the imaginary in New Guinea*. Oxford: Berg.

Kadhirvel, S. 1977. *A History of the Maravars, 1700–1802*. Madras: Madras Publishing House.

Kamma, Freerk C. 1939–41. Levend heidendom. *Tijdschrift Nieuw-Guinea* 4:206–13, 247–58, 320–33 and 5:22–35, 69–90, 117–35.

——. 1972. *Koreri: Messianic movements in the Biak-Numfor culture area*. The Hague: Martinus Nijhoff.

——. 1977. *Dit Wonderlijke Werk*. 2 vols. Oegstgeest, the Netherlands: Nederlandse Hervormde Kerk.

——. 1981. *Ajaib di Mata Kita*. 2 vols. Jakarta: Gunung Mulia.

——. 1982. The incorporation of foreign culture elements and complexes by ritual enclosure among the Biak-Numforese. In *Symbolic anthropology in the Netherlands*, ed. P. E. de Josselin de Jong and E. Schwimmer, 43–84. The Hague: Martinus Nijhoff.

Kamsteeg, F. 1993. The message and the people: The different meanings of a Pentecostal evangelistic campaign, southern Peru. In *The popular use of popu-*

lar religion in Latin America, ed. S. Rostas and A. Droogers. Amsterdam: CEDLA Latin American Studies.

Kapferer, B. 1983. *A celebration of demons: Exorcism and the aesthetics of healing in Sri Lanka*. Bloomington: Indiana University Press.

Kaplan, Martha. 1990. Christianity, people of the land, and chiefs in Fiji. In *Christianity in Oceania*, ed. J. Barker, 189–207. Lanham, Md.: University Press of America.

——. 1995. *Neither cargo nor cult: Ritual, politics and the colonial imagination in Fiji*. Durham, N.C.: Duke University Press.

Keane, Webb. 1994. The value of words and the meaning of things in eastern Indonesian exchange. *Man* 29:605–29.

——. 1996. Materialism, missionaries, and modern subjects in colonial Indonesia. In *Conversion to modernities: The globalization of Christianity*, ed. Peter van der Veer, 137–70. New York: Routledge.

——. 1997a. *Signs of recognition: Powers and hazards of representation in an Indonesian society*. Berkeley: University of California Press.

——. 1997b. From fetishism to sincerity: On agency, the speaking subject, and their historicity in the context of religious conversion. *Comparative Studies in Society and History* 39:674–93.

——. 1997c. Religious language. *Annual Review of Anthropology* 26:47–71.

——. 1998. Calvin in the tropics: Objects and subjects at the religious frontier. In *Border fetishisms: Material objects in unstable spaces*, ed. Patricia Spyer, 13–34. London: Routledge.

——. 2002. Sincerity, "modernity" and the Protestants. *Cultural Anthropology* 17:65–92.

——. 2006. Christian moderns: Freedom and fetish in the mission encounter. Berkeley: University of California Press.

Keesing, R., and R. Tonkinson, eds. 1982. Reinventing traditional culture: The politics of *kastom* in island Melanesia. *Mankind* 13:357–73.

Keller, Eva. 2004. Towards complete clarity: Bible study among Seventh-Day Adventists in Madagascar. *Ethnos* 69:89–112.

——. 2005. *The road to clarity: Seventh-Day Adventism in Madagascar*. New York and Houndmills: Palgrave Macmillan.

Kendall, Laurel. 1996. *Getting married in Korea: Of gender, morality and modernity*. Berkeley: University of California Press.

Kenji, Tsuchiya, and James Siegel. 1990. Invincible kitsch, or as tourists in the age of Des Alwi. *Indonesia* 50:61–76.

Kierkegaard, Søren. [1843] 1983. Fear and trembling. In *Fear and trembling/repetition*, trans. Howard V. Hong and Edna H. Hong, 1–123. Princeton, N.J.: Princeton University Press.

Knauft, Bruce M. 1978. Cargo cults and relational separation. *Behavioral Science* 13:185–240.

Knight, George R. 1993: *Millennial fever and the end of the world: A study of Millerite Adventism*. Boise, Idaho: Pacific.

Kopitoff, Igor. 1971. Ancestors as elders in Africa. *Africa* 41:129–42.

Kuhn, Thomas S. 1996 (1962): *The structure of scientific revolutions*. Chicago: University of Chicago Press.

Lacombe, P. 1892. Extract d'une lettre du P. Lacombe S.J. *Lettres des scholastiques D'Ucles*. 2d ser., vol. 2, 284–85. Shembagamur: Jesuit Madurai Mission Archives.

Ladurie, Emmanuel. 1981. *Montaillou*. Harmondsworth: Penguin Books.

Larmey, P. 1876. La danse du diable. *Scholastical de Vals*, 1876, 6–7. Shembagamur: Jesuit Madurai Mission Archives.

Leach, Edmund. [1972] 1983. Mechisedeck and the emperor: Icons of subversion and orthodoxy. In *Structuralist interpretation of Biblical myth*, ed. Edmund Leach and Alan Aycock, 67–88. Cambridge: Cambridge University Press.

Le Goff, Jacques. 1986. *The birth of purgatory*. Chicago: University of Chicago Press.

Lehmann, D. 1996. *Struggle for the spirit: Religious transformation and popular culture in Brazil and Latin America*. Cambridge: Polity.

Levine, Daniel H. 1995. Protestants and Catholics in Latin America: A family portrait. In *Fundamentalisms comprehended*, vol. 5 of *The fundamentalism project*, ed. M. E. Marty and R. S. Appleby. Chicago: University of Chicago Press.

Lévi-Strauss, Claude. 1995. *The story of lynx*. Chicago: University of Chicago Press.

Lewis, G. 1980. *Day of shining red: An essay on understanding ritual*. Cambridge: Cambridge University Press.

——. 2004. Religious doctrine or experience: A matter of seeing, learning, or doing. In *Ritual and memory: Towards a new comparative anthropology of religion*, ed. Harvey Whitehouse and James A. Laidlaw, 155–72. Walnut Creek, California: AltaMira.

Lewis, I. M. 1966. Spirit possession and deprivation cults. *Man*, n.s., 1:307–39.

——. 1971. *Ecstatic religion: An anthropological study of spirit possession and shamanism*. Harmondsworth: Penguin.

Lisboa, Marcos de. 1582–87. Relacion de las islas Filipinas. In *The Philippine islands, 1493–1898*, 55 vols., ed. E. H. Blair and J. A. Robertson, 5:34–187. Cleveland, Ohio: A. H. Clark, 1903–9.

Locher-Scholten, Elsbeth. 1994. Dutch Expansion in the Indonesian archipelago around 1900 and the imperialism debate. *Journal of Southeast Asian Studies* 25:91–111.

Lumbera, Bienvenido. 1986. *Tagalog poetry, 1570–1898: Tradition and influence on its development*. Quezon City: Ateneo de Manila University Press.

MAC (Meeting for African Collaboration) 1993. New Christian movements in Africa and Madagascar. *Catholic International* 4:28–36.

MacCormack, S. 1991. *Religion in the Andes: Vision and imagination in early colonial Peru*. Princeton, N.J.: Princeton University Press.

Magboo, Nemesio. 1922. *Ligaya sa langit at mundo: Catua-tuang pamgangnac ng mahal na Virgen sa maralitang cueva or portel ng Belen*. Manila: J. Martinez.

Marriott, McKim. 1976. Hindu transactions: Diversity without dualism. In

Transaction and meaning, ed. B. Kapferer. Philadelphia, Pa.: Institute for the Study of Human Issues.

Marriott, McKim, and R. Inden. 1977. Towards an ethnosociology of South Asian caste systems. In *The new wind: Changing identities in South Asia*, ed. K. David. The Hague: Mouton.

Marsden, G. ed. 1984. *Evangelicalism in modern America*. Grand Rapids, Mich.: Eerdmans.

Martin, David. 1990: *Tongues of fire: The explosion of Protestantism in Latin America*. Oxford: Basil Blackwell.

——. 2002. *Pentecostalism: The world their parish*. Oxford: Blackwell.

Marty, Martin E. 1992. Fundamentals of fundamentalism. In *Fundamentalism in comparative perspective*, ed. Lawrence Kaplan, 15–23. Amherst: University of Massachusetts Press.

Marty, M. E., and R. S. Appleby. 1992. *The glory and power: The fundamentalist challenge to the modern world*. Boston: Beacon Press.

——. 1993. Introduction: A sacred cosmos, scandalous code, defiant society. In *Fundamentalisms and society: Reclaiming the sciences, the family, and education*, vol. 2 of *The fundamentalism project*, ed. M. E. Marty and R. S. Appleby. Chicago: University of Chicago Press.

——. 1995. Introduction. In *Fundamentalisms comprehended*, vol. 5 of *The fundamentalism project*, ed. M. E. Marty and R. S. Appleby. Chicago: University of Chicago Press.

Marx, Karl, and Friedrich Engels. 1976. *The German ideology*. Moscow: Progress.

Marzal, M. 1983. *La transformación religiosa peruana*. Lima: Pontificia Universidad Católica del Perú.

——. 1991. La religion quechua peruana surandina. In *El rostro indio de Dios*, ed. M. Marzal, 196–97. Lima: Pontificia Universidad Catolica de Peru.

Matteson, Esther. 1954. The Piro of the Urubamba. *Kroeber Anthropological Society Papers* 10:25–99.

——. 1965. *The Piro (Arawakan) language*. Berkeley: University of California Press.

Mauss, M. [1924] 1954. *The gift: Forms and functions of exchange in archaic societies*. London: Cohen and West.

——. [1924] 1990. *The gift: The form and reason for exchange in archaic societies*. Trans. W. D. Halls. New York: Norton.

——. [1938] 1985. A category of the human mind: The notion of person, the notion of self. In *The category of the person: Anthropology, philosophy, history*, ed. Michael Carrithers, Steven Collins, and Steven Lukes, 1–25. Cambridge: Cambridge University Press.

——. 2004. *On prayer: Text and commentary*. Intro. W. F. S. Pickering. London: Berhahn Books.

Maxwell, David. 1998. "Delivered from the spirit of poverty?": Pentecostalism, prosperity and modernity in Zimbabwe. *Journal of Religion in Africa* 28:350–73.

——. 2001. "Sacred history, social history": Traditions and texts in the making of a Southern African transnational religious movement. *Comparative Studies in Society and History* 43:502–24.

McCauley, Robert N., and E. Thomas Lawson. 2002. *Bringing ritual to mind.* New York: Cambridge University Press.

McDannell, Colleen. 1995. *Material Christianity: Religion and popular culture in America.* New Haven: Yale University Press.

McHugh, E. 1989. Concepts of the person among the Gurungs of Nepal. *American Ethnologist* 16:75–86.

Meiklejohn, N. 1988. *La iglesia y los Lupaqas durante la Colonia.* Cusco: Centro Bartolomé de Las Casas.

Mellor, P., and C. Shilling. 1997. *Re-forming the body: Religion, community and modernity.* London: Sage.

Mendelsohn, Everett. 1993. Religious fundamentalism and the sciences. In *Fundamentalisms and society: Reclaiming the sciences, the family, and education*, vol. 2 of *The fundamentalism project*, ed. M. E. Marty and R. S. Appleby. Chicago: University of Chicago Press.

Meyer, Birgit. 1998. "Make a complete break with the past": Memory and postcolonial modernity in Ghanaian Pentecostalist discourse. *Journal of Religion in Africa* 28:316–49.

——. 1999. *Translating the devil: Religion and modernity among the Ewe in Ghana.* International African Library 21. Edinburgh: Edinburgh University Press, for the International African Institute, London.

Milbank, John. 1990. *Theology and social theory: Beyond secular reason.* Oxford: Basil Blackwell.

Miller, Daniel. 1987. *Material culture and mass consumption.* Oxford: Basil Blackwell.

Mills, Kenneth. 1994. The limits of religious coercion in mid-colonial Peru. *Past and Present* 145:84–121.

——. 1997. *Idolatry and its enemies: Colonial Andean religion and extirpation, 1640–1750.* Princeton, N.J.: Princeton University Press.

Mines, M. 1994. *Public faces, private voices: Community and individuality in South India.* Berkeley: University of California Press.

Miyazaki, Hirokazu. 2000. Faith and its fulfillment: Agency, exchange, and the Fijian aesthetics of completion. *American Ethnologist* 27:31–51.

Moffatt, M. 1979. *An Untouchable community in South India: Structure and consensus.* Princeton, N.J.: Princeton University Press.

Molina Rivero, R. 1986. Estrategias económicas y reproductivas en pampa aullagas-Oruro. In *Tiempo de vida y muerte*, ed. X. Izko and R. Molina Rivero. La Paz: Consejo Nacional de Población, Ministerio de Planeamiento.

Monast, J. 1969. *On les croyait chrétiens: Les aymaras.* Paris: Éditions du Cerf.

Moore, James. 1993. The creationist cosmos of Protestant fundamentalism. In *Fundamentalisms and society: Reclaiming the sciences, the family, and education*, vol. 2 of *The fundamentalism project*, ed. M. E. Marty and R. S. Appleby. Chicago: University of Chicago Press.

Moore, R. 1994. *Selling God: American religion in the marketplace of culture.* Oxford: Oxford University Press.

Morote Best, E. 1988. Dios, la Virgen y los Santos. In *Aldeas sumergidas*. Cusco: Centro Bartolomé de Las Casas.

Mosse, David. 1986. Caste, Christianity and Hinduism: A study of social organisation and religion in Rural Ramnad. DPhil thesis, University of Oxford.

——. 1994a. Catholic saints and the Hindu village pantheon in rural Tamil Nadu, India. *Man* 29:301–32.

——. 1994b. The politics of religious synthesis: Roman Catholicism and Hindu village society in Tamil Nadu, India. In *Syncretism/Antisyncretism*, ed. C. Stewart and R. Shaw, 85–107. London: Routledge.

——. 1997. Honour, caste and conflict: The ethnohistory of a Catholic festival in rural Tamil Nadu (1730–1990). In *Altérité et identité: Islam et Christiamisme en Inde*, ed. J. Assayag and G. Tarabout, 71–120. Collection *Purusartha* 19. Paris: Editions de L'Ecole des Hautes Etudes en Sciences Sociales.

——. 2003. *The rule of water: Statecraft, ecology and collective action in south India*. New Delhi: Oxford University Press.

——. Forthcoming. *The saint in the banyan tree: Popular Christianity and Hindu society in south India*. Berkeley: University of California Press.

Mulder, Niels. 1987. All Filipinos go to heaven. Working paper, Beilefeld.

Munn, N. D. 1986. *The fame of Gawa: A symbolic study of value transformation in a Massim (Papua New Guinea) society*. Cambridge: Cambridge University Press.

Nabokov, I. 1997. Expel the lover, recover the wife: Symbolic analysis of a south Indian exorcism. *Journal of the Royal Anthropological Institute*, n.s., 3:297–316.

Nash, J. 1979. *We eat the mines and the mines eat us*. New York: Columbia University Press.

Neill, S. 1984. *A history of Christianity in India: The beginnings to A.D. 1707*. Cambridge: Cambridge University Press.

Nelson, J. H. [1868] 1989. *The Madura country: A manual*. Madras: Asylum.

Nevett, A. M. 1980. *John de Britto and his times*. Delhi: Gujerat Sahitya Prakash Ananad.

Nies, Joyce (ed.). 1986. *Diccionario Piro (Tokanchi gikshijikowaka-steno)*. Serie Lingüística Peruana 22. Yarinacocha: Ministerio de Educación and Instituto Lingüístico de Verano.

Nock, A. D. 1933. *Conversion*. Oxford: Oxford University Press.

Numbers, Ronald L. 1976: *Prophetess of health: A study of Ellen G. White*. New York: Harper and Row.

Nyaundi, Nehemiah M. 1997: *Seventh-Day Adventism in Gusii, Kenya*. Kendu Bay: Africa Herald.

Obeyesekere, Gananath. 1981. *Medusa's hair: An essay on personal symbols and religious experience*. Chicago: University of Chicago Press.

Ortner, Sherry. 1995. Resistance and the problem of ethnographic refusal. *Comparative Studies in Society and History* 7:173–93.

Osborne, P. 1995. *The politics of time: Modernity and the avant garde*. London: Verso.

Osella, C. 1993. *Making hierarchy natural: The cultural construction of gender and maturity in Kerala, India*. PhD thesis, University of London.

Osella, C., and Osella, F. 1996. Articulation of physical and social bodies in Kerala. *Contributions to Indian Sociology*, n.s., 30:37–68.

———. 1999. Seepage of divinised power through social, spiritual and bodily boundaries: Some aspects of possession in Kerala. In *La possession en Asie du Sud: Parole, corps, territore*, ed. J. Assayag and G. Tarabout, 183–210. Collection Purusartha 21. Paris: Editions de L'Ecole des Hautes Etudes en Sciences Sociales.

Overing, Joanna. 1993. Death and the loss of civilised predation among the Piaroa of the Orinoco Basin. *L'Homme* 33 (126–28): 191–211.

Parry, J. 1980. Ghosts, greed and sin: The occupational identity of Benares funeral priests. *Man* 15:88–111.

———. 1985. The Brahmanical tradition and the technology of the intellect. In *Reason and morality*, ed. J. Overing. Association of Social Anthropologists Monographs 24. London: Tavistock.

———. 1986. *The gift*, the gift and the Indian gift. *Man*, n.s., 21:453–73.

———. 1994. *Death in Banaras*. Cambridge: Cambridge University Press.

Peel, John. 2000. *Religious encounters and the making of the Yoruba*. Bloomington: Indiana University Press.

Pelikan, Jaroslav. 1989. *Christian doctrine and modern culture (since 1700)*. Vol. 5 of *The Christian tradition: A history of the development of doctrine*. Chicago: University of Chicago Press.

Pemberton, John. 1994. *On the subject of "Java."* Ithaca, N.Y: Cornell University Press.

Pfeiffer, Baldur Ed. 1985: *Seventh-Day Adventist contributions to East Africa, 1903–1983*. Frankfurt: Peter Lang.

Phelan, John Leddy. 1959. *The Hispanicization of the Philippines: Spanish aims and Southeast Asian responses, 1565–1700*. Madison: University of Wisconsin Press.

———. 1970. *The millennial kingdom of the Franciscans in the New World*. Berkeley: University of California Press.

Philippine Bureau of Education. 1953. Documents on folklore, section headed "Camaligan." Manila: Bureau of Printing.

Pietz, William. 1985. The problem of the fetish, part 1. *Res* 9:5–17.

Pina-Cabral, Joao de. 1986. *Sons of Adam, daughters of Eve: The peasant worldview of the Alto Minho*. Oxford: Clarendon.

———. 1992. The gods of the gentiles are demons: The problem of pagan survivals in European cultures. In *Making history*, ed. K. Hastrup. London: Routledge.

Pitt-Rivers, Julian. 1954. *People of the Sierra*. Chicago: University of Chicago Press.

Platt, T. 1987. The Andean soldiers of Christ. Confraternity organisation, the mass of the sun and regenerative warfare in rural Potosí. *Journal de la Société des Américanistes* 73:139–92.

———. 1997. El sonido de la luz. Comunicación emergente en un diálogo chamánico quechua. In *Saberes y memorias en los Andes*, ed. T. Bouysse-Cassagne,

401–33. Paris: Centre de Recherche et Documentation sur l'Amérique Latine / Institut Français des Études Andines.

Platt, T., T. Bouysse-Cassagne, and O. Harris. 2006. *Qaraqara/Charka: Mallku, Inka y Rey en la "Provincia de Charcas," siglos XV–XVII*. La Paz: Ediciones Plural.

Pocock, D. 1973. *Mind, body and wealth*. Oxford: Basil Blackwell.

Pollock, Donald K. 1993. Conversion and community in Amazonia. In *Conversion to Christianity: Historical and anthropological perspectives on a great transformation*, ed. R. W. Hefner, 165–97. Berkeley: University of California Press.

Pouget, P. G. 1890. Un oracle du demon. *Lettres des scholastiques d'Ucles*, 2d ser., vol. 1, 283–84. Shembagamur: Jesuit Madurai Mission Archives.

Pouillon, J. 1982. Essay on the verb "to believe." In *Between belief and transgression*, ed. M. Izard and P. Smith. Chicago: University of Chicago Press.

Pyysiäinen, Ilkka. 2004. Corrupt doctrine and doctrinal revival: On the nature and limits of the modes theory. In *Theorizing religions past: Historical and archaeological perspectives*, ed. Harvey Whitehouse and Luther H. Martin, 173–94. Walnut Creek, Calif.: AltaMira.

Rafael, Vicente. 1988. *Contracting colonialism: Translation and Christian conversion in Tagalog society under early Spanish rule*. Quezon City: Ateneo de Manila University Press.

———. 1993. *Contracting colonialism: Translation and Christian conversion in Tagalog society under early Spanish rule*. Durham, N.C.: Duke University Press.

Raheja, G. 1988. *The poison in the gift*. Chicago: University of Chicago Press.

Ram, K. 1991. *Mukkuvar women: Gender, hegemony and capitalist transformation in a South Indian fishing community*. Sydney: Allen and Unwin.

Rappaport, R. 1968. *Pigs for the ancestors: Ritual in the ecology of a New Guinea people*. New Haven, Conn.: Yale University Press.

———. 1999. *Ritual and religion in the making of humanity*. Cambridge: Cambridge University Press.

Rauws, Johannes. 1919. *Onze Zendingsvelden, Nieuw-Guinea*. The Hague: Boekhandel van den Zendingsstudie Raad.

Ravuvu, A. D. 1987. *The Fijian ethos*. Suva: Institute of Pacific Studies, University of the South Pacific.

Reiniche, M.-L. 1979. *Les dieux et les hommes: Étude des cultes d'un village du Tirunelveli, Inde du sud*. Paris: Mouton.

Renck, Günther. 1990. *Contextualization of Christianity and Christianization of language: A case study from the highlands of Papua New Guinea*. Erlängen: Verlag der Evangelisch-Lutherischen Mission.

Retana, Wenceslao. 1894. *Un libro de aniterias: Supersticiones de los indios Filipinos*. In *Archivo del bibliofilo Filipino: Recopilacion de documentos historicos, cientificos, literarias y politicos, y estudios bibliograficos por W. E. Retana*. Madrid: Imprenta de la Viuda de M. Minuesa de los Rios.

Robbins, J. 2001a. Ritual communication and linguistic ideology: A reading and partial reformulation of Rappaport's theory of ritual. *Current Anthropology* 42:591–614.

——. 2001b. "God is nothing but talk": Modernity, language, and prayer in a Papua New Guinea society. *American Anthropologist* 103:901–12.
——. 2001c. Secrecy and the sense of an ending: Narrative, time, and everyday millenarianism in Papua New Guinea and in Christian fundamentalism. *Comparative Studies in Society and History* 43:525–51.
——. 2003. The anthropology of Christianity. Special issue. *Religion* 33(3).
——. 2004. *Becoming sinners: Christianity and moral torment in a Papua New Guinean society*. Berkeley: University of California Press.
Robbins, Thomas, and Susan J. Palmer. 1997. *Millennium, Messiahs, and Mayhem: Contemporary apocalyptic movements*. London: Routledge.
Robidé van der Aa, Pieter. 1879. *Reizen naar Nederlandsch Nieuw-Guinea ondernomen op last der Regeering van Nederlandsch-Indie in de jaren 1871, 1872, 1875–1876*. The Hague: Martinus Nijhoff.
Robin, R. W. 1982. Revival movements in the southern highlands province of Papua New Guinea. *Oceania* 52:242–320.
Rubin, Gayle. 1975. The traffic in women: Notes on the political economy of sex. In *Toward an Anthropology of Women*, ed. Rayna R. Reiter. New York: Monthly Review Press.
Ruel, Malcolm. 1982. Christians as believers. In *Religious organization and religious experiences*, ed. J. Davis. London: Academic Press. Reprinted in *A reader in the anthropology of religion*, ed. M. Lambek, 99–113. Oxford, Blackwell, 2002.
Rutherford, Danilyn. 1996. Of gifts and birds: The revival of tradition on an Indonesian frontier. *Cultural Anthropology* 11:577–616.
——. 2000. The white edge of the margin: Textuality and authority in Biak, Irian Jaya, Indonesia. *American Ethnologist* 27:312–39.
——. 2002. *Raiding the land of the foreigners: The limits of the nation on an Indonesian frontier*. Princeton, N.J.: Princeton University Press.
Rutz, Henry J., and Erol M. Balkan. 1992. Never on Sunday: Time and discipline in Fijian nationalism. In *The politics of time*, ed. H. J. Rutz, 62–85. Washington: American Ethnological Society.
Ryle, Jacqueline. 2001. *My God, my land: Interwoven paths of Christianity and tradition in Fiji*. PhD thesis, University of London.
Sabaté, Luis. 1925. Viaje de los misioneros del Convento del Cuzco a las tribues selvajes de los Campas, Piros, Cunibos y Shipibos por el P. Fr. Luis Sabaté en el año de 1874. In *Historia de las misiones Franciscanas y narración de los progresos de la geografía en el oriente del Perú; relatos originales y producciones en lenguas indígenas de varios misioneros, 1691–1921*, ed. P. F. Bernardino Izaguirre, 10:7–317. Lima: Talleres tipográficos de la Penitenciaría.
Sahlins, Marshall. 1993. Goodbye to tristes tropes: Ethnography in the context of modern world history. *Journal of Modern History* 65:1–25.
——. 1996. The sadness of sweetness: The native anthropology of Western cosmology. *Current Anthropology* 37:395–428.
Said, Edward. 1983. *The world, the text, and the critic*. Cambridge, Mass.: Harvard University Press.

Saignes, T. 1989. Borracheras andinas: ¿Porqué los indios ebrios hablan en español? *Revista Andina* 13:83–128.

———. 1995. Indian migration and social change in seventeenth-century Charcas. In *Ethnicity markets and migration in the Andes*, ed. B. Larson and O. Harris, 167–95. Durham, N.C.: Duke University Press.

Sala i Vila, N. 1994. Algunas reflexiones sobre el papel jugado por la iglesia y el bajo clero en las parroquias de indios en Perú (1784–1812). In *La venida del reino*, ed. G. Ramos. Cusco: Centro Bartolomé de Las Casas.

Salazar, Manuel B. 1971. *Tronco del mundo: An aguiagui kan kinaban bago magabot si Jesucristo sa ipag-awit*. Naga City: Cecilio.

Sallnow, M. 1987. *Pilgrims of the Andes: Regional cults in Cusco*. Washington, D.C.: Smithsonian Institution.

Salomon, F. 1990. *Nightmare victory: The meanings of Conversion among Peruvian Indians (Huarochiri, c. 1608)*. Department of Spanish and Portuguese, University of Maryland, working paper no. 7.

Samanez y Ocampo, José B. 1980. *Exploración de los Ríos Peruanos, Apurímac, Eni, Ucayali y Urubamba, hecho por Samanez y Ocampo en 1883 y 1884*. Lima: Privately printed.

Sangren, P. Steven. 1993. Power and transcendence in the Ma Tsu pilgrimages of Taiwan. *American Ethnologist* 20:564–82.

Santiago, Luciano P. R. 1988. Doctor Don Mariano Benerve Pilapil (1759–1818): Passion and transformation. *Philippine Quarterly of Culture and Society* 16:19–43.

Santos Granero, Fernando. 1993. From prisoner of the group to darling of the gods: An approach to the issue of power in lowland South America. *L'Homme* 33 (126–28).

Saulière. 1947. *Red sand: A life of St. John de Britto S. J., martyr of the Madura Mission*. Madurai: De Nobili.

Schieffelin, E. L. 1976. *The sorrow of the lonely and the burning of the dancers*. New York: St. Martin's.

Schmitt, Jean Claude. 2000. *Ghosts in the middle ages: The living and the dead in medieval society*. Chicago: University of Chicago Press.

Schrauwers, Albert. 2000. *Colonial "reformation" in the highlands of Central Sulawesi, Indonesia, 1892–1995*. Toronto: University of Toronto Press.

Schultze, Q. 1990. Defining the electronic church. In *Religious television: Controversies and conclusions*, ed. R. Abelman and S. Hoover, 41–51. Norwood, N.J.: Ablex.

———. 1996. Evangelicals' uneasy alliance with the media. In *Religion and mass media: Audiences and adaptations*, ed. D. Stout and J. Buddenbaum, 61–73. London: Sage.

Schumacher, John, SJ. 1981. *Revolutionary clergy: The Filipino clergy and the nationalist movement, 1850–1910*. Quezon City: Ateneo de Manila University Press.

———, ed. 1987. *Readings in Philippine church history*. Quezon City: Ateneo de Manila University Press.

Scott, W. H. 1983. Oripun and alipin in the Philippines. In *Slavery, bondage and dependency in Southeast Asia*, ed. A. Reid, 138–55. St. Lucia: University of Queensland Press.

——. 1984. *Prehispanic source materials for the study of Philippine history*. Quezon City: New Day.

——. 1994. *Barangay: Sixteenth-century Philippine culture and society*. Quezon City: Ateneo de Manila University Press.

Sebastián Pérez, E. Juan, B. Morán Zumaeta, and Joyce Nies. 1974. *Yine pirana 12: Gwacha ginkakle* (*Cartilla de lectura 12: Historia de los piros*). Lima: Ministerio de Educación.

Sharf, Robert H. 1999. On the allure of Buddhist relics. *Representations* 66.

Shiraishi, Takashi. 1990. *An age in motion: Popular radicalism in Java, 1912–1926*. Ithaca: Cornell University Press.

Shulman, D. D. 1980. *Tamil temple myths: Sacrifice and divine marriage in the south Indian Saiva tradition*. Princeton, N.J.: Princeton University Press.

Siegel, James T. 1979. *Shadow and sound: The historical thought of a Sumatran people*. Chicago: University of Chicago Press.

Silverblatt, I. 1988. Political memories and colonizing symbols: Santiago and the mountain gods of colonial Peru. In *Rethinking history and myth*, ed. J. Hill, 174–94. Urbana: University of Illinois Press.

Silverstein, Michael, and Greg Urban. 1996. *Natural histories of discourse*. Chicago: University of Chicago Press.

Simpson, Anthony. 2003. *Half-London in Zambia: Contested identities in a Catholic mission school*. Edinburgh: Edinburgh University Press.

Skog, M. 1993. The Mormons, Jehovah's Witnesses and the Faith movement in Sweden. Paper delivered to New Religions and the New Europe Conference, London School of Economics, March 25–28.

Smeele, Rogier. 1988. De Expansie van het Nederlandse Gezag en de Intensivering van de Bestuursbemoeienis op Nederlands Nieuw-Guinea, 1898–1942. PhD thesis, Institute of History, Utrecht University.

Smith, Michael French. 1980. From heathen to atheist: Changing views of Catholicism in a Papua and New Guinea village. *Oceania* 51:40–52.

Snow, David A., and Richard Machalek. 1983. The convert as social type. In *Sociological theory 1983*, ed. Randall Collins. San Francisco: Jossey-Bass.

Spencer, Jonathan, 1997. Fatima and the enchanted toffees: An essay on contingency, narrative and therapy. *Journal of the Royal Anthropological Institute* 4:693–710.

Spier, F. 1993. Rural Protestantism in southern Andean Peru. In *The popular use of popular religion in Latin America*, ed. S. Rostas and A. Droogers, 109–26. Amsterdam: CEDLA Latin American Studies.

Steedly, Mary Margaret. 1996. The importance of proper names: Language and "national" identity in colonial Karoland. *American Ethnologist* 23:447–75.

Stein, B. 1980. *Peasant state and society in medieval south India*. Delhi: Oxford University Press.

Stewart, C. 1991. *Demons and the devil*. Princeton, N.J.: Princeton University Press.

Stewart, Charles, and Rosalind Shaw. 1994. *Syncretism/anti-syncretism: The politics of religious synthesis*. London: Routledge.

Stewart, Michael. 1997. *The time of the gypsies*. Boulder, Colo.: Westview.

Stewart, Susan. 1995. Lyric possession. *Critical Inquiry* 22:34–63.

Stirrat, R. L. 1977. Demonic possession in Catholic Sri Lanka. *Journal of Anthropological Research* 33:133–57.

——. 1979. A Catholic shrine in its social context. *Sri Lanka Journal of Social Science* 2:77–108.

——. 1984. Sacred Models. *Man* 19:199–215.

——. 1992. *Power and religiosity in a post-colonial setting: Sinhala Catholics in contemporary Sri Lanka*. Cambridge: Cambridge University Press.

Stobart, H. 1995. *Sounding the seasons: Musical ideologies and the poetics of production in an Andean hamlet (Northern Potosí, Bolivia)*. PhD thesis, University of Cambridge.

Stoll, David. 1982. *Fishers of men or founders of empire? The Wycliffe Bible Translators in Latin America*. London: Zed Books.

——. 1994. "Jesus is Lord of Guatemala": Evangelical reform in a death-squad state. In *Accounting for fundamentalisms*, vol. 4 of *The fundamentalism project*, ed. M. E. Marty and R. S. Appleby. Chicago: University of Chicago Press.

Stoller, P. 1995. *Embodying colonial memories: Spirit possession, power and the hauka in West Africa*. London: Routledge.

Ströbele-Gregor, J. 1989. *Indios de piel blanca: Evangelistas fundamentalistas en Chuquiyawu*. La Paz: Hisbol.

Stromberg, P. 1993. *Language and self-transformation: A study of the Christian conversion narrative*. Cambridge: Cambridge University Press.

Szeminski, J. 1988. Why kill a Spaniard? In *Resistance, rebellion and consciousness in the Andean world*, ed. S. Stern, 166–92. Madison: University of Wisconsin Press.

Tambiah, Stanley J. 1970. *Buddhism and the spirit cults of North-east Thailand*. Cambridge: Cambridge University Press.

Taussig, M. 1993. *Mimesis and alterity: A particular history of the senses*. London: Routledge.

Taylor, Charles. 1989. *Sources of the self: The making of modern identity*. Cambridge, Mass.: Harvard University Press.

Taylor, D. 1985. Some theological thoughts about evil. In *The anthropology of evil*, ed. D. Parkin, 26–41. Oxford: Basil Blackwell.

Taylor, G. 1980. Supay. *Amerindia* 4:47–63.

Taylor, Isaac. 1849. *Loyola and Jesuitism in its rudiments*. London: Longman, Brown, Green, and Longmans.

Thomas, Nicholas. 1991. *Entangled objects: Exchange, material culture, and colonialism in the Pacific*. London: Harvard University Press.

——. 1994. *Colonialism's culture: Anthropology, travel and government*. Cambridge: Polity.

Thomson, Basil. [1908] 1968. *The Fijians: A study of the decay of custom*. London: Dawsons of Pall Mall.

Thornley, A. W. 1979. Fijian Methodism, 1874–1945: The emergence of a national church. PhD thesis, Australian National University.

Tibi, Bassam. 1993. The worldview of Sunni Arab fundamentalists: Attitudes toward modern science and technology. In *Fundamentalisms and society: Reclaiming the sciences, the family, and education*, vol. 2 of *The fundamentalism project*, ed. M. E. Marty and R. S. Appleby. Chicago: University of Chicago Press.

Tiongson, Nicanor. 1976. Pasyon: The best-known Filipino book. *Archipelago* 4 (3): 30–38.

Tomlinson, Matthew. 2002. Voice and earth: Making religious meaning and power in Christian Fiji. PhD diss., University of Pennsylvania.

Toren, Christina. 1988. Making the present, revealing the past: The mutability and continuity of tradition as process. *Man*, n.s., 23:696–717.

——. 1990. *Making sense of hierarchy: Cognition as social process in Fiji*. London: Athlone.

——. 1993a. Sign into symbol, symbol as sign: Cognitive aspects of a social process. In *Cognitive aspects of religious symbolism*, ed. P. Boyer, 147–264. Cambridge: Cambridge University Press.

——. 1993b. Making history: The significance of childhood cognition for a comparative anthropology of mind. *Man*, n.s., 28:461–78.

——. 1995a. Cosmogonic aspects of desire and compassion in Fiji. In *Cosmos and Society*, ed. D. de Coppet and A. Iteanu, 57–82. London: Berg.

——. 1995b. Ritual, rule and cognitive scheme. In *The crisis in text*, ed. Paul Wohlmuth, special issue, *Journal of Contemporary Legal Issues* 6:521–33.

——. 1998. Cannibalism and compassion: Transformations in Fijian concepts of the person. In *Common worlds and single lives: Constituting knowledge in Pacific societies*, ed. V. Keck, 95–115. London: Berg.

——. 1999a. *Mind, materiality and history: Explorations in Fijian ethnography*. London: Routledge.

——. 1999b. Compassion for one another: Constituting kinship as intentionality in Fiji. Malinowski Lecture. *Journal of the Royal Anthropological Institute* 5:265–80.

——. 2002a. Space-time coordinates of subjectivity in Fiji. In *Representing space in Oceania: Culture in language and mind*, ed. Giovanni Bennardo, special issue, *Pacific Linguistics* 523:215–31.

——. 2002b. Anthropology as the whole science of what it is to be human. In *Anthropology beyond culture*, ed. R. Fox and B. King, 105–214. London: Berg.

Trawick, M. 1990. *Notes on love in a Tamil family*. Berkeley: University of California Press.

Trilling, Lionel. 1972. *Sincerity and authenticity*. Cambridge, Mass.: Harvard University Press.

Tronchon, Jacques. 1986: *L'insurrection malgache de 1947*. Fianarantsoa: Ambozontany.

Tulving, E. 1972. Episodic and semantic memory. In *Organization of memory*, ed. E. Tulving and W. Donaldson, 381–403. New York: Academic.

Turner, Edith. 1992. *Experiencing ritual: A new interpretation of African healing*. Philadelphia: University of Pennsylvania Press.

Turner, Terence S. 1977. Transformation, hierarchy and transcendence: A Reformulation of van Gennep's model of the structure of rites de passage. In *Secular ritual*, ed. Sally F. Moore and Barbara G. Myerhoff, 53–70. Assen: Van Gorcum.

Tuzin, D. F. 1980. *The voice of the Tambaran: Truth and illusion in Ilahita Arapesh religion*. Berkeley: University of California Press.

——. 1992. Revelation and concealment in the cultural organization of meaning: A methodological note. In *Shooting the Sun: Ritual and meaning in West Sepik*, ed. B. Juillerat. Washington, D.C.: Smithsonian Institution Press.

Urton, G. 1981. *At the crossroads of earth and sky: An Andean cosmology*. Austin: University of Texas Press.

Utrechtsche Zendingsvereeniging. 1920. *Handelingen van de Utrechtsche Zendingsvereeniging*, 87–88. Oegstgeest, Neth.: Archives of the Hendrik Kraemer Institute.

van Baaren, Theodoor P. 1968. *Korwars and Korwar style: Art and ancestor worship in north-west New Guinea*. The Hague: Mouton.

van der Veer, Peter, and Harmut Lehmann, eds. 1999. *Nation and religion: Perspectives on Europe and Asia*. Princeton, N.J.: Princeton University Press.

van Hasselt, F. J. F. n.d. *Petrus Kafiar: Een Bladzijde uit de Nieuw-Guinea Zending*. Utrecht: Utrechtsche Zendings-Vereeniging.

van Hasselt, J. L., and F. J. F. van Hasselt. 1947. *Noemfoorsche Woordenboek*. Amsterdam: J. H. de Bussy.

Vance, Laura L. 1999. *Seventh-Day Adventism in crisis: Gender and sectarian change in an emerging religion*. Urbana: University of Illinois Press.

Vasavi, A. R. 1994. Hybrid times, hybrid people: Culture and agriculture in south India. *Man*, n.s., 29: 283–300.

Vial, Theodore. 2004. Modes of religiosity and popular religious practices at the time of the Reformation. In *Theorizing religions past: Historical and archaeological perspectives*, ed. Harvey Whitehouse and Luther H. Martin. Walnut Creek, Calif.: AltaMira.

Vilaça, Aparecida. 1997. Christians without faith. *Ethnos* 62:91–115.

Visvanathan, S. 1993. *The Christians of Kerala: History, belief and ritual among the Yacoba*. New Delhi: Oxford University Press.

Viswanathan, Gauri. 1998. *Outside the fold: Conversion, modernity, and belief*. Princeton, N.J.: Princeton University Press.

Viveiros de Castro, Eduardo. 1992. *From the enemy's point of view: Humanity and divinity in an Amazonian society*. Chicago: University of Chicago Press.

——. 1993. Le Marbre et le Myrte: De l'inconstance de le âme sauvage. In *Mémoire de la tradition*, ed. A. Becquelin and A. Molinié, 365–431. Nanterre: Société d'Ethnologie.

——. 1998. Cosmological deixis and Amerindian perspectivism. *Journal of the Royal Anthropological Institute*, n.s., 4:469–88.

Wadley, S. 1975. *Shakti: Power in the conceptual structure of Karimpur religion.* Chicago: Department of Anthropology, University of Chicago.
Wagner, R. 1986. *Asiwinarong.* Princeton, N.J.: Princeton University Press.
Walker-Bynum, Caroline. 1987. *Holy feast and holy fast: The religious significance of food to medieval women.* Berkeley: University of California Press.
——. 1996. *The resurrection of the body in Western Christianity, 200–1336.* New York: Columbia University Press.
Wallace, Alfred. [1869] 1986. *The Malay Archipelago.* Singapore: Oxford University Press.
Wallis, Emily Ethel. 1961. *The Dayuma story: Life under Auca spears.* London: Hodder and Stoughton.
——. 1966. *Tariri: My story, from jungle killer to Christian missionary.* London: Hodder and Stoughton.
Walsh, Andrew. 2002. Preserving bodies, saving souls: Religious incongruity in a northern Malagasy mining town. *Journal of Religion in Africa* 32:366–93.
Warner, Marina. 1976. *Alone of all her sex: The myth and cult of the Virgin Mary.* New York: Knopf.
Waterhouse, J. [1866] 1978. *The king and the people of Fiji.* New York: AMS.
Weber, Max. [1919] 1946. Science as a vocation. In *From Max Weber: Essays in sociology*, ed. H. H. Gerth and C. Wright Mills, 129–56. Oxford: Oxford University Press.
——. [1930] 1992. *Protestantism and the spirit of capitalism.* Trans. Talcott Parsons. London: Routledge.
Weiner, Annette B. 1992. *Inalienable possessions: The paradox of keeping-while-giving.* Berkeley: University of California Press.
White, G. M. 1991. *Identity through history: Living stories in a Solomon Islands society.* Cambridge: Cambridge University Press.
Whitehouse, H. 1992. Memorable religions: Transmission, codification, and change in divergent Melanesian contexts. *Man*, n.s., 27:777–97.
——. 1994. Strong words and forceful winds: Religious experience and political process in Melanesia. *Oceania* 65:40–58.
——. 1995. *Inside the cult: Religious innovation and transmission in Papua New Guinea.* Oxford: Oxford University Press.
——. 1996a. Apparitions, orations, and rings: Experience of spirits in Dadul. In *Spirits in Culture and Mind*, ed. J. M. Mageo and A. Howard, 173–94. London: Routledge.
——. 1996b. From possession to apotheosis: Transformation and disguise in the leadership of a cargo movement. In *Leadership and change in the Western Pacific*, ed. R. Feinberg and K. A. Watson-Gegeo, 376–97. London: Athlone.
——. 1996c. Jungles and computers: Neuronal group selection and the epidemiology of representations. *Journal of the Royal Anthropological Institute*, n.s., 1:99–116.
——. 1996d. Rites of terror: Emotion, metaphor, and memory in Melanesian intiation cults. *Journal of the Royal Anthropological Institute*, n.s., 4:703–15.
——. 1998. From mission to movement: The impact of Christianity on patterns

of political association in Papua New Guinea. *Journal of the Royal Anthropological Institute*, n.s., 4:43–63.

——. 1999. Comment. *Journal of the Royal Anthropological Institute*, n.s., 5:99–100.

——. 2000. *Arguments and icons: Divergent modes of religiosity*. Oxford: Oxford University Press.

——. 2004. *Modes of religiosity: A cognitive theory of religious transmission*. Walnut Creek, Calif.: AltaMira.

Whitehouse, Harvey, and James A. Laidlaw, eds. 2004. *Ritual and memory: Toward a comparative anthropology of religion*. Walnut Creek, Calif.: AltaMira.

Whitehouse, Harvey, and Luther H. Martin, eds. 2004. *Theorizing religions past: Archaeology, history, and cognition*. Walnut Creek, Calif.: AltaMira Press.

Whitehouse, Harvey, and Robert N. McCauley. 2005. *Mind and religion: Psychological and cognitive foundations of religiosity*. Walnut Creek, Calif.: AltaMira Press.

Wiles, M. F. 1996. *Archetypal heresy: Arianism through the centuries*. Oxford: Oxford University Press.

Williams, F. E. 1940. *The drama of Orokolo*. Oxford: Oxford University Press.

Williams, Rowan. 1987. *Arius: Heresy and tradition*. London: Darton, Longman and Todd.

Williams, Thomas. [1858] 1982. *Fiji and the Fijians*, ed. G. S. Rowe. Suva: Fiji Museum.

Wilson, J. and Clow, H. 1981. Themes of power and control in a Pentecostal assembly. *Journal of the Scientific Study of Religion* 10:241–50.

Wilson, Monica Hunter. 1971. *Religion and the transformation of society: A study in social change in Africa*. Cambridge: Cambridge University Press.

Wilson, R. 1995. *Maya resurgence in Guatemala: Q'eqchi experiences*. Norman: University of Oklahoma.

Witin, Fransiska. 1997. Belis dan Harga Diri Wanita. *Dian*, August 1, 6.

Wolters, Oliver W. 1982. *History, culture, and region in Southeast Asian perspectives*. Singapore: Institute of Southeast Asian Studies.

Worsley, Peter. [1957] 1970. *The trumpet shall sound: A study of cargo cults in Melanesia*. London: Paladin.

Wright, Robin M. 1998. *Cosmos, self, and history in Baniwa religion: For those unborn*. Austin: University of Texas Press.

Zupanov, Ignes G. 1996. Le repli du réligieux: Les missionnaires jésuites du 17e siècle entre la theologie chrétienne et une ethique paienne. *Annales Histoire, Sciences Sociales* 6:1201–23.

Contributors

CECILIA BUSBY was until 2006 a permanent lecturer in the department of anthropology at the University of Kent. She has conducted long-term fieldwork in South India and is the author of *The Performance of Gender: An Anthropology of Everyday Life in a South Indian Fishing Village* (2000), as well as articles on India and on English kinship. She has recently decided to redirect her skills toward a new career as a primary school teacher.

FENELLA CANNELL is a lecturer in anthropology at the London School of Economics and Political Science. She has carried out several periods of research in Bicol, Philippines. Her book *Power and Intimacy in the Christian Philippines* (1999) was awarded the Harry J. Benda Prize for Southeast Asian Studies in 2001. Her current research, on which she recently gave the Malinowski Lecture for 2004, concerns American Latter-Day Saints (Mormons). Her interests in both locations include new approaches to kinship and popular religion and the relationship between the two.

SIMON COLEMAN holds a chair in anthropology at the University of Sussex. He has carried out fieldwork in Sweden, England, and the United States, and his interests include charismatic Christianity, pilgrimage, and aesthetics. His books include *The Globalisation of Charismatic Christianity* (2000) and *Reframing Pilgrimage*, edited with John Eade (2004). His current fieldwork examines tensions between biomedical and other models of healing in the context of hospital space.

PETER GOW is a professor of anthropology at St. Andrews University in Scotland and author of *Of Mixed Blood: Kinship and History in Peruvian Amazonia* (1991) and *An Amazonian Myth and Its History* (2001). His work in the Amazon centers on myth, history, kinship, aesthetics, and mestizo identity.

OLIVIA HARRIS is a professor of anthropology at the London School of Economics and works with Andean people in Bolivia. She has distinguished publications on many aspects of Andean economics, politics, gender, and religion, among them *To Make the Earth Bear Fruit: Essays on Work and Gender in Highland Bolivia* (1999). She has recently completed a collaborative study of the same region from the period of Inca conquest to the consolidation of Spanish colonial rule, focusing particularly on the experience of historical time in the Andes.

WEBB KEANE is an associate professor in the Department of Anthropology and affiliate of the Center for Southeast Asian Studies at the University of Michigan, Ann Arbor. His work in Sumba, Indonesia, centers on problems of signification in social life, and his theory of verbal and material ritual communication is a key theme of his monograph on Sumba, *Signs of Recognition: Powers and Hazards of Representation in an Indonesian Society* (1997). He has also written extensively on themes in Protestantism, the theme of his next book, *Protestants, Missionaries, and the Paradoxes of the Modern Subject.*

EVA KELLER is a research fellow in social anthropology at the University of Zurich. She received her Ph.D. from the London School of Economics in 2002. Her book about Seventh-Day Adventism in Madagascar, entitled *The Road to Clarity*, was published in 2005. She is currently conducting research on representations of nature and conservation in Madagascar and Switzerland.

DAVID MOSSE is a reader in anthropology at the School of Oriental and African Studies in London. His work in South India combines a strong interest in popular religion with a focus on development and the environment. His extensive publications on these topics include *The Rule of Water: Statecraft, Ecology and Collective Action in South India* (2003) and *Cultivating Development: An Ethnography of Aid Policy and Practice* (2004).

DANILYN RUTHERFORD is an associate professor of anthropology at the University of Chicago. She is the author of *Raiding the Land of the Foreigners: The Limits of the Nation on an Indonesian Frontier* (1997). Her current research focuses on issues of sovereignty, identity, and audience in Dutch colonialism and Papuan nationalism in western New Guinea.

CHRISTINA TOREN is a professor of anthropology at Brunel University in London and director of the Centre for Child-Focused Anthropological Research (C-FAR). Her work in Fiji focuses on history, religion, and epistemology. She has written many well-known works on Fiji, including two books, *Making Sense of Hierarchy: Cognition as Social Process in Fiji* (1990) and *Mind, Materiality, and History: Explorations in Fijian Ethnography* (1999).

HARVEY WHITEHOUSE is a professor of anthropology and director of the Institute for Cognition and Culture at Queen's University, Belfast. A specialist in Melanesian religion, he carried out two years of field research on a cargo cult in New Britain, Papua New Guinea, in the late 1980s. In recent years, he has focused his energies on the development of collaborative research programs in the cognitive science of religion. His books include *Inside the Cult: Religious Innovation and Transmission in Papua New Guinea* (1995), *Arguments and Icons: Divergent Modes of Religiosity* (2000), and *Modes of Religiosity: A Cognitive Theory of Religious Transmission* (2000).

Index

FENELLA CANNELL is a lecturer in anthropology at the London School of Economics and Political Science. She has carried out several periods of research in Bicol in the Philippines. Her book *Power and Intimacy in the Christian Philippines* (1999) was awarded the Harry J. Benda Prize for Southeast Asian Studies in 2001. Her current research, on which she recently gave the Malinowski Lecture for 2004, concerns American Latter-Day Saints (Mormons). Her interests in both locations include new approaches to kinship and popular religion and the relationship between the two.

Library of Congress Cataloging-in-Publication Data

The anthropology of Christianity / edited by Fenella Cannell.
p. cm.
Includes bibliographical references and index.
ISBN-13: 978-0-8223-3608-2 (cloth : alk. paper)
ISBN-10: 0-8223-3608-1 (cloth : alk. paper)
ISBN-13: 978-0-8223-3646-4 (pbk. : alk. paper)
ISBN-10: 0-8223-3646-4 (pbk. : alk. paper)
1. Christianity and culture.
2. Ethnology—Religious aspects—Christianity.
3. Anthropology of religion. I. Cannell, Fenella.
BR115.C8A58 2006
306.6′3—dc22 2006010425